D1559623

ARGENTINA

ARGENTINA

the challenges of modernization

edited by
Joseph S. Tulchin
with
Allison M. Garland

A Scholarly Resources Inc. Imprint
Wilmington, Delaware

Scholarly Resources Inc.
104 Greenhill Avenue
Wilmington, DE 19805-1897

Library of Congress Cataloging-in-Publication Data

Argentina : the challenges of modernization / edited by Joseph S.
  Tulchin with Allison M. Garland.
    p.   cm. — (Latin American silhouettes : studies in history and
  culture)
    Includes index.
    ISBN 0-8420-2721-1 (cloth : alk. paper)
    1. Argentina—Politics and government—1983–   2. Argentina—
Economic conditions—1983–   3. Argentina—Social conditions—
1983–   4. Education and state—Argentina. I. Tulchin, Joseph S.,
1939– . II. Garland, Allison M., 1965–   . III. Series : Latin
American silhouettes.
F2849.2.A57   1997
982.06'4—dc21 97-24396
CIP

⊗ The paper used in this publication meets the minimum requirements
of the American National Standard for permanence of paper for printed
library materials, Z39.48, 1984.

Contents

Preface

"Argentina at the Wilson Center" was created in 1992 to bring distinguished political figures from Argentina to spend several months of reflection and study as Guest Scholars at the Woodrow Wilson International Center for Scholars. To complement the presence of these major public personages in Washington and to provide a unique platform in the United States for Argentina's decision makers and for the newly emerging private sector, the Wilson Center organized two major conferences in 1993 and 1994 to enable the project's scholars and sponsors to join with academics and policymakers from both countries to assess the challenges facing Argentina a decade after the restoration of democracy. The conclusions reached at these meetings form the basis of this publication.

"Argentina at the Wilson Center" was made possible by the generous support of a small group of leading members of Argentina's private sector. Beyond giving financial support, the sponsors participated with energy and intellectual vigor in the management of the program and in the public meetings held in Washington. "Argentina at the Wilson Center" exemplifies the meaningful contribution that the business community can make to enhance global understanding of one country's goals. This remarkable project has been applauded for bringing greater attention in Washington to events in Argentina and for enhancing the quality of dialogue between decision makers in a nonpartisan manner in the two countries.

The Wilson Center is grateful for the support and leadership provided by Dr. Antonio Estrany y Gendre, a member of the board of BRIDAS S.A. and president of the Consejo Interamericano de Comerico y Producción; Mr. Agostino Rocca, president and chief executive officer of Techint Group; Mr. Jorge E. Romero Vagni, executive vice president of Companía General de Combustibles S.A.; Dr. Fernando Jorge de Santibañes, chairman of the board of directors of Banco Crédito Argentino; and Mr. Guillermo Stanley, vice president of Citibank, N.A.

In addition, the Wilson Center would like to express its gratitude to Mr. Carlos Alberto Pulenta, president of Trapiche S.A.; Mr. Jorge Horacio Brito, president and chief executive officer of Banco Marco S.A.;

Mr. Jorge Vives, Massalin Particulares; Lic. Monica Madanes, Aluar; Mr. Victor Savanti, IBM Argentina; and Mr. George Stuart Milne.

The success of this program is also a reflection of the intellectual dedication of the four Guest Scholars selected to participate in this program. The Wilson Center owes a great debt to Eduardo Amadeo, José Octavio Bordón, Jesús Rodríguez, and Federico Storani for taking time away from the demanding schedule of political life to conduct serious academic analysis of the difficult challenges facing Argentina today. Their presence at the Wilson Center was a symbol of political pluralism and conviviality to the entire nation.

Finally, we would like to extend special appreciation to Alberto Föhrig for his valuable insight and thoughtful comments. His substantial contribution to the multiple phases of this project is evident throughout the volume. We also want to thank the Latin American Program staff—Cindy Arnson, Ralph Espach, and Michelle McCallum, and interns Dan Lenos, Meraiah Foley, Aimée Sutton, Angie Acosta, and Laura Alonso—for their indispensable help in organizing the conferences and in preparing the manuscript.

Introduction

The deep, lingering trauma of Argentine history is that somehow the nation never has achieved the greatness for which it was destined. For more than a century, Argentine leaders had spoken both privately and publicly of their expectations that their country soon would be accepted into the ranks of the world's great powers. Generations of Argentines were taught to believe that the nation's greatness would be recognized by the international community. But in the 1930s, evidence began to accumulate that the nation's destiny remained unfulfilled. The resulting bitterness, frustration, and alienation have been a constant element in the nation's politics and public policies since that time. Frequently, outside observers have found Argentina's international behavior odd. It has not been uncommon in the past half century for Argentine foreign policy to run counter to the country's stated objectives; those who formulated policy would blame one or more external actors for conspiring against their country. In the domestic political debate, it became the norm to blame one group or another for blocking the nation's road to greatness. So intense did the alienation become over time that in the 1970s the country fell into a virtual civil war that was ended only by a brutal military dictatorship that took the lives of more than ten thousand Argentine citizens without due process. The military capped its regime by invading the Malvinas/Falkland Islands and turning Argentina into a rogue state, an international pariah.

During the transition to democracy in 1983, there was a powerful sense that the nation was at a crossroads—that it had a historic opportunity to balance its accounts, to reset its national course, and to reinsert the nation into the international community. As president, Raúl Alfonsín referred frequently to the need for Argentines to reject the pretensions of the past, to see the world clearly, and to play a modest role in the world as they found it. Although he continued to insist, as had several of his predecessors, that Argentina could make a contribution to the world as a "moral power," and that it could play a role among the great powers because of its moral force, he made it perfectly plain that he considered Argentina a modest, developing nation and that it should comport itself as such on the international stage. His successor, Carlos Saúl Menem, has continued to emphasize the modest capacities of the nation and has deliberately linked

Argentina's reemergence onto the international scene to economic issues and on winning the friendship of the United States, which he considers the most powerful state in the international economy. As successive foreign ministers have indicated, the goal is to make Argentina a reliable partner.

In fact, Argentina has inserted itself into the world economy twice since it won its independence from Spain at the beginning of the nineteenth century, each time quite deliberately and self-consciously. Both efforts were designed to modernize the country and make it a more prominent actor on the world stage, and both were based on complex and multifaceted models of national development. The first, over a period of several decades during the second half of the last century, aimed at cashing in on the nation's comparative advantage in the production and sale of agricultural products. Argentina's vast area of unexploited land was used to satisfy the accelerating demand for food created by an urbanizing population in the industrialized nations of the Northern Hemisphere. The nation's leadership at that time, known as the Generation of 1880, used its control of the state to drive the indigenous population off the pampas and to pass the laws needed to attract the people and financing necessary to put the land into production and begin the export of foodstuffs. By any standard of measurement, the effort was hugely successful. Argentina enjoyed a run of economic growth unique in modern history. At the time of the nation's centennial in 1910, virtually every foreign observer considered Argentina a "modern" nation. What few imperfections remained were expected to disappear after a few more years of spectacular growth.

In retrospect, it is easy to see that while the sensational economic growth produced fabulous wealth and an elegant urban renewal for Buenos Aires, the federal capital, it did not lead to the diversification and strengthening of institutions that occurred among the northern industrialized nations. World War I demonstrated how dependent Argentina was on its external markets and how narrow the nation's autonomy was within the international community. The 1920s was a period of renewed growth, but the Great Depression finally destroyed the international trading system on which Argentina's economy had been based. World War II left Argentina without any leverage whatsoever in the international economy, its mode of production increasingly archaic. The domestic political debate became more and more divisive, characterized by stronger nationalistic overtones and an ever more prominent role for the military in the nation's politics, which became less tolerant. Under both civilian and military governments, the state assumed a greater role in the economy, which became still less efficient and less competitive. The dream of national greatness drifted further and further away, the nation's rank among international economies declining from its apogee of sixth place in 1928 to eighty-second in 1976.

Argentina's second entrance onto the world stage is very recent and still in progress. It began in 1983, after the transition to democracy following the war against Great Britain over the Malvinas Islands. This second entrance has been much less confident than the first. It has come at a time when Argentina seemed to have wandered in the wilderness for more than half a century. The economy was stagnant, the polity fragmented by dissension and intolerance and traumatized by years of violence culminating during the military regime that lasted from 1976 to 1983. During those years, more than ten thousand citizens were "disappeared" by the armed forces, acting in the name of the state and its struggle against subversion. The state, once the symbol of the nation's quest for greatness, had become bloated by inefficient enterprises, dragged down by a grossly overstaffed public sector, and unable to bring inflation under control. Endemic corruption was a constant embarrassment. The society, once the most equitable and educated in Latin America, with an enviable standard of living, had become less egalitarian and less well off. The citizenry, made leery by fifty years of kaleidoscopic changes of government, galloping inflation, and the gradual erosion of the rule of law, fell prey to cynicism and alienation.

The current reemergence onto the international scene has come in two steps thus far. The first, under the leadership of President Alfonsín, realigned the nation's moral center with the dominant values of the industrialized liberal democracies and reasserted the legitimacy of the institutions and rules of democratic governance. Alfonsín's greatest success was in facing down the elements of the military that refused to relinquish political control. He gave the greatest respect to the rights of free speech and assembly, and he encouraged the renovation of the press. He allowed the political parties to operate freely, but he was largely frustrated in his efforts to strengthen other democratic institutions. Alfonsín was convinced that the judiciary would not function in a democratic manner until the undemocratic judges appointed during the military regime were removed; that the congress would not fulfill its constitutional role until it had unlearned decades of obstructionist behavior; and that the economy would not function properly until the corporatist and corrupt unions were stripped of their monopoly over the labor market. The economy ultimately was his undoing, as he could not sustain support within his government for a macroeconomic plan and he was unconvinced that it was necessary to push ahead with the restructuring proposed by the World Bank and other external actors. By 1989 the economy was on the verge of collapse and the country was suffering through an episode of hyperinflation that threatened to tear the society apart. Alfonsín was forced to convince the president-elect to take office five months early to avert a breakdown in democratic governance.

The second step in the current insertion into the international community, taken by President Menem, was to restructure the economy in order to achieve macroeconomic stability and to make Argentina competitive once again in the international market. He called for the privatization of state-owned enterprises, hitched the value of the peso to that of the dollar, introduced labor and pension reform, and opened the economy to international trade and investment. To facilitate this process, Menem put an end to years of geopolitical wandering by aligning the nation unequivocally with the United States and by drawing closer to Brazil in the Mercado Común del Sur (MERCOSUR) trade group, along with Paraguay and Uruguay. Menem's goal was the modernization of the country, just as it had been for the Generation of 1880. So successful was Menem in selling his message that it became commonplace to evaluate government policies and even individual behavior by asking if that was how things were done in a "modern country." There is no question that the Menem administration has won the friendship of the United States and that it has pushed the restructuring process further than any other nation in South America. These achievements, together with Argentina's active participation in UN peacekeeping operations and the success of MERCOSUR, have won for the country a constructive role in world affairs, although it is a more modest role than had been anticipated by those whose fathers, grandfathers, and great-grandfathers had hoped for greatness.

Part of the modernization process, a painful part in some ways, has been learning more about the world outside Argentina and coming to see more clearly how Argentina fits into the global system. Given that a close relationship with the United States was central to Menem's plan and that such an alliance ran counter to a century of suspicion and tension with the United States, it is vital for the nation's leadership in Argentina both to establish good relations with the government and private sector of the United States and to convince the Argentine people that such a radical departure from the usual policy is in their best interest. In response to that need, in 1992 the Woodrow Wilson International Center for Scholars joined with a small group of leaders from the Argentine private sector to initiate the program entitled "Argentina at the Wilson Center." The program had three goals: to stimulate public discussion in Argentina on the issues stemming from the nation's reemergence into the international economy; to provide Argentina with a higher profile within the U.S. policy community; and to further mutual understanding between the two countries. To achieve these goals, the program organized two major conferences to bring together prominent academics and practitioners, as well as members of the private sector and nongovernmental organizations, in a public discussion of contemporary Argentine affairs. These unique encounters, the first such in Washington in many years, provided a neutral platform on which a wide variety of opinions could be expressed, creating a constructive environment for the debate of many divisive issues. In addition, these meetings brought the views of Argentines to the attention of policymakers, governmental officials, and academics in the United States, contributing to improved relations between the two countries. This volume is the product of those conferences.

One crucial component of the program brought prominent Argentine political figures to spend a period in residence at the center as Guest Scholars, where they might reflect upon issues touching on Argentine public policy. Each Guest Scholar, at the end of his stay, prepared an essay that served as the basis for the first four chapters of this volume. The Guest Scholars selected to participate in this program, José Octavio Bordón, Jesús Rodríguez, Federico Storani, and Eduardo Amadeo, represent the very best of the younger generation of leaders in Argentina. They were asked to study public policy questions of interest to them and to reflect on their personal experience as well as on the challenges facing their country ten years after the restoration of democracy and several years after the end of the Cold War. In this context of profound economic, political, and social change, the Argentine Guest Scholars reflected upon a future for their country, mapping out proposals to help shape their nation's future.

The career trajectories of these four practicing politicians since their stay at the Wilson Center reflect the tensions in contemporary Argentine politics and the problems remaining in the modernization process, which are the subject of the remaining thirteen chapters of the book. The reflections of these four active politicians complement the more academic analyses that follow of the country's attempts to consolidate democracy and transform its economy. Argentina has been modernizing at breakneck speed, with serious political and social repercussions. Understanding the perspective of these four politicians and the role that each has played in the country's transition illuminates the problems and challenges facing Argentina at the end of the twentieth century.

Building on eight years in politics as a Peronist member of the Argentine Congress and as the governor of the Province of Mendoza, José Octavio Bordón spent the early months of 1992 as a Guest Scholar at the Wilson Center to reflect upon the complex and interdependent relationship between Argentina's economic and political systems. Bordón's work demonstrates an increasing concern for issues of equity and of governmental accountability. He warns that corruption is becoming a serious obstacle to development. His essay highlights three major demands that the economic program has placed on Argentina's political system: the need for greater administrative efficiency, the need for ethics, and the decentralization of responsibility. Bordón does not believe that blind faith in the market will alleviate serious problems of poverty.

Upon his return to Argentina, Bordón was elected senator of Mendoza, playing a major role in Argentina's upper chamber. Bordón experienced growing tensions with the Menem administration and finally broke with the Peronist party in 1995, creating his own political party, Política Abierta para la Integridad Social (PAIS). In the 1995 presidential elections, Bordón's party formed an alliance with "Chacho" Alvarez, leader of the Frente Grande, to build a center-left coalition, Frente del País Solidario (FREPASO). As the FREPASO presidential candidate, Bordón campaigned on a platform of anticorruption and promised to address the social impact of economic restructuring—both concepts that had occupied his time at the Wilson Center. His efforts won over 29 percent of the vote, second to Menem, and put him twelve points ahead of the Radical party candidate, Horacio Massaccesi. In spite of this electoral success, the FREPASO coalition proved unable to contain the personalities of two strong leaders, which led to Bordón's break with the alliance. Bordón is now preparing a return to presidential politics, building a base of support beyond the Provinces of Mendoza and Buenos Aires. He currently heads a private think tank, the Fundación Andina.

Bordón's career reflects Argentina's fragile political party system and the country's long history of building mercurial electoral coalitions, both of which conditions have made it difficult to create a cohesive alternative to the ruling regime. In particular, Bordón's career is emblematic of the tensions within the very distinct factions that compose the Peronist party. President Menem will face an increasing challenge in holding together supporters that represent those that advance modernizing goals such as Bordón, the traditionalists led by Eduardo Duhalde, the governor of the Province of Buenos Aires, and those loyal to him personally, who support him for a third term. A succession crisis could fragment the Peronist party, particularly if a strong alternative candidate lures away disenchanted supporters. Menem's success through two presidential terms has hinged upon an unlikely alliance between the privileged and the poor, held together by the glue of economic growth and the passionate desire to avoid a return to the chaos of hyperinflation.

Jesús Rodríguez rose to power as a loyal Radical party supporter of Raúl Alfonsín. At the president's request, he stepped into the deteriorating situation in 1989 as minister for the economy, knowing that he was bound to become the target of heavy criticism for the collapse of the Alfonsín administration. Despite these attacks, Rodríguez returned to electoral politics with growing success as deputy for the Federal Capital. Specializing in budgetary matters, Rodríguez led the Unión Cívica Radical (UCR) in Congress to a position of responsible opposition, strengthening both institutions. Rodríguez directs a think tank, the Center for the Study of Structural Change (Centro de Estudios para el Cambio Estructural, or CECE), that examines major policy issues and formulates options for the Radical party block of the Congress.

Rodríguez's stay at the Wilson Center prepared him for his efforts to modernize the policy process in the Argentine Congress. As a Guest Scholar, Rodríguez was concerned with the political and institutional effects of Menem's reform process, foretelling the problems that would result from sacrificing respect for institutional procedures for the sake of efficiency. His chapter focuses on the absence of social and political consensus for a system of procedures and institutional operations. In fact, his own career has been a demonstration of the "winner-takes-all" aspects of a political system that obstructs progress. The efforts of the Alfonsín administration to implement needed state reform were thwarted by an opposition majority in the Senate, by the agitation of union leaders, and by the activities of provincial governors, most of whom belonged to the Peronist party. Since returning to the lower chamber, Rodríguez has been confronted by the disproportionate powers of the presidency about which he writes, facing the problems posed by Menem's style of governing through emergency decrees and bypassing institutions. He writes that the neutralization of the opposition (including political parties, the Congress, labor unions, and social organizations) ultimately excludes citizens from the process and devalues the instruments of a democratic system. These ideas have formed the basis of Rodríguez's political strategy in Congress as well as within his own party.

Federico Storani is one of the most dynamic and charismatic leaders of the Argentine Congress today. Storani's very different vision for the Radical party often places him in competition with Rodríguez. Following his stay at the Wilson Center, Storani has given greater emphasis to the work of his think tank, the Sergio Karakachoff Foundation, focusing on issues of public participation in the political process with an emphasis on social concerns and on issues of equity. Storani's base of support is drawn from the Province of Buenos Aires. Like Bordón, he faces the challenge of appealing to supporters beyond the confines of the province in which he is based.

Storani sees political parties as a principal agent in the transition to democracy. He has identified three basic problems with political representation in Argentina: lack of openness in party financing and the uncertain relationship between state and party; public wariness of political parties, resulting from the behavior of politicians; and a lack of accountability, defined as the difference between the behavior of a representative and the expectations of the electorate. If these problems are not addressed, he writes, democracy risks being eroded; it risks losing relevance as a form of government. Storani has dedicated his career since formulating these ideas at the Wilson Center to strengthening the links between party organization and the electorate. He has advocated an open system of internal party elections and advanced a system in which decisions flow from the local level, with the important participation of grassroots organizations. He believes that the Radical party is in crisis, unable to galvanize the country's popular forces to exercise a challenge to the Peronist consolidation of electoral power. Finally, like Rodríguez and Bordón, Storani is critical of the Menem administration for its failure to address the urgent demands of poverty, inequity, and unemployment, all of which have been exacerbated by the economic reform program. All three advocate a strong state role in human capital formation based on improved education, investment in infrastructure, and technological advances.

Eduardo Amadeo offers a response to these criticisms by outlining the Menem administration's strategy for addressing the challenge of alleviating the harsh consequences of adjustment without compromising the economic model. Amadeo came to the Wilson Center with a strong interest in social policy, having held a series of appointments by the Peronist party to policymaking positions. The dominant economic model advanced by the Menem administration had not provided sufficient support for the most vulnerable sectors of society, and Amadeo saw this flaw in the economic model as a major political liability for the government. He concentrated his efforts on addressing critical social issues with a strategy for human capital formation. Upon his return to Argentina, Amadeo won the support of the president for the plans he had formulated while at the Wilson Center. He was appointed secretary of state for social development. He was later raised to the rank of minister with an increased budget, as he had managed to convince key members of the administration of the political need to address the social impact of adjustment and the growing pressures of unemployment—even if those burdens are only short-term challenges. Amadeo deftly shifted the debate over policy instruments from entitlements and transfers to policy prescriptions for job creation and the formation of human capital. Menem's response to criticism had been to accelerate the reform process, arguing that labor reform was necessary for an increase in employment.

Amadeo plays a critical role within the Peronist party, offering a bridge between the president and his labor base. That role has become increasingly important as the "flexibilization" of labor (meaning that policies regarding hiring and firing are made more liberal) rises on Menem's reform agenda. Amadeo's program can close the gap between the economic debate outlined in the third section of this volume and the politics of reform detailed in the chapters by Jonathan Hartlyn, Liliana De Riz, and Torcuato Di Tella. Focusing exclusively on economics would tear the Peronist party in half, ripping the political superstructure away from its base and making the party incapable of winning elections without a charismatic leader like Menem. If macroeconomic policies result in increased unemployment—both white and blue collar—and if the flexibilization of labor further destroys union power, the Peronists stand to lose electoral support. Amadeo's ideas represent an effort to restore relations between Menem and his Peronist base within the context of modernization. Similarly, experts such as Jorge Balán, Cecilia Braslavsky, and Juan Carlos Del Bello, the authors included in the final section of this book, have brought international standards to human capital formation to buttress the efforts of the Menem administration to modernize the country. It is significant that all three took positions in the Menem government in an effort to put their ideas into practice.

The essence of Amadeo's argument is the need for social policies to address unemployment resulting from technological advances brought on by economic transformation and by "the inner dynamics of the government structures that prevent the country from attaining pre-crisis standards of living." Amadeo is primarily concerned with narrowing the gap between workers' skills and the skills demanded by new technologies. Argentina's sudden reemergence into the global economy has brought national firms into competition with higher international productivity levels and lower international wages, resulting in a significant rise in unemployment. "Education," Amadeo concludes, "is the pivot on which social policy hinges."

Amadeo's work at the Wilson Center also focused on inefficiencies in the administration of social policies, exacerbated by a reduction in resources caused by economic instability and later by the fiscal cuts required by Menem's reform program. Amadeo advances social policies that target beneficiaries and the issue of decentralization in an effort to improve openness and efficiency in social service delivery while at the same time encouraging community participation in decision making over the allocation of resources.

Emerging from the four essays by political leaders is a clear sense that one of the greatest challenges facing Argentina is the need for institutional development. Consolidation of democracy is possible only through a strengthened and independent political party system, legislature, and judiciary. Each of the Guest Scholars focuses on a different aspect of this dilemma. Rodríguez and Storani represent the internal conflict that has prevented the Radical party from emerging as a coherent challenge to Peronism. The path taken by Bordón reflects the fragility of the Menemist coalition, while Amadeo's career suggests possibilities for cohesion within the party. The experience and thoughts of all four, however, reflect an underdeveloped party system that lacks mechanisms for articulating the interests of the Argentine citizenry.

The weakness of the party system is a concern of academic analysts as well. Jonathan Hartlyn writes that the period between 1987 and 1994 has seen a decline in respect for civil rights in Argentina, marked by politicization, corruption, manipulation of the judiciary, media intimidation, and abuse of executive authority. The absence of structured parties and a party system, he writes, facilitates a neopatrimonial regime in which the president circumvents and marginalizes political institutions through direct, plebiscitary appeals and executive decrees. Over time, he warns, political institutions come to be avoided by alienated voters, and their growing irrelevancy comes at great cost to a democracy. Hartlyn sees a worrisome affinity between neopopulism and neoliberalism within neopatrimonial delegative democracies such as Argentina. Countries seeking to enhance international opportunities and to reconstruct the state must also find ways to strengthen the political institutions that are critical for generating consensus if they are to consolidate democracy.

Torcuato Di Tella and Liliana De Riz assess the prospects for the evolution of the Argentine party system, suggesting that a new structure of alliances is necessary for the normalization of the Argentine democracy. Di Tella predicts the emergence of a two-party or two-coalition system: a conservative alliance with right-wing Peronism and a renovated Peronism that attracts the independent left as well as the remainder of the Radical party, which, after undergoing a great transformation, will unite the country's trade unions with its progressive sector. Liliana De Riz interprets electoral data from the period between 1989 and 1995 to predict the emergence of a system comprising three strong parties as well as several significant minor parties. Electoral behavior is driven by voter expectations as well as by loyalty and voter identification with party values, she writes, explaining the Peronist party's success. Since 1983, the

Peronists have maintained a stable base of support of between 28 and 36 percent of the vote. In the wake of the Mexican peso crisis, voters turned to Menem for stability and continuity in the 1995 presidential elections. At the same time, the party system is beginning to feel the influence of third parties in legislative and provincial elections, she writes, focusing on the examples of the Frente Grande on the left of the ideological spectrum and Modín on the right. The challenge remains for third parties to make headway against the Radicals and the Peronists in the provinces, according to De Riz's interpretation of FREPASO's showing in the May 1995 gubernatorial elections. Both Di Tella and De Riz paint a grim picture for the Radical party, which appears to be unable to overcome intraparty conflict to transform itself into a reformist movement capable of channeling discontent and beating Peronism at the polls. Menem's second term has been marked by recession, with unemployment reaching 18.6 percent, giving rise to questions about equity in the distribution of the costs of adjustment and threatening to erode Menem's fragile coalition. A weak opposition, concludes De Riz, does not augur well for an easy future, or for the consolidation of resilient institutions.

Widespread allegations of corruption have called the quality of the country's democratic institutions into question. Many argue that if the Argentine Congress were able to increase its coherence as a governing body, a strong political party system might evolve. Others emphasize the importance of an independent judiciary as a necessary component of the reconstruction of the Argentine government and as fundamental to the country's consolidation of democracy. The chapters of this volume emphasize that there is now a historic opportunity for the reform of public structures in Argentina. Only when Argentina's main constitutional institutions enjoy widespread popular support will the country's long-term stability be guaranteed. Emilio Cárdenas, a lawyer and Argentina's former permanent representative to the United Nations, proposes a series of initiatives that would increase judicial productivity, efficiency, and quality, consolidating independence and transparency at both the federal and provincial levels.

Political accountability, judicial reform, institutional stability, and tolerance for dissent are the central challenges for Argentina's modernization, concludes Joseph Tulchin in his chapter on the geopolitical dimensions of Argentina's reemergence into the world economic system. Tulchin's chapter puts the Menem model into historical perspective and distinguishes between the short-term changes precipitated by the decision to link the nation's fortunes to those of the United States and the deeply rooted traditions of competition with the United States and Argentine exceptionalism. Those latter qualities will make it difficult for the country to adapt to its new role as a minor player in an open, competitive world economy.

Linking the political and economic policy options available to national leaders in Latin America to the international system, Jonathan Hartlyn argues that participation in the global system imposes severe structural constraints on the kinds of policies that Latin American states can pursue. None of the papers in this volume challenges the economic model guiding Argentina into the twenty-first century; rather, they propose different strategies for addressing the deleterious effects of economic adjustment on the population and its institutional resources. Section III of this volume is composed of four papers that trace the development of Argentina's economic transformation. Juan Carlos Torre argues that critical junctures in the Argentine economy have allowed for significant change in both the institutional rules and social coalitions governing Argentina's economic model. Torre argues that the transition to a market economy must be recognized as a political operation whose success was determined by political resources, institutional capabilities, and government leaders. Torre describes a political paradox in which Menem, a leader of the left, has been able to adopt right-wing policies without unleashing the wrath of his political base. Returning to the experiences of Bordón, Rodríguez, and Storani, it is evident that the absence of a realistic political alternative is relevant here. Similarly, the absence of mechanisms through which the most vulnerable sectors might express their political demands contributes to Menem's success, as he skillfully has managed to manipulate union leadership. Torre's chapter on economic change also raises the institutional issues outlined in the volume's section on the terms of democratic consolidation, suggesting that Menem was able to exploit fully the resources available within a presidential system through the large-scale use of decrees, emergency powers, and the manipulation of political institutions.

Daniel Marx, who served during Menem's first administration as the financial representative in Washington, evaluates the changes in public finance that have been undertaken since the restoration of democracy, suggesting that the context in which many of the Menem administration's reforms were adopted facilitated structural changes in the country's economy. Marx encourages further decentralization of decision making as well as continued privatization, with the help of state regulation to improve economic organization, efficiency, and productivity while helping to increase employment. He warns that the federal role, particularly in its relationship with the provincial governments, remains to be defined.

Juan Llach, who was subminister of the economy, and Fernando Cerro outline a "third stage" of Argentine growth and increased investment, defining a new relationship between the public and private sectors. Investment and exports will serve as the driving force for growth during the period between 1996 and 1999, they write. According to Llach and Cerro, continued structural reforms will reduce labor costs and strengthen prospects for increased investment. Ultimately, they argue, these changes will contribute to improved competitiveness and rising employment. As Torre suggests, the reform policies instituted by Menem are a race against time, a race between the destruction they provoke and the positive benefits they foster. Menem's truce with labor will depend on the success of Eduardo Amadeo's efforts to satisfy the demands of Argentina's popular sectors, thus deflecting attacks on the government. Amadeo's task will become increasingly difficult as the Menem administration embarks upon the "third stage" of growth advanced by Llach and Cerro, beginning with such labor reforms as changes in the collective wage bargaining system and the elimination of distortions created by union benefits.

The authors who have contributed to this volume repeatedly return to issues of equity raised by Menem's plans for economic restructuring and modernization. The research provided by Margaret Daly Hayes finds that many firms have benefited from economic recovery during the period between 1991 and 1994, but not all sectors have fared well. A dramatic consolidation of sectors has resulted from market opening, as smaller firms have been unable to compete with international products. Globalization, market opening, and trade liberalization have supported a dynamic export sector. However, most exports are dominated by a handful of large, Argentine-based multinational firms. Is Argentina's long tradition of a strong middle class threatened by Menem's economic model? Is wealth being concentrated in the hands of the elite? One of several policy challenges Hayes poses for the Menem administration is to develop a national education system that can address the demands for skilled labor necessary to compete in the global economy. In addition, she writes, Argentine universities and other research institutes are not well integrated into the industrial cycle.

In fact, the area of greatest convergence among the diverse contributors to this volume centers on the need to develop Argentina's human resources to adapt to technological advances and global trading patterns. The three chapters in the final section of this volume address the vast challenges to be faced in the human capital formation necessary to prepare the country for participation in a globalized economy. Braslavsky, Balán, and Del Bello explore current efforts to transform the Argentine education system and the obstacles facing the federal government, addressing institutional issues as well as the need to define a new relationship between the state and its citizens. Drawing lessons from the reform of higher education as implemented in Argentina in the 1960s, the authors of this section depict a system characterized by lengthy degree programs, part-time professors and students, scarce resources, and a lack of incentives for research—all of which contribute to high dropout rates and low numbers of graduates.

"Dynamism, strength, and democratization are not synonyms, but rather three distinct and necessary dimensions of federal government intervention in the overall process of reconverting the education system," concludes Braslavsky. Warning that decentralization without the articulation of a clear education reform agenda will only exacerbate problems, she advocates a strong role for the federal government in defining the skills for which training should be provided and in creating evaluation systems for regulation and accreditation.

Like Braslavsky, Balán argues that reform involves a fundamental change in the relationships between universities with their markets and the state. Balán details the crisis of an educational system expanding at an alarming rate, both in enrollment and in the number of institutions. Juan Carlos Del Bello builds upon the argument that the problems plaguing Argentina's university system are structural, recommending policy instruments to bring about positive change. The work of these three education specialists maps out an agenda for President Menem as well as for the private sector, offering means by which members of his administration as well as individual firms can introduce plans that might soften the impact of adjustment within the confines of the current economic model.

The first steps have been taken, and taken with considerable success. Ahead lie challenges in the consolidation of the nation's democracy, the reform of its social system, and the modernization of its educational system.

I

Forging a Political Consensus

Four Politicians Discuss the National Agenda

1

Argentine Democracy Ten Years Later

New Priorities

Jesús Rodríguez*

Eric Hobsbawm maintains that, for the purpose of analysis, just as the nineteenth century began in 1789 with the French Revolution and ended with World War I, so the twentieth century came to an end in 1989 with the fall of the Berlin Wall and the resulting collapse of the so-called real socialisms of Eastern Europe.[1] By the same yardstick, it could be said that, for Argentina, the 1980s began in 1983 with the restoration of democracy.

The aim of this essay, written in January and February of 1993 at the Woodrow Wilson Center, is to look critically and constructively, from the viewpoint of a practicing politician, at the characteristics that democracy is assuming in Argentina ten years after its inception. This work is divided into five sections, the first of which addresses specific features of the transition that began in 1983. The implications of the restructuring of Argentina's economy and the resulting social ramifications are analyzed in the subsequent sections. The fourth section deals with some of the political and institutional consequences that have grown out of the reform process itself. Finally, I have set out the minimum content of a strategy to make economic and social modernization compatible with a fully functioning democratic system. The object is to prevent elements of the modernization process from coming into opposition with the essential character of the democratic way of life.

At the end of the 1970s, approximately 90 percent of Latin Americans were living under authoritarian regimes. By the beginning of 1991, for

*I wish to acknowledge the collaboration of Alberto Föhrig in the preparation of this work.

the first time in history, all of the Latin American countries (with the exception of Cuba) had democratically elected presidents.[2]

In Latin America—this also holds true for Argentina—the authoritarian cycle was brought to an end by a number of factors, including the loss of legitimacy of the dictatorships, their failure socially and economically, changes in the international scene, and the fact that other political alternatives were ineffectual. This last factor is of no small significance given the manner in which the left developed in Latin America and its failure to make any headway by force of arms in all the variants in which that had been attempted. However, if Latin America had been at a different juncture in its history, if the political factors indicated above had not been operating, and if financial limitations had not been imposed by fiscal crises and the crushing foreign debt, there might have been a resurgence of one or another political system with populist roots.

The revival of political institutions, however, put an end to theories that claimed to establish a time sequence whereby economic development would precede political progress. Such theories also identified factors (in this case a minimum level of annual wealth per capita) that indicated that throughout Latin America the time was ripe for democracy. Today there is no doubt about the positive link between fully functioning democratic institutions and social and economic progress. It is generally recognized that countries with a relatively high degree of development are more able to establish and build on a democratic system. In the same way, nations with vigorous democratic roots have a better chance of speeding up social progress.[3] It is demonstrable that a fully operative scaffolding of democratic institutions, through the broad political consensus it engenders, is a prerequisite to economic and social modernization, making it possible to distribute more equitably the costs that are an inseparable part of the modernization process.[4]

One feature of Argentina's democratic restoration, which sets it apart from that of other Latin American countries, is that, unlike in Uruguay and Chile, in Argentina no agreement of a consensual nature existed between the outgoing regime and the opposition. And unlike in Brazil and Paraguay, in Argentina succession did not devolve on political sectors reconstituted from the authoritarian regime. Argentina's transition was devoid of any agreement on the rules defining democratization; in academic parlance, this type of transition is described as one of "rupture."

In restoring democracy, therefore, Argentina was faced with the challenge of constructing a social and political consensus not only in order to define the procedures by which the system was to function (its norms, institutions, and decision-making mechanisms) but also to grapple with a past of terrorism and unlawful repression. Moreover, the democratic institutions had to fit onto a social regime of accumulation—that complex mass of institutions and practices that arise during the process of accumulating capital—which at that time was in a state of collapse. In addition, the Argentine transition to democracy took place without agreement to leave on the part of the authoritarian regime. This situation was rendered more difficult by the lack of any significant agreement among the various political forces. Further, the ruling government was withdrawing in disorder because of its own internal collapse after the Malvinas defeat, a fact that left it no room for negotiation.

An institutional system such as Argentina's, in which an exaggerated amount of power rested in the presidency, fostered a lack of agreement on strategy. That fact led to a weakness in the institutions underpinning the country's party system, a weakness further reflected in and emphasized by the negligible policymaking powers vested in the Congress upon the restoration of democracy. The effect of a strong executive system is that, as the victorious party naturally concentrates all political power in its president, consensus among the opposition political sectors is difficult to obtain. This "winner-takes-all" situation further exacerbates the obstructionist, antagonistic posture of the defeated parties as the next election approaches. This phenomenon has such a strong influence that factions and candidates in the governing party also use it in their stance toward governmental policy.

During President Raúl Alfonsín's administration, for example, only in the months after the September 1987 election—which precipitated a restructuring of the Justicialista party—was it possible to pass basic, mutually agreed-upon legislation on topics as sensitive as national defense and the federal redistribution of taxes to the provinces. Unfortunately, this state of affairs did not even last until the start of the party primaries for the election of the president and vice president of the Justicialista party in July 1988. Then, in 1989, Argentina broke with the pattern of the past. In that year, economic crisis was not the prologue to yet another successful military coup. For the first time since the restoration of the compulsory secret vote, Argentines handed over the government from one civilian president to another, voted in by the will of the people, and from a different political background than his predecessor.

Argentina's financial problems are of long standing and are certainly not the offspring of democracy. In public and political debate, various explanations have been offered as to the origins of Argentine economic stagnation, the onset of which can be dated more or less to the mid-1970s. One hypothesis is that the country's financial difficulties stemmed from its isolation from the mainstream of world trade and investment. Others point to the growing influence of the public sector on economic life, whether directly on the manufacture of goods and provision of services or through regulation. Another possible explanation is the extraordinary increase in the informal sector of the economy.

These arguments, even if valid, do not account for the full extent of the problem. Other countries with no more access to the international market, or with greater state presence in economic decisions, or with a similar amount of unregistered financial activity have not had the continuous inflation and stagnation in production that Argentina has experienced.

In recent years, two continuously operating factors have influenced economic strategy—the huge budget deficit and the fact that no systematic, all-embracing policy has ever governed domestic financial decision making. Eclipsing both of these, and at the same time one of the elements that explains them, is the state's progressive loss of its authority to impose decisions and its growing inability to resist pressures and demands from the corporate sector.

The constitutional government that took over in December 1983 inherited a public sector whose main feature was lack of control. This can be seen from the levels of public spending (49.75 percent of GNP [Gross National Product]) and the deficit (15.15 percent in relation to production). At the same time, the problems created by a reduced amount of money in circulation were increased by a phenomenon that did not occur in other countries undergoing similar economic crises. Confronted by inflation and as a defense against it, financial agents removed savings from the national government's control by converting Argentine currency into U.S. dollars. The fiscal and financial crises that arose in the 1980s as a result of the foreign debt not only hurt public and private investment but also became lasting impediments to the restoration of growth.[5] The Alfonsín administration was able only temporarily to contain and partially reverse some of the effects of this economic deterioration.

For the first time, a contemporary democratic government had as a basic strategy integration into the world economy and reform of the state. This strategy involved the private sector's venturing into areas traditionally under public ownership, the privatization of state industry, and the use—under certain conditions, through open tender—of an anticipated cancellation of the foreign debt to finance new investment that would generate a positive balance of payments. All this took place in a context of continuing agreement among the authorities to bring about the real, massive, stable change needed for growth in an economy open to world competition, combined in turn with a lowering of protectionist import duties and the elimination of fiscal and quasi-fiscal subsidies.[6]

The results proved that this strategy could not overcome defects in government administration or the opposition party's obstructionist policies. Ensuring an atmosphere of tranquillity during the presidential election proved too hard a task. The price of political uncertainty this time was not military conflict but the effect on the exchange market: From December 1988 to June 1989, the rate of inflation doubled every month.

These events meant that the elected government had to assume power earlier than intended—in July 1989. Despite the fact that the new government, deriving its political power from constitutional change brought about by the restoration of democracy, was able to form a social alliance based on the support of the major industrial sectors and the acquiescence of the labor unions, the mood of crisis persisted until the beginning of 1991. The new administration carried out an audacious and—in the light of electoral promises—unexpected program of reforms. Owing to the gravity of the situation, the government was empowered to take exceptional measures. The uncritical acceptance of these measures by the public came as a result of the pressing nature of the circumstances, the demand for change, and a general sense of urgency.

The degree of social awareness during a political crisis in a country like Argentina is of major importance in dealing with structural reform within a democratic context. There is no doubt that critical situations are now faced far more effectively by the various sectors of Argentine society than they had been under the Alfonsín administration. At that time, two elements had contributed to the lack of understanding of the country's true situation. The government itself underestimated the gravity of the constitutional crisis and the need to solve it—a fact that was particularly evident during the first stage of the Alfonsín administration. By the same token, the strongly populist Justicialista party and the union movement controlled by it attributed the failure to meet social demands to the government's mistaken policies and its lack of concern for the most needy sectors of society.

The hyperinflationary episodes that followed brought about a change of attitude within some sectors of society with regard to solving some of the nation's basic structural problems. There is no doubt that this new attitude enabled the Menem government to put some of its policies into practice. Although sectors that had previously objected strongly to these policies did not take to them fervently when they were first announced, neither did they put up the active resistance that they had shown between 1983 and 1989.

The economic outlook of various ministers in the new administration is in line with the Washington Consensus.[7] This plan has been advanced as capable of overcoming the economic stagnation in Latin American countries. These ministers say that the stagnation was caused by the policy that downplayed industrial imports to give priority to goods sold on the domestic market, thus ignoring the opportunities presented by international trade. According to them, another cause of stagnation was the state's suffocating of economic activity by inefficiently allocating resources. The objectives of an economic policy to deal with this situation can be summed up as a search for a stable macroeconomic environment: the existence of a leaner, more efficient government; the development of an aggressive private sector; and, eventually, policies aimed at reducing poverty.

Of the three basic elements of the plan—stabilization, liberalization, and privatization—it is the last that requires special scrutiny. Such scrutiny should cover not only the amount of privatization in terms of mobilized resources and the sectors of production involved, but also the long-term consequences of the process. In Argentina, as in other countries, the expansion of state industry dates from the period immediately after World War II. The implicit assumption in those days was that the private sector could not attract significant long-term investment. Added to this, the argument went, the market lacked the ability to provide public services because of the existence of natural monopolies, economies of scale, and investments that cannot be divided into shares.

Around the middle of the 1970s, when the semiclosed economy—in which the state had the overall power to allocate resources and distribute revenue—began to show signs of collapse, Argentine state industry contributed 7.4 percent of total GNP while using up 20.5 percent of the total gross investment. Among industrialized countries, those figures were 9.6 percent and 11.1 percent, respectively.[8]

A private sector relatively protected from foreign competition and a public sector that went beyond natural monopolies could not be sustained. To a fiscal crisis that prevented the continued subsidy of tariff structures of distributive significance was added a lack of finance resulting from the scarcity of foreign exchange because of the debt crisis. Thus, defects in the state's assignment of resources, growing dissatisfaction with the social services provided by the state, a change in prevailing opinion about state intervention in the economy, as well as problems at the macroeconomic level—all led to the legitimization of change.

During Dr. Alfonsín's presidency, attempts to advance the reform and modernization of the state came up against the immovable barrier of a trio of opposing forces: an opposition majority in the senate, agitation by union leaders, and the activities of the provincial governors, the majority of whom were members of the Justicialista party. The Menem government, harried by demands for social change and the need to gain credibility by putting into practice the populist program it had set out in its election campaign, turned privatization into a synonym for modernization, thereby making it an objective rather than a tool. This confusion of reform with privatization was further enhanced by the abandonment of the state's non-delegable functions in areas such as public health and education, police services, and the administration of justice, all of which were showing marked deterioration. In the public presentation of its program, the Menem administration's privatization schemes are shown as a multipurpose tool: Their purpose is not only to solve recurring fiscal problems but also to provide additional financing for social programs while lifting the burden of the foreign debt and relieving the state of corporate pressures.

However, it has now become clear that Argentina's privatization schemes of the 1990s are merely the opposite side of the coin of the nationalizations of the forties. In those days, nationalization was held out as the perfect instrument for the solution of economic problems and public policy. Fifty years later, utopia is here again, with the same arguments but from the opposite direction. Thus, more on ideological grounds and with hopes of macroeconomic results than on solid microeconomic arguments, Argentina first nationalized and then privatized each and every one of its public services.

Privatization is often only vaguely defined. One of the most noticeable aspects of this vagueness is the way in which the privatization of a public industry is seen as the equivalent of selling off its assets. This perception is clearly incorrect. Privatization goes beyond the mere transfer of assets, which, moreover, is not the only way in which the private sector can take over the operation of public industries. In the case of public services, this can also be done by government concessions or by the outright takeover of the management of a state industry.[9]

However, any assessment of the long-term effects of privatization would demand consideration of elements of this policy other than the mere transfer to the private sector of benefits resulting from the operation of an industrial or service enterprise. Among such elements are the framework of regulations that the state sets up when privatizing an industry or service, the degree of competition in the market, and the concentration of ownership that results from privatization. In this regard, the result of Argentina's privatization policy has been to maintain the monopolist character of a considerable part of private industry, in some cases because these are natural monopolies but in others as a consequence of the standardizing process worked out in advance as a condition for privatization.

This situation has been aggravated by the fact that the government underestimated the need for a framework of laws and regulations to protect users from flaws in the market and from certain enterprises eventually becoming virtual monopolies in the hands of private operators. Even today, when a large section of industry has been transferred to private ownership and operation, there is still a lack of relevant rules and regulations. Where these do exist, their capacity to function is noticeably weak. Nor, in the experience of Argentina, is there a policy to give momentum to diversifying and extending ownership of public industry that has been privatized, except in a few cases. Concentration of ownership in the hands of the wealthiest groups, which accompanied the privatization policies in Argentina, makes it relevant to question the relationship between these groups and the state, and the capacity of the latter to control wealthy sectors in the future.

Meanwhile, on the macroeconomic level, privatization schemes have helped considerably to balance fiscal accounts in the short term.[10] As regards the foreign sector, however, not only must present incoming capital—which is at its greatest during the first years of operation—be taken into account, but so must its inevitable counterpart in terms of the renationalization of utilities.

Another effect on the economy as a whole, and one that certainly had repercussions on the foreign sector, is the inequality of incentives in the private sector, given the current structure of relative prices. This results in the existence of two subsectors in the Argentine economy (not counting agriculture). One, which yields high and often secure profits and is protected from foreign competition, is the service industry. Noncompetitive conditions in this sphere, much of it subject to great demand, allow price fixing of a monopolistic or oligopolistic type and the financing of investment with resources generated from the operation itself. The other subsector, manufacturing, functions without incentives to investment, and, being subject to international competition, is obliged to make a profit. That the emphasis of this economic strategy is more on restructuring services than on the manufacturing industry can be seen from the sale of a significant group of public companies to consortia in which foreign creditors have a major share. It is this part of the economic plan that is new.[11]

The serious instability of Argentina's economic system, coupled with the results of stagnation—a decrease in investment, high inflation, and an inability to generate employment—struck home on the domestic social scene. This aspect of the crisis imposed restrictions and conditions on any strategy for invigorating or expanding economic activity.

In Argentina, where the distribution of wealth used to be markedly more uniform than in other countries that were at the same stage of development, the gap between rich and poor began to increase starting in the mid-1970s. Until then—as a result of certain features of the structure of Argentine society, such as the slow rise in population and early urbanization—although growth was not taking place at great speed, the indicators of living standards were on aggregate acceptable, as was the distribution of wealth. Poverty was largely confined to certain rural areas outside the pampa and the outskirts of the big cities.

Now, however, analysis shows not only a widening of the gap between rich and poor, but also that poverty is no longer incidental. The picture of a country with growing social mobility among the middle sectors and geared toward social integration now seems a picture of the past. According to the permanent census of dwellings compiled by INDEC (the National Institute of Statistics and Census), in greater Buenos Aires in 1974, low-income homes received 11.4 percent of GNP. By 1990 they received only 9.7 percent. Meanwhile, high-income families, which had accounted for 28 percent of the total income in 1974, had increased their proportion to 35.3 percent over the same sixteen-year period. The increase in the income of families in the top bracket has been at the expense of both the poor and the middle sectors of the population.

Until the mid-1970s, state social policy was based on the assumption of regular economic growth, a consequent increase in employment, and the theoretical principle of universal benefits, the inclusion of new groups receiving social support. The present critical state of social policies has been caused by the bankruptcy of public funding sources during the 1980s, which saw the virtual extinction of traditional sources of finance, an increase in tax evasion, and the proliferation of subsidies for promoting private industry.[12] In addition to these factors, the legitimacy of state intervention has come under question among social sectors qualified to give an opinion.

Theoretically, a welfare state neutralizes the unequal distribution of wealth that arises from a market economy and that negates political equality in a "rule of law" society. That is why, although the grounds for disaster in Argentina's social policy were already in place, the crisis itself did not occur until democracy was restored. Only when the democratic system came into force could critical account be taken of the functioning of social institutions and of the gap between the law and its effective operation. Empirical evidence reveals that much of the state's social administration has been inefficient and ineffective. In general terms, it could be said that the concept of universality found its voice and brought about major differences in the degree of social provision and the quality of social services only as a result of fostering manifest inequalities.

The effects of the reform process, in particular of such a profound and substantial nature as is taking place in Argentina, are not confined to the economy alone. They spill over into the political sphere as well, affecting administrative institutions, the style of government, and society's perception of the democratic system—all as a result of the reform process itself.

President Menem's policy for restructuring the Argentine economy puts the need for efficiency before respect for institutional procedures and the rule of law. Resorting to emergency decrees—a method of government common in Argentina—has also become an important institutional tool in other Latin American countries. (For example, in Brazil, the administration of Fernando Collor de Mello issued fifty-five emergency decrees—or one every two days—in 1990 alone.)

In other regions of the world where reform took a similar course, other existing governmental institutions have been bypassed: The presidents of both Poland and Russia asked their respective parliaments for an extension of powers so that they could govern by means of decree. The fact that this phenomenon has become widespread suggests that the search for solutions to grave predicaments in an economy should not be allowed to degenerate into a series of institutional emergencies. Such a process enables the executive to assume almost full autonomy, thereby forcing other areas of government to submit to its dictates.

The argument that reform is inevitable—in itself, true—also led the Argentine government to operate in a particular way. Instead of trying to reach agreement on policy with political or social bodies by institutional means, an attempt was made to weaken parties, labor unions, and other organizations within the system. The objective was to neutralize the opposition. However, other countries that carried out economic reform, such as Spain, have proved that change can take place within a framework of political and social consensus—even if with a certain amount of conflict.

Recent experiences indicate that the governing style characteristic of an emergency goes beyond that emergency and becomes an accepted form of decision making; thereafter, the process is adopted even in areas that have no connection with the economy.[13] The direct result of all this is that citizens come to believe that there is no place in the democratic system for individual or group participation; this feeling of impotence also overtakes political parties, Congress, and labor unions.

Social apathy and financial emergency produce conditions that favor a particular type of corruption. The prevalence of this corruption rises in correspondence with the wealth normally present in the system; in some instances, government decision making is based on personal advantage to the officials concerned. That situation leads to a high degree of instability in the system, and society begins to break down. In the political sphere, the citizens' lack of confidence in state action becomes reinforced.

When, in addition, checks and balances are canceled out and doubt is cast on the independence of the judiciary, social apathy is accompanied by growing uncertainty about the reliability of the legal system. In the long term, this undermines the stability of democracy as a partnership. Participation shows itself to be not only futile but also unequal to the task of creating alternative solutions to problems or of influencing public decisions. [This essay was written before Menem was reelected in 1995—Ed.]

In its second term the Menem administration confronts, in the medium term, the challenge of strengthening and perfecting Argentine democracy. The first problem is that the reelection of President Menem ran the serious risk of a political regime being installed that is supported by an authoritarian party or movement. On the other hand, if an opposition party had won the election, its first task would have been the arduous one of rebuilding republican institutions and reestablishing their independence from the executive.

It is also clear that if full structural transformation of the economy takes place with minimum consultation and debate, there will be a wide margin for wrong decisions. Democracy is not just a formality that involves the periodic reelection of representatives; it also guarantees a certain type of outcome. Discussion is an inseparable part of the act of reaching decisions of a consensual nature, and such consensus offers a greater chance that those decisions will achieve their purpose. Consensus also endows the future sociopolitical scene with a greater degree of certainty, which is essential for the stability of the policies that govern restructuring. Thus, one of the political legacies of the economic reform carried out in Argentina has been the devaluation of the very instruments of a fully democratic system.

The 1980s have been christened Latin America's lost decade. In point of fact, the events of that critical period were the result of contradictions that were implicit in the development strategy that came into being after World War II. In Argentina, the problem seems to have been exacerbated in the 1970s by the unreasonable use of too much foreign capital, which contributed to the expansion of unproductive public spending (on the defense budget, on low-profit infrastructure, and so forth) and led to a wasteful policy of state subsidies of questionable effectiveness.

Today, ten years after the restoration of democracy, Argentina urgently needs to consolidate its political system. Argentine democracy must be brought to the point where it functions automatically by the logic implicit in its principles and by the dynamic that its political forces stamp on those who uphold the system. This process is not devoid of conflict or difficulty. Just as in 1983, when the challenge was to put an end to more than fifty years of institutional instability—the underlying cause of Argentina's decline—discussion today centers on the type of democracy to be constructed. One decade later, Argentina's democracy, like all forms of government, faces the task of generating public well-being, satisfying social demands, and creating economic growth with equity, participation, and a democratic example by the leadership.

Despite the remarkable advances the country has made since the return of democracy, the problem of growth has not yet been solved. If in the first period of democratic restoration there was a genuine attempt to learn coupled with a continuing sense of optimism stemming from the belief that Argentina's problems had been solved by the revival of its institutions and "international understanding," that state of affairs no longer holds. The risk is that one simplification of reality will be replaced by another, wherein the free market will revive "animal spirits," and success will be axiomatically guaranteed.

Fiscal prudence together with controlled management of public spending is a necessary condition for ensuring economic growth, but alone it is not sufficient. The lowering of protectionist barriers against foreign competition—a first step to commercial openness—does not guarantee the expansion and diversification of exports, especially manufactured products, unless it provides an adequate relative price structure. Rather, it generates uncertainties about the development of foreign trade.[14] The transfer to the private sector of manufacturing industries that were built up by the state, coupled with advances in the process of deregulation, removes obstacles in the way of the private sector but does not necessarily lead to growth. The task of creating a strategy that combines growth with equality will appear on the political agenda throughout the 1990s.

If Argentina is to generate an internationally competitive industry that will lead to dynamic growth, concerted efforts will have to be made to devise a political strategy that will incorporate at least three fundamental ideas—the reconstruction of the state, policies leading to technological innovation, and a planned attack on poverty. For the first, released from its industrial activities, the state must rebuild its capacity to regulate and, where feasible, recreate competitive markets. Seen from another viewpoint, the competitiveness of the economy does not depend only on initiative from the private sector; it is also the product of the collective expression of the community. As has been noted by the Organization for Economic Cooperation and Development, competitiveness has to be built in, and that depends on a large number of external factors.

For the second, market competition must be understood as a whole. There must be state policies in which technological research and innovation play a central role in the effort to add intellectual value to the fund of national resources. And for the third, owing to the continuing economic crisis and the chronic disarray of social policies, there is a need for a strategy to alleviate the despair of those who see themselves as continually slipping back and to cure the cynicism of others who are rarely able to obtain access to social services.

In redefining policies, Argentina must rid itself of ideological prejudice. Argentina must avoid a situation that, in the past, led to ignoring the inefficiency and lack of transparency in the state's "centralized and universal" decision making in the name of state supremacy. Today, those with the same dogmatic attitude wish to impose a "privatized and targeted" pattern of social policies that rely on the market as the sole factor that can bring about social integration.

To avoid repeating past mistakes, Argentina must take an alternative route to overcome its difficulties. The state must recover its ability to function. It must accurately identify those sectors of the population toward whom social programs should be directed, and recognize the wide variety of types of poverty. The state must also construct a capacity for institutional coordination, not only between levels of government through decentralization but also between social sectors through organizations that complement governmental institutions. Society's growing demand for greater self-government, to be implemented more independently, should be addressed by fostering nongovernmental organizations.

Concerted efforts to plan strategies—noticeably absent over the ten years of democracy thus far—should be translated into governmental action that requires political consensus as well as consensus of a social nature. Political consensus, however, is as yet no more than an agreement on party superstructure. Social discontent can, at best, be expressed only in a marginal way, or by disregarding conventional political activity. However, that could lead to the rise of and subsequent support for new leaders who function alongside the democratic system and whose ideology does not flinch at new forms of authoritarianism.

Another social demand to be met is that of participation. It must be remembered that democracy used only as a mechanism for electing leaders with no substantial content is a pathological variety of democracy—it is pure delegative democracy. Such democracy is typified by too much delegation within the institutions set up to administer the system. Personality cults, voting by referendum, and clientele voting find their way into parliamentary and party relationships. Although institutions are defined in terms of representative democracy, people begin to behave as if the system were delegative.

This means that any genuine strategy for modernization of the political system and for social progress requires the strengthening of civic institutions. Political parties must be created that can mediate effectively between the state and society. One characteristic of modern democracies is the increasing value they place on "public space," a concept that goes beyond the old choice between state or private sector and into the development of nongovernmental organizations. Social commitment to and participation in modernization not only help to make the process of change more effective but also reduce the power of interest groups wishing to hinder reform.

As regards the demand for democratic example, in Argentina's case the arguments for setting up legal checks are well known. For the most part, the ethical principle behind these checks is the need to make the institutional changes irreversible and to demonstrate the capacity of the government to achieve set goals, thus confirming its credibility. When an emergency overtakes democratic procedure, not only are the principal agents of the political process (parliament and the parties) robbed of their lawful powers, but in addition control mechanisms are neutralized and the functions of the judiciary are subordinated. Thus, illegitimacy leads to secrecy.

Just as centrally planned economies exercise total political power, a combination of concentrated wealth and a distortion of the true nature of the democratic system generate conditions favorable to the rise of authoritarianism. In fully consolidated democracies, debate centers on the various political strategies of the parties. In the new democracies, discussion is focused on the development and functioning of the system's institutions.

Democratically originated governments that derive their legitimacy from their results rather than from their procedures are essentially weak when they cease to produce results and when awareness of their imperfections begins to influence their procedures. The situation in Argentina today demands that the challenge be met not only in the results of governmental action—such as the choice of a model for society and social values—but also in governmental mechanisms—its political system, its procedures, and its norms. Once political and social groups have achieved the degree of maturity and sense of responsibility that is acquired by experience and an eye to future dangers, it should be possible to achieve a consensus on the style of development that will ensure increasing social integration within a framework of fully functioning democratic institutions.

Notes

1. E. J. Hobsbawm, *Age of Extremes: The Short Twentieth Century, 1914–1991* (London: Michael Joseph, 1994).

2. This statement does not imply a lack of recognition of the fact that republican institutions and democratic liberties can function at varying levels (as may be the case in Haiti, for example), or of the existence of systems with strong authoritarian components and governmental control over social organizations (as in the case of Mexico).

3. Clearly my aim is not to establish a purely mechanical relationship between a country's degree of development and its chances of consolidating a democratic system, which would be to ignore the importance that each nation places on its institutional traditions and history. The uncertain political future of the countries of Eastern Europe and the Russian Federation is an interesting example.

4. This final condition is necessary, for we have witnessed economic transformation being carried out by authoritarian methods—at great social cost—in Chile under Pinochet's dictatorship and, more recently, in China.

5. In 1983 the amount of the foreign debt was equivalent to a little less than 70 percent of GNP, while interest on it amounted to around 8 percent. The fiscal deficit was therefore equal to four times the total amount of notes and coins in circulation, plus current account deposits.

6. The financial cost in 1987 of subsidies via the national budget, the taxation system, and the costs of the nationalized industries has been estimated at around U.S.$4 billion at current rates. The opportunity cost of subsidies is equal to 70 percent of the real investment of the Argentine public sector and around 25 percent of the tax collected nationally in the provinces, in the city of Buenos Aires, and from the social security system in the same year.

7. "Washington Consensus" was coined by John Williamson, ed., *Latin American Adjustment: How Much Has Happened?* (Washington, DC: Institute for International Economics, 1990), to refer, loosely, to the package of stabilizing plans being touted by the International Monetary Fund, the World Bank, and the U.S. Treasury Department.

8. Until then, the performance of the Argentine economy could have been considered reasonably acceptable. In fact, in the period between 1964 and 1974 the economy grew at an average rate of above 4.5 percent, more than double the growth rate of the population and with no period of industrial recession. Manufactured exports, which made up 3 percent of the total in 1960, rose to 24 percent by 1975. The system's fragility is expressed by the deficit in the public sector; aggravated by the explosive inflation of 1975, it reached an equivalent value of around 15 percent of GNP in that year.

9. This last mode does not figure in the Menem government's privatization policy. My thesis, therefore, is that the urgent need for fiscal revenues constituted the central axis of that policy. For a more detailed discussion of regulatory issues, see "State Reform and Deregulatory Strategies," in *Regulatory Regimes and Competition Policy in Latin America*, ed. Moises Naím and Joseph S. Tulchin, forthcoming.

10. In fact, fiscal revenues in 1991 were identical to the transfers to international agencies. The amount, almost U.S.$3 billion, is equivalent to 60 percent of the fiscal surplus recorded that year.

11. Economic justification for privatization is not new. Over two centuries ago, Adam Smith declared that "in all the great monarchies of Europe, the sale of royal lands would produce very high sums which, if they were used to redeem

the public debt, would release much greater revenues than would have been possible by giving these lands to the crown. Once these properties passed into private hands, in a few years they would be much improved and better cultivated."

12. Surpluses in the social security system, direct taxes, and retentions on agricultural exports intended to take part of the income from the land, which in 1950 contributed a fiscal income of an equivalent of 10 percent of GNP, in 1986 represented a shift from the public sector of 0.5 percent of GNP.

13. A paradigmatic case, this is not the sanction of any law in particular but the working out of a body of laws, in this case the Código de Transito (Transit Code). This situation is in open violation of constitutional norms. Article 67, clause 11, of the National Constitution granted the Congress powers to frame and pass different national codes as well as laws of a federal nature.

14. The amount of capital required annually, assuming a 4 percent yearly growth rate, given the present relative price structure, will rise in the period from 1993 to 1997 to an annual average of around U.S.$18 billion.

2

The Implications of Change

The Political Challenge to Argentine Economic Stability

José Octavio Bordón

Since its transition to democracy, Argentina has undergone changes of nearly unprecedented depth and rapidity. Although everyone agrees on the fundamental importance of the reforms, there is no such unanimity in the evaluation of them. This divergence had caused widespread political debate on Argentina's institutional and socioeconomic future, as well as on its place in the world.

Despite the failures and shortages that the government and citizens have endured since 1983, it cannot be denied that Argentina has changed substantially in the past ten years. Today's politically and economically adjusted Argentina is the product of the restoration of continuously functioning democratic institutions, changes in patterns of political behavior, and the regular replacement of the country's leaders and representatives as support shifts from one party to another. Public opinion, the emergence of a newly empowered citizenry, and a free press have had considerable influence in this process.

There is a consensus in the nation that President Menem's economic stabilization program has made an important contribution to the country's improved image. While some disagreement still exists over the analysis of the features and the effects of the reforms, as well as over the state's new relationship with labor, capital, and production, there is basic agreement that the old political and economic system could not have maintained itself. Furthermore, many believe that decentralization, debureaucratization, and deregulation were necessary in order to make Argentine production and trade methods uniform with those of the rest of the world.

This consensus, however, is becoming blurred. In what areas? For what reasons? To what extent does this affect the predictability and stability of Argentina's economic and institutional system? It is crucial to the future of the country that enlightened debate take place on this subject, so that democracy may be strengthened, the quality of life improved, and stability and progress maintained in Latin America. At this stage of events, questions about the political aspects of economic change should not be wrongly interpreted as desire to know what conditions led to the creation of a stabilization program within the framework of ideas put forward in the "Washington Consensus."[1]

A majority of Argentines respect and value most of the initiatives that were adopted in the past to conquer hyperinflation. Now that the crisis has been overcome, however, many believe that mere political and economic stability are not sufficient. Some perceive that, while the market and its institutions provide the basic framework for economic stability, they do not in themselves guarantee self-sustained economic growth or equality in distribution.

Even among those who broadly support the policies of stabilization, a fierce debate has arisen on past and future policies. For example, many question the strategies enacted to combat inflation. Also, many have doubts about the policy of closing fiscal accounts by using resources produced by privatization schemes to service the national budget and the foreign debt. Some maintain that rather than create a deficit, the government should have used this capital to lay down a public and private source of funding for the modernization of industry, education, and services. Yet another criticism is that the government's stability policy seems to have placed limits on the process of equitable growth. Furthermore, the Argentine government must carefully analyze its ability to control and regulate potentially destabilizing shifts in the economic climate. For example, the government must keep close tabs on issues such as currency revaluations and export problems; the effect of the reduction of high expenditures on the nation's inefficient infrastructure, particularly the high tariffs placed on private services; the provision of highly trained workers for the production process; negotiations and explicit commitments concerning future production and export of hydrocarbons; and, finally, the future deactivation of strategic development plans.

Macroeconomic variables no longer provoke as much concern for the short term as they did from the mid-1970s to the early 1990s. Apart from questions surrounding salary for the armed forces, Argentina's institutional system faces no risk of alteration. International economic and political power centers veer from indifference to enthusiasm about the present situation in Argentina. Despite all the favorable aspects, a note of worry can be detected where optimistic enthusiasm might be hoped for. The volatility of the capital market, insufficient investment in the middle and long term, the trade balance deficit, and high interest rates are some of the economic factors that justify such worry. Tensions generated by attempts to reform the constitution so as to permit the reelection of the president and excessively electoralist posturing from the opposition as well as the government in power add political elements to this scenario. In this context it is important to point out that, although Argentina's political institutions are fully functional and there is unprecedented freedom of the press, a climate of doubt still exists as to the independence of the judiciary.

Argentine and foreign observers feel ambivalent, therefore, about judging what has taken place in Argentina, especially when evaluating its importance. While most people are optimistic about the country's future, there is worry that no plan has yet been established to ensure stability over the middle and long run. In order to forecast the future of the nation, therefore, one must consider both why and how Argentina has been transformed, the changes still to be made, the domestic and international position of the nation, and how it will evolve over the rest of the decade.

A Methodological Presentation

When analyzing social change, it is difficult to distinguish accurately between causes and effects. This is especially true in a case of such great complexity as Argentina. Thus, in order to establish a successful economic program after two consecutive periods of hyperinflation, the Argentine government must seek to alter both social and political behavior. In so doing, a two-way causal relationship will be formed whereby the economic system affects the political system and vice versa. This relationship is complex and its factors interdependent, and it should be treated as such.

Given that the initiative for structural change emerges most forcefully from the economic sphere, it would seem necessary to adopt a flexible approach in analyzing a) explicit objectives to which the economic program is to be applied, b) its immediate effects on the political system, c) new and continuing demands in the economic sphere arising from ongoing political change, d) a profile for a future political structure that will help to stabilize the country's transformation, and e) conditioning factors and possibilities offered by the international system and their effects on the economic sphere and the political system.

Implementing the Economic Program

The Argentine government's economic goals in the mid-1990s might be summarized as an attempt to give predictability to economic behavior. To avoid violent changes of course and speculative trends of any kind, it was rightly thought necessary that the frame of reference set up for government regulation and activity be stable, not only as a matter of form, but also—and especially—because of macroeconomic consequences.

As a result, top priority was given to the elimination of the budget deficit and the drastic reduction of state activity in the production of goods and services. It was hoped that these policies would effectively curtail hyperinflation by limiting both the government's demand for funds and the excessive printing of money to finance public expenditure. These steps also contributed to the improvement of tax collection; the privatization of a number of natural resource monopolies, for which regulations are needed; the transfer of control over education and health care from the central government to provincial and municipal authorities; and, finally, the establishment of substantial modifications in the management of labor and social services. Each of these initiatives, however, involves major adaptations in interpersonal institutional relationships that must completely transcend the economic plane both in practical and theoretical terms.

In the arena of international economic relationships, Argentina's program has also succeeded in adopting initiatives that greatly influence the political sphere. International free trade and competition as well as regional and continental integration will bring the economy forcefully into the sphere of traditional diplomatic activity. For instance, negotiators for a country with a closed economy must place emphasis on controlling the influx of merchandise across its frontiers. Future Argentine diplomats, on the other hand, must develop a capacity to generate new ties that encourage the influx of capital, technology, and commercial interchange.

Argentina's revived economic situation also has led to the creation of a new framework for renegotiating the country's foreign debt. Since Argentina submitted itself to the Brady Plan,* however, no substantial change has been observed in the consideration of Argentina's financial relations with other countries. Here it is important to note that since the signing of the Brady Plan in 1993, Argentina has succeeded in stabilizing its foreign

*The Brady Plan is an initiative designed by U.S. President George Bush's secretary of the treasury in 1989. It calls upon commercial banks to reduce their Latin American debt claims in exchange for repayment guaranteed by industrial nations and multilateral institutions.

debt, thus implying a clear recognition of both the existence of the debt and the need for refinancing in the future. In other words, Argentina has ceased to be a bad debtor and should move to organize its international financial relations from this new standpoint.

Immediate Effects on the Political System

Analysts of present-day Argentina are faced with a contradiction. On the one hand, they have before them a multifaceted reality that is developing as it goes along and for which, to a considerable degree, ex post facto theories are created to justify decisions that have already been adopted. On the other hand, they must be able to see the main direction in which events are heading so that they can make accurate predictions. In the first instance, they must cover a whole range of situations. The task of synthesis, however, demands a process of simplification and the loss of subtleties in exchange for gaining understanding of the essential facts. There are three important effects that the economic program set up in 1991 has had on the political system.

The Need for Greater Administrative Efficiency

Lack of economic control, caused by many years of institutional instability, substantially cut back the scope for political discussion. When the only subject of real intellectual breadth is personal survival, and instability makes it impossible to analyze causes or formulate remedies, the result is a pompous and exaggerated argument without the complementary need for practical political measures. In such circumstances, real power, if it resides anywhere, does not reside in the political leadership. Therefore, nothing really important is suggested because it will never be possible to put it into practice. Instability destroys all social structures and—in a way that is not fully understood—the power relationships that underpin the political system.

The result is not only that political groups cannot function, but also that a process of attrition attacks the very symbols that should unite the community. These symbols lose relevance from being applied frivolously and, because of the ongoing crisis, without practical results. Terms like "the nation's destiny," "the traditional way of life," "duty," "honor," "social values," and "family values" are emptied of all meaning. In such a situation, what is important is that a nation recover its underlying values, which are essential but intangible and not connected in any obvious way to an everyday reality that is out of control and inexplicable. It becomes vital to reconcile values with ideals, ideals with plans, and words with deeds.

Once the turbulence is calmed by economic orderliness, there arises a political duty to explain and respond to the social issues that stand revealed and that begin to take priority. An effective way to stimulate economic development, setting up a reliable social security system, rationalizing access to a megalopolis such as Buenos Aires, and restructuring of the railways are some of the most important technical subjects with political and social effects for which politicians must have concrete, practical proposals. Political leadership has a twofold role. On the one hand, it has a basic need to justify its existence to a society clamoring for ever more specific answers. On the other, the leadership must give due weight to the purely technical task of trying to formulate appropriate objectives, with the risk of giving inadequate attention to problem solving. Lowering prices, reducing public spending, and increasing state social spending are not always the only or chief factors that should go into determining any given course. To assign priorities, to bring sectoral policies into accord, to produce a consensus, to detect rapid international changes that may have a direct impact on Argentine life, to increase the productivity of public spending and to improve administrative systems— these are some of the problems that, in the country's new condition, will provide a challenge to leadership.

This responsibility can only be assumed by a new brand of politician, one different from those who, in the recent past, heroically survived personal and institutional insecurity. This is not a dogmatic observation but a recognition of the gradual change that has taken place in Argentina and the need to adapt to conditions that demand a new political profile.

This demand does not always receive adequate response from leaders who tend to draw comparisons between the present economically stable situation and the hyperinflationary crises of the past. Such a comparison inevitably leads to self-congratulation. While it should be acknowledged that the current situation is good compared with that of the past, the demand for a future of sustained economic growth and the satisfying of social demands must also be addressed. Seen from a middle- and long-term perspective, not all the signs are positive, nor are all the economic indicators favorable. On the political level, one unpredictable element is that matters for the next twenty years are being discussed as if they were important only for tomorrow. On the economic level, one reservation arises from the fact that the Argentine government still periodically resorts to cash from privatization schemes to finance spending. Nor is the international situation clear; in a world full of major upheavals, dependence on outside capital to finance the trade deficit involves an element of risk.

Moreover, the outlook for the transferable manufactured goods sector—the most important motor for growth in the long term—is not very encouraging. Major reforms in production are needed to enable Argentina to compete in world markets and to generate profitable businesses. A combination of political and economic uncertainty generates a feeling of ambivalence. In the short term, the economic picture looks positive, much better than it did just two years ago. However, there are still important areas that are not functioning. These, rather than a list of problems, are the ongoing agenda, which may in itself lead to a rational structure and greater predictability. Wide-ranging debate will be required to establish the necessary consensus over long-term policies, not only for the Argentina of today but also for the Argentina of tomorrow.[2]

The Need for Ethics

The most encouraging trend in this regard is the demand by the population for leaders who are not only efficient but also fundamentally honest. The general perception by the people of widespread, growing corruption that tinges all political groups equally is a serious obstacle, and its endangers the country's entire development. There is a need for thoroughgoing measures that will forestall and punish all corrupt practices. Although the economic sphere has created the necessary basic conditions for firm action against corruption, a clear policy in this field has not yet been envisioned. The gravity of this problem in Latin American countries should not be underestimated, for it is without doubt one of the most serious ills that democratic governments must strive to eradicate—as the crisis in Brazil's institutions, the political cataclysm in Italy, and the problems in Japan show. It is especially important at this stage in social reform that politicians stand for trust, transparency, and predictability. Those who decide to invest their savings in the middle and long term require leadership and rules that reject secrecy.

The growing role of a press that enjoys full freedom and a newly empowered citizenry that interacts positively with the mass media are new factors that have made political leaders more accountable to the electorate and have thus been a positive force in the struggle against corruption. However, the party in opposition tends to use the charge of corruption as an indiscriminate political weapon; the activities of that same party, when it is in power, prove that corruption is a deeply cultural problem and not the monopoly of any one particular party. In one way or another, the small corruptions that exist in everyone must be overcome, just as the tendency to moralize, which leads to a general condemnation of all politicians, must be avoided. The problem is cultural and institutional and, in the end, has to be solved on a national scale.

The situation demands fundamental changes that, by causing patterns of behavior to interact with structures, will really alter the course of events. Among such changes, an obvious one is an improvement in the process for selecting political leaders and representatives. In Argentina, as in other parts of the world, legal and institutional changes have begun. Party organizations are being opened up to give all citizens who are interested in the process of electing candidates a chance to take part, a chance to change the rules laid down by political parties for the tasks that congressmen will undertake, as well as to supervise the financing of political parties and to exercise greater control over the costs of electoral campaigns. Another subject that needs to be discussed in Argentina, as in the United States, is limiting the terms of office of representatives. A prolonged term in power often leads to an increase in bureaucracy, which in its turn can make openings for corruption.

An independent judiciary is fundamental. Such a judicial system must be committed to democracy, be speedy in its findings, and be accessible to all citizens. The creation of assemblies of magistrates and penal courts, greater speed and responsibility by the judiciary in dealing with paperwork, and a systematic effort to improve and modernize the administration of justice will not only better guarantee the protection of public and personal freedoms but also foster economic growth, which depends on investment just as investment depends on an honest legal system.

All these changes have set postmodern democracies in a framework wherein new forms of expression of citizen power through the mass media have deprived political parties of their monopoly to represent distinctive groups or social demands. This does not mean that political parties or representative democratic institutions have been abolished, nor that "abstract democracy" has been replaced by "corporate democracy." It means that more traditional forms of political representation are being complemented by new forms generated by the exercise of democracy throughout Latin America, just as new communication technology has led to new ways of expressing social demands and interests.

The Need for Decentralization of Responsibility

Argentina is a country of federal institutions with a long tradition of centralized power. Prolonged interruptions in democratic life have increased this concentration of power and have been a major influence on the behavior of politicians guiding the present democratic process.

From 1983 on, there have been various attempts to reach political agreements to bring the structure of the federal government closer to its declared intention of giving autonomy to the provinces. Several documents have been signed, but in practice little headway has been made. It is the economic program now under way that is giving special impetus to this process, even though this impetus stems from conflict rather than from any specific plan. Since the initial decision to rationalize the central government's finances, there has in fact been a massive transfer to the provinces of basic services, such as the administration of health and education and, more recently, of long-distance public transportation. Electricity generation and gas distribution have also been privatized with schemes for regional administration that will require provincial rather than national supervision.

This, in sum, has led to a massive transfer of responsibility—not always with proportionate financial resources or technical and management training—to local governments. These, in their turn, have had to collaborate with national agencies that either no longer exist or that are in the process of being dissolved. Like all sudden change that is not fully explicit or planned, this is a risky operation. However, insofar as its scope and potential can be assessed and its organization and implementation can be planned, decentralization may lead to a new kind of relationship between leaders and the community. Better contact between the respective levels of government would certainly reduce the likelihood of social demands being distorted, while increasing the chance of their being satisfied.

Similarly, the central government could formulate new policies for the services whose administration has been transferred. This seems an ideal opportunity to think in terms of a framework of educational and health policies able to deal with existing emergencies and to give the country a long-term view, with well-defined goals and ways of achieving them. This excellent opportunity, created by the trend to decentralization, must be used to evolve democratic institutions and increase social participation. The chance for success depends on whether politicians can bring to the subject the serious consideration it needs and create the structures to deal with it.

There must, in conclusion, be a federal fiscal contract to define the functions of the state at its three levels—federal, provincial, and municipal—and its commitment to and from the private sector. In the same way, setting up decentralized institutions by legal and political means should clearly define the functions of the state, the resources for each administrative level, and the resources that nonstate bodies should contribute to the state. This agreement should also imply a commitment to productivity on the part of state bodies. With these resources, the quantity and quality of the services offered would increase. Greater productivity from public spending, thanks to greater managerial efficiency, is one of the keys to growth with equality in Argentina. A more efficient state not only offers lower costs to private companies, making them consequently more competitive, but also gives the state greater legitimacy to "demand" higher productivity and social commitment from private enterprise.

Seen thus, growth does not involve only one particular administrative level—even if that is the state. It is rather the concern of the whole governing body, the various public agencies, the entire administrative spectrum, and the private sector—in short, the whole community. A federal fiscal contract is thus the grassroots institution needed to underpin a new growth strategy based on a culture of work, effort, and solidarity.

This recasting of the institutions concerned with fiscal relationships among the various governmental levels and between state and society is another essential requirement for consolidating the stability achieved by the economic program. Instability justified special rules, but the new stability must urge all those involved into an open, democratic debate to produce a consensus that will lay the foundations of a new pact. Stability cannot exist alongside secrecy. Such a political-institutional pact, molded by corresponding legislation, will underpin a situation of fiscal predictability, thereby clarifying to everyone which resources belong to the state and what it is providing in return. This will improve efficiency and obviate not only the duplication of function among the different administrative levels but also the failure to offer essential services as a result of fiscal chaos and irregularities.

Ongoing Demands and New Economic Demands

The essence of any plan for stability is to achieve predictability by means of personal and collective patterns of behavior. But what happens when large parts of the community reach this stage but nonetheless see the future as unsatisfactory? A significant paradox of present-day Argentina— and of any attempt to inject order into chaos—is that when a ship is sinking, being offered a rowboat can delude one into feeling safe. But the view from the rowboat—a calm sea and a blazing sun—can destroy all hope; each new day will be the same as today, just because it is predictable. When a community acknowledges the demand for present and future effort, the social demand it makes of a long-range economic program is that it offer a definite, credible hope of a better quality of life for everyone.

Pluralist democracies with market economies and social justice are not constructed to maximize individual selfishness. The mainspring of a fulfilled community is the individual and collective embodiment of people's dreams as a practical political program. Such a community is also based on coherent and efficient leadership and the fact that each citizen accepts responsibility for himself and accepts the social and institutional control that a republican democracy should exercise in the name of the people and of the aims they freely voice. The reasons behind and objectives of every effort to improve the lives of the people should always have the support and backing of the whole community. They should be objectives that all understand and agree upon. That is the political aspect of economic change. If such change does not bring with it achievable humanistic goals, identifiable as good and true, the people will neither believe in it nor embrace it. "A world population wanting an ever greater number of objects, growing pressure on the consumption of ephemera, the general demand for instant satisfaction, will in the end kill life."[3] There is a consensus on this subject in Argentina, and a number of measures to combat it are being considered. The most politically relevant will be discussed here.

It is first necessary to discover to what extent the market promotes a society's economic activity. The value of competition as a stimulus to human creativity is universally recognized. What, however, is the real possibility of genuine competition in today's economic climate? What is this possibility in Argentina? How do distortions in the market affect the common good? How should these distortions be offset? Such questions, which are being asked in Argentina and around the world, attract replies of varying accuracy and with a wide range of political consequences. This is clearly not a controversy in isolation but one that has essential relevance to the topics discussed here.

Despite the imprecision, swings in political theory, and the ideological wavering that market economics is subject to everywhere, every community at each period in its history must try to reach agreement on these questions. Only such a consensus makes it possible to define the role of the state, of individuals, of large corporations, of the political system, and of society as a whole. That situation does not exist in Argentina. There is, of course, a kind of official doctrine on the subject, which is manifested more by its practical execution than by any surrounding theoretical framework. But there has been no debate, either large or small, on how to achieve a uniformity of judgment that will become implicit in society and enable it to move on to more complex and concrete stages. On the contrary, a quasi-dogmatic belief in the self-activating and perfecting abilities of market mechanisms has been imposed either by the government or by other social sectors, thus creating an obstacle to enlightened debate and paralyzing any effort to create policies to support and improve the market. Argentina has moved from an almost total condemnation of market mechanisms in the past to virtually developing pride in it. Such swinging from one extreme to the other is clearly counterproductive. "Capitalism is not an ideology, it is a practice."[4]

Some other questions are, in one way or another, corollaries of this lack of debate. However, they have such relevance of their own that they cannot be ignored. This is the case with the attitude toward social policies and poverty. The crisis in the 1980s did not necessarily lead to a cut in social spending. What has been substantially cut has been public spending on effective, compensatory policies to do with technology and production. What has changed is the internal composition of social spending. The part designated to finance the growing deficit in the social welfare system and in assistance targeted to high-risk sectors has been increased. The budgetary victims are the elderly without insurance (who need more assistance) and recipients of universal social policies, such as health and education. The fact that all of these changes are occurring at the same time is undermining public services, lowering the skills of workers and professionals, and reducing the living standards of wide sectors of the population.[5] A competitive economy cannot be achieved by factories staffed by workers who cannot effectively bring expertise into the productive process, nor can such an economy come about in the midst of shantytowns. This whole problem requires more than policies targeted from the outside or a mere increase in social spending. It needs a modern participatory social policy that is not controlled by the state and that can interrelate public with private spending and worker relationships with flexible production.

Whatever the market's relative size, it is also axiomatic that competition means winners and losers. This is true for businesses as well as for individuals. It is also clear that once a high level of poverty has been created, that poverty tends to be fed simultaneously by a whole group of mechanisms, including individuals' technical skills, the state of their health, the infrastructure in their communities, their access (and that of their children) to education, and their tendency to social ills such as alcoholism, drug addiction, and theft.

Poverty in Argentina—and for that matter, everywhere else—is related in a variety of ways to other social conditions, and it cannot be cured by mere injections of money or by any policy of only limited scope. The subject needs a comprehensive approach for which mere assistance schemes, which sporadically supply goods but no new frameworks of reference, are not a substitute. Any new approach would certainly require new governmental structures capable of acting quickly and precisely, without bureaucratic rigidity, and offering models of social behavior rather than regulations.

Decentralization of responsibility for the provision of services categorically changes the nature of the state. Until now, not only was the administration of spending centralized but so was the right to generate resources; more seriously still, a whole system of closely associated values and power had developed. The current setup must inevitably give way to another in which local governments acquire more economic and financial autonomy. This will eventually give them more flexibility to attend to regional demands, which will stimulate still further demands, in a useful spiral that will permit greater attention to be paid to each community's practical needs. However, to bring about this state of affairs, central government must reformulate policies for public and private enterprise, which must be put into action with agreement from the provinces. That should result in the stable consensus fundamental for the next stage.

The Future Political Structure of Argentina

It would seem that the political system will consist of a distinctly smaller, more debureaucratized and more decentralized state than has been traditional in Argentina. The state's capacity to govern will be—that is, should be—substantially greater than that hitherto required. The entrepreneurial role of the state will disappear, and efficient administration will be almost a prerequisite. Above all, the political leadership will have to assume the role of model, facilitator, and supervisor in solving society's problems.

Any analyst of the present situation must remember that a central feature of the past has been isolation—not only economic but also political and even human. Therefore, it is essential that the political leadership head the long and painstaking process of tying in with other societies and encouraging cross-cultural exchange.

One fundamental corollary is accountability for both national and local governments, each on its own level. This will demand a homogeneous outlook that until now was not crucial to the political system. One requirement that the new reality makes of politics is that it interrelate national political parties with an ever more vigorous local democracy. A strong interaction is envisaged between social demands and political structures that must be adapted to the new times or else run the risk of putting the brakes on development. This means that politicians should become far more receptive than they now are to interaction with citizens. The demands of individuals and groups set institutional, economic, and social modernization in motion—but only to the extent to which the leadership is capable of avoiding isolation, demagoguery, and resignation.

Conditions and Possibilities Offered by the International System

The fall of the Berlin Wall in November 1989 marked not the end of one stage and the onset of another but the beginning of a period of transition that the breakup of the Soviet Union at the end of 1991 has not yet brought to a conclusion. The most obvious feature of the present international situation is its high degree of instability. The end of the Cold War signaled the end of a clearly defined order that has not yet been replaced. Events in Somalia, Yugoslavia, and the former Soviet republics are clear proof of this assessment. Other phenomena, such as the proliferation of weapons of mass destruction, which is a by-product of events in the former Soviet Union and which has been furthered by the decision of North Korea to withdraw from the Nuclear Non-Proliferation Treaty, bring to the fore, particularly in Asia, acute security problems that ending the Cold War might have been expected to solve.

Economic interdependence, which evolved under the influence of confrontation between the United States and the Soviet Union, has been a powerful force for integration all over the world. The dissolution of the Soviet Union and the end of the Cold War have released "fragmentary forces" based on national, ethnic, and religious factors that had for a long time taken a back seat to the dialectical tension between the two super-powers.[6] The impact of this fragmentation has been boosted by a world economic scenario in which growth figures produced by the principal powers record what has been described as "slow growth" or "controlled depression."

In the economic sphere, the world underwent a marked deceleration in economic growth beginning in 1990. While the growth rate of the international economy rose to an acceptable level (3.5 to 4.4 percent) during the second half of the 1980s, the 1990s signaled the onset of marked international deceleration. The growth rate fell to 2 percent in 1990, was practically nil in 1991 (0.1 percent), and was only 0.8 percent in 1992. Between 1991 and 1993, different types of developed economies went through periods of recession: the United States, Great Britain, and Canada (1991); Germany and Japan (1992); and France (1993).[7]

The reasons for this recession varied from region to region. In Europe, the high cost of German reunification led to an increase in the

Bundesbank's interest rates, which was passed on to the rest of the European Union. In Japan, the "bubble economy," the strong speculative currents of the 1980s generated by permissive fiscal and monetary policies, was brought to an end by its own contradictions and changes in regulations. In the United States, recession was caused by a restructuring and reduction of debt levels both of companies and of consumers that led to a fall in consumption and investment, as well as problems in the construction industry, the financial system, and reductions in defense spending.

One consequence of economic deceleration has been an increase in unemployment levels. In the developed countries as a whole, unemployment levels rose from 6 percent in 1990 to 8 percent in 1992. The situation in some regions and countries was even worse. France and Great Britain had rates of more than 10 percent, and Italy and Canada topped 11 percent. The United States also had a high rate, which climbed from 5.5 to 7.5 percent, and Germany, with a leap from 6 to 8 percent, about the average, was no exception. The single exception is Japan, which maintained full employment with an enviable unemployment rate of a little above 2 percent.[8]

Prospects for overcoming the recession are not obvious. Although macroeconomic indicators in the United States see a change of trend, which it is hoped will be maintained in the middle term, the projected rate of 3 percent annual growth, and, in particular, the Clinton administration's aim to increase levels of production and employment, suggest only a moderate increase in North American imports, such that it will be difficult for the United States to remain the driving force in the world economy it was at the beginning of the 1980s. However, the positive effect that reduction in the North American fiscal deficit will have on the international economy in general, due to controlled interest rates and to inflation levels significantly lower than those in past decades, should be recognized.

In this context, the developed countries should not waste the chance to reach agreement on a coordinated plan to stimulate growth at world level. The GATT should promote a fresh increase in world trade. However, the serious domestic problems faced by the majority of governments in the countries of the Group of Seven leave room for doubt that these objectives will be rapidly achieved. Even more uncertain are the consequences that any potential agreements may have both on the developed countries and on Argentina.

All this adds up to a panorama of the world that may well result in harmful shocks to Argentina's economic and political development. Slow economic growth on a world scale, together with the advance of protectionism (partly a result of slow growth), may exacerbate Argentina's overseas trade imbalance to a point where it cannot be financed by injections of foreign capital. The deteriorating situation in Russia may have a harmful impact on confidence in world financial markets and on international prices (not to mention the possibility of more serious problems of a military nature). The difficult economic situation and the fragmentation of political leadership in Europe and Japan, together with the trend in the United States to turn in on itself and its domestic problems, could bring about a deterioration in world economic and political conditions.

A positive scenario would be one in which a reactivation of the world economy and trade, together with stable financial conditions, would permit Argentina to finance a moderate deficit in its budget. At a more general level, economic reactivation and political stability demand that the United States, having overcome its domestic political "gridlock," not decide to take a vacation from the world or impose its will on other nations without providing the leadership needed to find a way out of the present situation, given that the various warring factions in Europe, Japan, Russia, and other countries in upheaval signal the need for commitment and cooperation in facing present difficulties. Argentina, however, cannot ignore the possibility that, if one or more of the elements in this positive scenario do not materialize, it could be adversely affected by reverberations from abroad in the near future.

One cause for concern in the political sphere is the breakdown of political institutions in Russia and the effects of that breakdown on its relationship with the other former Soviet republics, in particular the Ukraine. The dismemberment of the Soviet Union has not meant the disappearance of the strategic and tactical nuclear weapons that are in the hands of the four former Soviet republics that are signatories to START. Instability makes it impossible to see any easy way out of the problems between the newly independent states and Russia. It is imperative that the United States begins to evolve a vigorous foreign policy toward Russia. The critical situation there demands such a policy, not only to maintain stability in the countries of the former Soviet Union but also to satisfy the security interests of the United States.

On the other hand, the international situation might enable the U.S. government to form a policy that will justify the exercise of world leadership to which North America aspires. To do this it will have to evolve a new global strategy to replace the one that existed during the superpower standoff that lasted from the end of World War II until the collapse of the Soviet Union. Such new leadership, however, must coexist with an international power structure that—from an economic point of view, at least—is many-sided and that should therefore more resemble some form of shared power than the unilateral situation that now seems both economically and politically impracticable.

This might be an appropriate juncture at which to look at economic and political competition among North America, Europe, and the Asiatic Pacific, and among their respective leaders, the United States, Germany, and Japan. Despite the disappearance of the Soviet threat, contention among the three blocks should not be seen as inevitable. One group of variables is urging such contention. But there are other factors, too—the cooperation required to stimulate economic growth at the international level and the need for a collective defense strategy for dealing with the regional problems bequeathed by the Cold War and with new problems arising from disintegration and ethnic struggle. To address these problems will require a high level of cooperation and coordination among the three leaders.

The Clinton administration has, from the outset, concentrated its attention mainly on domestic policy, especially on the economy. Foreign policy matters have not been given their former priority, although the war in Bosnia and the crisis in Russia, as well as continuing negotiations in the Middle East, have achieved some level of attention. U.S. policy toward Latin America, like that toward other areas, lacks definition. Many people believe that the absence of major crises in Latin America may tempt the United States to slide back into its traditional attitude of "benign neglect."[9] The dangers of such a lack of policy have not only been widely studied by specialists but have also been demonstrated throughout the history of inter-American relations, in which some sort of economic, military, or political crisis has always followed periods of "benign neglect." There may be no serious likelihood today of an increase in military activity in Latin America, although events in Haiti, Venezuela, and Peru have shown that, in some cases, when economic crises go hand in hand with the breakdown of institutions, the results are serious complications for democratic structures in the region.[10] It is, therefore, important to stress the Organization of American States' commitment to the defense of democracy. With the reform of its charter, that organization will be able to make a significant contribution and, by eliminating confrontational, separatist, and isolationist tendencies, take a greater part in the consolidation of democratic regimes throughout Latin America.

At the same time, certain groups in the United States are beginning to perceive that, given the growing fragmentation and turbulence on the international scene, Latin American matters are of vital interest to the United States.[11] The post-Cold War international situation and the political and economic changes that have occurred in the majority of Latin

American countries provide an unequaled opportunity to reach a new stage in relations between the United States and Latin America.

Latin America, which many believed was doomed to vanish from the world political map once the stimulus behind the superpower confrontation disappeared, has made categorical changes in its politics and economics, including a change of attitude in its relationship toward the United States. The transformation that has taken place in the Argentine republic, in particular, rests on the change of outlook that overtook its people and leaders as a result of the turbulence in its recent past. The foreign policy of democratic Argentine governments has been built around that change. At the center of concern has been the need to redefine the context of relations with the United States. The accent in the bilateral relationship used to be on "asymmetry"; now it is on "alignment." The changes that have taken place within Latin America present a unique opportunity to lay the foundation of a partnership between the United States and Argentina based on the latter's key regional commitments in the Southern Cone. It is important to emphasize that this is an ideal juncture to interrelate the needs of the whole region so as to evolve a jointly agreed upon agenda of inter-American relations that truly represents the interests of all sides.

A dramatic change in the bilateral relationship between Argentina and the United States was planned and put into action by the Argentine government after 1989. Not only did the two countries agree on specific policies and ways of implementing them, but they also reached a decision to improve relations significantly. However, some of the ideas that fostered this policy, above all certain false conclusions arising from unrealistic expectations as to what should follow once the decisions had been adopted, must be revised if the foundations of a new stage in Argentina's relationship with the United States are to be laid down.

Historically the relationship has not been smooth, and to expect all differences between the two countries to disappear would be unrealistic and counterproductive.[12] This observation—one that rarely comes to the fore—seeks to obviate problems that might be generated by excessively high expectations of the results from a supposedly privileged relationship between two countries. It is, therefore, important to recognize Argentina's place in the world and the problems a country customarily faces when it does not occupy a central position on the international stage. Argentina's entry onto the world stage, like that of any other country, must be planned and carried out with a middle- and long-term perspective, for no exclusive alignment in a complex and multilateral world can solve the problems it will face.

These remarks should not be seen as a nostalgic call for a return to a past full of the sterile confrontations that arose from Argentina's tendency to see its international relations in the form of a series of intractable conflicts or zero-sum games. That attitude not only cost Argentina considerable sums of money but also used up scarce and important energies in the foreign sphere that could and should have been invested in creating firm, realistic relationships with other countries. This assessment, together with a recognition of what has been achieved, should be seen as a reasoned call to create a stable bond between Argentina and the United States, founded on the legitimate interests of both parties.

Systematic improvement in this bilateral relationship should have made the relationship strong enough for the parties to overcome disagreements through negotiation and a search for common advantage, when that is possible, as well as through recognizing their legitimate, distinctive, but divergent interests within a framework of mutual understanding. Normal disagreement between the two countries should not be seen as intractable, but as being open to solution for all parties concerned.

Not only must the two countries make good use of the cultural change that should go hand in hand with regularizing financial relations, but they must also capitalize on the advances that have been observed in this relationship over the past ten years—especially those stemming from the present Argentine government's efforts to place the relationship on a more equal footing. Such equality would not pretend to ignore the significant difference in power between the two nations, but it would demand a change in cultural attitudes on the part of Argentines to enable them to protect their legitimate interests without creating insoluble conflicts. On the part of North Americans, it would mean coming to understand and accept that a country with a leading role in the Southern Cone and in Latin America also deserves the right to protect its legitimate interests.

I do not want to conclude without airing some thoughts on the Mercado Común del Sur (MERCOSUR), and especially on relations between Argentina and Brazil and the development of their respective economies. Integration between the two countries, and the extension of that integration to the Southern Cone, is one of the main planks of Argentina's policy toward its neighbors. The problems that Brazil's political and economic instability and disagreements over macroeconomic policies have finally engendered among the members of the group, problems that have undermined MERCOSUR's viability, should be analyzed in the light of long-term needs and interests and solved in the short and middle term by implementing creative ideas that will satisfy all the members. Any plan for leveling out imbalances in dealings within MERCOSUR should take into account that such measures should aim to achieve the political and economic objectives of Argentina and her partners. The experience of MERCOSUR should be capitalized on, making it clear to everyone that the structural problems faced by the countries—such as their political and economic entry onto the international scene and the creation of a pattern of growth with equality for present and future generations of Argentines and inhabitants of the Southern Cone—can be solved only in a comprehensive and systematic way. If there is one feature common to all the countries that make up the exclusive club called the First World, it is their ability to evolve and implement strategies by which to confront problems presented to them by international economics and politics. Argentina will not acquire such abilities by changing its policies as problems arise but, rather, by showing that it is capable of fulfilling its commitments and that the unpredictability that plagued its past has finally been overcome.

Integration in the Southern Cone covers both political and economic relations between Argentina and Chile. This fact has led to an increase in financial interdependence, resulting not only in greater commercial links and the fact that capital investment from one country has a significant influence on the other, but also in the defusing of age-old sources of contention between the two countries, which share one of the world's longest borders. These moves toward greater integration have had positive effects on mutual security, such as the negotiations between Argentina and Brazil over safeguards in nuclear energy programs that culminated in the recent ratification of the Treaty of Tlatelolco by the Argentine Congress and also by Brazil and Chile, and the initiatives under way among the three countries of the Southern Cone to abolish chemical weapons.

The evolution and improvement of MERCOSUR and its association with and extension to other neighboring countries should be seen as one of the most positive developments in foreign policy in the Southern Cone of South America. MERCOSUR is producing a market of major significance to the world, with a population of approximately 200 million and a joint GNP of almost U.S.$500 billion. It should also lead to the consolidation of peace and democracy in the region. These integration efforts should not, however, be seen as an alternative to regional or hemispherical integration but as a natural complement to a strategy for entry onto the international scene and, far from being wasted on the Southern Cone, posits the need to make commercial links in wider spheres.

Conclusion

Interaction between a country's economic mechanisms and its political structure is a two-way causal relationship whose constant flux precludes treatment designed for static situations. Any analysis must of necessity be complex and will not lend itself to easy postulation of miraculous, all-embracing answers. By now, Argentines have learned the painful lesson that without general well-being and without well-planned economic programs that can be implemented in any political context—even one in which institutions are subordinate to the initiatives of professionals—there can be no stable democracy.

Therefore, to understand the political aspects of economic transformation, the course of the interaction must be followed. This will identify the political needs of the moment, the economic needs that will result, and all the elements of the political scene at the end of a first cycle of interaction.

The implementation of Argentina's present economic program has many virtues, but it also presents many imponderables. Value judgments apart, the program has generated a need to resolve numerous problems of a political nature. The common denominator of these problems seems to be the need to move closer to a political scene that is stripped of most of its formality and that redefines the importance of the role filled by each individual within the framework of society.

Industry must become competitive, and to do so it must foster a greater role for every employee. Diplomats must negotiate on a more participatory level than that to which an isolated country has been accustomed. If this happens, each of these sectors will see the need for greater dialogue and participation. Argentina will not be able to make such a major change of attitude unless the politicians themselves take a lead in adopting it, and that will happen only if relationships are redefined among the political leaders themselves. They must understand that they cannot be lulled by stability, nor can they be driven headlong by the goal of leading a third transitional government. These politicians must first turn institutional and economic normalization into a modernizing process that will permit growth with social justice. This will not be possible if what has already been achieved is not safeguarded and the foundations have not been laid for a more egalitarian, transparent, creative Argentina. To achieve that goal, an attitude is needed whereby the honest search for a consensus becomes a common denominator of the government and the opposition—a consensus reached between them in order to make governing possible, and a consensus with the people in order to guarantee the functioning of the political system and the state. What will be required will be an understanding of the importance of a division of power and the need to agree to and respect federal and production contracts as a demonstration of the capacity to move forward from democracy as an abstraction and to realize its essential values to the fullest.

Notes

1. See José Octavio Bordón, *Una década de democracia en la Argentina mientras el Muro de Berlín se caía de ambos lados* (Washington, DC: Woodrow Wilson International Center for Scholars and Center for Latin American Studies, Georgetown University, 1992).

2. José Octavio Bordón and Carlos Ponce, "Bien en el corto plazo, pero . . . ," *Boletín de Coyuntura Económica del Instituto de Economía y Organización de la Fundación Andina* (Mendoza, Argentina) 2, no. 5 (March 1993).

3. Jacques Attali, *Lignes d'horizons* (Paris: Fayard, 1990).

4. Michel Albert, *Capitalism against Capitalism*, trans. Paul Haviland (London: Whurr, 1993).

5. On this subject, see Ernesto Aldo Isuani, *Estado de Bienestar, conflicto social y desigualdad*, presented at the "Latin America Seminar on Social Policies in the Nineties," Instituto de Investigación y Formación en Administración Pública, Universidad Nacional de Córdoba, October 22–24, 1992.

6. For the concepts of "integratory and fragmentary forces," see John Lewis Gaddis, *The United States and the End of the Cold War* (New York: Oxford University Press, 1992).

7. Economic data obtained from *World Economic Outlook* (Washington, DC: International Monetary Fund, October 1992), and *Interim Assessment*, January 1993.

8. Ibid.

9. See, for example, Peter Hakim, "Clinton and Latin America: Facing an Unfinished Agenda," *Current History* 92, no. 572 (March 1993): 97–101.

10. This danger is discussed in Abraham Lowenthal, "Latin America: Ready for Partnership?" *Foreign Affairs, America and the World* 72, no. 1 (1993): 74–92.

11. For the concept of "turbulence" in world politics, see James N. Rosenau, *Turbulence in World Politics: A Theory of Change and Continuity* (Princeton: Princeton University Press, 1990).

12. Joseph S. Tulchin, *Argentina and the United States: A Conflicted Relationship* (Boston: Twayne, 1990).

3

Legitimacy and Transition in Latin America

Social Forces and the New Agenda of Consensus

Federico Storani

Democratic Dogma: Are the Legitimate Origins of Power the Primary Basis for Consensus?

Representative, pluralist democracy derives its legitimacy from a system of beliefs and values based on the free expression of people's sovereignty. In the agonistic phase of political activity—the struggle for power and ways of holding onto it—this system of beliefs has, with certain exceptions, never become part of the political tradition in Latin America. Not only do Latin American governments threaten the institutions of the continent's incipient democracies, but they also try to find new ideological justification to uphold their former activities.

In Latin America today, there are two possible threats to democratic legitimacy. The first is that of sui generis coups, such as Peruvian President Alberto Fujimori's move on April 5, 1992, to dissolve congress and weaken the country's judiciary. The second concerns the type of democracy to be imposed in Latin America. The period of transition is over, and we must now clarify the type of democracy we want. Because a large part of society has lost confidence in the democratic system, the tendency will be to increase repression. This will inevitably lead to social conflict rather than greater public participation in government and a consequent increase in social integration. The breakdown is already under way, and today's political challenge is no more or less than how to make democracy remain legitimate.

Legitimacy can be subdivided into complex abstractions. What these add up to, however, is a need for mechanisms that, as a prerequisite for freedom, will guarantee citizens a structure to which they owe loyalty but that at the same time will take heed of their grievances against that structure. One of the foundations of democratic legitimacy is the recognition of a majority and a minority, represented politically in the form of a government and an opposition. Majority and minority are two parts of a sovereign will that is expressed as two opposing wills. "The majority has the right to govern and the minority that of exercising opposition and criticizing, in an attempt to become, in its turn, the majority," the Italian historian Guglielmo Ferrero has written. "This is why in democracies the opposition is as vital an organ of the sovereignty of the people as the government itself. To suppress the opposition is to suppress the sovereignty of the people."[1]

Latin American governments have demonstrated little consensus on the question of democratic legitimacy. Why? Max Weber, in *Economy and Society,* makes a classic distinction between different kinds of legitimate rule. One is the rule of law, which rests on a belief in the legality of the norms of a given order and on the right of whoever exercises authority according to those norms to govern. Another is traditional authority, which rests on a belief in the importance of tradition and in the authority exercised as a consequence of it. A third is charismatic authority, whose legitimacy is based on respect for a given leader's exceptional qualities, exemplary behavior, or heroism, and consequently for the norms he dictates.[2]

When Latin American democracies lose their legitimacy, what seems to happen is a kind of cross-fertilization, making for mutual influence between the three types of legitimacy. Leaders of the charismatic type who do not show exemplary behavior erode their own legitimacy. Evidence of this result can be seen in the general disillusionment with democracy caused by continual corruption. People begin to feel that such leaders think themselves above the law, generating further disillusionment with the mechanics of legal democracy.

A second important element in the decline in legitimacy in new Latin American democracies is the relationship between the economic and political systems. Liberal democracies are founded on two basic systems— a system wherein the state is responsible to its citizens and in which citizens have rights, and an economic system that generates, and more or less fairly distributes, wealth. In sum, if the system is to be legitimate it must have, both in the economic and in the political sphere, the uncoerced loyalty of its citizens. Political priorities must coexist alongside economic ones. Lack of legitimacy in either of these areas eventually erodes the legitimacy in the other.[3]

Avoiding a Legitimacy Crisis in the Argentine Transition: Rebuilding the State and Political Parties

The term "transition" has been used, according to political convenience, to mean several different things. A remark regularly made about Latin America—and about Argentina in particular—by authoritarian governments and military dictatorships is that "people are not mature enough to live in a democracy," suggesting that until maturity is reached, the path to democracy cannot begin. This is absurd. Mature democratic behavior is not something achieved from one day to the next but is a process of apprenticeship that can be undertaken only through practice under a democratic regime.[4]

This view of transition, a legacy of authoritarian thought, has been very restricting. Summed up graphically, it might be termed freedom in small doses. Those subscribing to this view see transition as a process whereby freedom must be only partial, and, to continue the metaphor, the dose should be administered slowly, drop by drop. Clearly, there are a number of different possible processes that suit the historical, political, and social conditions of a given country. In Argentina, the greater the amount of freedom, the more quickly people learned the social routines that formulate and validate rules about pluralism, tolerance, and norms of living together that ultimately reinforce democratic behavior.[5]

With the restoration of democracy in Argentina in 1983, a broad political transition began without restrictions or conditions. Two things made this possible: the government, by its political will, decided that it should be so; and the transition involved a complete break from the previous regime. In this, Argentina's situation differed from that of Brazil, Uruguay, Chile, or Paraguay, which were forced to make their transitions to democracy by pacts with previous governments. Argentina's defeat in the Malvinas in 1982 hastened the dictatorship's downfall and left it too weak to impose conditions. It tried to, by declaring an amnesty for any members of the armed forces involved in human rights violations between 1976 and 1983, but, apart from the defeat, the dictatorship had also performed poorly in social and economic spheres. All these factors prevented the military junta from negotiating a better deal for themselves. The attempt to wrest sovereignty over the Malvinas by force had, among other aims, that of gaining the dictatorship prestige and public acceptance, both of which had then sunk to an all-time low. Two days before the islands were invaded, there were large protest demonstrations in several Argentine cities. The protests were violently repressed, resulting in many arrests and a number of people being killed or wounded.

Despite the fact that the transition to democracy involved a complete rupture with the past, the legitimate government in Argentina has faced huge problems. In some ways, the total break has given the government greater freedom and room to implement its policies. At the same time, however, the break has also meant greater public uncertainty. Argentina's political transition faced three main challenges: a) the legacy of the so-called Dirty War, the seven-year campaign of state-sponsored terror that followed the military coup of March 1976, b) international isolation and border clashes, and c) economic crises and foreign debt.[6] The transition was both broad and deep. Evidence of this lies in the trials of those responsible for state terrorism. These trials gave the new democracy a moral base from which to operate. This led to the solution, in 1984, of the long-standing border dispute with Chile; to a search for regional integration, which culminated in the MERCOSUR pact; and to state reform being placed at the center of the political agenda.

Transition, as the word indicates, contains the notion of movement—in this instance, movement toward full democracy. A functioning state of law is not enough. The aim of transition is a democratic society, and in that respect Argentina still has a long way to go, for the country contains a residue of authoritarianism whose expression is the defense of vested interests and corporate behavior. A democracy built on pluralist representation—political, social, and economic—has several participants. In a full democracy, however, with enough legitimacy to sustain stable institutions, the principal agents are the state and the political parties.

The State and Its Crisis

In Latin America, the role of the state in the accumulation of capital has been fundamental. The entrepreneurial, interventionist, *dirigiste* state sprang out of the need to promote development, to involve new social sectors, to offer a modern infrastructure, and to educate workers to confront need, shortage, and the private sector's inability to perform these functions. Had it not been for state intervention, Latin America today would be in even worse circumstances than it is. Mistakes and abuses apart, the state set developments in motion that allowed the economy to emerge from its early stage as an exporter of raw materials into an industrial entity, thus totally and positively changing the character of the chief Latin American countries.

There is no happy ending to this tale, however, nor does it constitute a belief that the market can solve everything. In the nation, state politics articulated social consensus and created conditions for economic activity. The economic functions of forming a society were subsidiary to the political. The political function of the state offered guarantees of equilibrium and stability.[7]

The trend today is to turn the market into the state by means of the influence that the market exercises over the state's functions. This lessens the sway of politics and leaves social matters to be resolved by the "efficiency" of the market. In peripheral countries, the dominant view is that the economy is society's chief organizer. As a result, political primacy disappears in the structure of the state, which is reorganized to underpin the market.

Although these are the main trends, they cannot answer the basic questions surrounding the legitimacy of social organization. How does the state represent the deprived, the poor, the uneducated, and the ill-informed, none of whom has access to power? How can the decline in public participation be halted if people think that public participation cannot solve their problems? The state is not "their" state. Nor are they integrated into a market from which they have become excluded. What is the impact of this schism on the legitimate bases of democracy?

The whole world is talking about the crisis of the state. The Western welfare state is under grave pressure; the real socialist state has collapsed, together with its ideology; the "interventionist-benefitist" state in Latin America is in shambles. Even in the most advanced nations, a reappraisal of the relationship between the state and society is taking place.

The dominant political outlook today is neoliberal. Its aim is to reduce the economic functions of the state to a minimum. In Latin America there has been a rush to apply the market economy blindly. The state in its previous form was breaking down, lending legitimacy to these policies.

The breakdown of the state also had a social dimension. Inefficiency in the provision of public services, an increase in public spending, an unjust assignment of resources, profiteering by government employees, an increase in the number of laws and a decrease in their observance, and a pretense of equal distribution of wealth in the face of rising inequality nourished a feeling of alienation from and distrust of the state.[8] The state's connection with illegal repression during dictatorial and authoritarian periods, known as "state terrorism," further lowered the prestige of state institutions.

The international context contributed to a reform of the economy. The collapse of real socialism ended a process that was already under way, and economics took on a universal character. Democratic Latin American governments that came to power in the 1980s faced economic crises while they were in the transitional stage. The situation led to a certain instability, with a promise of more to come, and the solution did not lie in a reversion to populist demagoguery. That would only postpone the crises, ultimately making them worse. Rather, the solution lay in acknowledging the need to press on with structural changes that would deal decisively with the problems of an unwieldy state.[9]

The causes of the breakdown of the state and the need for reform have not yet been pinpointed. Some observers believe them to have been state interventionism, political patronage, the exaggerated size of modern states, overregulation, the application of Keynesian politics contrary to the principle of financial balance, and monetarism. The Washington Consensus offered financial stabilization achieved by sudden strict measures, privatization, and the removal of economic barriers. Others have argued that the causes of the crisis lay not in the functions themselves but in how the state performed them.

According to the first group, the state's functions should be the basic ones that all states perform—administration, justice, government, maintaining relations with other states, and, with reservations, social welfare. The second viewpoint places emphasis on generating the conditions for growth. As well as carrying out its basic functions, the state should assume an economically active role. It should promote savings and investment, develop selective strategies in the industrial sector, and promote exports. However, by the public and private sectors complementing each other and by state reform—both necessary components of a competitive economy—the two positions converge in a redefinition of the public sector.[10]

Discussions about reforming the role of the state began generally with the oil crisis in the 1970s, but they did not take place in Latin America until the mid-1980s. Any redefinition of the relationship between state, society, and market brings with it a profound cultural change in social demands and social policies. In Latin America, this cultural disparity carried a high political price, paid principally by the first democratic transition governments.

For Argentina, with a considerable public sector tradition and nationalized companies in both industry and services, the task of reform was not simple. Alfonsín's Radical government began the social debate, but it could make no practical headway in the face of large-scale resistance from labor unions and the Justicialista party. One observer stated: "For the first time the declared strategy of a contemporary democratic government was state reform along with integration into the world."[11]

President Menem came to power in 1989 professing total opposition to state reform and, in particular, to the privatization of Aerolíneas Argentinas and Entel, the state-owned airline and phone companies. He then changed his position and worked to further Alfonsín's reforms. This is not the place to analyze Menem's about-face, but it is worth pointing out that his task was made easier by steadily worsening hyperinflation and by the opposition's tolerance and understanding, which helped to sanction a legal framework—the Administrative Emergency Law and the Economic Emergency Law—that permitted state reform.

Stabilizing strategies, such as the Plan Austral of 1985 (a heterodox program that introduced a new currency, the Austral, while freezing prices and wages in an effort to halt inflation), which enjoyed broad social consensus, together with the crisis in the state, created the conditions that legitimized the reforms and produced change in the behavior of society. Despite serious mistakes in its conception and execution, the state reform policy was widely accepted. Its main conceptual error was to equate state reform and modernization with privatization.[12] It was also a mistake to use a substantial part of the funds generated by privatization to pay for foreign debt by means of the worst of its mechanisms—capitalization itself.

The big question in most of Latin America today is what happens after reform. There is widespread concern about desertion by the state of its basic functions, generally acknowledged as nondelegable. The treatment of social concerns becomes important not only for ethical reasons but also because of the need for skilled workers if Argentina is to achieve a developed economy. Integrating the economy into the international market requires an increase in the quantity and quality of exports. To accomplish this, the training of workers is essential. So are improvements in education, the development of a policy for science and technology, and investment in the infrastructure.[13]

Political Parties and the Problem of Representation: An Agenda for Reform

If Latin American democracy is to be consolidated, there must be political parties. A robust party system, a high level of trust in institutions, and public loyalty to the majority parties are essential characteristics of consolidated democracies. Such features give democracies flexibility and strength.[14] It is impossible to talk about democracy without stressing the importance of political parties.

The need for a representational system is not under discussion in contemporary Latin American democracies. The controversy is over the ways in which purely representational democracy, semidirect forms of democracy, and citizen participation should complement each other. Direct democracy and representational democracy are not opposite poles but points on a continuum.[15]

In Latin America, and in Argentina in particular, the problem of representation has three basic aspects. First is the lack of transparency in party financing. In all of the developed democracies of the world, there is a clear relationship between state support of parties and the elimination of potential sources of corruption associated with private contributions. Second, public wariness over political parties is much more clearly a result of the past behavior of politicians, who are often not good examples of integrity. Countless Latin American officials have grown rich illegally and remain immune from justice. Third, and most important, are the several nonfinancial aspects that contribute to the problem of representation. The concept of representation implies a certain degree of identification between the representative and those he represents. To represent a constituency implies acting in the interests of those who are represented and responding to them. The representative should act in an independent way, using discretion and judgment. But those represented should be seen not simply as subjects of public policy but as people capable of action and of evaluating the representative independently. The representative should work in such a way as not to engender conflict with those he represents. If conflict should arise, the representative should be able to explain why, in his opinion, the interests and desires of his constituents are not necessarily one and the same.[16]

There is, in fact, a breach between the behavior that the electorate expects of its representatives and the way they in fact operate. The aim should therefore be to generate mechanisms to lessen this gap. The institutions governing electoral systems must change. In Latin America, representation is usually proportional. A viable option would be to promote a mixed system, such as that currently used in Germany, which allows for two votes to be cast. One is a vote to elect a candidate within an electoral district; the second is a vote for a party.[17]

An ideal course would take advantage of the best elements of the proportional representation system as well as those of the single vote system. Proportional representation tends to result in a larger number of parties being represented within the government. However, the party ticket system prevents the voter from deciding which representatives he wants to be included in the nomination of candidates. The single vote system, on the other hand, can lead to polarization between two parties. A second disadvantage of that system is the tendency to revitalize politics by means of vested interests. There is potential inequality of access to the elected representative by groups in a position to influence his selection.

In the ticket system, this problem is mitigated by the fact that the electoral districts are larger. Without doubt, the greatest advantage of the single vote system is that it ensures that the individual representative is directly responsible to a fixed geographical section of the electorate. The mixed system combines the attributes of both systems, and, when it is applied correctly and with sufficient publicity, many of its problems can be avoided.

A second element in need of change in Latin America and particularly in Argentina is the system of internal elections. Election of a party's candidates for public positions is now done by its members. This practice should be replaced by a system of open elections, in which any taxpaying citizen of an electoral district can vote for the candidates who will represent the party in the general elections. This is not a question of taking away from the parties their monopoly over appointing candidates for public office, for that would work against the party system, but rather of ensuring that internal elections do not contribute to political patronage or fraudulent negotiations between those responsible for mobilizing voters. Anyone who wishes to be proposed at an election of this type must be a member of a political party and have the signed endorsement of a stated number of party members.[18]

The problems of political parties go far beyond the way in which they function. The Latin American sociopolitical structure has been in a critical state ever since the collapse of the old oligarchies, giving rise to problems of legitimacy. The risk is that democracy, having triumphed, may then be eroded in such a way as to lose relevance as a form of government. And even if democracy is not replaced by another form, a process of decay may occur whereby the tasks that a government should perform are passed on to corrupt or criminal factions.[19]

From a philosophical and practical point of view, popular disenchantment with politics has a number of causes. One is the influence of the news media; another is an increase in participation with the arrival of democracy; and a third is a disillusionment with blanket solutions to ever more specific problems. Still, in the Latin American context, the lack of liaison between representative and electorate is so great that there is much to be done before even approaching the deeper debate on the relationship between society and politics.

The aim is to reverse the flow of power. Social democratization means that, in more and more areas, decisions are taken at the base of the pyramid rather than the top. A chain of communication founded on participation must be established. Through daily discussion, those affected by political decisions can evaluate proposals under consideration. If reasoned agreement can be obtained, we may assume that correct steps are being taken. In this way, the gap between what is imposed and what is recognized as valid will shrink.[20]

Political parties are no exception. There is a crucial need for more direct links between the party organization and the electorate. Such links cannot be made by patronage alone. Any benefit that practice may bring, especially in needy areas, as well as being morally dubious also alienates much larger sectors of society from politics. Other internal matters to which attention should be paid include solidarity and loyalty between party workers and leaders as regard their rightful task of deciding what or whom to vote for. All these factors should be taken into account during the course of party restructuring.

Ideological incoherence among party leaders and gaps between promise and deed discourage members from participating in internal matters.[21] A direct consequence of this is that party workers give too much of their time to internal matters, paying more attention to political problems than to the problems of society.

It is essential that both national and local subjects be discussed at the local level. There are many activities of a social nature that can be performed and that have an ideological slant but in which ideology does not need to enter directly. For those taking part in these activities, both as givers and receivers, politics becomes linked with the benefits that the work brings, which are then set in a broader ideological and political context. The result is psychological identification between community work and the party the workers belong to. These activities must have relevance to a given party's values in that they promote solidarity or help the less well off. Discussing abstract values is of less use than putting such values into practice. Practice endows the tasks that are undertaken with symbolic validity.

Civil society's relationship with political parties and the state should be substantially modified. During the military dictatorships in Latin America, the proscription of political parties generated a new kind of social participation in nongovernmental organizations that had little to do with traditional parties. Many of these organizations were formed to counter state repression, and one of their objectives has consequently been to avoid any identification with party or state affairs.

In the present circumstances, one way of giving grassroots organizations a chance to act is to bring them into the state, where they may be able to participate in the design and implementation of policy. Such participation would eliminate ad hoc governmental structures, which increase the cost of programs and lead to patronage. A democratic process of policy development can ensure effective participation by the public in decision making, preventing the imposition of state policies that are inappropriate. The public sector can make an important contribution to policymaking by assuming responsibility for planning. In addition, public sector institutions must take a leading role in coordinating the efforts of nongovernmental organizations to implement state initiatives.

As for the relationship between grassroots organizations and parties, public protest and participation in social action must be channeled into politics. Every grassroots organization tends at some point to question the established power, so that its participation ultimately becomes political. Such organizations cannot assume that by maintaining a distance from electoral politics they can uphold their principles and at the same time achieve their goals. To do so would mean to disappear when the events that gave birth to them are over. Furthermore, if the demands of these organizations are to be met, they must be put into perspective alongside programs proposed by other organizations. Their demands must also be economically viable and sustainable.[22]

Two dangers must be avoided. These are manipulation and coercion, which are dimensions of the wider phenomena of appropriation and political patronage. To ensure a mutually fruitful partnership between political parties and grassroots organizations, the immediate objective should be to maximize the autonomy of the groups within a framework of mutual cooperation.

Argentine Parties and Their Problems of Representation

Since the country's return to democracy in 1983, both principal political parties have been in government. The Radical Civic Union (UCR), the oldest party in Argentina, was in power during the first part of the democratic takeover. This party has a classic liberal outlook. Its organs are the National Convention, which is composed of twice the number of members the party has in the national parliament, and the National Committee, which, with twenty-five members, is the party's principal executive organ. In addition, each province has a party convention and provincial committee, a fact that illustrates the strong federal character the party has had since its foundation in 1890. By origin, the party represents working people, and in particular the middle classes. Certain groups have traditional links with the party. One is Franja Morada, a student Radical group that has maintained a strong influence within Argentine universities. Since the return to democracy, it has run the Argentine University Federation.

The party structure is apparently closed. Only party members take part in internal elections to choose party officials and candidates for public posts, from councilor to congressman and from mayor to president.

The word "apparently" should be explained. The party has a large membership in comparison with other parties in Latin America or Europe. At present, the Radicals have approximately 2.5 million members throughout Argentina. That is about 15 percent of the nation's electorate. In the October 1993 parliamentary elections, the party polled a little more than five million votes—double its number of members and 30 percent of the total vote.

The figures may give the wrong impression, because membership numbers are far greater than the number of active party workers. Many members, on average about 30 percent nationwide, do little more than vote in party elections. This flaw in the system arises because many join the party in return for some political favor. Political patronage has spread. There is pressure to increase the number of party members, who then have value as "political capital" at the time of party elections. That, in turn, has a considerable influence on the selection of candidates for public office. The practice worsens in time of crisis and destroys the nature of the party, undermining its ideological values and solidarity and cutting the party off from the community. However, party membership is no guarantee of voter loyalty. The growing number of options in the restricted vote, added to the effects of political patronage, produces situations in which the number of votes in general elections are lower than the number of party members. In the elections for governor in the province of Tucuman in 1991, the UCR polled 20,000 votes, while the number of party members in that district was 80,000. In the 1993 elections in Gonzalez Catan township in La Matanza in the Province of Buenos Aires, the number of votes in the general election was also lower than the number of party members.

The ruling Justicialista party, Argentina's other large party, is difficult to define as such. Its own leaders and workers prefer to be called the National Justicialista Movement, and they point out that the party is only a section within the movement. This reflects the history of the party's foundation by the then-Colonel Juan Domingo Perón and the "national movements" that were in vogue in the 1930s and 1940s. It also explains why the party's main social support base, the labor movement, shares its vertical, centralized nature with the party. The phrase that usually springs to the lips of any Peronist leader is "The union movement is the backbone of the National Justicialista Movement." Increasingly weak unions are playing a diminishing role within the party. On the other hand, and in keeping with the party's traditions, a new movement has been initiated—"Menemism." The coalition that backs President Menem reflects an alliance among the economic conglomerates that benefited from the privatization of state-owned enterprises, conservative and provincial parties with an authoritarian leadership, and a large portion of the unions' leaders coopted by the president with posts and payoffs. This populist-conservative coalition is composed of Argentina's higher classes as well as the country's poor.

An internal movement called "Peronist Renewal" brought in a system of direct participation by members in the selection of candidates. It ended up both undemocratic and authoritarian. Rule from above continues in the party, as Menem himself picks candidates—often not party members—without significant opposition; for example, the president's candidate for senator from the federal capital was Avelino Porto, a nonparty member, who tried to bring about a new power alliance and who was defeated in 1994 by the Radical party senator Fernando De la Rua.

The Justicialista party is composed of an executive organ, the National Justicialista Council, and provincial councils. The party has over three million members. These figures have grown as a result of political patronage, handouts, and chains of corruption. The Justicialista party uses the state apparatus indiscriminately and, internally, has less of a democratic tradition.

As for social representation, an analysis of the party's support in the 1995 elections—42 percent nationally—reveals loyalty among the less privileged sectors and rising support among those who are better off. There is no doubt that the success of the Convertibility Plan (a 1991 law that established an exchange rate between the Argentine currency and the U.S. dollar at a fixed parity of one to one), which produced a substantial drop in the inflation rate, has brought credit to its architect, Domingo Cavallo, the finance minister from 1991 to 1996. We shall see in time whether the less well-off sectors, who are hardest hit by the cost of restructuring, will continue to support the party. The latest development within Menemism is a new conservative alliance that identifies fully with government policy. The UCD, the Union of the Democratic Center, virtually disappeared in the 1995 elections, and many of its leaders joined the Justicialista party.

In spite of the fact that the main opposition party, the Unión Cívica Radical, is currently in crisis, the Argentine party system is being consolidated. In the elections of October 3, 1993, the two parties together polled 73 percent of the votes, while the remainder was divided among a large number of political groups spread over a wide ideological spectrum.

The best electoral alternative to the Peronist government would be the formation of a coalition of economic, social, and political forces with a shared belief that the present path of Argentine development, both in political and economic terms, will ultimately undermine the country's democratic legitimacy.

Conclusion

Latin America's current cycle of democratic governments is very recent and was preceded by a painful history of authoritarianism. We must not lose this chance to consolidate our democracies. Lack of tradition and practice conspire against such a consolidation; beset by difficulties, we may be tempted to ignore basic principles.

The aim of any analysis of democratic transition is not only to define the difficulties that must be faced but also to indicate the characteristics of each stage of the process. The threat to democratic stability arises from many factors, all of which operate concurrently. Any study of this threat must identify the dominant factors and the framework in which they evolve. The moral authority of democratic legitimacy rests upon the actions and behavior of the main agents of the democratic process: the state and the political parties. Other participants are involved in the transition, but our aim here is to identify those with a decisive role now and in the future.

Political parties must be fully democratized. When applied to parties competing in a democratic atmosphere, this statement may look like a truism. But that is not the case. After the euphoria following the restoration of democracy and the end of authoritarianism, old vices arose that, owing to public apathy and tolerance, may one day again serve to justify coups. To prevent that, the parties must not look like fortresses of privilege, sinecures, and political patronage, or like machines ready for the attack. In democratic transitions, when effort and sacrifice are called for, moral values should still be guaranteed.

As well as expressing morality, mechanisms exist that can help to decrease uncertainty and improve representation and modes of political action. Among these we stress an ethical code of political behavior and the creation of a specific court to address electoral matters. In the case of Argentina, the country's legislative branch must draft legislation to modify party and general electoral systems, with particular attention to issues of finance. Internal party elections should be made open so that all of the people may participate in politics. One possible strategy is that such elections take place at the same time for all parties, with special outside control.

We have said that the electoral system that would suit Argentina best would be a combination of the party ticket and the restricted vote. During transition it is important to keep up momentum, and the ticket system would fulfill that requirement. But the quality of representation must also be improved. The best way to do so is for representatives to be fully responsible to their constituencies as well as to their party.

Links between the parties and the community must be strengthened. Nongovernmental organizations and the parties must complement each other by performing joint tasks that preserve the identity of each while at the same time providing a full ideological context for efforts that individually would accomplish little.

The other main agent, the state, is at present the object of much inconclusive debate. Exhaustion of its previous role has been cited, but it would be wrong to conclude that the state should be reduced to the role of mere spectator of the market.

In addition to the basic functions that it is generally acknowledged to have—which are far from efficiently carried out in Latin America—the state has other fundamental responsibilities that it must assume if society is not to disintegrate.

An ambivalence is developing in Latin American societies. The reason is that restructuring policies have been primarily short-term economic initiatives that have not taken fully into account either social questions or the role the state should play in them. Matters such as education, health, science, technology, social security, and justice—the very core of the state's role—are often ignored. The state's relationship with society and the market must be redefined.

The present situation, with increasing marginalization and poverty, cannot continue. The risk of creating a highly fragmented society in economic, social, and cultural terms undermines the possibility for evolution—in the long term for Argentine society and for the consolidation of democracy. The current pattern of economic and political development creates a society deeply divided into two groups: those who can integrate into the new organization of the economy and those who cannot. The sad conclusion about this game is that it has no winners in the long term. Deep divisions within Argentine society are changing long-standing patterns of social behavior. Criminality, violence, and insecurity are increasing both in frequency and scope, even altering the life of society's well off. Argentina is ceasing to be a well-educated, egalitarian, and socially mobile society.

The following points demand urgent state action: a) a plan for industrial growth, identifying sectors that can compete in the international market; b) investment in infrastructure that will optimize resources by lowering the cost of production and exports; c) the development of human resources, not only for ethical reasons but also to provide the basic education and skills necessary to build a competitive nation; d) the establishment of frameworks of regulation to prevent monopoly in the private sector; e) the promotion of integration policies within Latin American countries that build markets on a scale compatible with those in other regions; and f) policies to redistribute income and reduce inequalities created during a period of unusual concentration of wealth in the upper classes.

Notes

1. Guglielmo Ferrero, *El Poder* (Buenos Aires, 1943), 196.
2. Max Weber, *Economía y sociedad. Un esbozo de sociología comprensiva* (Mexico: Fondo de Cultura Económica, 1992), 215.
3. W. Connolly and Stephen Lukes, *Legitimacy and the State* (New York: New York University Press, 1984), 227.
4. Federico Storani, *Revista Generación '83* (Buenos Aires, 1985).
5. Carlos Raimundi, "Desafíos de la modernidad," unpublished document prepared for internal discussion, Junta Coordinadora Nacional de la Unión Cívica Radical, Buenos Aires, 1986.
6. Federico Storani, "Los condicionantes de la transición democrática" (Paper presented to the National Committee of the Unión Cívica Radical, Buenos Aires, 1987).
7. Brian Thomson, "La reestructuración del estado y la superación de la pobreza," Institute of Latin American Studies (University of Texas at Austin), Conference, Toluca, Mexico, 1993.
8. Alejandro Médici, Pedro Pratt Seminar Thesis, "Crisis del Estado," *Derecho Político* (La Plata, December 1993).
9. Luiz Carlos Bresser Pereira, "Economic Reforms and Economic Growth: Efficiency and Politics in Latin America," in *Economic Reforms in New Democracies: A Social-Democratic Approach*, ed. Luiz Carlos Bresser Pereira, Adam Przeworski, and Jose Maria Maravall (New York: Cambridge University Press, 1993), 81.
10. J. E. Lane, *The Public Sector: Concepts, Models, and Approaches* (London, 1993).
11. Jesús Rodríguez, "La democracia argentina diez anos después: Nuevas prioridades" (Washington, DC: Woodrow Wilson International Center for Scholars, 1993).
12. Ibid.
13. Alberto Föhrig, "Hacia una superación del neoliberalismo: Nuevas prioridades y modos de acción estatal" (Paper presented at the XIV Congress of the Institute of Latin American Studies Student Association, Austin, Texas, March 4–5, 1994.)
14. Larry Diamond, Juan Linz, and Seymour Lipset, eds., *Democracy in Developing Countries: Latin America* (Boulder: Lynne Rienner Publishers, 1989), 20–21.
15. N. Bobbio, *The Future of Democracy: A Defence of the Rules of the Game* (Cambridge: Polity Press, 1987), 53.
16. Hanna Pitkin, *The Concept of Representation* (Berkeley: University of California Press, 1972), 209–11.
17. Kathleen Bawn, "The Logic of Institutional Preferences: German Electoral Law as a Social Choice Outcome," *American Journal of Political Science* 37, no. 4 (November 1993): 965–89.
18. "Draft Law for Open Primary Elections" (Presented by provincial congressmen Horacio Aispuro, Marcelo Elías, Fernando Acedo, and Gustavo Aldo

Pera to the Honorable Chamber of Deputies of the Province of Buenos Aires, Period 117, Number 733, September 28, 1989).

19. Manuel Antonio Garretón, *Los partidos y la transformación política de América Latina* (Santiago de Chile: Ediciones Facultad Latinoamericana de Ciencias Sociales-Chile, 1993): 9.

20. Jürgen Habermas, *Legitimation Crisis* (Boston: Beacon Press, 1973), 104–5.

21. Susan Stokes, "Representación y redemocratización en América Latina: Un balance crítico" (Work presented to the Institute of Peruvian Studies, Lima, April 22, 1993.)

22. Jorge Castañeda, *Utopia Unarmed: The Latin American Left after the Cold War* (New York: Alfred A. Knopf, 1993), 364.

4

Poverty in Argentina

Toward an Integrated Social Policy

Eduardo Amadeo *

This study examines ideas about poverty and the policies for dealing with it that are currently prevalent in academic and political circles. The basic assumption underlying this essay is that the best social policy is full employment with decent wages. However, there are two barriers to achieving these ends. One is that Latin American countries are involved in a process of transition in which technological change leads to a high degree of instability in employment. The other is that even if Argentina were to achieve a higher growth rate than it has succeeded in doing for many years, such dynamics would not be enough to overcome the social gap that has accumulated—hence, the need for active social policies.

The present work sets out to understand the various options available, both in terms of theory and of political reality. Those options are then related to Argentina's needs as well as to its limitations. There are no perfect paradigms for social policy. Fortunately, the dynamic of social thought invariably leads to a revision of concepts. At the same time, policy is applied to specific realities at given times. That, by definition, is a dynamic process, and we must be able to cope with this complex reality in our decisions. To manage uncertainty and change is the essence of politics.

Poverty in the United States

Given the effort needed to establish the new economic order, involving a reduction of state power, macroeconomic restructuring, and the new

*My research was carried out in the stimulating atmosphere of the Woodrow Wilson International Center for Scholars, thanks to a generous scholarship from the Center's "Argentina at the Wilson Center" program.

challenges posed by globalization, many of the old and new questions about poverty remain unanswered. Basic questions about how to avoid exclusion in the context of rapid technological change are the new key issues of social policy and the subject of a new and fresh debate. Therefore, an adequate framework of concepts is still being developed within which strategies governing the nature and future implementation of social policy can be put into practice. New economic policies have been much better conceptualized than new social policy.

This sense of a lack of conceptual or political structure does not apply only to Latin America. In his inaugural address in January 1993, President Bill Clinton admitted that his country, the most powerful in the world, faced severe difficulty in its efforts to defeat poverty and its most immediate consequence, violence. In a retreat to a more conservative position, Clinton proposed to reduce wholesale dependency on the "welfare state" as a step along the road toward the restoration of the traditional values of American society—work, family, and community. Among other things, this implies recognition that unemployment programs have not succeeded and have instead generated a subculture of poverty that ultimately discourages the poorest from working even in times of economic expansion.[1] It also means accepting, as U.S. Secretary of Labor Robert Reich has done, the failure of many of the programs designed to stimulate employment through the creation of job centers or by the provision of incentives from the private sector. Because these schemes either failed to provide job security or merely reinforced participation in a marginal labor market of low-wage jobs, it is necessary, according to Reich, to find new ways of coping with unemployment.

In his address, Clinton also acknowledged that a serious breakdown of the most basic elements of American society had occurred. By the year 2000, one in three children born in the United States will live in one-parent families. There will be a similar spread of intergenerational poverty, while social divisions will deepen and violence and marginalization will increase. As a consequence—although the cost is far greater than Latin American countries can begin to imagine—U.S. society is speeding up its search for new models and new measures for defeating poverty.

The debate goes beyond mere ways and means; it examines such key issues as how a society functions, the common good, and the treatment of the poor. Here we should mention the work carried out by a group of writers who, in pure Tocquevillian tradition, have been exploring those values and institutions as they were influenced during the 1980s by the tide of conservatism.[2] Meanwhile, the complexity of the subject must be underscored. The point of mentioning the United States is to discourage simplistic assumptions, such as the claim that social problems can be solved by economic growth alone,[3] or beliefs that there are ready-made models to which easy access is possible. In fact, a World Bank report recently concluded that even with the most optimistic rates of growth, it will be difficult to regain the balanced society that existed fifteen years ago. Consequently, a much greater and more creative effort must be made in the area of social policy.[4]

Poverty, the State, and Inflation: The Need for a Model in Latin America

A study of the literature on the causes of poverty in Latin America reveals a clear conceptual break between what was written before 1991 or 1992 and what has been written since. Until then, everything on the subject noted a direct correlation between the continent's long decline, mistakes made in the course of adjustment, and the explosion of poverty. The economic and social deterioration of Latin America during the 1980s has been well documented. A fatal combination of circumstances reigned: an excessive foreign debt, the abrupt cessation of capital investment, a rise in international interest rates, ill-conceived restructuring policies, and political instability. The frenzy into which Latin America fell was marked by a succession of programs intended to slow inflation by contracting domestic demand, frustrated attempts to generate exports through a series of devaluations, and indiscriminate cuts in public spending. In each case the result was counterproductive—production decreased and debts rose, as did inflation, poverty, and inequality.

Crushed by their inability to understand what was happening, politicians and intellectuals of the period blamed either the Right or the Left, according to their own ideological leanings. The fault, they claimed, lay in external factors (terms of trade, protectionism among developed countries, high interest rates, flaws in the IMF's plans for economic adjustment) or internal factors (economic politicization and protectionism, chronic statism, bad social policies).[5]

Whatever the case, it became clear that there was a strong link between these economic policies and the increase in poverty.[6] The poor, unable to protect themselves against either inflation or adjustment, became the principal victims of such insensitive policies. It was not only faulty macroeconomic policies that further impoverished the poor, but also a financial system that automatically transferred resources to the upper classes, with extremely low returns in productivity and reinvestment. The state thus became a sort of Hood Robin, using its power to benefit the rich by stealing from the poor.

In the literature on the subject, the perception of the relationship between macroeconomics and poverty changed after 1991 or 1992, when some of the benefits of a rational macroeconomic structure began to be witnessed in the region. Even those who were least disposed to accept the need for change in the structure of the economy were able to see the positive effect that stability had had on improving conditions for the poor. The figures are incontrovertible. In Argentina, for example, Eduardo Bustelo—who writes critically of post-1990 policies—acknowledges the reduction in the number of destitute in greater Buenos Aires as a result of the improvement in the economy between 1989 and 1992 (see table).[7] However, not all that has been written has been "refreshed" by the new reality. Many authors go on indiscriminately using the term "adjustment" to denote the macroeconomic expansion of the early 1990s. Few of those who criticize recognize the increase in disposable financial resources pro-

The Decrease in Poverty: Percentage of Households and Population below the Poverty and Extreme Poverty Lines[a] in Greater Buenos Aires, 1988 through 1993[b]

		Percentage of Population below Extreme Poverty Line	*Percentage of Households below Poverty Line*	*Percentage of Population below Poverty Line*
May	1988	6.4	22.6	29.9
October	1988	7.8	24.2	32.4
May	1989	6.3	19.7	25.9
October	1989	12.7	38.3	47.4
May	1990	9.1	33.7	42.6
October	1990	5.0	25.3	33.8
May	1991	3.8	21.8	28.8
October	1992	2.4	13.7	17.8
May	1993	2.9	13.6	17.8

Source: Executive Committee for the Study of Poverty in Argentina and INDEC.
[a]The statistics are based on incomes declared in the Instituto Nacional de Estadísticas y Censos (INDEC) study of households. There is an underestimate on the order of 20 percent, while the percentages in the table are overestimated and should be considered above all as indications of trends.
[b]The extreme poverty line is the cost of a basket of consumer goods. The poverty line is approximately double the line for extreme poverty.

duced by stability and the possibilities that it has opened up. Above all, there is a lack of fresh thinking—both by the Left and the Right—on the new structure of social relationships created in Latin America by exposure to international competition and the need for greater all-round efficiency. In five years of economic transformation, intellectual energies have been geared toward understanding the transition process and, in particular, to searching for and applying methods of privatizing the economy.

During this process, the state has not disappeared. It has become a new state, and it must respond more efficiently to its own historic functions, which, in certain cases, have been enlarged. New ways of expressing social demands have emerged, and the prevailing political thought decrees that the state must shed its nonessential control of the means of production so as to concentrate on its basic tasks. People are now demanding this. An atmosphere of stability and growth produces greater demand for social equality.

How is this new state to be organized? How centralized will it be? What are its new functions? These questions require a new vision that is still being explored in writing and that has not yet been identified by politicians. One danger during transition is that a new thought or power structure may tend to block attempts at inquiry or lateral thinking. We must, therefore, open our minds to the subject of the state and our need for social policies.

Another theoretical and political problem that recent literature is beginning to explore is the connection between macroeconomic equilibrium, the opening up of markets, and social policy. In other words, to what extent is the integration of social and economic policy possible when there is an urgent need for increased productivity?[8] A serious lack of investment and the gap between workers' existing skills and the skills demanded by new technologies have aggravated the problem throughout Latin America. Thus, technology itself has accelerated rates of unemployment. If the problem is not resolved, we shall face a situation in which economic growth leads to exclusion from employment. Should that happen, it will be even more difficult to reverse the damaging effects of the lost decade.[9]

One final political-theoretical problem that must be solved is that of the contradiction between the need for wide social coverage (a universal social policy) and the requirements of rapid economic growth, which may demand investment in policies that offer quick results (for example, specialized education). Sometimes it is a trade-off between excellence and equality that remains to be resolved.

Poverty in Argentina

During the period between 1989 and 1993, economic stabilization had a striking effect on the circumstances of those most in need. Lack of control over economic variables hurts the poorest sectors of society. Over the last fifteen years, almost the entire Argentine population has suffered a continuous decline in its standard of living. In fact, reports from Comisión Económica para América Latina and the National Institute of Statistics and Census note that Argentina is the only country in Latin America in which the incidence of poverty rose between 1975 and 1990.[10] Dramatically reversing what had been a gradual improvement in social integration, the number of those with incomes below the poverty line in 1989 was six times greater than it had been in 1974.[11]

Disposable income, however, which has risen noticeably in recent years, does not reflect the depth of Argentina's social deterioration. Despite the positive impact of the stabilization program, when income rose in 1992 it was still 14 percent below its 1986 level, with the poorest sectors recovering a lower percentage of their income than those with higher incomes.[12]

The relevance of statistics on poverty must be improved. Measures of absolute income fail to take into account criteria that define living standards, which should be considered first in any evaluation of the spread of poverty. For an accurate assessment of the social situation, the following variables should be considered: a) the reduction in the quality of basic services provided by the state, a statistic that affects both the poor and the middle classes, who had to abandon higher-quality private services; b) the deterioration of economic and social infrastructure in the more densely populated urban areas (the percentage of people served by municipal drinking water dropped from 58.8 percent in 1975 to 55.38 percent in 1990, at a time when, in the nineteen districts of urban Buenos Aires, 56 percent of the population had running water, a figure comparable to that in places like Santiago del Estero and Misiones, provinces with predominantly rural populations)[13]; c) the deterioration in the quality of assets accumulated by those most affected by impoverishment, especially with regard to their dwellings; d) the falling income of workers in the informal sector,[14] which further marginalizes those with less ability to enter the job market; e) the loss in production capacity of certain low-income activities, owing to low investment or repeated cycles of low prices (this last phenomenon is typical of certain single-product provincial economies and, in large part, explains the rise in poverty in those areas); and f) changes in family structure as a result of women being forced to work outside the home, thereby delegating household tasks to children incapable of undertaking them, resulting in a reduction in strong, extended-family ties, and, finally, an increase in de facto unions among young couples ill equipped to cope with the demands of running a home.[15]

Another fact to be taken into account when assessing poverty is the high level of instability in poor homes. One set of statistics shows that homes with incomes just above or just below the poverty line are the most vulnerable to changes in employment and income policy, and they have the greatest difficulty in later recovering.

However, because of the sharp increase in social spending between 1990 and 1995, some of the key social indicators (such as infant mortality, malnutrition, and access to water and housing) have shown remarkable performance, reversing previous trends. What is most revealing of serious decline in the quality of services provided by the state during the last twenty years is education. Problems with the quality of the educational system were first made public in a dramatic report published by the Ministry of Education in February 1994.[16] The report confirmed that differences in the quality of education have produced sharp divisions in society. Such disparity in levels of education undermines the progress essential to the construction of modern Argentina, a nation built on the premise of equal opportunity and based on a system of universal public education. The new educational system created by the new Federal Law of Education is reversing these negative trends, but it will take at least a generation before the full impact can be seen.

The picture of poverty given here will allow, later in this study, for the formulation of a more comprehensive strategy. This picture will also help in assessing the extent of the effort needed to reacquire a standard of living acceptable to Argentine society. Not only is there a need for more money—and a satisfactory way of distributing it—but funds are also necessary for restoring the social infrastructure, reorganizing the educational system, taking direct action to alleviate the most immediate social problems, and creating programs to prevent poverty from being handed down from generation to generation. The middle class must regain its ability to save money so that it may recover its previous living standards, recapture its old status, and help its children participate, once again, in the "model of progress."

The present generation of Argentines faces an enormous challenge of good administration and growth, especially in view of the macroeconomic limits and social problems that must be confronted. Although the economy has performed spectacularly, a fact that has been translated into record social spending, it is clear that the country cannot recover quickly from twenty years of decline. This generation must produce not only the income for its own present welfare but also the resources needed to pay their inherited debt and to save for their future. This enormous burden can hardly be alleviated with additional public debt, at least not until the administration reaches a balanced budget. Therefore very careful management of public spending, massive inflow of private capital for basic services, and a creative social strategy are needed to navigate this path.

Models for a Social Policy

Strategies for confronting poverty are not limited solely to matters of technique. The problem is closely related to society's ideological perspective and values at any given time and expressed in the mandate bestowed upon democratically elected representatives. The violent ideological shifts in the Western world over the last ten years clearly demonstrate how a framework of ideas defines the conception and application of social policy. No one today can seriously claim that views on social progress or on the state's relationship with society or on society's tolerance of poverty have remained static over recent years. It is clear, for example, that we can no longer blame capitalism itself for poverty, nor can we demand violent changes in the structure of property. Reality led us to reject the concept of the "casino society"[17] advanced by Ronald Reagan at the height of his influence, according to which a government should aim all its effort toward providing opportunities so that "anyone could become rich"[18] before allocating resources. Surveys today reveal that North Americans do not care how large the state becomes so long as it ends poverty and violence. This represents a complete turnaround in opinion from ten years ago.[19]

The pendulum, then, has begun to swing. Intellectuals and politicians are looking for ways to integrate society more closely. Many subjects are under discussion—the common good, a sense of success and freedom, public institutions, individual responsibility, and the relationship between ethics and economics.[20] Stimulating and wide-ranging debate prompts us to return to basic values that will ensure that democracy, as defined by Robert Bellah, functions as a "permanent moral questioning."[21] Perhaps, as Walter Lippmann writes, the process will bring "an open search for new ways of finding the common good."[22]

This debate is not purely theoretical. If we agree that a society functions properly only to the extent that its members feel united in a certain ethical identity, we can analyze each of its institutions in that light. Government, family, school, church, and political institutions form a network of relationships that ensures a shared prosperity.[23] All these can be analyzed and if necessary changed so that they contribute to the common good. This notion of properly functioning institutions ensures the common good, placing limits on the omnipresent claims of the state (and the economy) to direct the social life. It is, above all, the vitality of our institutions that demands our greatest energies. For an individual to change does not make sense if he cannot project his actions into society through its institutions.

When society finds these basic responses, a clearer framework for social policy emerges. Society needs harmony and stability if it is to function to its full capacity. Through such harmony we find principles beyond the purely technical by which each of our institutions can operate. Thus, for example, schools are not only successful to the extent that they hand out formal knowledge but also "when the school itself, its head, and its teachers have a firm concept of their mission, when each child has a solid family behind it, and when the community helps to organize families to support schools."[24] In other words, when the school educates human beings in the full sense of the word it empowers them to develop in every area of life.

In Argentina today the demand for sustained macroeconomic stability and order that has been repeatedly expressed in recent elections has led to the building of a framework for social policy. There is also wide-ranging consensus that an economic policy should form an adequate basis upon which the "model of progress" can be built. In any case, and as always happens when a society is restructured, success at one stage in terms of political openness brings new demands. Because of this, but above all for purposes of basic social solidarity, it is necessary to begin to develop steps directed toward the rapid alleviation of poverty.

Because permanent social change must take place alongside economic and political transformation, there has to be a consensus in debate and action on society's basic institutions. As has been said, this is not simply a technical matter. Nor is it a question of increasing the number of school exams or buying computers. New ways must be found of linking schools with their communities and educating the whole person. The same applies to political institutions, the church, the workplace, and direct social action.

Toward an Integrated Social Policy

A middle-of-the-road approach to the causes of poverty makes it possible to think in terms of an integrated social policy. Violent changes in property ownership, exclusively free market policies, and simple direct assistance policies are not under discussion. But as often happens when the lure of ideology fades, the need arises to articulate more complex, wide-ranging alternatives. Ethically, theoretically, and politically, the idea of an all-embracing policy is appealing to Latin American countries. Having concentrated our energies on economic reform, we are willing to give our attention now to integration between the economic, social, and political spheres. What does such integration involve?

One of the central issues of economic reform has been its effect on society. The failure of the social reforms of the 1980s, which involved the shrinking of consumer demand and indiscriminate reduction in public spending, highlighted the contradiction between instability and the welfare of the poorest sectors of society.[25] The most detrimental aspect of these reforms was that they closed doors. Additionally, they hampered progress as the state's finances deteriorated and no ideological alternatives were advanced. Safety-net programs were then abandoned because of falling production and investment. Nor did the possibility exist for reform of the structures administering social programs, the quality of which quickly deteriorated.

Only when stability is achieved is it possible to posit a clearer relationship between the social and economic spheres. Louis Emmerij rightly says that although it is clear that rapid economic development is essential to reduce poverty and achieve social progress, such development is not successful if we take the length of the transition period into account. No one denies that economic development is successful in the long term in achieving social objectives and in fighting poverty, but the process can take from three to five generations. In other words, the period of transition would be humanly unacceptable and politically irresponsible.[26]

The World Bank, a champion of structural reform, also acknowledges that even the most optimistic projections for the GNP in Latin America are not sufficient to restore greater social equality. One of their recent reports states that Latin American countries have ignored the social sector for too long, and this has resulted in growing levels of poverty and the most unequal wealth distribution in the world. Today, the poorest 20 percent of Latin Americans receive 4 percent of the GNP, and because of this, one of our fundamental aims should be to concern ourselves vigorously and urgently with fighting poverty, improving living conditions, and giving stability to the new economic system. Failure to confront poverty aggressively may well lead to conflict about income distribution, discontent, and perhaps a return to populism.[27]

Integration between the social and economic spheres, then, depends principally on growth and investment, with full employment and adequate wages. A plan for economic progress is necessary for long-term improvement across the board. However, even assuming a sustainable political will, additional conditions are necessary if the period of transition, which will be difficult for society for economic, political, and human reasons, is to be shortened. The first step is to improve fiscal resources and their administration. Argentina has experience with the most effective methods for achieving this. An extremely aggressive policy for collecting taxes not only led to a record social budget but also met a long-term social debt—namely, the payment of old-age pensions.[28] Severe macroeconomic readjustment during the 1980s led to the greatest transfer of funds to the richest sectors;[29] that transfer can then be reappropriated by means of aggressive tax collection. The transfer came about through the appropriation of funds from individuals and from the state's inability to cope with the taxation system during inflation. The collecting of taxes is as socially fair as it is economically sensible.[30] The conclusion is that a healthy fiscal system is necessary if the social and economic spheres are to be integrated.

The second element of the relationship between the economic and social spheres is employment. The problems inherent here underlie the new policy of integration into world markets that dominates Latin American economies. On the one hand it is clear that, beyond its importance to society, full use of available labor ensures the success of any economic program. There is no more reliable mechanism for ensuring increased demand. However, stability will not be achieved in the long term unless productivity levels match those of other competitive markets. Any policy that maintains levels of remuneration out of proportion with productivity inevitably leads to fluctuations in prices, to balance-of-payments crises, and, eventually, to high inflation.

One fundamental problem for Latin America is that the sudden opening up of the economy means that prices must be rapidly readjusted to much higher international productivity levels, to much lower international wages, and to industries that incorporate labor-saving technology. The result may be a significant increase in unemployment.

What, then, are the solutions? Recent experience suggests that we must discard policies that distort the relative price structure. It is true that no country in the world practices a policy of totally open borders or complete lack of intervention in its commercial markets. It is also true that for the effect of these "sins" to be kept to a minimum, certain conditions, such as a steady macroeconomy following a long period of stability of key variables, must be met. We also need competitive technology and investment that is relatively compatible with a more competitive market.

Argentina is wagering on another possible outcome. The aim is to induce as much growth and investment as possible within the present economic system in the hope that future full employment will compensate for the unemployment generated on the way by advancing technology. The danger of this is that any jobs that are created may result in a low-skilled workforce, suitable only to an earlier period, that will find it more and more difficult to enter the modern work market.

We must think seriously about how to cope with an increase in structural unemployment and the marginalization of certain types of workers.

In accordance with its social values, each society develops a different way of resolving its unemployment. Some of these can be seen today in studies of the various capitalist systems. In the American system, there is an extremely mobile manual workforce with a safety net of welfare programs for the poorest. The European system limits mobility but sets up safety nets in the form of generous publicly financed social security systems. In evaluating the two systems, the ethical aspect must of course be considered as well as the economic. By looking at the amount that European countries spend on maintaining their programs for the unemployed, we can see the enormous cost such a system would entail for Latin America.

In view of the difficulty of intervening in the price structure or massively financing unemployment, a more rational solution for what may be a problem inseparable from economic adjustment would be to make our low-productivity areas more competitive by improving the technological skills of the labor force, as well as by lowering the institutional barriers that limit the full economic integration of those who are currently excluded.

A very rigid tax system, overly expensive contributions to the retirement system, the formal limitations of bureaucracy, and corruption at the municipal level all act as sources of exclusion for the microentrepreneurs and self-employed. In order to remove these barriers, we must evaluate these instruments from the point of view of the economics of the low-productivity sectors. These sectors find it almost impossible to obtain credit from the formal financial sector, and that fact jeopardizes their chances to improve productivity or profits. Hence, if we expect to close the gap between the high-productivity nucleus of the economy and those who are at the borders, the government must tackle both the problem of the institutional barriers and the lack of access to credit.

The Human Dimension

Looking through the rich bibliography on the successes and failures of programs to fight poverty, we may conclude that many of the failures have resulted from lack of thought about the human dimension that lies beyond technicalities and material considerations. Through charitable works, emergency employment programs, job centers for the poor, and food handouts, millions of dollars have been wasted in unsuccessful attempts to improve social conditions. In some cases, this was due to lack of continuing incentive. In others, the policies themselves became a disincentive to the recipients to improve their condition.

It may be worth pointing out a phenomenon now taking place in the United States that highlights the need to think of integrated social policy from a human standpoint. That is the emergence of a marginalized underclass who do not think of work as a positive value and who remain resistant to the material incentives offered by an eventual improvement in their finances.[31] In fact, statistics over the last ten years have shown a significant relationship between not working and poverty; and while the level of poverty has declined in the nation as a whole, marginalization has become entrenched in the parts of society typified by chronic unemployment. All of this takes place in a society that theoretically maintains a high degree of social mobility and in which poor immigrants, who have a culture in which work is valued, can make rapid progress.

The resistance to work may have its roots in the destruction of self-esteem brought about by continuous failure. Being poor becomes preferable to looking for work because working means giving up the benefits of social assistance programs. In addition, society often inadvertently sets up support systems that reinforce poverty. Job centers turn into places where marginal workers meet employers who want workers with low qualifications to whom they can pay low wages. The most serious aspect of this subculture is that its patterns may be reinforced by being passed from one generation to the next, thereby defeating the positive message education can bring during the formative years.

An integrated social policy, then, should not only look for a way to solve an immediate need; it should also look for cultural guidelines that allow individuals to overcome their poverty permanently through their own efforts. That is where education comes in. With its capacity for instilling cultural guidelines, education is the pivot on which social policy hinges. The aim of education is not only to provide information; a complete education provides multiple dimensions: knowledge, self-esteem, information, motivation, and social recognition. When an individual absorbs these values, he is fit to take part in the general plan for progress, or perhaps in the opportunities offered by the community, and—in the case of the poor—to sever the link that transmits poverty from one generation to the next. But it is not only schools that provide these values. The school interacts with society, and it is that interaction that ensures that the formal knowledge passed on by the educational system is accepted and valued. A society that grants social and individual recognition permits a person to cultivate his self-esteem and feel that he is recognized; it also motivates him by means of economic incentives.

All of the above elements must be taken into consideration in any strategy meant to address the problem of poverty. A situation may occur in which values instilled at one stage in an individual's life vanish at another for lack of continuity—a conclusion backed by much research. The initial effects of education often disappear either because of lack of continuity and support or because the social milieu is aggressive enough to neutralize them. Education is no different from other social policies. Any educational system must, as well as being adequately financed, also lead to enablement, so that individuals can negotiate their situation with understanding, motivation, and self-esteem. In this way, social support is seen not as a stigma but as an appropriate temporary step. If a correct balance is achieved, the act of receiving support will result not in the isolation of the poor but in the social recognition of their basic human condition.

In contrast to the utilitarian school, with its "colder" view, one writer, Amartya K. Sen, stresses the importance of taking the human factor into account in economic decisions. Sen's remarks are so pertinent that they are worth quoting here at length. Any policy to fight poverty, he writes, needs to address the question of the nature of poverty:

> What is the shape of the beast we are trying to tackle with variable amounts of targeting? The policy literature on poverty has been deeply concerned with the perspective of income deprivation. I have tried to argue elsewhere for seeing poverty as the failure of some basic capabilities to function—a person lacking the opportunities to achieve some minimally acceptable levels of these functionings. . . . The functionings relevant to this analysis can vary from such elementary physical ones as being well nourished, being adequately clothed and sheltered, avoiding preventable morbidity, and so forth, to more complex social achievements such as taking part in the life of the community, being able to appear in public without shame, and so on. . . . If we insist on seeing poverty in the income space (rather than directly in terms of capability failure), the relevant concept of poverty has to be *inadequacy* (for generating minimally acceptable capabilities) rather than *lowness* (independent of social and personal characteristics). . . . It is important to see human beings not merely as recipients of income, but as people attempting to live satisfactory lives, and to see poverty not simply as low income but as the lack of real opportunities to have minimally adequate lives.[32]

Success in the fight against poverty, therefore, depends on achieving a simultaneous balance of the following three elements: a) an economic framework that can offer opportunities, b) the incorporation of a group of values through education, and c) the removal of adverse conditions in the immediate social milieu that make it difficult for individuals to plan strategies and that result in intergenerational poverty.

The Application of Social Policy

In the past, when it justified itself merely by existing, the state did not need to show any accountability to society at large, not only because macroeconomic disorder impeded a rational approach to public spending, both before and after the fact, but also because a lack of transparency was created by political patronage. Throughout most of Latin America, this resulted in the following: social policies with a low degree of targeting, except when arising from political patronage; a lack of adequate planning before, or evaluation after, the results; the total administrative and executive centralization of social policy through macroministries for social action; and the lack of coordination among the different sectors on policies with potential social impact.

Both literature and the experience of recent years provide plenty of examples of ineffective social policy in Latin America. The inefficiency quoted above was made still worse by the reduction in available financial resources produced by economic instability. Even where resources existed, however, the system did not work. A clear instance of this occurred in Argentina, where for years the social areas of the government have been unable to spend all their budgets because of administrative inefficiencies. This confirms the statement that new economic policy has been conceived more quickly than social policy. Although the reasons are many, the most plausible seems to be that during the adjustment period governments were leery of touching social areas because they could not be sure of the impact on the already compromised circumstances of the poor. The only instance in which economic and social restructuring took place simultaneously was in Chile during the dictatorship, and the results there were mixed.[33] What is clear is that much close intellectual and political study must take place if we are to find a new way of implementing social policy on principles that have already been explored and that in some cases are derived from the most basic administrative logic—early planning, evaluation, targeting, and decentralization.

Targeting

None of the literature on the subject of social policies leaves any doubt that, either in universal or compensatory actions, adequate targeting is always needed.[34] Some analysts,[35] however, have raised points that should be considered, the first of which is cost. To target implies identifying a subject (that is, a section of the population), putting together a structure to locate the subject, and controlling the policy's application. For these reasons, targeted policies are said to be more expensive. The reply is simple: The effectiveness of targeting should be assessed by the amount of resources that reach those who need them, and that should be compared with the total cost of systems that have a high leakage rate. If this is done, the effectiveness of targeted programs becomes unquestionable.[36]

The second issue to consider is stigma. It has been argued that policies directed toward a specific group of people stamp them with the stigma of poverty, and that this has the counterproductive effect of reducing their self-esteem. Often, it is said, people reject support that stigmatizes them. The response to this varies. Not all targeted policies isolate a group in such a way as to stigmatize it. The policy of nutritional assistance for young mothers at risk carries no stigma. It is, moreover, possible to envisage a self-targeting technology whereby people voluntarily choose the services to be provided on the basis of location, methods of distribution, and other specifications.

The third factor in targeting social policy involves borderline cases. One danger of targeted policies is that they may miss people on the fringes of poverty, people who need help if they are to avoid sinking further. This risk is increased by one of the worst aspects of poverty in many parts of Latin America—the poor's lack of social organization. The response here is a technical one, which concerns the extent to which the subjects of the policy understand the dynamics of poverty. It is also a political one, in that it is through social organization that the poor can gain the ability to make demands.

Decentralization

Decentralization of social policies is both a technical matter and an important political option. Decentralization not only cuts administrative costs and corruption and addresses the inability to tap into grassroots sentiment—defects of elephantine systems—it also stimulates community organizations, the only lasting way of dealing with social problems. Those opposed to greater degrees of decentralization claim that they undermine the state's ability to guide the system as a whole and to compensate for geographical and social differences. In the case of education, the strongest argument centers on the state's duty to present educational guidelines derived from a unified concept that embraces the whole country.

In Argentina, however, there is serious contradiction in the form of a society in which thousands of intermediary organizations run side by side with a centralized, inefficient social policy infrastructure. On the one hand there are model children's homes financed by the community; on the other, there are enormous "people depots" run by the government in which children are little more than numbers and where the maintenance cost for each of them far exceeds that of the community institutions.[37]

Experience in direct social action with high community participation, such as the mass vaccination programs in Colombia (which involved students, nongovernmental organizations, the armed forces, and local government), the emergency food programs that the Province of Buenos Aires used during the hyperinflation of 1989, or the Glass of Milk Program in Lima in 1984, show the capacity for mobilization and social and economic effectiveness that this type of initiative can have.

One of the main outcomes of decentralization is the deterioration of the political patronage apparatus, which depends on public funds that are administered with little social control. In political terms, that is a mistake because it does not take into account the new social awareness in which political power is derived more from an administration's degree of openness to people than from the illicit maneuverings of political bosses. In the 1993 mayoral elections in Argentina, the voting mostly favored those who had been efficient in the use of public funds and penalized those who had increased public sector employment by political patronage. In other words, manipulation of the party structure no longer ensures electoral victory.

Within the idea of decentralization as an efficient tool of social policy, social fund organizations have a particularly important contribution to make. The Fondo Participativo de Inversión Social (FOPAR) in Argentina, the Fondo de Solidaridad e Inversión Social in Chile, and the Emergency Social Fund in Bolivia should be analyzed in detail. Each has extremely positive aspects. They promote social organization and lead to the correct defining of social priorities. As direct participants in the programs that they themselves have prioritized, citizens pay close attention to the administration of their resources, and when people control administration the costs of public works are noticeably lower.[38] One criticism directed at these funds is that they do not reach the poorest sectors, which do not have any capacity to organize, and therefore the programs cannot function. But no universal policies will deal with that problem. The poorest sectors should be targeted by social policies that can fulfill their basic needs and help them to improve their capacity to organize until they can take advantage of the above programs or similar ones. In sum, theory and practice are unanimous in their view of the importance of programs that use social energy as a tool for dealing with immediate social or structural needs, and special effort should be devoted to evolving new schemes based on that principle.

Finally, we must consider the decentralization of education as a tool of social policy. All theory and common sense indicate that education is social integration's most reliable tool. Social programs that try, after the fact, to rescue individuals with basic educational shortages either fail or have serious limitations. Educational statistics indicate, however, that beyond the improvement observed in the figures for matriculation, the various countries of Latin America face a serious problem of quality, a problem that becomes more evident the more the economy opens up. There are various remedies, but they are costly, and it takes a long time for their effects to be noticed. The question, then, is how to reduce the length of time it takes to improve the quality of education and how to increase its socializing effects. This problem is the subject of much research. Community participation, however, is especially important in the educational process as a way of improving the quality of education itself and of developing feelings of social obligation within the community.

No single strategy exists for decentralizing education. Any strategy has to take into account the needs of a given society at a given moment. In Chile, there is still fierce controversy over the educational and social benefits of the extreme decentralization that emerged during the military dictatorship. In North America, the federal government is trying to take a larger part in monitoring the quality of education in the states and in the development of compensatory programs. In Argentina, we have just transferred all school administration to the provinces and there is a new role for the national ministry of education.

Be that as it may, education should be drawn into the community in two ways. First, because it is the community that does the true educating, the home, church, community associations, and local political organizations should have an educational function that is at least as important as that of the school.[39] Second, in the allocation of knowledge and the development of the child's value structure, parents have an irreplaceable role to play. The present-day reality of our civilization gives little help in wielding these two weighty educational tools. Community life is dominated by negative signals, from violence in the media to a decay in social institutions (the family, political institutions, and even religion). There are no longer any points of reference.

Parents' participation in their children's education is fundamental everywhere in the world. In a recent unusually harsh and sincere speech, the U.S. secretary of education said that the destruction of the American family and the isolation of its members—even in intact families—has had a profound and enduring effect on the education of our children. Parents must slow down their lives so as to help their children grow. In a recent inquiry on violence in the schools, half of the pupils with lower than average scores said that their parents did not share with them anything related to school.[40]

There is an added problem involved in bringing education closer to parents and to the community. This is the ambivalent attitude of teachers, who know they need greater backup from parents but are resistant to what they see as interference in the school. Such resistance is also noticeable in the political positions of the unions that represent the teachers. In Argentina, "municipalization" of the educational system has been used as a banner for the unions to wave to resist any attempt to decentralize education further, since that would give parents greater say.

Technical-political solutions must be found to this problem. The political solution rests on an explicit decision to bring about integration among school, community, and parents by whatever means are possible at any given moment, while maintaining the conceptual unity of education throughout the country, as is the state's fundamental role. The technical solution must suit the characteristics of the different communities and be politically viable. In the context of an integral social policy, it is essential that education be brought closer to the people and that methods are found to achieve this objective.

Notes

1. Lawrence Mead, *The New Politics of Poverty* (New York: Basic Books, 1992).

2. See, for example, the works of Robert Bellah et al.: *The Good Society* (New York: Alfred A. Knopf, 1991), and *Habits of the Heart* (Berkeley: University of California Press, 1988). See also, Oliver F. Williams and John Houck, eds., *The Common Good and U.S. Capitalism* (Lanham, MD: University Press of America, 1987).

3. A magnificent article on this subject was written by Robert J. Samuelson in the *Washington Post*, January 7, 1993, under the descriptive title "It's Not the Economy, Stupid."

4. See "Human Resources in Latin America and the Caribbean. Priorities and Action," *Latin America and the Caribbean Region Report*, no. 13662 (Washington, DC: World Bank, January 1993).

5. Or, as the World Bank says, having committed the worst sin of using the macroeconomy as a tool for redistributing income.

6. See, for example, Samuel A. Morley, *Poverty and the Distribution of Income during Latin American Adjustment in the '80s* (Washington, DC: World Bank, 1992).

7. See Eduardo Bustelo, "Hood Robin. Ajuste y equidad en America Latina" (Paper presented at the seminar "Models for Development and Poverty in Latin America," December 1–3, 1993, Woodrow Wilson International Center for Scholars, Washington, DC). It is curious that Bustelo uses the title of a previous article of his even when the facts demonstrate that his basic hypothesis, that adjustment is essentially perverse, was wrong.

8. In this respect, Louis Emmerij puts forward an interesting conceptual thesis in a document entitled "The Social Question and the Interamerican

Development Bank" (Washington, DC: Inter-American Development Bank, December 1993).

9. See "Implementing the World Bank's Strategy to Reduce Poverty" (Washington, DC: World Bank, 1993).

10. Argentina, Ministry of the Economy, "Informe sobre la pobreza en la Argentina" (Paper presented at the Extraordinary General Assembly of the Organization of American States on Poverty, Mexico, D.F., February 1994).

11. Ibid., 37.

12. Ibid., 40.

13. Secretaría de Recursos Hídricos de la Nación, *Informe* (Buenos Aires: Ministry of Public Works, 1993).

14. See "La diferenciación interna de los asalariados del Gran Buenos Aires," Programa Pronatass, Ministry of Labor and Social Security, Argentina, September 1992.

15. "Informe sobre la pobreza en la Argentina," 34.

16. This problem was anticipated in an excellent report by Inés Aguerrondo, "La calidad de la educación en la Argentina," research paper prepared for the Ministry of Education, Argentina, December 1992.

17. As Michel Albert calls it in *Capitalism against Capitalism*, trans. Paul Haviland (New York: Four Walls Eight Windows, 1993).

18. Quoted by Bellah in *The Good Society*, 87.

19. Mead, *The New Politics of Poverty*.

20. See, for example, Bellah, *The Good Society* and *Habits of the Heart*; see also *The Common Good* and works by Daniel Bell and Reinhold Niebuhr, among others.

21. Bellah, *The Good Society*, 20.

22. Ibid., 9.

23. Walter Lippmann, *The Good Society* (Boston: Little, Brown, 1937).

24. James Coleman, Thomas Hoffer, and Sally Kilgore, *High School Achievement: Public, Private and Catholic High Schools Compared* (New York: Basic Books, 1982).

25. See, for example, Luis Beccaria and Ricardo Carciofi, "Social Policy and Adjustment during the 1980s: An Overview of the Argentine Case" (Washington, DC: Brookings Institution, 1992).

26. Emmerij, "The Social Question."

27. *Latin America and the Caribbean Region* (Washington, DC: World Bank, 1993); *Latin America and the Caribbean: A Decade after the Debt Crisis* (Washington, DC: World Bank, 1993), 142.

28. See *Argentina, invertir y crecer* (Buenos Aires: Ministry of Economy, 1993).

29. See Juan José Llach, "Hiperestablizaciones sin mitos" (Buenos Aires: Instituto Di Tella, 1991).

30. See "Latin America and the Caribbean," 142.

31. Mead, *The New Politics of Poverty*.

32. Amartya K. Sen, "The Political Economy of Targeting," in *Public Spending and the Poor*, ed. Dominique van de Walle and Kimberly Nead (Washington, DC: Public Economic Division, Policy Research Department, World Bank, 1993), 15–17.

33. See "Modernizar con todos," report by the pilot mission of the Social Reform Program of the Inter-American Development Bank, Washington, DC, January 1994.

34. See, for example, Margaret Grosh, "From Platitude to Practice: Administering Targeted Social Programs in Latin America," *World Bank Regional and Sectoral Studies Monograph Series*, Washington DC, August 1993.

35. See works by Frances Stewart and others in van de Walle and Nead, eds., *Public Spending and the Poor.*

36. Grosh, "From Platitude to Practice," 46.

37. For a dramatic example of an unmanageable social welfare system, see the case study "Toward an Effective Social Reform Policy in Venezuela," prepared by the Inter-American Development Bank by the pilot mission of the Social Reform Program, December 1993.

38. See, for example, Steen Jorgenson, Margaret Grosh, and Mark Schacter, eds., "Bolivia's Answer to Poverty, Economic Crisis and Adjustment: The Emergency Social Fund," *World Bank Regional and Sectorial Studies, 1992* (Washington, DC: World Bank, ca. 1992), esp. 65–66.

39. Bellah, *The Good Society*, 146.

40. Richard W. Riley, U.S. Secretary of Education, "State of American Education" (Speech delivered at Georgetown University, Washington, DC, February 15, 1994).

II

The Terms of
Democratic Consolidation

5

Democracies in Contemporary South America

Convergences and Diversities

Jonathan Hartlyn*

In an opinion article entitled "Can We Govern?" the Washington columnist David Broder highlighted the fact that "governments in democratic societies around the globe are notably weak these days." He then went on to cite the examples of Japan, Italy, France, Germany, Great Britain, and Canada as well as the United States. Citing Bill Brock, he noted how "the virtual erasure of national boundaries to the flow of capital and the location of manufacturing and service facilities lessened governments' ability to control their national economies." Broder noted how three major governing institutions—parties, Congress, and the presidency—were extremely weak, while interest groups and the news media appeared to be growing in power. Because interest groups and the media are not oriented toward constructing consensus, one of the central intended goals of political institutions, this situation was severely complicating the ability of nation-states to address important problems and generate effective policy.[1]

The vast implications of changes in the global economy and the difficult challenges of governance are also familiar themes in contemporary

*This is a revised and updated version of a paper presented at the "Segundo Encuentro de Estudios Políticos sobre el Mundo Andino," Villa de Leyva, Colombia, April 1994, and published in Madrid, Spain, in *Síntesis: Revista de Ciencias Sociales Iberoamericanas* 22 (July–December 1994): 17–51. Text that originally appeared in Jonathan Hartlyn and Arturo Valenzuela, "Democracy in Latin America since 1930," in *Cambridge History of Latin America*, vol. 6, Part II, *Latin America since 1930: Economy, Society, and Politics*, ed. Leslie Bethell (New York: Cambridge University Press, 1994), 100–101, is reprinted by permission of Cambridge University Press.

Latin America. However, the seeming similarity of some of these issues should not obscure their very different analytical significance in a region seeking to construct or reconstruct democratic institutions in a context of severe social inequalities, while also confronting or emerging from often severe state and economic crises. The challenges in Latin America are even greater than those in industrialized countries. Changes imposed on them by the global economy come on top of the exhaustion of the model of import-substituting industrialization, the debt crisis, and the fiscal collapse of the state—the collapse in the region's more industrialized countries of what Marcelo Cavarozzi has termed the state-centric matrix.[2] Democratic governance confronts difficult questions of how to build consensus to confront seemingly intractable economic problems in countries with often profound historical legacies of weak democratic institutions. Similarly, many of these countries face basic questions regarding the appropriate roles of state institutions. In some countries, following extended crises, occupants of the presidential office have taken considerable power upon themselves, often with the acquiescence of large sectors of the population, to enact significant neoliberal economic reforms; thus, governance has come at the cost of open debate and democracy. At the same time, Latin American social groups, especially popular ones, appear weaker and more disarticulated, though there are some countertendencies.

Latin America is undergoing a broad transitional process—actually, a set of partially linked transitional processes—with socioeconomic and cultural dimensions as well as political ones. These processes involve decomposition and destruction—of state and societal institutions, groups and forms of behavior—as well as (in many cases still unclear or uncertain) recomposition and restructuring, generating often contradictory trends. It is still not apparent which phenomena are peculiar to the transition phase and which will be longer lasting, thus making meaningful, broad comparative statements even more difficult.

Nevertheless, it is evident that the implications of these complex transitional processes with regard to politics are profound. Empirically, but in an uneven process throughout the continent, the state and the sphere of politics no longer have the same importance they once did as the dominant forger of identity and the organizer of conflicts, or as locus of conflict and decisions—even as the parties, campaigns, constitutional designs, and electoral rules continue to be important, but in different ways. Social conflicts and actors are more complex and diversified, often with their own international ties and ramifications.[3] They are no longer fused to overarching goals or to political and economic actors, as they have been in many countries in the region in the past. One analytical consequence is that the old "master" paradigms, modernization and dependency, and the newer one of neoliberalism, all of which in different ways highlighted the central importance of socioeconomic and cultural factors, have not been replaced by other single-focused paradigms and are unlikely to be. There is a growing recognition that there are multiple causal interactive logics, within and across political, societal, and economic dimensions.[4]

Indeed, it is not surprising that in a thought-provoking review of democratizing tendencies in the region at a conference held in Villa de Leyva, Colombia, in 1988, Laurence Whitehead underscored "the impressive diversity of national experiences."[5] He chose to explain the seeming diversity across Latin America on the basis of the quality of political leadership; inflation; drug trafficking, crime, and associated corruption; social and political polarization (leading to guerrilla violence and "dirty war" responses); and economic crisis caused by the external debt.

In 1994, there is some evidence of a convergence at the level of types of regime on the continent: "up" from the harshest types of authoritarian rule but also "down" from unrestricted democracies, with few unambiguous cases of democratic consolidation. Furthermore, one could argue that the existence of significant international forces and influences impose severe constraints on the nature and kind of economic and social welfare policies that governments can enact. The continuance of democratic regimes, even if some remain limited or even contrived, suggests that national experiences are likely to be structured within a narrower set of political and economic options than in previous decades, especially the 1970s.[6]

Yet, in disentangling these apparent convergences, diversities and occasionally unexpected "movement" by countries, as well as some explanatory factors for them, emerge. The factors Whitehead enumerated can be regrouped to emphasize two in particular: a) international factors, which through their contradictory political and economic effects help explain some aspects of the "convergence" phenomena in Latin America; and b) the nature and extent of challenge to state coherence and the rule of law, including the impact of social and political polarization, drug trafficking, inflation and economic crisis, and restructuring policies.[7]

Furthermore, there is another factor of central importance, foreshadowed by Broder, that should not be overlooked in explaining the "diversities" within "convergence." This one relates to historical continuities and discontinuities regarding political institutions, particularly political parties, party systems, and constitutional arrangements. Underscoring the importance of this factor is the belief that one should reject mechanistic explanations of politics, in terms of its being "explained" by other social or economic phenomena. To the extent that democracy depends upon channeling conflict and building enduring institutions that can generate consensus and encourage compromise, the parties, party systems, electoral laws, and constitutional structures are essential. Strong parties and party systems favor democratic rule, but only with the appropriate mix of appeals and with party organization that is neither too loose nor too rigid. And presidentialism in Latin America has been problematic, especially in the context of multiparty systems (and even more so if they are weak and fragmented parties). At the same time, one should also reject mechanistic explanations from politics. A specific institutional configuration will not necessarily ensure democratic consolidation. Multiple factors affect democratic prospects, and in some cases tensions across social groups, conflicts, and economic and social crises may be especially intractable or unresolvable.[8]

To make this chapter more manageable, I will focus on the seven South American countries with the most democratic experience on the continent since 1930 (Argentina, Brazil, Chile, Colombia, Peru, Uruguay, and Venezuela).[9] Like the work by Whitehead cited above, this is written in the spirit of a review essay rather than as a test of formal hypotheses; the comparative analysis remains incomplete. Much more detailed work would be required to clarify the differential impact of different factors and the importance of different sequences of interaction across factors and events in the various countries.

Optimism with regard to the evolution of democratic patterns in Chile and Uruguay appears based in part on the relative absence of economic crisis, the strength of their state structures, and the significance of past patterns of democracy and how structural changes and political learnings over time have modified them. At the same time, without reform of the constitutional structure of those countries, there are reasons to believe that serious future challenges to their democracies could arise. Argentina, Brazil, and Peru, which also had transitions from military rule in the 1980s, have all experienced declines in the quality of their democracies over time (in the first two instances) or actual breakdown and partial reequilibration (Peru). In the short term, there is unlikely to be dramatic improvement, though based on issues of presidential leadership the situation would appear a little more hopeful for Brazil. Venezuela, the only consolidated democracy of the seven countries in 1980, has moved toward partial deconsolidation and fragmentation of its party system. In Colombia, significant democratic political reforms have been combined with remarkable political party continuity and economic restructuring, but also with state crisis and profound internal violence. As a consequence, Colombia's overall democratic evolution, historically constrained, has also deteriorated over this past five- to ten-year period.

Conceptualizing Democracy

In this paper, the meaning of democracy will be restricted to a procedural definition, making possible a debate of how different countries in Latin America exemplify different degrees or types of democracy, and the implications that different features of the state, of the regime, and of political and party institutions have for democracy. At the same time, it is clear that within each country the meaning of democracy will remain contested and debated.

"Democracy" or "political democracy" incorporates three critical dimensions.[10] The first, to use Robert Dahl's term, is contestation. In a democracy, the government is constituted by leaders who successfully compete for the vote of the citizenry in regularly scheduled elections. The essence of contestation is the acceptance of the legitimacy of political opposition, the right to challenge incumbents and replace them in the principal positions of political authority. Contestation requires state protection for the freedom of expression and association and the existence of regular, free, and fair elections capable of translating the will of the citizenry into leadership options. Particularly significant for political contestation is the development of consolidated party systems, in which the interaction among parties follows a predictable pattern and their electoral strengths remain stable. Parties promote distinct programs or ideologies, sponsor individuals for elected office, and serve as critical links between civil society and the state.

The second dimension is constitutionalism, or respect for the constitutional order, embodied in constitutional documents and practices, often in contravention to the strict application of the principle of majority rule. It is in this sense that contemporary democracies must be understood as "constitutional democracies." A constitutional democracy, while guaranteeing the right of the opposition to challenge incumbents by appealing for the support of a majority of the citizenry, defines and restricts the powers of governmental authorities. It also places limits on the hegemony of electoral majorities and their representatives, with a view toward protecting the rights and preferences of individuals and minorities, the options of future majorities, and the very institutions of democracy itself. These institutions and rules vary and include such provisions as restrictions on presidential reelection and the partial insulation of judicial, electoral, and security organs from elected leadership. They also include the use of qualified legislative majorities and complex ratification mechanisms when fundamental changes in the nation's constitution and basic laws are at stake. Finally, they make provisions for power sharing and minority representation, an essential element for the protection of the opposition and encouragement of the concept of a "loyal opposition." In practice, constitutional democracies diverge on the degree to which contingent majorities or their representatives are constrained by constitutional and legal restrictions.

The third dimension is inclusiveness or participation. By definition, democracies are based on the concept of popular sovereignty. As democracies evolve, the constitutional provisions for citizenship broaden to include larger proportions of the adult population, through the elimination of restrictions on suffrage based on property, literacy, gender, race, or ethnicity. Changes in formal rules, including residency and registration requirements, and the effective involvement of the population in politics through the expansion of parties and movements, lead, over time, to full inclusiveness.

A constitutional democracy may be viewed as consolidated when contestation and respect for the constitutional order are widely accepted and citizenship and effective electoral participation have been extended to all adults possessing minimum qualifications. This definition of democracy is often supplemented by a concept of citizenship that incorporates formal equality (universal suffrage) and legal protection from abusive state power. It also includes notions of material satisfaction and education sufficient for participation to be deemed meaningful rather than manipulated. One need hardly underscore how often these elements are problematic in Latin America.

What factors appear to help the process of consolidation? Analysts have focused on a vigorous and active civil society and a functioning, viable economy. Yet, what has been clear across much of Latin America recently for somewhat differing reasons (following an excessive faith in simplistic neoliberal prescriptions and the harsh reality of economic restructuring, or brought about by the consequences of ignoring the realities of international economic constraints or the impact of drug trafficking) is that what is of central importance is a functioning, coherent state that is democratically controlled and a "political society" that is institutionalized and relatively autonomous, involving political parties, leaders, and actors.

Patterns of Democracy in Latin America Today

Over the past seventy years in Latin America, one can observe two historical cycles with regard to democracy: one from the late 1920s to the late 1950s (with a subcycle in the late 1940s), and another from the late 1950s to the late 1980s and continuing to the present. Both began with a predominance of civilian regimes, many of which succumbed to military rule only to return subsequently to rule by civilians, though the number of countries involved has been greater more recently. Prior to 1990, the most auspicious moment for democracy in the region occurred in the late 1950s. The pendulum swung sharply back in the 1960s in the aftermath of the Cuban revolution, and at that time the nature of dictatorship changed in qualitative terms. Between 1962 and 1964, eight military takeovers took place. Military coups in Brazil, Argentina, Peru, Chile, and Uruguay would also inaugurate bureaucratic authoritarian or military regimes that sought to rebuild the institutional order, either in direct response to threats from the Left or in an attempt to preempt that threat. During the 1970s there were from twelve to sixteen authoritarian governments in Latin America at any one time, most intent on modernizing and transforming their societies by excluding not only the old politicians but the citizenry as well.

Then, in the 1980s, in the throes of the worst economic crisis since the Great Depression, the most dramatic political reversal took place on the continent since the 1930s. Over the period between 1988 and 1991, for the first time in the history of the continent, presidential elections were held in every single country except for Cuba.[11] For the first time in its history, all of the countries of the region with the exception of Cuba were led by elected presidents according to constitutionally prescribed provisions, however circumscribed the democratic nature of many of these regimes and problematic the electoral processes that brought some of them into office.

Political democracy, although limited and constrained in several countries, appeared triumphant on the continent as never before in the history of the region as the last decade of the century began. This current shift in the region ran parallel to a broader international trend toward democracy. The number of states that the Freedom House annual survey rated as "free" (an approximation of political democracy), grew from 42 in 1972 to 52 in 1980 to 76 in 1992.[12] At the same time, simplistic renditions of an "end of history" argument suggested that international legitimation of democracy also presaged its consolidation.

However, by 1995, it was clear that optimism about this latest "democratic wave" had to be tempered, both worldwide and in Latin America. As the total number of countries listed by Freedom House grew from 183 in 1992 to 191 in 1995, the percentage of free countries fell from 42 percent to 40 percent, and that of partly free countries from 36 percent to 32 percent.[13] In Latin America, we can point to both dramatic and ongoing processes that underscore the fragility of democracy in the region. Dramatic negative events in the early 1990s—a successful coup in Haiti, failed coup attempts in Guatemala and Venezuela, an *auto-golpe* in Peru—were followed by the reinstallation of Aristide to power in Haiti in 1994, and the reequilibration of a form of very restricted democracy in Peru. Yet other worrisome events occurred, such as military challenges to Chilean authorities and continued political assassinations in Colombia. Furthermore, more gradual but no less significant processes were evident in numerous countries related to problems with ongoing human rights violations and even basic electoral processes.

Shifts in the measures generated by Freedom House of political rights and civil liberties over the period from 1980 to 1994 provide another indicator of the progress and then stagnation in democratic progress in Latin America and the Caribbean. Transitions to democracy in the 1980s in the region are evident by the increase from seven countries with a population greater than one million that were rated "free" in 1980 to thirteen countries in 1987: Argentina, Brazil, Costa Rica, Dominican Republic, Jamaica, Trinidad and Tobago, Uruguay, and Venezuela (scoring 2–4) and Bolivia, Colombia, Ecuador, Honduras, and Peru as more restricted democracies (scoring 5) (see Table 1). However, in the period from 1987 to 1994, there has been movement both "upward" and "downward," toward a somewhat greater convergence of more mixed kinds of semidemocratic regimes. Between 1987 and 1994, Chile, Panama, and, to a lesser extent, Paraguay and Nicaragua had moved "upward" from the most authoritarian categories. However, there was also considerable movement "downward" toward the middle level of categories. According to these rankings, nine countries (instead of thirteen) were "free" in 1994, with five of those nine

Table 1. Freedom House Scores of Latin American Countries with Populations of over One Million*

Category	1980	1987	1994
Free (2–4)	Costa Rica (1,1)	Costa Rica (1,1) Trinidad and Tobago (1,1)	
	Venezuela (1,2)	Argentina (2,1) Venezuela (1,2)	Costa Rica (1,2)
	Ecuador (2,2)	Uruguay (2,2)	Chile (2,2)
	Trinidad and Tobago (2,2)	Dominican Republic (1,3) Jamaica (2,2)	Trinidad and Tobago (2,2)
		Brazil (2,2)	Uruguay (2,2)
Free (5)	Colombia (2,3) Dominican Republic (2,3)	Colombia (2,3) Bolivia (2,3)	Argentina (2,3) Bolivia (2,3)
	Jamaica (2,3)	Peru (2,3) Ecuador (2,3) Honduras (2,3)	Ecuador (2,3) Jamaica (2,3) Panama (2,3)

Partly Free *(6–11)*	Belize (3,3)	Guatemala (3,3)	Brazil (2,4) El Salvador (3,3) Honduras (3,3) Venezuela (3,3)
	Brazil (2,4)	El Salvador (3,4)	Colombia (3,4)
	Mexico (3,4)		Dominican Republic (4,3) Paraguay (4,3)
		Mexico (4,4)	Mexico (4,4)
	Peru (5,4)		Guatemala (4,5)
	El Salvador (5,4)		Nicaragua (4,5)
	Guatemala (4,5)		Peru (5,4)
	Honduras (6,3)		
	Nicaragua (5,5)	Nicaragua (5,5)	Haiti (5,5)
	Panama (5,5)	Panama (5,5)	
	Paraguay (5,5)		
	Argentina (6,5)	Chile (6,5)	
	Chile (6,5)	Haiti (5,6)	
	Haiti (6,5)	Paraguay (5,6)	
Not free *(12–14)*	Cuba (6,6) Uruguay (6,6)	Cuba (6,6)	Cuba (7,7)

Sources: *Freedom in the World: Political Rights and Civil Liberties 1987–88* (New York: Freedom House, 1988) and *Freedom in the World: The Annual Survey of Political Rights and Civil Liberties 1993–1994* (New York: Freedom House, 1994). Inspiration for the table comes from Larry Diamond, "Democracy in Latin America," 1993 manuscript (note 12). *Combined Freedom House scores: political rights (high of 1 to low of 7) and civil liberties (high of 1 to low of 7)

listed as restricted democracies (scoring 5). The list in 1994 now excluded Brazil, Colombia, Dominican Republic, Honduras, Peru, and Venezuela, but it added Chile and Panama; furthermore, Argentina and Jamaica fell within the democratic category and Guatemala also declined further in both political rights and civil liberties. Another way of indicating the movement toward the middle is by noting that, in 1987, eight countries had very low (democratic) scores and six countries had very high (authoritarian) scores; in 1994, that had fallen to four countries with low (democratic) scores and one with a high (authoritarian) score (see Table 2). Although we may quibble with individual placements of countries or the inevitable simplifications of the exercise, these rankings illustrate the general trends we are currently witnessing in the region.

The primary conclusion is that if over the last several years there has been movement away from the harshest types of authoritarian rule, there has also been a decline in progress toward unrestricted political democracies. The existence of "movement" across categories suggests that there has been difficulty as well in consolidating *restricted* democracies.

Table 2. Summary Scores for Latin America, Selected Years

	1980	1987	1992	1993	1994
Free (2–4)	4	8	5	4	4
Free(5)	3	5	6	4	5
Partly Free (6–9)	7	3	8	11	12
Not Free (10–14)	8	6	3	3	1
Total	**22**	**22**	**22**	**22**	**22**

Source: Table 1.

The seven countries of South America with the greatest experience with democratic rule since 1930—Argentina, Brazil, Peru, Chile, Uruguay, Colombia, and Venezuela—exemplify this more general regional pattern. From 1980 to 1990, the first five of these countries underwent democratic transitions from military rule, with Chile being the last country to do so, in 1990 (although with significant constitutional restrictions remaining). With the enactment of the 1991 constitution, it could be said that Colombia underwent an important transformation in a democratizing direction, as numerous restrictions on effective contestation were finally removed.[14] Venezuela also carried out a number of more modest political reforms during this period. Yet, except for Chile and Uruguay, the other countries all had worse scores on civil liberties in 1994 than they had in 1987, and three of them (Colombia, Peru, and Venezuela) had worse scores on political rights as well (see Table 1).

The International System: Sustaining a Political-Ideological Floor for Democracy? Collapsing or Helping to Rebuild the Socioeconomic Roof?

At the international level, discussion can focus on economic, political, and security dimensions. At the level of politics and security, current international trends favor democracy in the region, though clearly less than was the case for southern European democratic transitions. Ideologically, there is no other model of rule competing with democracy in Latin America. The Cuban revolution, which had such a profound impact on actors across the entire ideological spectrum, inspiring or strengthening guerrilla movements, counterinsurgency doctrines, liberation theologies, and reformist impulses, no longer serves as a model. With the end of the Cold War, the central goal of "stopping communism," sometimes complicated by a "dual track" of U.S. civil-military diplomacy, has molded toward a consensus around promoting democracy. This has permitted multilateral, if still somewhat timid, international actions seeking to "defend" democracy in the hemisphere.

At this political-ideological level, the United States and other international actors have played positive roles in these seven countries. They have helped to limit "slippage" to outright military authoritarianism more than actively to enrich democracy. One could mention the support of the National Endowment for Democracy for the opposition forces in the 1988 plebiscite vote against Pinochet, discussions with the Peruvian military during the Alan García administrations, and pronouncements surrounding the 1993 elections in Venezuela. At the same time, it is clear that there are limits to and ambiguities concerning these actions, as is evident in the evolution of relations between the United States and the Fujimori administration in Peru. Concerns for democracy and human rights in U.S. policy toward Peru have been balanced by desires to continue working with the Peruvian government on antinarcotics issues and to show support for the government's sweeping market-oriented reforms.[15] The "constitutionalization" and hybrid authoritarianism of the Fujimori government following the April 1992 constitutional breakdown showed responsiveness to international political pressure; in a different international context, given the severity and nature of the crisis in Peru (or in other countries), the response might well have been a coup d'état or more overt authoritarian rule.

With regard to the military, the situation in Latin America remains decidedly mixed for the fundamental reason that it is not obvious what an appropriate professional role for them should be that would facilitate their removal from active involvement in domestic politics. There is no clear international organization or externally oriented mission for the Latin American militaries, and involvement in international peacekeeping missions or regional defense efforts is not a fully equivalent proxy.[16] To the extent that the military retains an active role in internal security or in combating drug trafficking (sustaining or increasing their budgets and size), the risk of more extensive military involvement remains acute, and current problems of human rights violations by state agents may be added to the challenges of addressing past ones. Historical legacies of entrenched prerogatives and privileges will be difficult to dismantle, whether because of the military's continued presence following a democratic transition (including, in the case of Chile, constitutional guarantees) or because of civilian abdication of responsibility for internal security matters.[17] As J. Samuel Fitch notes, it may be unavoidable to have Latin American militaries play an active role in internal security. Civilians must "take seriously their responsibility in internal security," including enforcing norms and doctrines regarding the rights of combatants and noncombatants appropriate for democratic regimes. Democratic leaders must "develop a basic consensus with respect to the missions to be assigned to the armed forces," and those leaders must work to integrate the military within democratic regimes by generating new institutional mechanisms if necessary.[18] The extension of military missions into involvement in noncombatant domestic roles, such as in civil engineering projects, providing disaster assistance or relief, or doing environmental work, has clear risks for the civilian leadership and does not eliminate the need to address difficult issues related to budget, force size, and professional identity. Probably the most negative U.S. role in terms of this dimension has been played in countries like Colombia and Peru, where particularly in the mid to the late 1980s there was an emphasis on "militarizing" the war on drugs. At the same time, the United States and other international actors have discouraged military coups, although the reluctance of powerful domestic societal actors or of political leaders to support such actions have also been important. In sum, although a "floor" is being sustained, it appears to be a wobbly one.

If international political-ideological currents generally favor democracy, it is clear that international economic currents have not played a similar role in the region. The international system and the kinds of societal changes and balances of power induced within countries are imposing severe structural constraints on the kinds of economic models that Latin American states can pursue—and thus on the kinds of economic goals that can be successfully pursued through political participation. Even as the democratic quality of many Latin American countries has suffered, poverty and inequality both prior to and after the initiation of stabilization and initial reform efforts have increased. This is not to argue that some kind of economic stabilization and market-oriented reforms were not necessary, but to underscore that those that were implemented almost certainly increased poverty (see Table 3).[19]

Although the impact of international economic ideologies, forces, and flows must be factored in, initial conditions and continuing policy deci-

Table 3. Poverty and Extreme Poverty in Selected Countries, 1970–1992

	Households under the Poverty Line—		Households under the Extreme Poverty Line—	
	Total	*Urban*	*Total*	*Urban*
Argentina				
1970	8	5	1	1
1980	9	7	2	2
1986	13	12	4	3
1990	na	16*	na	4*
1992	na	10*	na	1*

Brazil				
1970	49	35	25	15
1979	39	30	17	10
1987	40	34	18	13
1990	43	39	na	22
Chile				
1970	17	12	6	3
1987	38	37	14	13
1990	35	34	12	11
1992	28	27	7	7
Colombia				
1970	45	38	18	14
1980	39	36	16	13
1986	38	36	17	15
1990	na	35	na	12
1992	na	38	na	15
Peru				
1970	50	28	25	8
1979	46	35	21	12
1986	52	45	25	16
Uruguay				
1970	na	10	4	na
1981	11	9	3	2
1986	15	14	3	3
1990	na	12	na	2
1992	na	8	na	1
Venezuela				
1970	25	20	10	6
1981	22	18	7	5
1986	27	25	9	8
1990	34	33	12	11
1992	33	32	11	10
Latin America				
1970	40	26	19	10
1980	35	25	15	9
1986	37	30	17	11
1990	39	34	18	13

Source: Comisión Económica para la América Latina (CEPAL), Panorama Social de América Latina, 1994 (Santiago: CEPAL, 1995), 158–59.
*Buenos Aires only

sions also matter. In contrast to the "transition" Latin American countries (with the partial exception of Chile), governments in countries like Spain in the post-Franco era benefited from inheriting low levels of public domestic debt and modest levels of public expenditures as well as a coherent, functioning state apparatus.[20] Table 3 provides estimates for poverty and absolute poverty rates for the seven South American countries. What they show is that only two countries, Uruguay and Colombia, had urban poverty rates in the 1990s that were lower than or the same as what they had been in 1970. Even as Chile, Argentina, and, to a lesser extent, Venezuela showed declines in poverty rates from 1990 to 1992, Colombia showed an increase. Urban poverty rates in Argentina and Chile in 1992 remained twice what they had been in 1970. In Venezuela they were one and one-half times what they had been in 1970, and in Brazil, Colombia, and Peru they remained tragically high, ranging from 38 to 45 percent of the population. As CEPAL notes, economic growth, declines in rates of inflation, increases in employment and in average wage rates (and in some cases of the minimum wage) helped the poorest groups in countries like Argentina and Chile in the past several years more than redistribution; only in Uruguay did distribution help decrease poverty.[21] In Chile, the one country of the seven that is most clearly past the difficult stage of implementing economic restructuring, these socioeconomic constraints are evident in the kinds of strategies that the democratic governing coalition has been implementing. For example, its successes in alleviating poverty have been based primarily on employment generated by economic growth (especially in the low-wage sectors) rather than on governmental redistribution of income or assets. The Chilean socialists have sought to downplay welfare-type transfer payments and instead target social investments that give the poor more access to education, training, and other benefits to ease their integration into the market economy.[22] In sum, these constraints may be seen as limiting the policy options and goals of actors within these countries and paving the way for continuing social and political tensions.

The kind of response that national leaders construct can have a significant impact on how international investors respond, on enhancing the lives of those integrated into the new model, and in terms of how those "left out" of the new economic model respond—even if overall constraints limit the extent of poverty alleviation possible, at least in the short and medium term. This underscores the argument of Acuña and Smith, that "inferring politics from economics is bad methodology . . . especially under Latin America's current highly constrained economic conditions."[23]

Therefore, if the international system has provided a "wrecking ball" for the "economic roof" in several Latin American countries, it must be recognized that the roof had been eroding over many decades and in some cases had been actively dismantled from within by the choice of domestic policies. Furthermore, the nature and pace of the dismantling of the old roof and construction of the new one also has had substantial short-term effects. Over the next decade, the nature, height, and diversity of "roofs" will continue to be determined by the complex interaction of international and domestic actors and institutions. To the extent that international investment and other capital flows continue to be disproportionately distributed in the region, a "diverging" impact upon the countries of the area may more clearly be felt over the years ahead, and international aid may help some countries to rebuild more than others. It is also clear that new patterns of production are generating more diversified linkages to the global economy, which cut across national boundaries and constrain what national economic policymakers can hope to act upon even as economic integration schemes open up additional opportunities and constraints. At the same time, democratic consolidation implies more active participation by an engaged citizenry and more effective accountability of elected officials. In seeking a viable path through these contradictory demands, the state and political institutions will remain key domestic actors.

The State: From Overcommitted to Underengaged or Reconstituted?

The "crisis of the state" visible in most of these South American countries over the 1980s and early 1990s was an uneven combination of several factors. One was associated with fiscal crisis linked to debt, the collapse of the old import-substitution industrialization model, and the need to respond to the challenges of the new global economy. Another factor has been the inability to provide the basic functions of order, security, and justice. A third has been the question of greater access to the state by individuals in the context of the other two crises, usually combining aspects of state decentralization with democratizing and decentralizing reforms. As governments in several countries reasserted control over economies in sharp decline and reestablished a minimal sense of political order, state capacities also began to increase in certain, albeit still limited, respects. Indeed, although disputes still range about the appropriate scope of state action, there is now widespread recognition that a viable, reconstructed state is essential not only for democracy but for sustaining a healthy economy as well. As Joan Nelson has cogently argued, the market-oriented agenda of reforms, by itself, lacks a plan for strengthening the state that disintegrated under the weight of past policies and economic processes, and such a plan is crucial for both the market economy and political democracy.[24]

Variations among countries in state coherence and the rule of law are correlated with democracy, though not reducible to it. The link between these issues and the quality of democracy is drawn concisely in the *Human Rights Watch World Report 1993*:

> Periodic elections and transfers of power have not automatically led to an improvement in the quality of democracy experienced on a daily basis by the majority of citizens. Impunity for serious human rights violations committed by state agents is still appallingly pervasive; for the most part, military and police forces are accountable to courts and to civilian authorities on paper only. The courts fail miserably in providing citizens with a fair and impartial forum for the resolution of private disputes, and even more miserably in protecting them from abuse at the hands of the state, or in redressing those abuses.[25]

Not surprisingly, where historical legacies of state coherence are present and where conjunctural socioeconomic or Hobbesian state crises have not taken place, democracy has had greater chance of success. Comparative review suggests that it is a more difficult task for a democratic regime to build a state than it is for such a regime to transform an existing, functioning, even if authoritarian, state in a more democratic direction. The Chilean democratic regime is almost certainly better off with its state (with all of its authoritarian constraints) than is the Colombian regime with its weak state. Countries such as Spain and Portugal had lean but powerful and activist state apparatuses (not only in terms of bureaucracies but also in terms of penetration) before they were democratic, and that helps explain their democratic evolution, including the extension of citizenship.

The two major immediate causes of diminished state coherence in the region have been economic crisis on the one hand, and drug trafficking and guerrilla violence on the other. Where stabilization and adjustment have been both delayed and chaotic, the extent of state destruction has been considerable. It further weakened the ability of states to deliver basic services, collect taxes, and retain personnel with the necessary skills and morale, although the level of the crisis appeared most severe in Peru. As Guillermo O'Donnell and others have suggested, after complex fits and starts, effective stabilization and restructuring emerged as viable only when the crisis appeared to have reached "the very bottom" (his examples were Chile under Pinochet, Bolivia under Paz Estenssoro, and Argentina under Menem).[26] This also helps to explain the initial successes of Fujimori in Peru, as well as the failure of Carlos Andrés Pérez and the initial reluctance of Rafael Caldera to institute market-oriented economic reforms in Venezuela. Pérez sought economic reforms in as autocratic a fashion as his Argentine and Peruvian counterparts, but in a context of less severe crisis in which the population largely blamed the international system and corrupt politicians for the severity of the crisis.[27] Severe economic crisis has also tended to exacerbate issues related to the judiciary, the rule of law, and protection from crime as well as from arbitrary treatment by state officials, leading to the growing "privatization" of security for those who can afford it. This secular decline in the functioning of the state, on top of more dramatic state failures, has clearly impaired democracy.

Many authors have emphasized that initiating market-oriented reforms, especially in a context of severe crisis, usually requires concentrated executive authority, whereas sustaining, deepening, and consolidating them may well require a broader, more accountable, and more institutionalized political process. However, no Latin American country has yet successfully to achieve both consolidated market-oriented reforms and democracy, and the powers granted to executives to address state crises have made movement to more institutionalized practices difficult. The first two kinds of state crises (socioeconomic and related to the rule of law) have been linked in countries like Argentina, Brazil, Peru, and even Venezuela, weakening the state and encouraging a kind of plebiscitarian, neopatrimonial, "delegative democracy" (in contrast to representative-institutional democracy), as O'Donnell has highlighted.[28] As he notes, a perverse cycle was generated in which the fiscal crisis of the state and privatization led to decreased state autonomy, to corruption, fragmentation, and colonization of the state, helping in turn to feed the disaggregation and disorganization of society. Indeed, although privatization should reduce patronage and opportunities for corruption, in the short term, decisions both about who will purchase the state assets and how the revenues generated by them will be spent have actually fed these processes in several countries. Argentina and Peru in the mid-1990s, where incumbent presidents Menem and Fujimori were reelected, highlight how voters may well reward leaders who put a stop to economic decline, restoring order and the functioning of at least parts of the state. Those leaders, in turn, ably manipulated the fear of a return to chaos to achieve reelection, blocking more institutional processes from proceeding, at least in the short term, processes that appeared necessary both for economic reforms to proceed and for democracy to strengthen and consolidate.

In this context, Colombia stands out as quite anomalous in comparison to the other six countries, because a series of substantial market-oriented economic reforms were enacted in the absence of an economic or foreign exchange crisis. This anomaly is in part explained by a previous anomaly: Rather than an "overcommitted state" or a "state-centric matrix," as in most of the other countries considered here (although in the case of Peru only after the Velasco reforms, if then), in Colombia the

state has always been quite weak, and many significant social and economic processes were not processed through it. At the same time,
Colombia's economic policy had been marked by moderation and prudence for many decades, which had permitted it to avoid the heavy in-
debtedness and the severe stabilization programs that afflicted so many
of its neighbors. Colombia has undertaken a surprising amount of restructuring with a weak state. It is easier to restructure if there is "less distance
to go" in terms of moving to market-oriented practices, and if the strength
of societal actors favoring it is high (financial conglomerates are heavily
diversified, and many have strong export-oriented interests). It was also
true that in spite of the fact that the Colombian state underwent a severe
decline, important sectors of the economic policymaking bureaucracy
retained both high technical competence and high morale.[29]

Colombia, however, symbolizes a second kind of challenge to state
coherence and to the rule of law, one generated by guerrilla violence and
by the reaction and counterreaction to state efforts to control drug trafficking, which led to a spiral of incredible violence and to the collapse of
the country's judicial apparatus. Even as one set of reforms has been oriented toward moving the country away from the straitjacket of coalition
rule, another set of efforts has been directed at enabling the state to carry
out some of its most basic, sovereign functions.[30]

Not surprisingly, where there is a confluence of both kinds of state
crises—economic and "Hobbesian"—the risk to the state and to the regime is even greater. Considering Peru in 1980, one would have never
imagined the set of circumstances that would come together so tragically
as to induce the spiral of decline that the country entered into. At the
same time, democratic breakdown in 1992 did not lead to a full-blown
authoritarian regime but to the establishment of a hybrid authoritarian-
democratic neopatrimonial regime dominated by Fujimori. Fujimori has
been able to control inflation, resume growth, and reduce terrorist violence; he sustained his popularity (since eroded) through the use of resources generated by privatization and other state revenues, among other
tactics. The state that is emerging from the earlier chaos is not necessarily democratic or eager to extend the rule of law; rather, it is leaner and
more efficient but also more centralized and militarized.[31]

Thus, in many countries the processes both of economic crisis and of
stabilization and adjustment critically weakened Latin American state
capacities while often concentrating government power in the hands of
the president. Even now, as countries such as Argentina and Peru have
moved beyond the worst moments of crisis and state capacities are re-
emerging in such areas as revenue collection and the ability to maintain
order, key issues remain with regard to state linkages to citizens in ways

that matter not only for their economic well-being but also for citizenship and democracy. In this regard, the Freedom House indicators are tragically eloquent in highlighting the decline in respect for civil rights from 1987 to 1994 in Argentina, Brazil, Colombia, Peru, and Venezuela. The immediate causes for the decline in the indicators reflect some common themes around issues such as the politicization, corruption, or manipulation of the judiciary, media intimidation, or abuse of executive authority. In Brazil, Peru, and especially Colombia, overall levels of violence and the inability to control abuses by state agents are also important.

The collapse of the "overcommitted" state threatens an "underengaged" state because of a combination of lack of vision, resources, and human capacity. The rule of law does not require democracy, though it may well facilitate democracy, just as democratic regimes not only require a functioning rule of law in order to become consolidated but also seek to deepen and extend it. In Latin America in the mid-1990s, degree of stateness and of extension of the rule of law and the extent to which the criteria of political democracy are satisfied were most clearly correlated positively in the cases of Uruguay and Chile and were in a joint if uneven process of decline in Venezuela and Colombia. In Colombia, there has been a remarkable (but declining) divergence between its seemingly stable political and party patterns and the weakness of state institutions and the rule of law in the face of powerful, undemocratic social actors and uncontrolled elements within the state. Argentina and especially Brazil showed more divergence between a greater respect for political rights and a growing absence of the rule of law. The Peruvian case provided an example of a state emerging from chaos that would not necessarily reconstitute itself as democratic or be eager to extend the rule of law (beyond seeking to enhance contract enforcement and property rights).

Political Institutions: Compromise or Polarization? Inclusion, Marginalization, or Alienation?

International and state factors are clearly relevant in explaining the convergences and diversities throughout Latin America and in the experiences of the seven South American countries. As important as these issues are to the stability and the quality of democracy in those countries, political parties and political institutions and their changing roles and impact also have their own independent effect.

There is an inevitable tension between governability—which seeks to maximize consensus and efficient decision making—and democracy—whose exercise involves the expression of multiple interests and conflict. In this context, two kinds of arguments can be highlighted. One is that a key way democratic regimes have moderated this tension—indeed we could say a requirement for consolidated democracy—is to have strong political institutions and parties in a coherent party system. The contrast cited above between Chile and Uruguay on the one hand (whose democratic transitions led to "representative-institutional democracy") and Argentina, Brazil, and Peru on the other (which became instead examples of "delegative democracy") has already anticipated a historical argument about the deep roots and central importance of political institutions and the difficulty of building them in a context of crisis. The recent Latin American experience suggests that countries can sustain party systems in the context of crisis but that it is difficult to forge one, though Venezuela is a partial exception to the first of these generalizations and Argentina appeared to be a partial exception to the second one until the most recent set of elections highlighted growing party fragmentation.

A stable party system may be said to exist where a country's major parties are institutionalized; adopt a coherent but not necessarily unchanging position vis-à-vis the state and society; effectively incorporate all relevant groups in society, including economically dominant groups, employing a mix of ideological, programmatic, and clientelistic appeals; and where the interactions between or among those parties occur with an expected regularity and with electoral strengths within more or less understood parameters. Parties that rely purely on ideological or programmatic appeals may encourage an excessive sectarianism and polarization in society (for example, Chile in the early 1970s). Those that rely almost exclusively on clientelism or specific material or instrumental benefits may ultimately breed excessive corruption and cynicism about the political process, encouraging some social groups increasingly to employ means outside of electoral channels to express their political demands while alienating others (for example, Colombia from the late 1970s). Parties that appear too undifferentiated and too undemocratically centralized in their leadership patterns may also generate significant discontent (such as Venezuela from the mid-1980s).

A second argument is that the dilemma of governability vs. democracy is more difficult to resolve in Latin America in a manner favorable to democracy because of presidentialism. The historical experience of these seven countries also suggests that in presidential systems democracy is much more likely to be successful where such a stable party system revolves around two or two and one-half parties. Chile is a partial exception.[32] Obversely, those countries with shifting party loyalties, inchoate party systems, and greater electoral volatility are less likely to be on the road toward democratic consolidation. It is not surprising to witness in a context of severe crisis and vast changes that the expression of demands and frustrations is channeled through new parties and movements, especially in countries with two parties (particularly Venezuela, and to a lesser extent Uruguay; Colombia again is a partial exception). But, to the extent that more parties emerge, it becomes more difficult to achieve consensus and for the executive and the legislature to agree on policy. When presidentialism and multipartyism are combined, as Scott Mainwaring notes, the "desire of elites and citizens to compromise and create enduring democratic institutions" become the central pillar of support for democratic stability; it would be better if institutional mechanisms could reinforce those desires.[33]

It is in situations in which a society's multiple interests are represented by a large number of parties, particularly where those parties are strongly ideological, that a parliamentary system would appear to be of particular assistance in potentially mitigating explosive political conflict. In presidential systems, cohesiveness and centripetal competition are much more likely to occur in a two-party system. However, those two parties are more likely to be of the "catch-all" nature; they may rely more strongly on clientelist and brokerage claims, and they may tend to collude with each other in excluding other parties and interests while either becoming excessively centralized (as in the case of Venezuela) or factionalized and incoherent (as in the case of Colombia). In this context, seeming stability at the electoral level may well disguise the fact that parties are not adequately representing societal interests, and conflict is likely to express itself through other, often violent, means. Societies with potentially explosive conflicts may well be better off having them expressed in the political arena through a multiplicity of parties than through what may be perceived as an extremely constrained two-party system. In that case, a parliamentary system would be preferable to presidentialism because it has more incentives and mechanisms with which to encourage coalition-building and compromise.

Comparisons of historical experiences with party systems to contemporary circumstances suggest both the ability of consolidated party systems and parties to adapt (though as everywhere around the globe, with difficulty) to new economic challenges, social demands, and campaign technologies and the difficulty of constructing strong party systems where none previously existed. Thus, as we might expect based on past patterns of strong party institutionalization, Uruguay and Chile appear consolidated—democratically in the case of Uruguay, semidemocratically in the case of Chile. In the two countries, "political learning" and moderation by strong, coherent party actors appear to be important factors in explaining these patterns, though both also possess problematic, political-institutional arrangements. Brazil and Peru are the two countries in this group with the weakest parties and party systems, and both have significant contemporary problems with regard to democratic consolidation. However, Peru in 1997 is weaker in terms of its parties and party system than expected from historical projections, whereas Brazil may finally be emerging from a dramatic period of party instability. Argentina remains approximately in the intermediate position it was in historically, though in part because of contradictory trends—on the one hand, the country's "stalemated" party system has ended with the dramatic changes in the Peronist party, but, on the other hand, in the mid-1990s the country moved away from consolidating a stable two-party system.[34]

Venezuela presents the most apparent anomaly. In a context of decentralizing, democratizing reforms and economic crisis, Venezuela underwent a process of partial democratic deconsolidation, punctuated by two failed coup attempts in February and November of 1992 and the forced resignation of President Carlos Andrés Pérez in May 1993. That was followed by apparently "realigning" elections in December 1993 and a fragmentation of its two-party system (which appeared beginning in the 1973 elections). Colombia remains a difficult case to categorize because surprising party continuity (eroded in part by party factionalism leading to new parties in some cases) has been juxtaposed with serious challenges to its state institutions, continuing human rights violations, and the absence of the rule of law. At the same time, in spite of a weak state presence, Colombia cannot be categorized as a delegative democracy, and there have been democratizing reforms and processes (particularly following enactment of the 1991 constitution).

The extent of the link between historical patterns and contemporary outcomes may be partially illustrated by a review of electoral volatility rates (changes in shares of votes by parties from one election to another) in these seven countries. As Michael Coppedge argues, changes in party vote shares may be viewed as desirable if they reflect the "gains and losses of parties engaged in healthy competition for the loyalty of the voters." They may be undesirable if they reflect more the "proscription of parties, boycotting of elections, the splintering of political parties, fragmentation of the party system, and the lack of consolidation of the regime."[35] One simplistic hypothesis would be that as a consequence of the debt crisis and economic restructuring, one would expect substantially greater volatility in the region over this past decade than previously. However, Coppedge's analysis of legislative elections in eleven Latin American countries over the twentieth century highlights how problematic that argument is. This is because Coppedge found that average volatility per decade in the region has changed only slightly from one decade to another from the 1930s to the 1980s. Furthermore, as has been widely believed, he confirms that electoral volatility in Latin America, on average, has been much greater than in Europe and that much of it is due to the "undesirable" features of changes in vote shares more problematic for democratic consolidation. Of the countries of interest here, Uruguay and Colombia had low levels of electoral volatility, similar to those of European countries. Venezuela had volatility rates close to the Latin American average. Argentina, Brazil, Peru, and (to a lesser extent) Chile had extremely high average volatility indices, far above the Latin American average.

More recent trends in electoral volatility in the region point to the mix of continuity and change across the seven countries (see Table 4). Data in the table indicate a continuation of past historical patterns of low volatility in Uruguay, but a decrease in volatility in Chile (overstated in the table because the calculation is based on seat allocation and not votes). Colombia and especially Venezuela show an increase in volatility.[36] Peru shows continuity in the fact that elections continue to be marked by remarkably high levels of volatility (the highest of the seven countries), whereas Brazil showed first a pattern of somewhat higher than expected volatility and then a decline to levels of volatility that were still high. Argentina has the most irregular pattern, showing first a relative decline and then an increase in volatility with the emergence of the Frente Grande as a new opposition voice, as disgruntled voters increasingly turned away from the Radicals.

In turn, each country faces certain risks because of the mix of political-institutional arrangements it possesses. Uruguay may well have consolidated its democracy, as Linz and Stepan argue. Yet, as they also insist, Uruguay remains "risk-prone" to breakdown because of a combination of continuing economic malaise, lack of democratic control over the armed forces, and what González and Gillespie call "the potential for a politico-institutional stalemate [that] keeps pace with the increasing fragmentation of the party system."[37] The country's party system was almost equally divided into thirds in the past election, and it might well have fragmented more if not for the apparent party loyalty of older voters and the relatively old age profile of the population (in Colombia, the most analogous case to Uruguay, extremely high abstention rates especially among the young may serve as a functionally alternative prop to the traditional party system). There is evidence of "political learning" about the value of democracy among political actors across the political spectrum. In the short term or even the medium term, given moderate, prudent leadership, especially in the presidency, there is no necessary reason to forecast a breakdown, especially in the current international conjuncture. Yet, the continuation of presidentialism, fractionalization of the major parties,

Table 4. Recent Trends in Electoral Volatility: Selected Latin American Countries

Country	Elections	Volatility Index
Argentina	1983–85	19.1
	1985–87	23.8
	1987–89	9.7
	1989–91	16.5
	1991–93	10.9
	1993–95	28.5
Brazil	1986–90	38.6
	1990–94	19.9
Chile	1989–93	12.1
Colombia	1982–86	12.0
	1986–90	11.4
	1990–91	21.9
	1991–94	18.0
Peru	1980–85	50.0
	1985–90	51.6
	1990–95	55.3
Uruguay	1984–89	13.4
	1989–94	13.1
Venezuela	1978–83	11.6
	1983–88	6.9
	1988–93	42.3

Sources: Dieter Nohlen, ed., *Enciclopedia Electoral Latinoamericana y del Caribe* (San José, Costa Rica: Instituto Interamericano de Derechos Humanos, 1993); Scott Mainwaring, "Parties, Electoral Volatility, and Democratization: Brazil since 1982" (Paper presented to the nineteenth International Congress of the Latin American Studies Association, Washington, DC, September 1995); Claudio Fuentes, personal communication; Gary Hoskin, "The State and Political Parties in Colombia," ms. dated April 1995; Michael Coppedge, personal communication; Luigi Manzetti, personal communication. The research assistance of Eduardo Feldman in calculating the indices is gratefully acknowledged.

Argentina: 1993 based on incomplete, unofficial results, 1995 based on results for presidential election; Brazil: based on seats, not votes; Chile: based on seats, not votes; Colombia: Conservative and Liberal factions each treated as one party; Venezuela: 1993 based on results for the presidential elections. Results based on presidential elections tend to increase volatility rates somewhat.

Volatility index: $V = 1/2 \sum |P_i,t - P_i,t-1|$, where P_i,t is the percentage of the vote won by party i at time t and $P_i,t-1$ is the percentage of the vote won by party i at the time t−1, the previous election. This difference is calculated for all parties, added together, and divided by half. V ranges from 0 to 100, and may be viewed as the percentage of the national vote that is gained or lost in the aggregate by all parties from one election to the next. See Michael Coppedge, "(De)institutionalization of Latin American Party Systems" (Paper presented to the convention of the Latin American Studies Association, Los Angeles, September 1992).

and the fragmentation of the party system with the continuing emergence of the Frente Amplio is a recipe for legislative impasse and short-lived policy coalitions (electoral reforms that might mitigate these possible negative outcomes were approved in December 1996).

Chile also reflects elements of continuity and change. At one level, there is an apparent continuity of electorates and parties in the Right, Center, and Left. Yet both the structural and constitutional context of the 1990s is completely different from that of the 1960s and 1970s, even as many of the parties of the center and center-left have revalorized political democracy and accepted the economic model, in the context of a constrained transition and a fear of authoritarian reversal. With a strong ideological Right, a military with high prerogatives, continued constitutional constraints on full democracy, and a society that is both organizationally weaker and more fragmented, a new model of party-society relations is emerging.[38] If previously the risk in Chile was one of an excessive ideologization and polarization of politics, it was also the case that, for many, political activism was "ethically guided." Now there is a danger of going to the other extreme: having a politics that seeks to avoid conflict as it is more pragmatic, more consensual, and less confrontational—but at the risk of ignoring larger questions about how to improve society and replacing broader ethical concerns and goals for societal change with pure personal interest and the potential for corruption.[39] Thus, the politico-institutional context remains problematic, but to date the broad consensus on policy goals and the strength of the consociational *Concertación* pact has facilitated governance; the problem of presidentialism and multipartyism has been "solved" by means of an overarching pact between the Center and the Left. Yet, it is unlikely that the alliance can be long term, or that it should be. In that case, the extraordinarily strong presidency inherited from the Pinochet constitution may become problematic from the perspective of deepening democracy in the country. And political institutions may serve more to foster alienation than compromise.

As already noted, in terms of the style of democratic institutionality, Brazil, Peru, and Argentina have provided the greatest contrast to the cases of Uruguay and Chile; in those three countries, political institutions have often been marginalized, short circuited by direct, plebiscitary appeals and executive decrees. The neopatrimonial features of these countries' current regimes were clearly facilitated by the absence of structured parties and party systems interacting with socioeconomic and state crises. Further highlighting the role of short-term political maneuvering over long-term institutionality (and building upon numerous past precedents in the region, but this time with the added element of majority support), in Peru and Argentina popular incumbent presidents arranged constitutional reforms permitting immediate (and thus their own) presidential reelections. Thus, the most recent round of presidential elections in these three countries highlights how voters rewarded economic stability, voting for *continuismo* (indirectly in Brazil and directly in the other two cases), albeit in conditions strongly manipulated by the governing parties.[40] The preceding crisis-ridden terms of Collor in Brazil and Fujimori in Peru both starkly illustrated the problems of presidentialism in weak, fragmented, multiparty systems—including executive-legislative impasse and plebiscitarian and authoritarian actions by the president. In the other five countries, it is almost (but after Italy, only almost) unimaginable to have an extra-party or very weak party figure elected president (such as a Fujimori or a Collor). In Brazil and Peru, having a president elected in a second round rather than in the congress (as in Bolivia) may also have enhanced the president's plebiscitarian role and decreased effective coalition building with the congress. In Brazil in 1989, for example, Collor's party received 5 of 81 seats in the senate and 41 of 502 seats in the chamber, while he received 30 percent of the popular vote in the first-round presidential election and 53 percent in the second round. Cardoso won a convincing 54 percent of the vote in the first round and sought to build a broad-based coalition that would provide him with majority support in congress. To what extent political leadership can effectively shift a country down a more institutional road in the face of contrary incentives is currently being put to the test in Brazil. In Peru in 1990, Fujimori's party received only 17 percent of the vote for chamber seats, and he was elected president only in a second-round election by a deceivingly high vote of 62.5 percent. Five years later, Fujimori won a sweeping electoral victory in the first round (64 percent) and his party and movement also carried legislative elections providing him with solid legislative support for his second term (67 of 120 seats). Just as dramatically, the four dominant parties of the 1980s (American Popular Revolutionary Alliance [APRA], Acción Popular, Popular Cristiano, and Izquierda Unida) combined received only seventeen seats in the new congress.[41] Fujimori's openly antagonistic attitude toward parties and political institutions does not bode well for the strengthening of democratic institutions.

Argentina has witnessed many critical changes. To highlight one, business groups that previously "vetoed" the Peronists now trust them, whereas they largely distrust the military that previously helped them to block the Peronists from coming to power. And, as in Uruguay and Venezuela, a new party has emerged protesting neoliberalism and the corruption of the governing neopopulist leaders. Unlike Brazil under Collor or

Peru under Fujimori prior to 1992, though, the neopatrimonial features of Argentina under Menem were not the result of lack of support for the president in the congress (which is one factor helping to explain the different fates of Collor and Menem).

These neopatrimonial delegative democracies have illustrated a surprising, if fragile, affinity between neopopulism and neoliberalism.[42] Although neoliberal technocrats have had a different core constituency than neopopulists, they also seek bases of support within the urban informal sector and the rural poor from among those who had been largely excluded from the previous economic model. In addition to surprisingly sharing an overlapping social base of support, these types of policymakers and politicians both prefer policy to be enacted by authoritative executives from above—thus, neopatrimonialism and economic reform by centralized, decree-making overlap. To the extent that neoliberal policies lower inflation and enact programs to alleviate poverty, neopopulists may retain a popular base of support. Ultimately, however, the neoliberal goal of rules set either by a free market or neutral procedures (and with a bias toward internationally competitive firms) may clash with neopopulist efforts to retain discretionary power, patronage, and clientelism. Only in the context of more institutionalized party systems would this tension appear more likely to be resolved, which brings us back to our starting point, the weakness of party systems in these countries.

Is the type of delegative democracy more or less represented by these three countries, then, one that can endure (O'Donnell), or are these more "transition phenomena" (Cavarrozi)?[43] The bundle of neopatrimonial attributes this concept captures is found in countries that either had similar regimes in the past or that had little or no prior democratic experience; they are also countries that had weak party systems (though maybe a strong party) in a presidentialist context. For these countries, the confluence of state and socioeconomic crises reinforced these historical attributes. Alfonsín, for example, may have been capable of taking significant steps toward promoting greater institutionalization of politics in Argentina if socioeconomic crisis and hegemonic aspirations had not helped to undo his presidency. Yet, we now see that "second-wave" neopopulists are more accepting of the constraints imposed by the international system. The overlap of social bases and desired strategies of neoliberalism and neopopulism have led to surprising affinities between the two and to personal successes for leaders such as Menem and Fujimori, although it is doubtful they will be able to sustain their popularity over time. Nevertheless, the ability of Menem and Fujimori to sustain their grip on power suggests that this type of politics may survive beyond a simple "transition" period, although in some cases only after "corrections" such as Fujimori's *auto-golpe*. Yet inherent contradictions would appear to preclude democratic consolidation without profound modifications.

Of the seven countries we have been discussing, Venezuela and Colombia are the two that appeared on the surface to have the best fit between presidentialism and a two-party system. Their differing kinds of parties and electoral systems, however, combined with socioeconomic and state problems previously indicated to impact significantly on the quality of their democracies. The Colombian party system has factionalized, incoherent, "irresponsible" parties with weak penetration of civil society; as the crisis unfolding since President Ernesto Samper's inauguration surrounding the role of illegal campaign contributions by drug traffickers illustrates, the problem is more the ability of societal groups—many of them undemocratic—to penetrate the parties. Yet, Colombia has avoided becoming a "delegative democracy." Although one could not argue that Colombia's current problems of governability are directly due to presidentialism, the initial rigidity of its pacted transition in 1958 and of the power-sharing arrangement between the two major parties, which was so difficult to overcome, is associated with it. And, in the context of its democratizing 1991 constitution, if new parties do emerge to challenge the hegemony of the traditional parties, the dilemmas of presidentialism previously identified may more clearly affect the country.[44]

The Venezuelan party system was very hierarchical, with strong penetration of organizations in civil society—a *partidocracia*. There is a clearer connection between the nature of the parties and their National Front agreement and subsequent crisis in Colombia than in Venezuela, where it seems more that a socioeconomic crisis following the end of a poorly planned and employed oil bonanza became a political crisis and then a military one. The election of Caldera in 1993 as a minority president at the head of a new party that broke away from the established Comité de Organización Política Electoral Independiente (COPEI) party has raised for Venezuela issues previously discussed about the dilemmas of governability versus democracy, especially in the context of presidentialism in a multiparty system. The Caldera presidency will also be a clear test of whether having had an institutionalized party system precludes a turn to delegative democracy, or whether a context of sufficient socioeconomic and state crisis and of party fragmentation, regardless of historical legacies, is sufficient.[45]

In the dilemma between governability and democracy, political institutions and parties are intended to serve as channelers of demands and forgers of compromise. Unlike what has occurred in several countries in previous decades, political institutions today do not appear to be instruments of polarization in society. The greater risk in the 1990s is that they will be circumvented by plebiscitarian leaders or avoided by alienated voters, in either case potentially becoming irrelevant, at great cost to democracy. Although historical legacies matter, the role of political institutions and the possibilities for democratic consolidation in the region will be determined by responses to current challenges.

In Lieu of a Conclusion

If Broder's observations that began this paper are relevant for the United States, with due weight given to the significant differences in contexts, he has identified problems that are even more acute for Latin America. Individual countries in the region, while seeking to enhance international structural opportunities in a difficult context and to reconstruct the state, must also continue to find creative ways to strengthen the political institutions critical for generating consensus within democracy if they are to consolidate democracy. As we have seen, the ability of political institutions to do so in most countries is challenged not only by significant conjunctural factors but also by historical and institutional issues related to the "fit" across constitutional structures, party systems, and electoral codes.

From the above discussion of issues related to the international system, the state, and political institutions, one can draw ideal-type pessimistic and optimistic scenarios for the region. Pessimistic scenarios (though not the worst one could imagine) would be that forms of restricted, nonconsolidated democracies perdure—without institutionalization—as the international "legitimacy" of democracy remains unchallenged in the region and in the absence of domestic "threats" to the established order that would provoke military intervention or societal pressure for such an intervention. The international system would place severe constraints on economic policies and options, particularly with regard to redistribution (though not necessarily in terms of poverty alleviation). The state, battered by debt and fiscal crises and withering away under neoliberal reforms, becomes underengaged from a desperately needy society both in terms of ensuring a modicum of the rule of law and of promoting socioeconomic growth with equity. Parties and political institutions, instead of serving as arenas of discussion and of compromise, or even of presenting ideologically and ethically charged and potentially polarizing visions of society and of policies, instead become marginalized from the alienated, distrusting public as neopatrimonial rulers govern.

Optimistic scenarios, in turn, would see the current international circumstances as particularly propitious not only for democracy, but also
for market-oriented reforms and for advances in regional integration
throughout the continent. Emerging from the traumatic process of economic restructuring will be a state that may be smaller in size and more
modest in its goals and its reach, but more efficient and more capable in
what it does do, which includes meting out justice, implementing targeted programs of poverty alleviation, as well as instituting ambitious
programs in education and in health. And, although many issues are no
longer channeled through the state or processed by political means, political parties and institutions reemerge as important forums for debate,
discussion, and compromise, responding to an invigorated civil society.

Countries are unlikely to fit neatly into either ideal type; none is likely
to approximate the rosy scenario, though the diversity of national experiences is likely to lead countries to array across the spectrum, even if the
most likely apparent outcome is that a larger number of them cluster toward the more pessimistic scenario.

Notes

1. David S. Broder, "Can We Govern?" *The Washington Post*, January 31–
February 6, 1994, National Weekly Edition.

2. See Marcelo Cavarozzi, "Beyond Transitions to Democracy in Latin
America," *Journal of Latin American Studies* 24, no. 3 (October 1992): 665–84.

3. There are numerous examples. For an analysis of the rubber tappers in
Brazil, see Margaret Keck, "Social Equity and Environmental Politics in Brazil:
Lessons from the Rubber Tappers of Acre," *Comparative Politics* 27, no. 4 (July
1995): 409–24. For how Ecuadorian indigenous groups, with the assistance of
international NGOs, are pressing a lawsuit against a petroleum transnational enterprise in the United States, see Glenn Switkes, "Ecuador: The People vs.
Texaco," *NACLA—Report on the Americas* 28, no. 2 (September–October 1994):
6–10.

4. These themes are nicely highlighted in Manuel Antonio Garretón M., *La
faz sumergida del iceberg: Estudios sobre la transformación cultural* (Santiago:
CESOC-LOM, 1993), esp. 7–12.

5. Laurence Whitehead, "Generalidad y particularismo de los procesos de
transición democrática en América Latina," *Pensamiento Iberoamericano* 14
(July–December 1988): 309.

6. For an analysis that emphasizes that international influence is not a constant and that the international environment was far more economically permissive in the 1970s, see Barbara Stallings, "International Influence on Economic
Policy: Debt, Stabilization, and Structural Reform," in *The Politics of Economic
Adjustment*, ed. Stephan Haggard and Robert R. Kaufman (Princeton: Princeton
University Press, 1992). Politically, of course, the 1970s in South America were
marked by various kinds of military regimes, with the exceptions of Colombia
and Venezuela.

7. A third, the quality of political leadership, will largely not be dealt with here, but I also concur that it is an important and sometimes overlooked factor.

8. Substantial changes have taken place in the social structures of Latin American countries and in the forms and types of organization of social groups. Similarly, there are important differences in the evolution of civil-military relations across countries. A more complete analysis would incorporate a direct analysis of these issues as well.

9. For a historical review of these countries (and of Costa Rica), see Jonathan Hartlyn and Arturo Valenzuela, "Democracy in Latin America since 1930," in *Cambridge History of Latin America*, Volume VI, Part II, ed. Leslie Bethell (New York: Cambridge University Press, 1994), 99–162.

10. The debt to Robert Dahl's influential work for the first and third points in this characterization of democracy is obvious. See Robert Dahl, *Polyarchy: Participation and Opposition* (New Haven: Yale University Press, 1971). The definition of democracy that emphasizes the importance of competition for political leadership as a critical element stems from Joseph A. Schumpeter's pioneering work, *Capitalism, Socialism, and Democracy* (New York: Harper, 1942). These four paragraphs are taken from Hartlyn and Valenzuela, "Democracy in Latin America," 100–101. Reprinted by permission of Cambridge University Press.

11. For a review and analysis of these elections, see Rodolfo Cerdas-Cruz et al., eds., *Una tarea inconclusa: Elecciones y democracia en América Latina, 1988–1991* (San José: IIDH-CAPEL, 1992).

12. Larry Diamond, "Democracy in Latin America: Degrees, Illusions, and Directions for Consolidation," prepared for the Inter-American Dialogue, November 1993 (draft), for data on 1972 and 1980. For 1992 and subsequent data, see Freedom House Survey Team, *Freedom in the World: The Annual Survey of Political Rights and Civil Liberties 1993–1994* (New York: Freedom House, 1994), 8. Freedom House ranks countries on separate scales for political rights and civil liberties, in which 1 is the highest score and 7 is the lowest. Countries with combined scores on these two scales of 2 to 5 are rated "free," a useful if imperfect proxy for democracy.

13. Ibid. Countries whose combined scores on the political rights and civil liberties scales fall between 6 and 11 are ranked "partly free" by Freedom House.

14. As Pilar Gaitán notes, this unprecedented process of political transformation in the country (unprecedented because of the origin and nature of the political and social actors that played important roles and the democratizing goals and intentions) was neither a democratic foundation, nor a democratic restoration, nor was it based on a *ruptura*. See "Algunas consideraciones acerca del debate sobre la democracia. Los partidos frente a la crisis política: El caso colombiano," unpublished manuscript, Bogotá, February 1994, 5–7.

15. For a critical review, see Coletta Youngers, "After the *Auto-golpe*: Human Rights in Peru and the U.S. Response," Washington Office on Latin America, July 1994.

16. As Linz and Stepan argue, the situation in Southern Europe was different. Although Greece and Portugal had been NATO members as authoritarian regimes, in the 1980s NATO membership for them and for Spain facilitated missions and identities that enhanced military professionalism without involving intervention in domestic political or social processes. See Juan Linz and Alfred Stepan, *Problems of Democratic Transitions and Consolidation: Southern Europe, South America, and Post-Communist Europe* (Baltimore: Johns Hopkins University Press, 1996), 219–20.

17. For an interesting analysis of the historical roots of their embeddedness in constitutional texts in Latin America, see Brian Loveman, *The Constitution of Tyranny: Regimes of Exception in Spanish America* (Pittsburgh: University of Pittsburgh Press, 1993).

18. See his "Democracy, Human Rights, and the Armed Forces," in *The United States and Latin America in the 1990s: Beyond the Cold War*, ed. Jonathan Hartlyn, Lars Schoultz, and Augusto Varas (Chapel Hill: University of North Carolina Press, 1992), esp. 201–3.

19. For a useful, critical discussion of the claims of both defenders and critics of neoliberalism, see Stephen Haggard and Robert Kaufman, *The Political Economy of Democratic Transitions* (Princeton: Princeton University Press, 1995), 309–34, although it may underplay somewhat the role of international constraints on domestic policy choices. It is not simply that there might be international "punishment" and domestic capital flight for wrong domestic policy choices, but sometimes, as following both the debt crisis in 1982 and the peso debacle in December 1994, the "tequila effect" of investment withdrawals may occur simply for being in the wrong "region" of the world.

20. See Haggard and Kaufman, *Political Economy*, 311–12. In addition, for Portugal and Spain, entry into the European Common Market meant significant transfers of income rather than the outflows that marked much of Latin America from the onset of the debt crisis until the end of the 1980s; these European countries also never had to deal with the dramatic surges of inflow and then outflow of capital that followed for countries like Mexico and Argentina in the early 1990s.

21. CEPAL, *Panorama Social de América Latina* (Santiago: CEPAL, 1994), 13.

22. Kenneth Roberts, "Rethinking Economic Alternatives: Left Parties and the Articulation of Popular Demands in Chile and Peru" (Paper presented to the eighteenth International Congress of the Latin American Studies Association, Atlanta, March 1994), 14–15.

23. Carlos H. Acuña and William C. Smith, "The Political Economy of Structural Adjustment," in *Latin American Political Economy in the Age of Neoliberal Reform*, ed. William C. Smith et al. (New Brunswick: Transaction Publishers, 1994), 19. I also agree with them when they argue subsequently that "divorcing politics from economics is also bad methodology" (p. 23), though in the end I might focus somewhat more on the political dynamics and institutions that they mention.

24. Joan Nelson, "How Market Reforms and Democratic Consolidation Affect Each Other," in *Intricate Links: Democratization and Market Reforms in Latin America and Eastern Europe*, ed. Joan Nelson (New Brunswick: Transaction Publishers, 1994), 19–20. She also notes the need to develop agreement on the extent to which and the ways in which inequality generated by market processes will be mitigated. International financial institutions have begun to pay increased attention to issues of state rehabilitation.

25. Human Rights Watch, *Human Rights Watch World Report* (New York: Human Rights Watch, 1992), 69, cited in Larry Diamond, "Democracy in Latin America," unpublished manuscript, Stanford University, 24.

26. Guillermo O'Donnell, "The State, Democratization, and Some Conceptual Problems (A Latin American View with Glances at Some Post-Communist Countries)," in Smith, ed., *Latin American Political Economy in the Age of Neoliberal Reform*, 175.

27. For an excellent, more comprehensive analysis, see Louis W. Goodman et al., eds., *Lessons of the Venezuelan Experience* (Washington, DC: Woodrow Wilson Center Press and Johns Hopkins University Press, 1995).

28. For O'Donnell: "Delegative democracies rest on the premise that whoever wins election to the presidency is thereby entitled to govern as he or she sees fit, constrained only by the hard facts of existing power relations and by a constitutionally limited term of office. The president is taken to be the embodiment of the nation and the main custodian and definer of its interests." In "Delegative Democracy," *Journal of Democracy* 5, no. 1 (January 1994): 59–60.

29. For a more favorable review of Gaviria's economic liberalization measures, see Miguel Urrutia, "Colombia," in *The Political Economy of Policy Reform*, ed. John Williamson (Washington, DC: Institute for International Economics, 1994); for a more critical one, see José Antonio Ocampo, "Economía y Economía Política de la Reforma Comercial Colombiana," *Serie Reformas di Politica Publica No. 1* (Santiago: CEPAL, 1993).

30. For an extensive, excellent review of the nature of the "state crises" in Colombia and the efforts to respond to them, see Ana María Bejarano, "Recuperar el estado para fortalecer la democracia: Alcances y límites de la reforma del estado en un contexto de crisis: El caso colombiano" (Paper presented to the convention of the Latin American Studies Association, March 1994).

31. See Bruce Kay, " 'Fujipopulism' and the Liberal State in Peru, 1990–1995," *Duke University of North Carolina Working Paper Series*, no. 19, December 1995.

32. In a two-party system, each of the parties would be expected to be able to win a presidential election, even if one of the parties usually gains presidential office. In a two and one-half party system, there would be a third party that receives some consistent percentage of the vote and maintains a minority presence in the legislature but that is not considered a significant contender for the presidency.

33. Scott Mainwaring, "Presidentialism, Multipartyism, and Democracy: The Difficult Combination," *Comparative Political Studies* 26, no. 2 (July 1993): 223. See also Juan Linz and Arturo Valenzuela, eds., *The Failure of Presidential Democracy* (Baltimore: Johns Hopkins University Press, 1994).

34. For a useful analysis of the stalemated party system and the "impossible game" of party politics it generated in Argentina, see Ruth Berins Collier and David Collier, *Shaping the Political Arena* (Princeton: Princeton University Press, 1991).

35. Michael Coppedge, "(De)institutionalization of Latin American Party Systems" (Paper presented to the convention of the Latin American Studies Association, Los Angeles, September 1992), first quote from p. 1, second from p. 17.

36. They also show an increase in abstention rates. Colombia has always had high abstention rates (over 60 percent five times in elections for the chamber of deputies since 1958), but the estimated abstention of 67 percent in the 1994 legislative elections was the highest since 1958, followed by the 65 percent rate of the 1991 election. In Venezuela in 1993, the abstention rate was nearly 40 percent, a dramatic increase from past presidential year elections.

37. Luis Eduardo González and Charles Guy Gillespie, "Presidentialism and Democratic Stability in Uruguay," in Linz and Valenzuela, eds., *The Failure of Presidential Democracy*, 247.

38. Mary Alice McCarthy, personal communication with author, Santiago, Chile, August 1995.

39. Garretón, *La faz sumergida del iceberg*, 7–12.

40. For a sympathetic view of Cardoso that still makes clear the active nature of government support for his campaign, see Carlos Eduardo Lins da Silva,

"Plato in the Tropics: The Brazilian Republic of Guardians," *Current History* 94 (February 1995): 81–85; on Fujimori's abuse of incumbency and how other features of the new constitution gave him even further advantages, see David Scott Palmer, "Peru's 1995 Elections: A Second Look," and other articles in the same issue of *LASA Forum* 26 (Summer 1995): 17–20.

41. Fujimori's percentage appears more decisive than in fact it was because based on the new constitution it consisted of the valid vote only, excluding the 17 percent blank and spoiled ballots (as well as the 28 percent who abstained from voting); under 1995 election rules, Alan García would have won with 69 percent of the vote in 1985, not the 46 percent he received. See Palmer, *Peru's Elections*, 19.

42. This paragraph is based on Kurt Weyland, "Neo-Populism and Neo-Liberalism in Latin America: Unexpected Affinities" (Paper presented to the convention of the American Political Science Association, New York, September 1994).

43. See O'Donnell, "The State," 157–80; and Marcelo Cavarozzi, "Politics: A Key for the Long Term in South America," 127–55, in Smith, ed., *Latin American Political Economy*.

44. For a more extensive discussion of presidentialism in Colombia, see Jonathan Hartlyn, "Presidentialism and Colombian Politics," in Linz and Valenzuela, *The Failure of Presidential Democracy*, 294–327.

45. At least one Venezuelan specialist has argued that Caldera's strengthening of the executive's power and weakening of the rule of law in the country mean that Venezuela has already become a "delegative democracy," even as he sees the emergence of a hybrid democratic-authoritarian regime in the country that could be long lasting. Although Caldera has found support from the anti-Pérez faction of Acción Democrática (AD) in congress—"the product of fear, of the realization that the democratic system is in real danger"—he has also simply overridden it by executive decree when necessary. See Aníbal Romero, " 'Rearranging the Deck Chairs on the Titanic': The Agony of Democracy in Venezuela" (Paper presented to the nineteenth International Congress of the Latin American Studies Association, Washington, DC, September 1995), 22.

6

Evolution and Prospects of the Argentine Party System

Torcuato S. Di Tella

Problems with Argentina began when the country had to confront the challenge of higher-level industrialization, especially since the 1940s. But even during the era of agrarian prosperity there were already some traits that differentiated Argentina from other settler nations. One of them, quite well known, was the extreme concentration of land ownership, which throttled the development of a strong rural middle class. Admittedly, that rural (and small-town) middle class was and still is quite large by Latin American standards, but it falls far short of the influence its counterparts wield in Australia or Canada.

The other sign of danger that might have been observed during Argentina's heyday was the very large proportion of foreigners among the bourgeoisie and the skilled workers, who formed over two-thirds of the total (between 1880 and 1930). As they did not take up citizenship, the two most strategic social classes for capitalist growth and institutional consolidation were, in practice, almost disenfranchised. Even more serious, the feeling of ethnic superiority they held toward the majority of the country's inhabitants bred attitudes that were transmitted for a couple of generations, making it difficult to develop a national consciousness. On the other hand, some sectors of the traditional elites felt threatened by the inflow of people who quickly acquired high positions in the economy, jumping over most of the native middle classes, in contraposition to what happened with immigrants to Western Europe or the United States. Local elites reacted with a resentful variety of nationalism that idealized the Hispanic past and its modern reincarnations in Falangismo and Fascism.

A particularly dramatic chasm existed between that nationalism, espoused by sectors of the upper classes, especially in the provinces, and the mass of the foreign-born middle class and their early descendants. Argentina, then, became what Domingo Faustino Sarmiento had predicted in his later years: a rich commercial Carthage, with successful entrepreneurs from all over the world but not enough responsible citizens, a deficiency especially significant among the better-off urban sectors.[1] To use a more modern phraseology, it was a country in which political development ran far behind economic growth, in contrast with that South American Athens, Chile. While in Argentina foreigners constituted 30 percent of the total population (and 60 to 70 percent of the bourgeoisie and urban working class), very few of whom took up citizenship; on the other side of the Andes, their total scarcely reached 4 percent. The upper layers of the stratification pyramid being more predominantly national in Chile, their participation in politics was more organic. The result was an early alternation between Conservatives and Liberals, to which the Radicals and the Socialists were later added. The "European" pattern of Chilean politics is due, then, to that country's economic and social similarity to southern Europe and to the absence of a large foreign population.

In Argentina, by contrast, during the formative decades around the turn of the century, the bulk of the bourgeoisie and the urban working class did not have the vote, and therefore they had much less political strength than would have been the case in a similar country with no equivalent nationality problems (such as Australia or New Zealand). The result of this electoral and political weakness is that the political parties that might have expressed the views of those two classes were very rickety or nonexistent, while corporatist patterns of pressuring the authorities were an essential alternative.[2]

Thus there was no real bourgeois liberal party, and attempts to organize one by Bartolomé Mitre and his followers were short-lived. The early Radical party might have performed that role, especially in its Bernardista wing, or later in its Antipersonalista variant, but both those factions were always very weak. Often it is taken for granted that such a group of *galeritas* would have few votes, but examples from Great Britain to Chile, including Brazil and Colombia, show that similarly distinguished gentlemen could be more successful at party-building, given adequate circumstances.

It may be argued that the real equivalent of a bourgeois liberalism was the Partido Autonomista Nacional (PAN), President Julio A. Roca's political machine. This is only partly so, and it was precisely the weakness of circulation of elites between the urban bourgeoisie and the political scene that gave too much relative weight to the landowners, however modernizing, within that party.

If we now look at industrialization in a comparative way, we may see that in Brazil the large number of potential internal migrants facilitated a type of development with "unlimited supply of labor," as Arthur Lewis has called it. In Argentina such conditions did not exist, the effect being an early growth of trade unionism, which already by the beginning of the century could match the militancy and strength found in unions in some southern European countries. Politically it found expression in anarchism, and later in socialism and communism. Significantly, the Socialist party has been capable of winning elections for the senate in the capital city since 1913, and it could get a very good proportion of the electorate there for decades, till the advent of Peronism.

Internal migrants in Argentina, apart from being less numerous, proportionally, than in Brazil, did come, to a large extent, from quite prosperous rural areas in the pampas. This, combined with the existence of a strong labor movement, is responsible for the difference between Argentina's and Brazil's varieties of populism. Varguismo never had such an important trade union component as Peronism. The rise in Brazil, in recent years, of a socialist type of party created by trade union leaders is a different phenomenon, one based on the new industrial reality of São Paulo. If it is capable of extending to the rest of the country, however, that would be due to its alliance with an important faction of the Church. The formation and expansion of the Partido dos Trabalhadores (PT), which has no equivalent in Argentina, is an indication of the more advanced level of industrialization now existing in Brazil. In a sense, Argentine Peronism—at least in its traditional guise, before the changes brought about by President Menem—was a mixture between the PT and Leonel Brizola's Partido Democrático Trabalhista (PDT), capable of getting between 40 and 50 percent of the vote in a country with a much greater urban base and a stronger trade unionism. Within that weaker Brazilian trade unionism, though, there is a very important sector controlled by the PT and other leftist groups, which is more autonomous and responsive to rank-and-file participation than its Argentine counterpart.

The enormous proportions of internal migration in Brazil, associated with the increase in size of its main cities and industrial centers, create a lack of social memory among its population. This is the opposite of what happens in the other three Southern Cone countries, where the present urban population is much more likely to have been bred in the same urban environment as its parents. Political traditions, memories, and prestige are more lasting, and that is markedly so in Chile and Uruguay. Thus the persistence of the party spectrum in these countries should come as no surprise.

The Weakness of the Right in Argentina

At the time of the 1930 Uriburu coup, the conservative forces did not appear to have the capacity to counteract President Hipolito Yrigoyen's "excesses" by appeal to the vote. This electoral weakness of the Right in Argentina is part of the problem and not part of the solution, as progressive optimists have long believed. That weakness, which is becoming increasingly the focus of new research, has been often considered the logical result of the elite's unwillingness to accept the moderate sacrifices necessary to coopt at least the middle classes. This interpretation tends to paint the Argentine upper classes in excessively dark colors, or by contrast to whitewash their peers in Chile, Colombia, or Brazil—not to mention most of Western Europe, Japan, and the United States, where conservative parties capable of getting a large percentage of the vote have existed or continue to thrive.[3]

Admittedly, the prospects for a strong conservative party are rosier in the Northern Hemisphere because of the operation of the international economic system, which helps incorporate not only the middle classes (transforming them into the bulk of conservative vote) but also the lower ones, which are channeled into moderate social-democratic-type parties or increase the numbers of working-class tories. In the Third World or in Latin America, straitened economic circumstances make a consensual politics more difficult, but not impossible. The example of Chile is quite pivotal, as there an electorally strong right has existed for decades and continues in good health after the demise of General Augusto Pinochet. The same is true in Colombia, which has social conditions quite opposite those dominant in Chile. In Brazil, though the system of political parties is much more unstable than in Colombia and Chile, the União Democrática Nacional (UDN) maintained an important presence at the polls during the period between 1945 and 1964, and so has its successor during the military regime, the Aliança Renovadora Nacional (ARENA), and its offspring the Partido Progressista Brasileiro (PPB) and the Partido da Frente Liberal (PFL), up to this day.[4]

Similar situations have developed in Peru and Bolivia, and in Venezuela the Christian Democratic party (COPEI) functioned for decades as an updated right-of-center party, similar to its European counterparts. In Argentina, for at least fifty or sixty years, nothing like that has existed, despite the quip that, short of one, there are three conservative parties: the Peronists, the Radicales, and the "liberal" Unión de Centro Democrático (UCD). In fact, Peronism, though incorporating undoubtedly conservative elements, is basically a populist, not a conservative, party, with very few moorings among the upper classes. Its recent conversion to the free market must be interpreted in the light of similar reorientations among social democratic parties throughout the world.[5] The Unión Cívica Radical (UCR) remains in a middle-of-the-road position, even if under Raúl Alfonsín it was capable of getting the votes, if not the heart, of the upper classes. The Right, despite its programmatic hobbyhorses having acquired greater legitimacy among both specialist and popular opinion, continues to be divided into several small groups with scant electoral appeal. Its present support for the Menem government is mostly a tactical alliance, focused on the circles in power rather than on the party as such.

What we have had for decades in Argentina, as a result of its intermediate level of industrial and cultural development, is a peculiarly complex equilibrium or social stalemate, an *empate social*. This remains basically true, with the inevitable ups and downs, even if the popular sector has been weakened, both by international economic trends and by local policies.

Social Stalemate as a Step toward a System of Checks and Balances

A social stalemate, or *empate social*, is not necessarily a bad thing, but it is a costly one. In fact, it is the condition existing in consolidated democracies, but it arises in them only after the early stages of capital accumulation have been completed. In its full sense—that is, when an *empate social* incorporates as one of its participants the organized working class— it certainly did not exist for Great Britain or the United States during their early stages as industrial nations. This does not mean that there was no equilibrium of powers in those countries, but it did not include a strong, politically organized working class as a component. Thus its effects over capital accumulation were very different. Admittedly, in Australia a situation nearer to that in Argentina arose quite early in this century, with a strong trade union movement and a labor party that came to power nationally before World War I. But Australia has the peculiarity of having evolved as an offshoot of Great Britain overseas, benefiting from its advanced institutions and transferring from the mother country a population that came almost entirely from it. The human stream reaching Australia was somewhat akin to an internal migration, and thus quite different from what happened in the Río de la Plata. Argentina had to build its own institutions, its own nationality, and that posed a far more complex challenge, especially because its political and cultural inheritance was from nations where industry, science, and modern government had been lagging far behind Europe.

Another model of development often extolled for Argentina is that of the Southeast Asian nations. None of these countries has any degree of *empate social*. On the contrary, they toil under a strong authoritarianism that pervades their whole social life, despite the fact that they have a remarkable degree of egalitarianism. But this egalitarianism has been imposed from above, in order to make society more efficient. It has not been the result of internal pressure, but rather a response to a Communist threat from outside. Besides, their economy has been centrally controlled, with protectionism and subsidies applied when necessary in a discriminating way by a powerful state. Nor did Japan have an *empate social* during its formative years as an industrial power, before World War II. Even afterward, quite apart from American predominance, there was not much internal sharing of power, despite democratization. Neither the trade unions nor the Socialist party have been capable of mounting a serious challenge to the ruling elite till very recently. The dominant groups, once purged of some elements associated to the past and after undergoing a process of land reform inspired by the foreign occupation, developed a high sense of solidarity and established their hegemony on the basis of a combination of modern attitudes and a strong deferential pattern inherited from feudal times. None of that is applicable to Argentina.

The remarkable economic growth experienced by Mexico and Brazil until a few years ago was also based on a very different social reality from the one prevalent in Argentina, as it has taken place under stable semiauthoritarian or authoritarian regimes unchecked by a powerful popular organization. In Mexico, true enough, there was a revolution, but that was long ago. Over its million dead a new power structure was built, capable of controlling the peasantry and the working class, channeling them into the tasks of capital accumulation in a way that certainly might be envied by Argentine capitalists.

Argentina's relative stagnation during the last several decades is a consequence of its uneasy *empate social*. The country is too modernized to follow the Southeast Asian path, too independent to become another Australian-type British offshoot, too full of veto groups to emulate the Brazilian or Mexican pattern, and it has arrived too late to copy the American or British models. No wonder perplexed social scientists put it in a category by itself when they classify the world's countries as developed or underdeveloped.

During the last fifty years, many alternative economic and political projects have been attempted, some under very repressive regimes, but to no avail. Argentina, in contrast to Brazil, Mexico, or Chile, was unable up to 1983 to establish a presentable authoritarian or semiauthoritarian military or civilian regime. It is significant that among all the supposedly developmentalist military dictatorships since the sixties, Argentina's have been the least successful. That was probably due to the fact that there was always some group among the elites prepared to mobilize the threatening, even if not really revolutionary, popular movement in order to overcome its enemies. However, once the new coalition was in power, its Peronist component proved to be intractable and menacing, thus forcing a breakup of the alliance.[6]

The social stalemate, though also existing in varying degrees in other parts of the continent, occurred in Argentina at an excessively early stage of development, because of the country's peculiar social conditions. But then are the trade unions the main culprits in blocking a strong economic upsurge? That would be a half truth—in other words, a falsehood. One might just as well claim that Argentina's stagnation is due to its high level of education, its excessively low infant mortality, or its omnivorous reading habits. More to the point one could argue, still getting at only a partial explanation, that the brakes on development are due to the lack of land reform (so important in Japan and Southeast Asia), to the speculative tendencies of entrepreneurs, to the bourgeoisie's habits of capital flight, or to the armed forces' authoritarianism.

In Argentina the "liberal" Right has been arguing, with increasing response from the public, that what is necessary is to weaken or dissolve all corporatist pressure groups as much as possible so as to allow the free work of market forces. This approach ignores the fact that no process of economic growth or consolidation, especially in its early stages, has ever taken place simply as the result of market mechanisms: It has always been prodded by a strong state, even if a lean one.

The fact is that Argentina is condemned to pluralism, and an all-encompassing form of pluralism at that, with the politically organized lower strata included. This might have been a blessing rather than a curse, but it came too early, when the country was still culturally (and otherwise) too near its roots, in the "amoral familism" so poignantly described by the Banfields in their study of a southern Italian town.[7] However, the light could be appearing at the end of the tunnel if the traditional "amoral stalemate" were to be replaced by a legitimated variety that thereby ceased to be a stalemate and became a democratic system of checks and balances with adjudicating mechanisms that make governance possible.

The Democracy of the Undemocratic—Corporatism as a Precondition of Democracy

Ancient lore has it that the only way out of a labyrinth is upward. Maybe that is applicable to the Argentine setting. Let us first explore the walls

and the cul-de-sacs against which we are likely to bump, in trying to get
out of the trap:

1. Many if not most Argentines are authoritarian and at the same
   time quite organized. Therefore pressure groups are likely to be
   powerful, authoritarian in their internal structure, and intolerant
   toward others, despite their declarations to the contrary. And this
   is not going to change in the short run.[8]
2. Organized interests include the working class. But given the form
   that industrialization took during World War II and early
   Peronism, industrial and trade union groups have been based on
   state support and shun economic competition or freer associ-
   ationist forms, relying excessively on bureaucratization and
   caudillismo, the political system shaped in the nineteenth century based on networks of patronage and personal allegiances to
   powerful leaders.
3. The attempt by President Juan Domingo Perón to consolidate
   capitalist development with strong state prodding was unsuccessful because of the class polarization of Argentine society, which
   transformed his projected multiclass integrative party into a populist one excessively oriented toward redistribution and clientelism.
4. As a result of the above factors, the state lost its power to arbi-
   trate among warring factions and became increasingly an impo-
   tent bystander. Pressure groups have been long capable of
   resisting and vetoing each other's hegemonic attempts, but unable to establish their own.

One suggested way out is to force the democratization of the corporatist interests. This was attempted without success by President Raúl
Alfonsín during his first years in office. The aim was commendable, but
it was very difficult to implement. It got confused with a general on-
slaught against the organized labor organizations, and as such lost legitimacy among a certain sector of the rank and file who might have otherwise
favored the attempt. Besides, it should be taken into account that in no
country in the world are trade unions excessively democratic in their internal structure, as has been stated repeatedly by social scientists from
Robert Michels to Seymour Martin Lipset.[9]

The inroads that are necessary on the privileges and the status quo of
all vested interests, including those of the poor, trade unionists, and state
employees—and, of course, those of the rich (such as protected and sub-
sidized entrepreneurs, tax evaders, and financial speculators)—are such
that authoritarian solutions are tempting. But history has proved that these
solutions have become inefficient and unworkable. On the other hand, it

is not possible to replicate the Japanese, Taiwanese, or Korean types of development, in which the state-fed privileges of some groups, however arbitrary and irrational, became in time the basis for a portentous surge of capital accumulation and technological progress, turning rentiers or state profiteers into zaibatsu. Much less is the present Chinese pattern applicable to Argentina.

So the necessary gradual disengagement of entrenched privileges must be undertaken with care, avoiding the intention of destroying or seriously maiming any of the corporative groups. Modern pluralist democracy has been shown to consist, to a large extent, of an unwritten pact of coexistence between neocorporative interests.

Argentina is on the verge of consensual pluralism, but it is not yet there. Since the downfall of the military regime in 1983, great strides have been made in that direction in a complementary way during the Raúl Alfonsín and the Carlos Menem presidencies. Alfonsín, leading a centrist party with conservative electoral support, helped the transition by bringing to power a coalition of a basically moderate nature, calculated not to threaten the interests of the establishment regardless of the presence near the president of a few reformist elements with a leftist past. On the other hand, Peronism, despite its transformations, continued to be seen as menacing by a wide sector of the public. That was so much the case that the hyperinflation that struck the country during the last months of the Radical administration was due, to a large extent, to the fear of confiscatory Peronism's winning the 1989 presidential elections—almost a certainty from the beginning of that year, according to opinion polls.

At that moment, president-elect Carlos Menem, with a small group of advisers, decided to take a step quite unprecedented in the traditions of Peronism. He made an explicit pact with the Right, personified (in the absence of a large conservative party) by the largest industrial and exporting corporation in the country. This pact was unnecessary in terms of votes but essential in order to break the image of confrontation and fear that existed not only in the minds of the more nervous members of the bourgeoisie but also of the intelligentsia, who anticipated a repetition of the maltreatment they had been subjected to during the early Perón presidencies. Of course, the Peronist militants were despondent and felt betrayed. Admittedly, the whole operation was undertaken without much consultation or previous ideological preparation, but its mentors have had no shortage of comparable international experiences from which to draw.

The violent popular reaction that accompanied the first bout of hyperinflation at the end of Alfonsín's government did not repeat itself as feared, and after a couple of years Domingo Cavallo took the reins of the economy and succeeded in taming inflation and—perhaps—initiating a period of moderate growth. There was throughout this process a serious though mostly latent opposition in the Peronist party, and a much more open one among the trade unions, whose central organization, the Confederación General del Trabajo (CGT), was divided between supporters and opponents of the economic program. The relationship between organized labor and President Menem in his second term has been increasingly strained. In September 1995, the CGT staged a general strike to protest government attempts to make the labor market more flexible.

The Radical party has taken a sharp oppositional stance, though solidly in favor of the preservation of the democratic system. Surprisingly, in several by-elections the main loser was the Radical party, because the coalition engineered by Alfonsín started disintegrating: Conservative voters, no longer fearing Peronism, feel free to vote for whomever they prefer, whether safe Menemista candidates, the "liberal" UCD, the authoritarian Gral Antonio Bussi in Tucumán, or other regional forces. The leftist sector of the Alfonsinista electorate, disenchanted by the crisis of the last presidency and much more so by the Pacto de Olivos, basically has also abandoned the party, and tends toward independent left-wing voting, feeding the looming new coalition of the Frente País Solidario (FREPASO). On the other hand, within Peronism the coexistence of rightist elements, some of them openly courting the *carapintadas*, with more leftist ones and with a majority made up of pragmatic reformists will become ever more difficult.

Tensions within the Argentine Party System

The consolidation of consensual politics in Argentina is coming about as a result of an agreement between corporative interests. That is how it should be, given the realities of politics and of what pluralism is about. Raúl Alfonsín and his Radical party—the most convincedly democratic group in the country—tried to do it on the basis of appeals to a responsible citizenry, attempting to curtail and democratize the pressure groups. It would have been nice if it had worked, but unfortunately the program was inadequately connected with the forces that make a country move. Radicalismo's heyday has now passed, as has that of similar centrist forces such as the British Liberals and the French or Chilean Radicals. In Chile, the Radicals, and then the Christian Democrats, performed a pivotal centrist role for many decades, with occasional alliances with either the Right or the Left. The more recent developments in Chile, given the consolidation of the Right, also seem to forecast a new role for the Christian Democrats as the more moderate component of a popular alliance, shorn of its more extreme elements (such as the Communist party) but including the Socialists.[10]

In Argentina, radicalism, which occupies a position similar to Christian democracy in Chile, needs to undergo a great transformation before such a convergence can take place. That would involve an alliance with the bulk of the trade unions, or with a "progressive" sector of Peronism, against the Right. For that type of coalition to take place, it is first necessary to have the strength of both major parties severely reduced. That can happen, and, what is more, it is necessary in order to consolidate Argentine democracy. One of the prerequisites of a stable democracy is the presence of a strong conservative party, by that name or any other, with any ideology but incorporating the bulk of the upper classes and capable of winning elections. For that to happen, votes can be garnered only from Radical or Peronist supporters.

By the above criteria there is no strong conservative party in Argentina, though there are several small nuclei attempting to perform that function. It is often stated, however, that Menemismo, if not Peronism, is now such a party. It certainly looks like one, especially if its top circles are taken as evidence. But on second consideration, and once its total social composition and spread of attitudes is considered, Peronism cannot really pose as a serious and trustworthy conservative party. Nor is it possible to base one's argument on the difference between Menemismo and Peronism, unless a split were to occur among their ranks. Because as things stand at present (mid-1997) the Peronist, Menemista, or Justicialista party (as you may choose to call it) is too full of trade unionists and the wrong type of pressure groups to be a really solid party of the establishment. The establishment, and especially its more calculating elements, are certainly supporting President Menem, but one can wonder how long that predicament can last, especially once Menem's term of office comes to an end.

If a conservative party or solid alliance were to appear as a new political actor, it would surely conjure up on the other ideological hemisphere a social democratic type of coalition, as is the case in Chile and in most moderately to highly industrialized nations. The Conservative party I am imagining—eventually under Menemista leadership—would mop up its many kindred souls, which are today dispersed among practically all political tents.

This polarization would make it easier for a large chunk of dissident Peronists to become the nucleus of an oppositional coalition, converging with the FREPASO. For the moment, the FREPASO cannot be considered to be such a coalition, especially because of its excessive fascination with the traditional models of the Left. But things are likely to move in that direction, and the new coalition, if it takes real momentum, will surely include some Radicals. As a matter of fact, events are already pointing in that direction in the Radical party, as a part of its leadership is attempting to recover its tarnished social democratic image. That attempt, if taken too far, is likely to further antagonize the main electoral base of the party, which is very moderate, as shown by its preference for Fernando de la Rúa in the mayoral election in Buenos Aires. But such a split would create a highly qualified though small political machine, like the British Liberals, eventually prepared to enter into alliances with other groups on the Left or with dissident Peronism.

Regarding the future of Peronism, its heterogeneous nature, which is a very well known fact, must be taken into account. We must distinguish, however, between the Justicialista party and the present ruling coalition, which is the result of an alliance with independent conservative entrepreneurial sectors. The analysis of such a coalition must be differentiated from a description of the party as such. If this type of distinction were not made, one might end up believing that the Spanish Socialist party has a Catalanist ideology because of its long alliance with Convergencia i Unió, or that there are no differences between the Catholic Popular party and the Social Democrats in Austria, because of the Grand Coalition they have formed for decades.

With these caveats, considering the Justicialista party, its conservative sector has three quite clear structural sources and a less clear fourth one. The first and more traditionally conservative element is the caudillo-type leadership from the interior or underdeveloped provinces (of which Menem is an example, though not a perfect one, because he had a period of leftist involvement during the seventies). The second rightist sector within Peronism is made up of the minority of industrialists and other business people who are at odds with the majority of their class and who have joined the movement for a variety of reasons.[11] The third element is formed by the ideologically authoritarian intellectuals and political leaders who still are present in the movement; though they are in the process of being "converted" to democracy, these ghosts still make their appearance, and more often than they should in a popular movement prepared to perform a role in the consolidation and advancement of democracy.

Finally, the trade union bureaucrats are often considered as a strongly rightist component of Peronism. Though it would be impossible to deny the ample evidence of that, the statement should be more closely considered. Conservatism should not be mixed up with mere authoritarianism, rampant also among the Left, or with anticommunism, a trait shared by many Social Democratic unionists all over the world. Many Argentine labor leaders have a mixture of what might be called "Third World authoritarianism" plus a basic pragmatism that can easily turn into bread-and-butter unionism. They would of course be on the moderate or rightist sector of a labor or popular movement, but they (at least most of them) are not likely to end up as members of a party of the Right, if such a party were clearly established as such, under any name.

On the ideologically leftist fringe of Peronism, and among some trade unionists in and out of the CGT, rumblings of discord are quite apparent. But only if the bulk of the more pragmatic trade unions decide to take an independent path—probably under "authentic" national-popular colors—will a serious transformation of the political scene take place. This is possible in the medium run, as even a successful economic recovery will not, for some time, spill its effects over among the lower strata of the population. If the pragmatic trade union leaders do not take an opposi-tional stance, they might see their followers abandon the fold. Admit-tedly, a well-organized party may withstand these internal conflicts, as has, by and large, Spanish socialism. But Peronism is a much less disci-plined movement, especially given the nonexistence of a really charis-matic father figure like Perón. Besides, its Right, based on the above-alluded provincial caudillos and other ideological elements, is much stronger than in any Social Democratic party and thus more intractable as a partner.

Among trade unionists, those who more radically oppose the present economic policies (most of them of a leftist orientation, with some Peronists) have formed a new independent federation, the Congreso de los Trabajadores Argentinos (CTA), which includes teachers and one of the two state employee unions, both sectors very vulnerable to budget cuts in government. A more moderate rejection of the Cavallo plan is expressed in an internal current within the CGT, eventually capable of splitting away but for the moment uneasily remaining within the fold—the Movimiento de los Trabajadores Argentinos (MTA), still basically Peronist.

The trade union leadership is torn between its attraction to power and its realization of the negative impact of economic policies on their rank and file. Given the fact that, despite everything, a rule of law is being established in Argentina, strong-hand methods in trade unions will be-come increasingly isolated and open to challenge, as has happened in other Latin American countries. The Peronist leadership itself, particu-larly its middle rungs, which are much less corrupted than usually be-lieved, will thus feel increasingly predisposed to express the sentiments of their members, even at the cost of alienating official favor. A new struc-ture of potential alliances, and maybe a "normalization" of the Argentine party system, will then be the order of the day.

Patterns of Change

The next years will be very tense, because a reformulation of the party structure may create at times conditions of ungovernability. On the basis of the previous analyses, it is possible to look into the future and posit, with some hesitations, the following sequence for the next decade or so:

1. At first there might be a maintenance and slight adjustment of the present party system, with a slow growth of an independent Left allied with dissident Peronist factions (as in the FREPASO), a weakening of the Radical party, and the consolidation of an electorally viable Right encompassing quite a few authoritarian elements (as with Bussi in Tucumán, or other provincial parties). Peronism continues to be dominant and mostly united, except for minority sectors involved in such alternative alliances as the FREPASO. Authoritarian elements within Peronism feel an increasing attraction to the rising Right, where they find many kindred souls.

2. In a second stage, the continued deterioration or very low recovery of living conditions for the lower strata could produce a division within Peronism, with most of the trade union sector becoming an opposition. The "verticalista," possibly Menemista or a conservative wing of the party, retains control of most of the less developed provinces and some other structures, benefiting from the exercise of power.

3. In a third stage, perhaps toward the end of Menem's second term in office, the party system might show a high fragmentation. There could then be a strong conservative force, with enough authoritarian elements to appeal to the Right of Peronism but not sufficient to get involved in military *golpismo*. The latter is also unnecessary, because of the lack of serious menaces and the prospects of acceding to the government via elections—or at least of having important bargaining power in Congress. The Radical party is reduced to a rump, and as a strategy of despair it develops a leftist orientation, hoping to regain votes but in fact alienating its traditional middle-class support. Right-wing Peronism continues to exist as a sizable force, its strength based upon the interior provinces and some business interests. The split-off and much renovated Peronism, with trade union anchorage, becomes established in a "pragmatic center-left" position, extending the experience of the FREPASO, under that or some other rubric. An

independent Left with high emotional and ideological commitments might continue to exist among the intelligentsia, though no longer hegemonic there and with little electoral appeal. Party fragmentation makes this the most dangerous moment in the sequence, raising the specter of ungovernability.

4. Finally, if Argentina is ever to follow the Western European pattern—which is not impossible, taking into account that even Eastern Europeans are doing it—a two-party or two-coalition system must eventually evolve. One way that could happen is if the Conservatives coalesce with right-wing Peronists and bring about, on the opposite side, an alliance or fusion between the renovated and trade-union-supported Peronists, the remainders of the Radical party, and the burgeoning independent Left. Of course, a change in the nature of Argentine trade union leadership is the hardest variable to predict in this formula, but, if the above considerations are valid, it is quite possible. Equally large an impediment to the formation of a wide though moderate Left is the resistance intellectuals have toward elements associated with Peronism.

To return to more immediate matters, what we have in Argentina is a situation in which, for the first time in its history, practically all important organized groups have a legitimated representation in the system, with no one being barred from attempting to influence it. Paradoxically, this happens at a moment when the marginalization of the poorer strata, who are bearing the brunt of the conversion from a statist to a competitive market economy, is most severe. That is so much the case that the possibility exists that they may lose their faith in being represented, either by Peronism or by a noninsurrectionary Left. If that happens, the clock would be set back indeed, and violence could become endemic.

But the "pacto a la argentina," first agreed on in 1989 between Peronism and the Right and then reproduced in a different context between Menem and Alfonsín in 1994, is in the process of showing its solidity despite occasional setbacks or the presence of dissidents. It has come about as a paradoxical attempt at doing away with the country's peculiar brand of stagnationist corporatism, using its own components as levers of change. It may turn out to be the responsibility of the present leadership of the Peronist party to use their corporatist connections to control the worst effects of "corporatism left to itself," and maybe to succeed in creating a new type of civic coexistence—but at the cost of altering the Argentine party system out of all recognition.

Notes

1. Domingo Faustino Sarmiento, *Facundo o civilización y barbarie* (Caracas: Ayacucho, 1977).

2. I have argued this point at greater length in "El impacto de la inmigración en el sistema político argentino," *Estudios Migratorios Latinoamericanos* 4, no. 12 (August 1989): 211–30. For a contrasting view, see Hilda Sabato and Ema Cibotti, *Hacer política en Buenos Aires: Los italianos en la escena pública porteña, 1860–1880* (Buenos Aires: Cisea-Pehesa, 1988).

3. See Atilio Borón, *State Capitalism and Democracy in Latin America* (Boulder: Lynne Rienner, 1995); and Edward Gibson, *Class and Conservative Parties: Argentina in Comparative Perspective* (Baltimore: Johns Hopkins University Press, 1996).

4. During the 1994 elections, these two parties practically opted out of the presidential race, but between them they won 30 percent of the seats in the lower chamber.

5. See Seymour M. Lipset, *Political Renewal on the Left: A Comparative Perspective* (Washington, DC: Progressive Policy Institute, January 1990).

6. This argument is similar to Guillermo O'Donnell's in "Un juego imposible," in *Modernización y autoritarismo* (Buenos Aires: Paidós, 1972), 180–213.

7. Edward C. Banfield and L. F. Banfield, *The Moral Basis of a Backward Society* (Glencoe, IL: Free Press, 1958).

8. Edgardo Catterberg, *Argentina Confronts Politics: Political Culture and Public Opinion in the Argentine Transition to Democracy* (Boulder and London: Lynne Rienner, 1991).

9. Seymour Martin Lipset, *Unions in Transition: Entering the Second Century* (San Francisco: Institute for Contemporary Studies, 1986).

10. Something in this line has happened in Italy, with the breakup of its centrist Christian Democratic party and the incorporation of its main successor, the Partito Popolare, into the moderate left coalition including the erstwhile Communist party.

11. This group must not be confused with the much more numerous conservative entrepreneurs who have been supporting Menem's policies, forming what I have described as a tactical alliance.

7

From Menem to Menem

Elections and Political Parties in Argentina

Liliana De Riz

In a country in which political instability has dominated recent history, presidential succession according to the constitution is without a doubt a major achievement.[1] The 1995 election is the eighth national election to have taken place in the twelve years following the return of democracy. This is particularly important because Argentine society lacks an electoral tradition. Previously, elections were held every ten years, and what occurred in the interim would overshadow the results of the most recent vote.

For the third time in little more than a decade, Argentina has elected a president under a competitive and nonexclusionary system. In 1989, Carlos Saúl Menem succeeded Alfonsín and, for the first time in six decades, power was passed peacefully from one political party to another. Menem was reelected in 1995, reviving the Peronista tradition that began with Perón himself in 1951. The object of this chapter is to analyze changes within the structure and dynamics of party competition as reflected in the results of elections between 1989 and 1995. Changes in the rules of political competition, as established in the 1994 constitution, will be analyzed as well.

Shifts in the electoral map make up part of the backdrop to the transformations that began to take shape between 1983 and 1989. It is therefore necessary to begin with an assessment of the most significant trends during that time. The assessment reveals a tendency by the electorate to vote for parties other than the two main political powers and volatility in voter preferences.[2]

Weaknesses in the two-party system born in 1983 did not lead to the emergence of a third political party with sufficient national electoral support to compete on an equal level with the two traditional parties. On the contrary, minor political parties, which in 1989 represented about one-quarter of the electorate, had little electoral support at the national level and strong support at the provincial level. Moreover, these parties had a heterogeneous base of support (De Riz and Androgüe, 1991).

In the presidential elections of 1989, the coalition that supported Alfonsín—composed of Radicals, former Peronismo supporters, and both right-wing and left-wing parties—lost to a new coalition formed in support of Menem.[3] With 46 percent of the vote, Menem defeated the Radical candidate Eduardo Angeloz by ten points. Voters switched to Justicialismo and the Center-Right in response to inflationary pressures that had burst forth two months before the election and that shortly thereafter gave rise to hyperinflation and the anticipated resignation of President Alfonsín.

Most significant among the changes noted in the 1989 national elections for deputies are the clear dominance of the Partido Justicialista (PJ) and the significant growth of Center-Right parties (see Table 1).

National Elections for Deputies

As opposed to presidential elections, in which the formation of a government is at stake, in elections for deputies the performance of the incumbent government becomes a key issue. This would explain the polarization of the electorate during presidential elections, while elections for deputies allow room for diverse political forces and accentuate the importance of nonpartisan voting.

The 1991 National Elections for Deputies

In 1991 elections for the partial renewal of the National Chamber of Deputies, the first to be held during Menem's term, resulted in a clear triumph for the government, with 40.7 percent of the vote. However, electoral support for the government fell 4 percent from 1989. The Unión Cívica Radical (UCR), the Radical Civic Union, received 29 percent of the vote, an amount slightly higher than it had obtained in 1989 (see Table 2). The UCR watched its electoral support fall dramatically in provinces such as Tucumán, San Juan, Salta, Neuquén, and Corrientes. The PJ won in fourteen provinces, the UCR carried five provinces, and minor provincial parties carried four (see Table 2). The two main parties combined received 69 percent of the vote. This reflects the growing electoral strength of the minor provincial parties, a trend that began in 1985.

Table 1. Results of the National Deputy Elections, 1983, 1985, 1987, 1989 (%)

	PJ	*UCR*
1983	33.5	47.4
1985	34.6	43.2
1987	41.5	37.2
1989	44.7	28.3

A new right-wing party, the Movimiento por la Dignidad y la Independencia Nacional (MODIN), the Movement for National Dignity and Independence, headed by former Colonel Aldo Rico, received 3.5 percent of the vote. MODIN came in fourth place, behind the Unión de Centro Democrático (Ucedé), the Union of the Democratic Center, which received 5.3 percent of the vote. In Buenos Aires province, MODIN came in third place with 9.2 percent of the vote and won three seats in the Chamber of Deputies.

A comparison can be made between the 1991 and 1985 elections, the latter being held during the Radical administration. In both cases, the electorate ratified a successful stabilization policy: in 1985 the Austral Plan and in 1991 the Convertibility Plan. Political competition remained bipolar. Innovations were introduced for the 1991 elections. Four separate rounds of voting by different groups of provinces were established and carried out under a wide variety of electoral systems. The simultaneous double vote, known as the Lemas Law, was applied in eleven provinces. In a majority of these provinces, this system was inaugurated the very same year.[4] The number of people who abstained from voting increased from an average of 15 percent during the 1980s to 22 percent in 1991.

1993 National Elections for Deputies

In the second national election for deputies, in October 1993, the PJ won with 42.3 percent of the vote—its electoral strength having grown since 1991—compared with 30 percent for the UCR, the main opposition party (see Table 2). Electoral support for the two main parties combined grew to 72 percent, yet it was still far below the 78 percent recorded for the 1985 and 1987 elections (De Riz, 1992). The party system remained bipolar, with smaller third parties carrying weight in the legislative and provincial elections.[5]

The election results demonstrate the growing predominance of the PJ. Viewed against the backdrop of Argentine political history, the October elections did away with the model that had reigned since the defeat of Peronismo by a military coup in 1955. Since then, in effect,

Table 2. Elections for National Deputies;, 1991–1995 (%)

	PJ			UCR			FREPASO*		
	1991	1993	1995	1991	1993	1995	1991	1993	1995
Buenos Aires	44.6	48.1	52.0	23.1	25.9	18.0	2.7	4.2	23.9
Catamarca	36.9	39.4	49.9	4.7	47.4	33.2	–	–	13.9
Córdoba	34.9	36.5	42.4	46.8	44.1	37.3	–	–	12.3
Corrientes	33.4	36.7	32.2	14.9	12.6	13.7	–	–	5.9
Chaco	36.6	37.3	41.2	21.4	23.7	31.8	–	0.4	7.0
Chubut	47.3	44.8	42.4	36.5	43.3	38.7	–	–	8.4
Entre Ríos	49.5	45.5	47.3	44.2	42.3	37.2	–	2.4	12.7
Federal Capital	29.0	32.5	23.0	40.3	29.9	20.3	3.7	13.6	35.0
Formosa	44.3	56.4	49.3	34.0	39.8	33.6	–	–	13.9
Jujuy	39.8	37.2	28.8	20.6	26.2	23.5	–	–	13.2
La Pampa	48.3	43.9	50.7	29.8	19.6	24.9	–	1.9	6.6
La Rioja	63.0	61.5	76.7	24.1	35.0	19.8	–	1.7	2.4
Mendoza	50.0	48.7	45.0	30.2	30.6	16.8	–	–	19.5
Misiones	51.1	50.6	50.6	44.0	44.2	39.8	–	–	7.5
Neuquén	30.0	27.3	27.4	14.5	29.2	11.9	–	2.7	22.3
Río Negro	38.4	41.9	44.0	38.4	41.9	43.1	–	2.6	11.6
Salta	36.3	39.7	34.5	7.6	17.8	13.4	–	–	10.0
San Juan	31.6	23.4	48.2	8.2	11.5	8.9	–	–	3.4
San Luis	47.8	51.4	58.8	36.6	34.0	18.9	–	–	19.3
Santa Cruz	47.9	57.5	58.8	37.0	33.8	22.9	–	–	14.9
Santa Fé	34.9	37.9	34.4	27.1	34.9	16.5	–	1.3	27.6
Santiago del Estero	25.6	–	45.0	44.0	–	22.7	–	–	5.2
Tucumán	47.0	40.9	34.3	5.7	20.9	15.9	–	–	19.3
Tierra del Fuego	31.1	42.3	45.9	16.9	23.4	22.4	–	1.6	6.0
National Total	40.7	42.3	43.0	29.0	30.0	21.8	1.5	2.5	21.2

Source: Dirreción Nacional Electoral, Ministerio del Interior.

*In 1991, FREDEJUSO (Frente por la Democracia de la Justicia Social). In the 1993 elections, Frente Grande (Fredejuso and Frente del Sur). In the 1995 elections, FREPASO (FG, Unidad Socialista, and PAIS-Política ABIERTA para PA INTEGRIDAD Social, and Christian Democrats no government had been able to survive the fourth year of its term. Military coups ousted Arturo Illia and Isabel Perón before they could pass the electoral test. President Arturo Frondizi's defeat in elections that were held after four years in power brought about the authority crisis that ended in a military coup. That was the beginning of a downfall that ended with President Raúl Alfonsín's leaving office before the end of his term.

In light of the high social costs of the government's adjustment policy, the outcome of the 1993 elections rejects any immediate connection between the severity of the economic adjustment and social discontent. How can the behavior of the electorate be explained? It is obvious that electoral behavior is influenced by expectations. Peronismo's success at the ballot box was tied to the certainty created by the relative stability of prices. This achievement was able to neutralize the impact of the social exclusion of an increasing portion of the population, allegations of corruption, and scandals that touched the Supreme Court on the eve of elections.[6]

Nevertheless, solely interpreting the outcome of the 1993 elections in terms of the political benefits of economic stability obscures a key political fact. In order to understand the behavior of the electorate throughout a decade of restored democracy in Argentina, the fact that the PJ won in 1993 (as they had been doing in 1987, 1989, and 1991) must be taken into account. Peronistas remained loyal to the party in spite of the drastic changes Menem had made in traditional Peronista policies. Since 1983, the number of those voting Peronista has remained stable, at levels between 36 and 38 percent of all voters. This figure is considered to be the foundation of the Peronista electorate over the last decade. That fact confirms that identification with the PJ is not based on programs or specific policies, but rather on values such as social justice and on a certain leadership style—a combination of loyalty and effectiveness, charisma and pragmatism—introduced by Perón and replicated by Menem.

Electoral support for Menem over and above the base of the 36-to-38 percent Peronista votes has fluctuated since 1989, in line with the swing in votes by the traditionally non-Peronista portion of the electorate. This sector of the population, sensitive to changing conditions, was influenced by the memory of hyperinflation, which, in turn, helped the government.

Two political forces from both sides of the ideological spectrum, the Frente Grande (FG), the Large Front, a left-wing coalition headed by breakaway sectors of the PJ and the Left, and MODIN, to the right, emerged as channels for social protest and ideological votes.[7] However, in 1993, MODIN received only 5.8 percent of the vote and the Frente Grande received 2.5 percent (the Left as a whole received 4.7 percent of the vote).

A more detailed analysis of the 1993 electoral results reveals that the pattern observed in 1991 was not sustained. In the Federal Capital, a district traditionally dominated by the UCR, the PJ won the first minority with 32.5 percent of the vote versus 29.9 percent for the Radicals. It also won in twenty of the twenty-eight local elections. These results contrast with the 1991 election figures: 40.3 percent and 29 percent received by the UCR and the PJ, respectively (see Table 2). Voters from the Center-Right threw their support to the PJ, as shown by the catastrophic fall of the Ucedé, the Partido Democrático (PD), the Democratic party, and the Partido Demócrata Progresista (PDP), the Progressive Democratic party, which together received only 7 percent of the vote. Support for the Ucedé, which had obtained 22 percent of the vote in 1989, fell to 8.6 percent in 1991 and even further to 3 percent in 1993. The data from 1993 suggest that an electoral coalition supporting Menem was created that included voters from both the high and low ends of the social ladder. The new political party, the Frente Grande, climbed to third position in the Federal Capital with 13.6 percent of the vote.

In the Province of Buenos Aires, which represents around 37 percent of the electorate, the PJ won with 48.1 percent of the vote versus 25.9 percent for the UCR. Support for the UCR increased from the 23.1 percent received in 1991, but the gap between the UCR and Peronismo widened. With close to an absolute majority, the PJ—four points higher than in 1991—gained the first minority in eighteen of the nineteen districts that make up greater Buenos Aires. The Buenos Aires metropolitan region is a heterogeneous conglomerate that includes the very poor, the impoverished middle classes, and industrial workers fighting to keep their jobs.[8] The right-wing party, MODIN, received 11 percent of the vote, making it the third most powerful force in this district.

The UCR lost votes in the Federal Capital and in Córdoba (where it retained its first minority status). Electoral support for the UCR remained steady in Buenos Aires, Catamarca, Jujuy, Entre Ríos, and San Luis, and increased in a majority of the districts. The 1993 elections clearly showed that Justicialismo had conquered areas previously controlled by the Radicals, which heavily influenced the government's political strategy.

The Constitutional Reform

The October 1993 elections were carried out under unique circumstances dominated by the government initiative to reform the constitution. The stated goal of the reform was to legalize a second presidential term and ensure Carlos Menem the right to be reelected in 1995. What was the impact of the electoral results on the government initiative for constitutional reform? How did these results influence UCR strategy?

The will of the electorate—as expressed at the ballot box—indicated that constitutional reform could be achieved only through a difficult process of negotiation and an agreement between the major parties.[9] However, that was not how the government interpreted the electoral results. The 1993 election results for the Federal Capital and greater Buenos Aires unleashed an arrogant attitude—referred to as "Menemazo"—that inspired the decision to hurry the constitutional reform project through the Senate.[10] Through obscure negotiations with minor parties to gain the needed two-thirds' support, the Senate approved a project that it had become familiar with only minutes before the voting took place (see Table 2).

Immediately following Senate approval of the reform project, the government called for a nationwide plebiscite to allow the electorate to vote either for or against the reform. The plebiscite was to take place on November 21. The fact that a plebiscite was called while the issue was still being addressed in Congress removed any doubt that it was being used to pressure the lower house. Two-thirds of the members of the Chamber of Deputies must vote in favor of the reform in order for it to be passed, a number that, in principle, was unlikely to be obtained.[11]

The "Olivos Pact" and the April 1994 Elections for Delegates to the Constitutional Reform Convention

To the public, the UCR seemed to be faced with the dilemma of either refusing to ratify constitutional reform, as the party convention had decided, and face possible defeat in the plebiscite, or to agree to negotiations and avoid electoral confrontation.[12] The approach adopted by ex-President Alfonsín, elected president of the UCR by a narrow margin, favored negotiation with the government. Alfonsín, together with Menem, endorsed an agreement on the contents of the reform, known as the "Olivos Pact." At the beginning of December, the UCR national convention approved the decision to negotiate a reform and, shortly thereafter, a consensual reform project was born.

The new pact to reform the constitution was made possible through a compromise between the reelection ambitions of the president and the efforts of the opposition to limit presidential authority through the introduction of new rights and the creation of a less powerful presidency. This pact was passed into law with congressional approval.[13] Alfonsín was once again able to play a major role in the negotiations for constitutional reform. However, the UCR was in the midst of a crisis arising from its failure as a government and its successive electoral defeats since 1985. Lacking a leader capable of giving direction to the party and convincing public opinion of its ability to govern, the UCR found in the negotiations a way to try to head up an opposition coalition. The October 1993 election, in which the UCR received 30 percent of the vote, fueled this hope.

After the constitutional convention elections in April 1994, a system composed of three major parties and several minor parties emerged (see Table 3). Together, the PJ and the UCR received 57 percent of the vote.

Table 3. Constitutional Convention Elections, 1994 (%)

	PJ	UCR	FG
Buenos Aires	42.8	15.7	16.4
Catamarca	44.3	44.0	—
Córdoba	32.6	42.6	5.7
Corrientes	28.5	10.1	—
Chaco	41.9	26.3	5.4
Chubut	38.7	44.2	6.4
Entre Ríos	41.4	24.1	12.4
Federal capital	24.5	15.2	37.6
Formosa	55.5	31.3	—
Jujuy	21.8	23.1	—
La Pampa	44.1	27.9	7.4
La Rioja	57.0	32.4	4.0
Mendoza	38.2	17.2	—
Misiones	44.5	34.9	—
Neuquén	23.9	12.9	29.2
Río Negro	42.7	42.7	9.7
Salta	38.5	10.8	—
San Juan	18.3	5.4	—
San Luis	52.8	24.6	—
Santa Cruz	56.0	34.1	—
Santa Fé	36.2	12.0	10.2
Santiago del Estero	52.8	40.4	—
Tucumán	39.0	8.0	3.6
Tierra del Fuego	37.6	13.8	5.1
National Totals	**37.7**	**19.8**	**12.7**

Source: Dirreción Nacional Electoral, Ministerio del Interior.

Support for the PJ fell from 42.3 percent in 1993 to 37.7 percent, a figure below its historical low of 1983. Support for the UCR dropped from 30 percent in 1993 to 19.8 percent, and the Frente Grande emerged as a third national political power with 12.7 percent of the vote. Support for MODIN grew from 5.8 percent of the vote in 1993 to 9.2 percent in 1994.[14] Questions were raised regarding the future of the two-party system in response to the UCR's electoral debacle—the party had entered elections with an internal split over the legitimacy of the Olivos Pact. The strong growth of the Center-Left—represented by the Frente Grande and personified by Carlos "Chacho" Alvarez—and, to a lesser extent, the growth of MODIN also fueled this debate. Although MODIN had not grown as rapidly, its support was more evenly distributed according to district.

In the Federal Capital, electoral support for the Frente Grande climbed to 37.5 percent of the vote, making it the largest minority. The FG was twenty-two points above the UCR and thirteen points above the PJ. In Buenos Aires province, electoral support for the FG quadrupled, shooting up from 4.2 percent in the legislative elections of 1993 to 16.3 percent in the constitutional convention elections in 1994. It also ousted the UCR from its position as second largest minority.

Nevertheless, because this election was not to reelect political authorities, which permitted a "freer" expression by the electorate, the outcome did not permanently alter the electoral strength of the parties. During this election, misinformation and indifference ran high, and abstentions rose to 24 percent.

The Amended Constitution

Institutional reforms, unanimously approved by all parties, redefined the key rules of the game (Sabsay and Onaindia, 1994). The electoral system was modified for the ninth time since 1987. The amended constitution established the direct election of the president and reduced the presidential term from six to four years, bringing it in line with those of the deputies. A variation of ballotage was chosen so that a candidate would be elected after the first round if a) the candidate obtains more than 45 percent of the validly marked votes, or b) the ticket receiving the most votes in the first round obtains at least 40 percent of the validly marked votes and there is at least a 10 percent difference between the number of validly marked votes received by the two parties receiving the most votes.[15] The opposition initially proposed a classic ballotage system, requiring that an absolute majority be obtained, but the above formula was finally adopted. This process encourages polarization during the first round of voting, which, in turn, provides an incentive for forming an opposition coalition.[16]

Article 90 of the amended constitution permits the reelection of the president for only one term and calls for elections every four years. Additional changes made to the electoral system include the direct election of senators, the addition of a third senator representing the minority in each province, and the reduction in senatorial terms from nine to six years with biannual renewal. Other reforms reflect attempts by the opposition to limit the exceptional powers of the president: the creation of the position of chief of cabinet, who oversees all administrative matters, has

federal authority, and reports directly to Congress; and the constitutionalization of the "need" and "urgency" decrees, prohibiting their application in penal, tax, electoral, and legislative cases, and calling for their
ratification by Congress without a fixed deadline.[17]

The amended constitution transferred to the legislative branch the
power to pass special laws for regulating bodies and structures essential
to the functioning of the new state apparatus. This included, among other
things, determining who will sit on the magistrate counsel and the trial
jury. It also referred to decisions on the "need" and "urgency" decrees
submitted to Congress, with opinions given by the newly created permanent ad hoc bicameral commission; set limits on the authority of the public defender; and defined the criteria for electing the attorney general.[18]

The 1995 Elections

The Presidential Elections

The presidential elections held on May 14, 1995, were carried out under
the new rules established in the constitutional reform. Anxiety created by
the introduction of ballotage brought election polls to the forefront of the
political debate. Discussion of the figures superseded debate on actual
proposals. Pollsters took the place of political analysts, and television
focused on the ever-changing data. The presidential campaigns of opposition candidates challenged the policies of President Menem but were
unable to produce credible alternatives. Menem visited cities and rural
areas, inaugurating schools, hospitals, and roads, and demonstrating the
accomplishments of his government as if he were running for governor.
He refused to debate his adversaries.

In 1995, Menem was challenged by a rival within the ranks of
Peronismo: the Peronista senator from the Province of Mendoza, José
Octavio Bordón. He was the presidential candidate for the Frente del País
Solidario (FREPASO). A Center-Left coalition created by Bordón and composed of an alliance among the Frente Grande, the Unidad Socialista and
the Christian Democrats, and the País party FREPASO came into existence a few months prior to the elections. During the month of February,
Bordón and Alvarez, the candidate from the FG, ran against each other in
open internal elections for the presidential nomination. To the surprise of
many, five hundred thousand citizens voted in internal elections to decide
which of the two candidates would head the presidential election ticket.

The image of Bordón, as recalled by the president of Brazil, Fernando
Henrique Cardoso, was that of a modern intellectual who represented the
liberal and democratic ideals of Peronismo, a moderate and a moderator

with successful experience governing Mendoza province. His slogan, "For a safe change," was much more moderate than that of the Radical presidential candidate, Horacio Massaccesi.[19] In spite of the incentives created by the new electoral system, FREPASO and the Radical party did not join together as an opposition front. The heterogeneity within FREPASO—a coalition against Menem more than a true alliance—and the lack of national leadership within the UCR conspired against that goal. Divisions within the opposition and the PJ's greater resources contributed to its failure.

At the time of the elections, the choice appeared to be between the government, which, paradoxically, was benefiting from its handling of the initial consequences of the Mexican peso crisis—that is, its continued rule offered a guarantee against chaos—and an opposition that could not guarantee that "history would not be turned back." In essence, FREPASO was not able to transform itself from a party of social protest into a party capable of ruling; the UCR could not rid itself of its image as a failed government. Menem received 47.7 percent of the vote in the first round. The two-party system that had emerged in 1983 had been replaced by a three-party system with various minor parties. The UCR, with 16.4 percent of the vote, was succeeded by FREPASO, which received 28.2 percent, as the second largest minority (see Table 4). Twenty points above FREPASO, the Menem-Ruckauf ticket represented a party that clearly dominated the political scene. The PJ won nationwide with the exception of the Federal Capital, where FREPASO won with 44.1 percent of the vote versus 41.5 percent for the PJ (see Table 5).[20]

The results of the March 1973 presidential elections were reproduced in the 1995 elections. In 1973 the PJ had received about 50 percent of the vote against an opposition, at that time divided into three sectors (the UCR with 23 percent, the Center-Right with 16 percent, and the Left with 7 percent).

Table 4. National Presidential Elections by Party, 1983, 1989, 1995 (%)

Parties	1983	1989	1995
Radical (UCR)[a]	50	36	16.4
Peronista[b]	39	46	47.7
Center-Right[c]	4	10	—
Left[d]	4	5	1
Right[e]	—	—	1
FREPASO[f] (Center-Left)	—	—	28.2
Blank and null ballots	3	3	4.1

Source: Dirrección Nacional Electoral, Ministerio del Interior.
[a]Radical: 1989 UCR and Confederación Federalista Independiente (CFI), Independent Federalist Confederation

bPeronista: 1983 PJ; 1989 FREJUPO (Frente Justicialista de Unión Popular [Justicialista Popular Union Front]); 1995 PJ
cCenter-Right: 1983 Ucedé, Alianza Federal (Federal Alliance), Alianza Socialista Democrática-Demócrata Progresista (Democratic Socialist Alliance-Progressive Democrats); 1989 Alianza de Centro (Ucedé, Demócrata Progresista, Demócrata [Democrats], Pacto Autonomista Liberal [Autonomous Liberal Pact]), Fuerza Republicana (Republican Force), Bloquista (Blockists), Movimiento Popular Neuquino (Neuquén Popular Movement), other provincial parties.
dLeft: 1983 Partido Intransigente (Intransigent party), Frente de Izquierda Popular (Popular Leftist Front), Partido Obrero (Workers' party), Movimiento al Socialismo (Movement toward Socialism), Partido Demócrata Cristiano (Christian Democratic party), Movimiento de Integración y Desarrollo (Movement for Integration and Development), Partido Socialista (Socialist party); 1989 Alianza Izquierda Unida (United Leftist Alliance), Socialistas (Socialists), others.
eRight: MODIN, Fuerza Republicana (with 0.38 percent), the FR was included together with MODIN and the Frente para la Coincidencia Patriótica ([FRECOPA] Patriotic Coincidence Front) in 1989.
fFrente Grande Alliance (Unidad Socialista [Socialist Unity], Democracia Cristiana [Christian Democratic party] and Alvarez's followers) with Bordón's País party.

Table 5. Presidential Elections by District, 1995 (%)

	Ticket		
	Menem-Ruckauf	*Bordón-Alvarez*	*Massaccesi-Hernandez*
Buenos Aires	51.84	29.71	13.90
Catamarca	53.30	15.40	30.14
Córdoba	48.20	20.72	28.87
Corrientes	46.08	33.85	16.10
Chaco	56.82	18.03	22.89
Chubut	57.07	15.25	25.59
Entre Ríos	45.99	24.85	26.60
Federal Capital	41.53	44.19	10.67
Formosa	49.37	16.66	31.40
Jujuy	46.85	22.76	21.49
La Pampa	50.63	23.87	22.87
La Rioja	75.82	6.26	16.79
Mendoza	51.94	33.66	12.12
Misiones	50.85	9.03	37.90
Neuquén	53.80	25.46	16.18
Río Negro	44.00	16.03	37.32
Salta	55.50	24.77	16.69
San Juan	59.23	30.27	9.66
San Luis	52.21	25.35	20.19
Santa Cruz	58.00	22.71	17.30
Santa Fé	46.82	37.38	12.76
Santiago del Estero	63.90	10.02	25.05
Tierra del Fuego	61.14	22.42	13.28
Tucumán	45.47	29.11	12.36

Source: Dirección Nacional Electoral, Ministerio del Interior.

In the 1995 elections, the minor parties virtually disappeared from the presidential race. In 1989 the Ucedé received 10 percent of the vote, and in 1995 it supported the PJ presidential ticket. The minor parties, which combined had captured 15 percent of the vote in 1989, received only 2 percent in 1995 (see Table 4). The Left, which in 1989 received 5 percent of the vote, threw its support to FREPASO.

The 1995 National Elections for Deputies

In the national elections for deputies, the PJ received 43 percent of the vote, compared with 21.7 percent for the UCR and 21.2 percent for FREPASO. Support for minor political parties dropped from 27 percent in 1993 to 14 percent in 1995. The latter figure is close to the percentage of the vote—13 percent—that they received in 1983. MODIN received only 1.6 percent of the vote, and Ucedé received 2.9 percent. The remaining parties, both right-wing and left-wing, did not obtain even 1 percent of the vote (see Table 2).

A sharp contrast can be observed in the presidential and congressional election results for the opposition. Electoral support for FREPASO in the presidential race was eight points higher than in the congressional elections. Electoral support for the UCR, however, was five points higher in the congressional elections than in the presidential election. This reflects the inability of FREPASO to establish an electoral base at the provincial level. Unlike the UCR, FREPASO was successful at the national level but not in the election for deputies. The UCR, on the other hand, was able to maintain power, although diminished, at the congressional level. The high degree of electoral support the PJ presidential ticket received indicates an anomaly among supporters of the right-wing alliance who voted explicitly for the PJ ticket, and among non-Peronistas who split their vote, voting Peronista in the presidential elections while supporting their own parties in congressional elections.

In these elections, the number of votes split between the presidential ticket and congressional candidates reached about 20 percent of all valid votes, a figure considerably higher than the 5 to 7 percent historical average.

Gubernatorial Elections

The results of the gubernatorial elections, which took place in fourteen provinces in May 1995, showed that the PJ and UCR parties received, in general, more support at the ballot box for their gubernatorial candidates than for their presidential tickets (see Table 6). This underscores the influence of local politics on voter preferences. FREPASO did not win one governorship, reflecting its weak electoral base at the provincial level. The UCR retained governorships in three provinces (Córdoba, Río Negro, and Chubut) and gained Catamarca. In Misiones, the preliminary electoral results showed its candidate to be the winner with 48.4 percent of the vote versus 46.5 percent for the PJ candidate. However, a recount requested by the UCR proclaimed the Peronista candidate the winner by a narrow margin.

Table 6. Gubernatorial Elections, 1995 (%)

	PJ	Parties UCR	FREPASO	Difference PJ/UCR
Buenos Aires	56.7	17.3	21.0	+35.7
Catamarca	42.7	54.0	0.0	-11.3
Córdoba	40.0	47.2	5.1	-7.2
Chubut	32.4	57.9	2.6	-25.5
Entre Ríos	48.9	43.9	5.2	+5.0
La Pampa	54.2	22.3	4.7	+31.9
La Rioja	82.4	15.7	1.3	+66.7
Mendoza	43.1	20.5	16.5	+22.6
Misiones	47.7	45.0	2.9	+2.7
Río Negro	44.5	44.9	9.3	-0.9
San Juan*	47.4	22.8	0.0	+24.6
San Luis	71.5	16.5	11.0	+55.0
Santa Cruz**	66.5	0.0	0.0	+66.5
Santiago del Estero	66.5	17.8	1.06	+48.7

Source: Dirección Nacional Electoral, Ministerio del Interior.
*Civic Alliance, included the *sublemas* (subparties) Social Justice, Cruzada, Frente Grande, and UCR
**Encuentro Santa Cruceño received 32.3 percent

Elections in the other eight provinces—staggered over the period between July and October—resulted in the loss of two provinces to the opposition: the UCR in the Chaco and the anti-Menem sector of the Movimiento Popular Neuquino (Neuquén Popular Movement) in Neuquén. In Tucumán, the Fuerza Republicana (the party of retired General Antonio Bussi) won, and in Tierra del Fuego, the Movimiento Popular Fueguino (Fueguino Popular Movement) won, twenty-two points ahead of the PJ candidate. The PJ regained Formosa, Jujuy, Salta, and Santa Fé. The elections in Santa Fé are not included in this discussion because of allegations of fraud.[21] The gubernatorial political map is divided as follows: 60 percent of the governorships are held by the PJ, 22 percent by the UCR, and 18 percent by local parties.

Following the Justicialista victory, the traditional Peronist tendency to behave as if no other political force in government counted continues to strengthen. As a consequence, the internal disputes and the urge to transform them into state issues persist. Conflicts between the government and its internal opposition have proved to be more crucial to the evolution of democratic goverance than the misadventures of the opposition parties (De Riz, 1996).

The Post-Election Scenario

Menem began his second term amid a climate of indifference, which contrasted sharply with the magnitude of his victory. The new Menem government was inaugurated in the midst of an economic crisis that had been kept hidden from the public. In July, Argentines learned that the unemployment rate had reached 18.6 percent, an unheard-of level for a country with a long history of full employment. Public opinion polls indicated a fall in the popularity of the president. Initial confidence in the future turned into uncertainty. The change in the economic outlook—now characterized by recession, unemployment, and a serious fiscal crisis threatening the provinces—heightened the conflict within the administration: on one side, the political sector, in the hands of men who had been with the president since his days as a populist candidate, and on the other, the technocrats, led by Minister Cavallo, responsible for the economic reforms. The tactical alliance between the two sectors had been sustained during the party's economic and electoral successes. Following the electoral triumph in May 1995 over a "pulverized" opposition (in the words of the president), the severity of the economic crisis fueled the struggle for control within Peronismo. Cavallo's reputation among the general public and in the business world, in addition to his political ambitions, led to uneasiness among Menem's followers. During the month of August, Cavallo denounced the existence of mafias operating within the government. This revelation hung a cloak of suspicion over all three branches of government. The political crisis unleashed by Cavallo put the spotlight on the weakest aspect of Argentine democracy: the frailty of its institutions, infiltrated by corruption.

Menem was obligated to reaffirm his support for the minister of the economy in order to maintain calm in the markets. This appeared to be more a truce than a solution to the problems generated by the crisis. As a result, in an economy troubled by the impact of its economic program, the general sense of uncertainty continued (Gerchunoff and Machinea, 1995). As the future appeared less promising in the eyes of the public, the social costs of the economic reforms implemented by the Menem government became less tolerable (Halperín Donghi, 1994; Minujin and Kessler, 1995).

Following victory at the ballot box, opposition to the government increasingly came from within the ranks of Peronismo itself, more than from other political parties. Succession within Peronismo is at the heart of these struggles.[22] The rivalry between Menem and Duhalde, the governor of Buenos Aires province, took center stage. Eduardo Duhalde, by having been successfully reelected governor, had placed himself in a position to become a presidential candidate in 1999. The September 3 gubernatorial election in Santa Fé province, one of the four most important electoral districts in the country, was a preview of the conflict to come.[23]

Twelve years after the restoration of democracy in Argentina, is the commitment to reconstruct democratic institutions strong enough to prevent a return to the past? In the current political context, the continuity of democratic institutions is not in question. Praetorianism is not a threat today. Freedom of expression and the strength of a pluralistic society are the watershed that divides the two eras. At present, the margin for testing alternative economic policies has been restricted, and, therefore, the space for dissension has been reduced. Economic reform has not been questioned, but the "spirit" that propels it has been. What is in question is the quality of the management of the reform and its related institutions, specifically the absence of an independent judiciary and corruption and inequalities in the distribution of social costs attributed to the changes implemented by Peronismo.

In Argentina, as in other new democracies, differences between the parties exist, but clear profiles are not generated to help the public discriminate among them; politics becomes personalized, the leaders are increasingly discredited, and the number of citizens who do not identify with a political party grows.

A weak opposition and the manner in which the government operates do not facilitate the consolidation of institutions capable of braking the centrifugal forces within Peronismo or exercising the necessary control over whoever is in power. Nevertheless, the self-renewal process initiated by the UCR alters this scenario. Toward the end of 1995, Rodolfo Terragno was named president of the party and began to restructure its organization. Terragno, who does not have a history as a Radical—he joined the UCR in 1987—represents the desire to disassociate the party from its traditional image. Terragno presents himself as a reformer, the direct opposite of Menem's "bulldozer" style of leadership. His goal is to re-create a modern state, strong and clean, in contrast to the Peronista strategy—that is, indiscriminate reduction of the state and corruption. Whether this "renewal" of the UCR will be translated into a reform movement capable of channeling discontent and defeating Peronismo at the ballot box remains to be seen.

FREPASO, however, survived a crisis that brought an end to the dual leadership that had emerged after the May 1995 elections. In spite of having had a significant electoral triumph with its candidate, Graciela Fernandez Meijide, who was elected senator for the Federal Capital in October 1995, FREPASO split at the beginning of 1996. Differences between Bordón and Alvarez over the strategy to be adopted for the *intendencia* (mayoral) elections for the city of Buenos Aires culminated with Bordón and a group of his core supporters in the País party abandoning the coalition.[24] Following the quick rise of Graciela Fernandez Meijide, FREPASO had a new dual leadership marked by a high degree of internal competitiveness between Meijide and Alvarez.

Will the system composed of three major parties and several minor parties that emerged following the 1995 elections be maintained? Will Peronismo be able to resolve the internal struggle for succession without destroying the institutions of government?

Since the May 1995 elections, the Argentine political map remains in flux. It is still too soon to predict the future electoral strength of the various political parties.

Notes

1. The military coup of 1930 was the first of a series of coups that disrupted the constitutional order. Others occurred in 1943, 1955, 1962, 1966, and 1976.

2. In 1983, the UCR and the PJ received 85.86 percent of all the votes in the country. In 1989, the percentage of total votes for both parties reached only 72 percent. The PJ has won in all of the national elections since 1987. Its electoral support has grown mainly by luring voters away from provincial parties and by gaining the support of people not affiliated with a party who are sensitive to changing circumstances.

3. Fifty-eight percent of those who voted for Alfonsín the first time voted for him again; 27 percent voted for Menem, 9 percent voted for Alsogaray, and the remaining 6 percent either voted for the left-wing parties or abstained (Catterberg, 1989).

4. Bear in mind that, according to the federal organization of the Republic of Argentina, provinces have the authority to legislate over electoral issues (De Riz, 1992).

5. With respect to the power distribution in Congress, these "third parties" form miniblocs, and, in many cases, often have just one representative. Yet they can play a decisive role when their vote can tip the scale in favor of one of the two major political parties.

6. The 1993 electoral campaign was marked by the virulence of accusations by both sides. In the end, the Supreme Court appeared to be subject to government influence and factional disputes. The negative character of this electoral campaign led to a growing respect for the 1991 campaign. The success achieved

in controlling inflation continued as the leitmotiv of the government. However, in 1993, the slogan for keeping Menem in power was "So that history does not come to a standstill." Bear in mind that in Argentina neither the exact starting date nor the duration of the electoral campaign is specified. As in Uruguay, legislation regulating electoral campaigns is scarce. However, in Argentina there is no control like that exercised by the Uruguayan Electoral Court, which ensures clean campaigns (Lauda, 1994).

7. In 1993 the Frente Grande formed an alliance with the Frente del Sur (Southern Front) and Oscar Allende's Partido Intransigente (Intransigent party).

8. It is important to remember that the social composition of greater Buenos Aires, which represents almost 60 percent of the population in the province, has changed, and that the metropolitan area no longer represents the heart of the industrial proletariat.

9. The constitutional reform project introduced by Alfonsín during his term did not obtain the consensus needed. He was unable to overcome the resistance of those who were not convinced by his clear renouncement of a second term—that is, those who still thought that the reform project was tailored for Alfonsín's benefit. He was also unable to neutralize the mistrust Peronistas and Radicals felt for a semipresidential government system (Nohlen and De Riz, 1991).

10. In the Senate, the PJ relied on its own quorum. In the Chamber of Deputies, with only 127 seats, the PJ did not have its own quorum. However, it was able to direct the will of this body, with a total of 257 representatives, aided by the support of only three deputies from minor parties.

11. Article 30 of the 1853 constitution requires the support of two-thirds of the members of Congress in order to declare the need for reform. The PJ maintained that two-thirds of the members in attendance of the lower chamber were sufficient to sanction the need for reform.

12. Please note that, according to surveys carried out immediately prior to the plebiscite, constitutional reform was supported by about 50 percent of Argentines (Sofres [French polling association]-IBOPE [Brazilian Institute of Public Opinion], September 1993).

13. In the Senate, Radicals and Justicialistas rejected a reduction in terms for senators from nine to four years. Finally, a six-year term with renewal every two years was agreed upon in the constitutional convention.

14. The FG won in the Federal Capital with 37.5 percent of the vote, compared with 24.5 percent for the PJ and 15.2 percent for the UCR. In the Province of Buenos Aires, the FG became the second minority, slightly ahead of the UCR, with 16.3 percent of the vote.

15. The decision to consider only the validly marked votes (that is, to exclude blank votes) generated debate, because in Argentina blank votes have traditionally been an expression of protest.

16. Peronismo's first defeat in free and nonrestricted elections in 1983 was due to the broad coalition formed in support of Raúl Alfonsín. Argentine politics, since the appearance of Peronismo, has always been characterized by a divided opposition.

17. Between 1989 and 1993, President Menem dictated 308 "need" and "urgency" decrees, which constituted a clear and systematic violation of the principle of the division of power. Furthermore, the magnitude of these decrees was unprecedented in the history of constitutional governments (Fernández Rubio and Goretti, 1994).

18. Through July 1997, Congress had failed to pass legislation associated with the constitutional reform. The time period stipulated for the passage of a

majority of the laws has expired. The chief of cabinet was designated by decree and not by special law, as stipulated in the constitution.

19. In UCR internal elections, which took place in November 1994, the Radicals chose the presidential ticket of Horacio Massaccesi and Antonio Hernandez. Massaccesi, governor of the Province of Río Negro, was nominated in an election in which only 30 percent of registered Radicals voted. Close to the party old guard and more inclined to negotiate with than to confront Menem, Massaccesi did not inspire enthusiasm among most party members.

20. In the Federal Capital, the UCR won only 10.6 percent of the vote, the lowest figure ever recorded. This figure is comparable only to the percentage of votes the UCR received in San Juan during the same election.

21. The governorship in Corrientes was not up for election at this time. The governor is currently a member of the Autonomous Liberal party.

22. The political movement built around the charisma of Perón reverted to the people by the will of its creator. Perón resisted the institutionalization of the political force that he had created. The weakness of Peronismo's organizational structures and its dependence on a strong leader to direct the party left the problem of succession unresolved. The intentions of the "renovation" Peronistas—a political sector created by a coalition of congressmen and governors following the electoral defeats of 1983 and 1985—to create a party and limit the influence then exercised by the labor unions, faded with the rise of Menem to the presidency in 1989 (De Riz, 1995a).

23. The general suspicions of fraud, generated by the less than transparent provisional counting of the votes, led the provincial political parties to refuse to recognize the results and to initiate a recount (in Santa Fé, the Lemas Law has been in effect since 1991). Following a vote-by-vote recount, the initial winner—the candidate endorsed by President Menem—had to admit defeat. The recount showed the winner to be the candidate endorsed by Governor Duhalde thirty-eight days after elections had been held. The scandal of the Santa Fé elections once again raised the question of the ability of Peronismo to resolve internal disputes without destroying political institutions. (For an analysis of Argentine politics between 1946 and 1989, see Torre and De Riz, 1991.)

24. Bordón supported the candidacy of Gustavo Beliz, former minister of the interior and founder of the Nueva Dirigencia party (New Leadership party), for mayor of Buenos Aires City (*intendente*). Bordón wanted to widen FREPASO's territory to include Peronista voters disenchanted with Menemism. Bordón resigned from his seat in the Senate after having been accused of corruption by a provincial tribunal in relation to irregularities in government contracts negotiated while he was governor of Mendoza.

Bibliography

Canitrot, Adolfo, and Silvia Sigal. "Economic Reform, Democracy, and the Crisis of the State in Argentina." In *A Precarious Balance: Democracy and Economic Reforms in Latin America*, ed. Joan M. Nelson, 2:95–140. San Francisco: Institute for Contemporary Studies, 1994.

Catterberg, Edgardo, and M. Braun. "Las elecciones presidenciales argentinas del 14 de mayo de 1989: La ruta a la normalidad." *Desarrollo Económico* (Buenos Aires) 29, no. 115 (October–December 1989).

Corradi, Juan. "Menem's Argentina, Act II." *Current History* 194, no. 589 (February 1995): 76–79.

De Riz, Liliana. "El debate sobre la reforma electoral en Argentina." *Desarrollo Económico* 32 (July–September 1992): 126.

———. *Radicales y Peronistas en el Congreso Nacional: 1983–1989.* Buenos Aires: Centro Editor para América Latina, 1995a.

———. "Reforma constitucional y consolidación democratica." *Sociedad* 6 (April–May 1995b): 61–76.

———. "Argentina: Democracy in Turmoil." In *Constructing Democratic Governance: Latin America and the Caribbean in the 1990s*, ed. Jorge Domínguez and Abraham Lowenthal, 147–66. Baltimore: Johns Hopkins University Press, 1996.

De Riz, Liliana, and Gerardo Androgué. "Polarizzazione e depolarizzazione nelle elezioni in Argentina (1983–1989)," *Quaderni dell' Observatorio Elettorale* (Florence) 26 (July–December 1991): 7–52.

Fernández Rubio, Delia, and Mato Goretti. "El gobierno por decreto en la Argentina." *El Derecho* 32, no. 8525 (June 27, 1994).

Gerchunoff, Pablo, and José L. Machinea. "Un ensayo sobre la política económica después de la estabilización." In *Mas allá de la estabilidad: Argentina en la epoca de la globalización y la regionalización*, comp. Pablo Bustos, 29–92. Buenos Aires: Fundación Ebert, 1995.

Halperín Donghi, Tulio. *La larga agonía de la Argentina peronista.* Buenos Aires: Espasa Calpe/Ariel, 1994.

Lauda, Martín. "La Campaña electoral en América Latina: Propaganda, período, prohibiciones." Working Paper No. 17. University of Heidelberg, 1994.

Machinea, J. L. "Stabilization under the Alfonsín Government: A Frustrated Attempt." Centro de Estudios de Estado y Sociedad (CEDES) Document No. 42. Buenos Aires: CEDES, 1990.

Minujin, Alberto, and Gabriel Kessler. *La nueva pobreza en Argentina.* Buenos Aires: Editorial Planeta, 1995.

Nohlen, Dieter, and Liliana De Riz. *Reforma institucional y cambio político.* Buenos Aires: Legasa, 1991.

Sabsay, Daniel, and José M. Onaindia. *La Constitución de los Argentinos.* Buenos Aires: Errepar, 1994.

Torre, Juan C., and Liliana De Riz. "Argentina since 1946." In *The Cambridge History of Latin America: 1930 to the Present*, ed. Leslie Bethell, 73–194. New York: Cambridge University Press, 1991.

8

Refurbishing the Argentine Judiciary

A Still-Neglected Theme

Emilio Jorge Cárdenas

An adequate judiciary is fundamental not only to the proper working of any government but also for the survival and consolidation of democracy. Further, it is essential to achieve a basic level of legal security, both in connection with the citizen's individual relations with the public sector and with respect of the need to guarantee that the sanctity of private contracts and transactions will always be safeguarded. The absence of public justice leads to the absence of private justice. In fact, an independent and effective judiciary is truly a prerequisite for democracy.

It is sometimes relatively easy to achieve modernizing changes, including legal ones, but it seems difficult to develop a truly independent and effective judiciary. Neverthless, it must be done. Antiquated judiciaries, like the Argentine one, become incapable of making the law effective. Sooner or later, they stall economic growth. There is no doubt that investors do take into account the quality of the judiciary when considering where they may decide to risk their money. They certainly should.

Of all the neglected themes of the recent years of Argentina's deep and rapid transformation, the need to refurbish the judiciary is probably the most important one. It is, in fact, a key factor in the urgent need to complete the reconstruction of the Argentine government. As Felipe A. M. de la Balze has recently pointed out, "Growth fundamentally depends on private initiative, entrepreneurial creativity and innovation, and the ability, training, and motivation of a country's people. Nevertheless, a well-organized government is a necessary condition for accelerated growth."[1] This last includes, naturally, a competent judiciary.

Up to now, Argentina has never been able to organize a good professional civil service. In fact, the staff of its fragile public institutions, including the judiciary, has, over the years, deteriorated in terms of its quality. The ongoing shake-up of all public structures (after Argentina decided to both break the historical deadlock in which the country had been caught and reinsert itself into the international arena) gives Argentina a historic opportunity to undertake a complete reform of its judiciary from the bottom up. This must be understood as an integral part of present efforts to return to the developmental path that Argentina strayed from in the 1940s.

The Constitutional Framework

Argentina has a federal judiciary headed by a federal supreme court whose nine members are appointed for lifetime tenure. They are chosen and appointed by the president and subject to confirmation by the Senate. All other federal judges will now also be appointed by the president in a public session, at the proposal of the new Magistrates' Court. Appointments will be made taking into account the professional qualifications of the individual candidates. This appointive system is the prevalent one in the provinces.

The Supreme Court, it must be remembered, acts both as constitutional court and as the final court of appeals. Since 1992 an intermediate court of appeals, known as the Tribunal de Casación, has reduced the volume of the Supreme Court's difficult caseload. Since the enactment of the 1994 comprehensive amendment to the Argentine constitution, and specifically under its new Article 114, a special magistrates' council (Consejo de la Magistratura) is in charge of selecting and monitoring the behavior of federal judges and managing the judiciary, thus replacing the Supreme Court in this area. This is a major step in the direction of consolidating both the federal judiciary's independence and providing a fair degree of transparency in the selection process.[2] Judges will now have to be appointed through a process that is both public and competitive.

This council—the structure and operation of which has still to be regulated by law—will also be in charge of monitoring and responding to allegations against unfit federal judges, and, eventually, of undertaking disciplinary action against them when required. To remove such judges, if and when the council decides to start the pertinent procedures, a special ad hoc jury is to be organized. Both the Magistrates' Council and the juries that may eventually be required will be jointly governed by a diversified group of officers of the executive power, legislators, judges, and practicing lawyers.

While we wait for the regulations necessary to put this mechanism into motion, we must remember a fundamental issue. The impeachment and, even more, the removal of judges from office must remain a difficult task. The removal procedures must be used only in connection with serious breaches of conduct and to preserve the necessary independence of federal judges, protecting them against undue harassment. Independence, however, must mean not only that the judiciary is free from influence by the other powers of government but also that it is beyond the direct influence of popular majorities. As in the United States, judges are protected against financial coercion from other branches of the government; the constitution states that they shall be remunerated with a compensation that shall not be diminished during their continuance in office. In fact, this particular guarantee is intended to free judges from even the fear of retaliation for their decisions.

Argentina also has individual provincial judiciaries. Under the federal constitution, all provincial governments must adopt the republican and representative structure and be structured following the traditional division of powers—between an executive, a legislative, and a judiciary branch. Each province's judiciary is, in fact, organized along lines similar to those of the national judiciary. Each is independent within its own jurisdiction, which may reach as far as the provincial legislatures. Final decisions rendered at a provincial level can be appealed to the federal Supreme Court if a matter of a federal nature is being discussed.

A Few Hard Facts

The public image of Argentina's judiciary is certainly not very bright. The general public believes that the judiciary is not only too slow but also too expensive. A recent poll indicated that 80 percent of those interviewed do not "believe in" the Argentine judiciary.[3] To many, the wheels of Argentina's justice are, at best, square wheels, and must be changed. Labor cases tend to last, on average, more than seven years per case before being decided by the court. In today's world, such a delay is unacceptable.

In fact, Argentine civil courts decide only 20 percent of the cases they receive every year, while the productivity of the commercial courts seems only a little better; they decide 50 percent of their caseload. Justice delayed, it must be recalled, is frequently justice denied. Furthermore, there is also a well-entrenched view that some in the judiciary are infected by a certain degree of corruption. There is no agreement or hard evidence about the extent of corruption within the Argentine judiciary, and thus any debate on the issue tends to be supported only by extremely subjective views or anecdote. But personal integrity is critical if the judiciary is to be able to carry out its responsibilities. Otherwise, justice and judgment lie a world apart.

According to a recent study,[4] Argentina has approximately thirty-one hundred judges, a figure that covers both federal and provincial positions and excludes only the so-called peace judges, who are in charge of very minor cases. These judges are assisted by the work of about fifty thousand officers and employees. In a country of roughly thirty-four million people, every year almost two million new cases reach the court systems, and the total operating cost of the federal and provincial judiciaries is U.S.$1.7 billion, equivalent to 0.65 percent of Argentina's GNP. The ratio between expenses devoted to the federal judiciary and the aggregate expenses of the federal administration recently has been improving with an increase in proportionate spending. In 1983, judicial expenses were 0.8 percent of aggregate public expenses; in 1994 they were approximately 3.2 percent.

Litigation is significantly less common in Argentina than in other countries. Argentines in fact file only one-third the number of cases that are litigated in the United States, and 50 percent of the number that normally go to court in the "mother country," Spain. Having said this, if one compares the budgets of those three countries, one finds that Argentina spends twice the amount of money per case spent in the United States and two and one-half times the amount spent in Spain.

On the other hand, Argentina's judiciary operates with twice the personnel of the Spanish or U.S. system. This is a serious problem. For each federal judge the system has almost twenty-six court officers and employees. In fact, the particular ratio at the Supreme Court level is even higher: one justice for 142 officers and employees. This situation appears to be somewhat better at the various provincial levels, since for each provincial judge there are, on average, only about fifteen officers and employees. Money spent in personnel, when calculated on a "per judge" basis, is roughly U.S.$500,000 per year. It can, therefore, be preliminarily concluded that Argentina's problems seem to derive not necessarily from a lack of funding but instead from questions of efficiency and productivity.

Argentine judges have not, up to now, been selected predominantly on the basis of their professional qualifications. No process fine-tuned to carefully scrutinize legal abilities has ever been in place. Instead, political affiliation still seems to play the major role. That is another serious problem, because the real independence of the federal judiciary is critical to Argentina's constitutional structure.

Independence is the only tool capable of insulating judges from improper pressures in the discharge of their duties. When, on August 18, 1995 (the date on which the Magistrates' Council became operative), the completion of a rushed appointment of thirty-six judges was published in the *Official Bulletin*, the cause of independence was again materially damaged.

Being a good judge is quite a difficult matter. Judges might, it has been argued, be divided into four categories: a) judges with neither head nor heart—they must always be avoided; b) judges with head but no heart—they are almost as bad as the former; c) judges with heart but no head—these are ordinary, likable people with little talent. No system can entirely avoid them, but one should not have too many of them. They are always risky although preferable to the prior two groups; and d) judges possessing both head and heart, who are definitely rare—they are the ideal judges.

The performance of Argentine judges is not subject to periodical reviews and assessments to grade their quality or to determine their professional ability. Other countries, like France or Germany, do assess the performance of their judges annually. Judicial independence cannot be interpreted as meaning that judges are completely free from scrutiny. At stake is nothing less than ensuring judicial accountability. Nevertheless, one should not act in haste, and one must keep in mind that reform in this particular field should be cautious, since otherwise instruments designed to guarantee the judges' responsibility could be abused and used against their independence. A delicate balance must be found.

The public must also be educated, as "consumers" of judicial services, about the complaint procedures that have been structured into law and are at everyone's disposal. Also, Argentina's judges should be required to attend "refresher" courses or undertake graduate training. Such courses are important not only to improve their professional skills but also to focus on ethical issues and judicial temperament. The judiciary must be aware of the needs of litigants and attorneys, to be able to react in an effective and sensitive manner to them.

It must be noted that the salary levels prevailing in the Argentine judiciary, which traditionally were below those of other countries, are no longer substantially different from the ones prevailing in countries such as Spain or the United States. Unfortunately, the Argentine judiciary's "devotion" to work—when compared with the number of days effectively put in by other public servants or the private sector—is not good. Judges average only 132 days per year, while the public sector aggregate average is 164 days and the private sector is 231 days. In other words, it can be argued that the Argentine judiciary works only 57 percent of the days worked by the private sector and 80 percent of the days worked by the public sector as a whole. The reasons for this discrepancy seem to be shorter daily working hours and excessively lenient working regulations, allowing too many days free.

Judges in Argentina must consider their work a full-time job. Nevertheless, they are specifically authorized by law to teach and to perform related academic duties. There apparently have been some abuses in this connection, and a close look must be taken into this matter to determine whether corrective action should be undertaken. All other "side work" is definitely not allowed.

The Need for Action

There is no doubt that the time has now come to remedy the present situation. There is really not much room for trying only to patch up the present structure. The need is for an "integral" plan capable of delivering a modern system to a country that badly needs it. Such an approach will necessarily take some time and require both talent and resources. It must, unavoidably, start with trying to determine where, in fact, we are at present.

The urgency to restructure and modernize the Argentine judiciary goes deep into the heart of society. What Alexis de Tocqueville once stated about America is also applicable to countries like Argentina that have a similar constitutional structure: "The peace, the prosperity and the very existence of the Union are vested in the hands of the federal judges. Without them, the Constitution would be a dead letter."[5]

Modern conditions of liberty can be based only on an efficient and carefully structured judiciary. People cannot perceive impunity as being a normal and acceptable condition. The need to ensure virtuous government cannot be based on heroic individuals or civic discipline. It must, instead, be structured on a system containing all the proper checks and balances. Only through it can the rights of all be guaranteed and freedom be protected, minimizing governmental coercion. But also only through democratic autonomy, a political order marked by respect for authority and law, can it be sustained.

The federal Ministry of Justice has already developed a comprehensive strategy that has been designated "judicial reordering." The following are its main components:

1. A "mediation" and conciliation alternative is to be organized. The ministry would like to make mediation and conciliation mandatory, for a short period of time, prior to allowing any formal

lawsuit to begin. This particular "filter" suggestion—because of its mandatory nature—has already raised some opposition from the local bar association. It is true that other alternatives, like arbitration, are available and could also be promoted, but they could take years to implement and gain the necessary public support. Prompt action is imperative.

2. All matters that are not controversial and that are today handled through the judiciary such as "estate procedures" in which there are no contested issues could, in the short term, end up being handled out of court, through the good offices of Argentine notaries public, an institution based on its Continental equivalent.

3. A substantial procedural reform is to be undertaken that would focus on simplifying both discovery and the filing and production of evidence and considerably reducing the length of time during which evidence may be produced.[6]

4. All experts acting in court are to be paid fixed fees. The present system is based instead on the amount involved in the respective transaction, and it can, therefore, easily become exorbitant.

5. Malicious lawsuits, in the future, will generate fines to be paid by the lawyers representing the party whose behavior is determined to be malicious.

6. The presently abused possibility of litigating *in forma pauperis* will be reduced. Only exceptional situations will be allowed to enjoy such an advantageous position, which frees the beneficiary from normal court expenses. Today, judges are extremely generous in granting such a privilege, thus allowing the promotion of many lawsuits that otherwise would simply not be heard.

7. The payment of the tax charged by the state in every lawsuit is very frequently delayed for long periods of time. The ministry's proposal is to police its payment strictly, so that such delays are avoided.

8. Every debtor who is being sued for lack of payment of a debt, will, in the future, be registered in a special registry, which will be open to the public. It is hoped that all lenders or counterparts in a transaction will have a fair chance to determine whether the party with whom they are about to close a deal has an impeccable credit record.

9. Every worker who collects an indemnification related to a working accident or to a disability caused by his work may have to be registered in an ad hoc special registry, the purpose of which is to try to avoid the "industry" generated by workers (and their lawyers) who "shop around" various jobs with the main purpose

of suing their employers and collecting indemnities, again and again, for faked "accidents" or disabilities.

10. The ministry further proposes that authorization be given to the judges to order the immediate restitution to the corresponding owners of all real estate that becomes the object of litigation. It is a present practice that, for example, leasees will try to stay in the property they occupy while being sued by lessors for lack of payment of the rent or for other contractual defaults.

11. Another proposal involves the reordering of the present system through which property—in particular, real estate—is auctioned as a result of court orders. The present situation is that a "league" frequently operates in such auctions, distorting market prices.

12. The world of checks will, in this context, be reregulated. An increase of the penalty applicable to those who do not, when requested, cover the checks they issue is being considered. It will include possible fines. In this particular connection, negligence will cease to be an excuse, justification, or even an extenuating circumstance for nonperformance regarding the issuance of checks. Penalties for uncovered checks will be extended to reach the corporations represented by whoever may have signed an unpaid check. Finally, all penalties according to issuers of uncovered checks will be waived, should the debtor cover the check a short period after the corresponding collection request is filed in court.

13. If the proposals by the Ministry of Justice are accepted, the workload of courts will become more subject-oriented, thus specializing its activity and personnel as much as possible. It is expected that this will expedite the performance of the courts' duties. The ministry is trying to cope with a situation in which, today, the size of courts' workloads raises serious questions about their overall efficiency and effectiveness.

14. Judicial infrastructure and related facilities will also be improved. In fact, one of the projects presently under consideration is a very ambitious one, since it involves calling for bids for the construction of an entire new "judicial city."

15. Peripheral privatization of various services is also being considered and proposed. Filing, communications, computer processing, and information services could all be contracted out with the private sector. These proposed moves will save money and mean greater efficiency.

16. The ministry also suggests resorting to retired magistrates—on a onetime-call basis and during a single year only—to try to help

the acting judges to bring down their present workload. This program envisages an across-the-board action, covering the whole federal court system and that of the city of Buenos Aires.

Those are the principal proposals that have been put forward by the Ministry of Justice to date. They are definitely interesting. One can certainly argue in favor or against some or all of them. The real problem however, from the point of view of action required to improve the present judiciary, is that the proposals by the Ministry of Justice do seem to be some kind of a mosaic. They should, instead, be part of a medium-term master plan.

There is a lot that can and must be done rapidly, such as carefully regulating the judicial selection mechanism derived from the 1994 constitutional amendment. A high-level and independent task force appointed to deal with the issue could guarantee that, while ongoing urgencies are taken care of, a more healthy and integral medium-term plan can be shaped.[7] Matters such as reviewing all procedural codes in operation, or drafting a code of judicial conduct (which Argentine judges do not have), for example, may not look urgent, but they must be dealt with as we move forward with the reshaping of the judiciary. Judges must not only comply with ethical standards, but they should also participate in defining, drafting, and enforcing them. A task force structure could allow them to be involved in the related work. The effort to rebuild the Argentine judiciary is an imperative of modernism. It is also connected to the important task of institution-building. That is not to be forgotten, because only when the main constitutional institutions of a country have gained widespread popular support is that country's long-term stability guaranteed.

Notes

1. Felipe A. M. de la Balze, "Mora y aruajo, noguera y asociados," *La Nación*, August 11, 1993.

2. Santiago H. Corcueva, "Consejo de la Magistratura," *La Ley*, July 17, 1995; Nestor Baraglio, "Consejo de la Magistratura," *El Derecho* 8806 (August 4, 1995): 1; Rafael Bielsa and Luis Lozano, "Quién controlará al Consejo de la Magistratura?" *Clarín*, November 24, 1995; Eduardo D. Craviotto, "El Consejo de la Magistratura. Consecuencia de la crisis de la Administración de Justicia?" *La Ley*, February 13, 1995.

3. Felipe A. M. de la Balze, "Remaking the Argentine Economy" (New York: Council of Foreign Relations Press, 1994), 14.

4. Asociación de Bancos Argentinos (ADEBA), "La reforma del poder judicial en Argentina," *Trabajo de investigación de la Fundación de Investigaciones Económicas Latinoamericanas (FIEL)*, (Buenos Aires: ADEBA, 1994).

5. Alexis de Tocqueville, *De la démocracie en Amérique* (Paris, 1888), 1:171 et seq.

6. Articles 14, 15, 17, 19, 20, 22, 24, 26, 27, 28, 34, 36, 45, 80, 81, 84, 142, 143, 144, 163, 310, 315, 316, 398, 410, 429, 460, 525, 528, 551, 571, 572, 594, 598, 680, and 684 will eventually be subject to amendments in a comprehensive, but still partial, procedural reform.

7. See Enrique V. del Carril, "Reforma Judicial. Decisión política demorada," *La Ley*, November 9, 1993; and Horacio M. Lynch and Enrique V. del Carril, "La Justicia. Un plan integral de reforma al sistema judicial argentino" (Buenos Aires: Fundación Banco de Boston, 1992).

9

Continuity and Change in Argentine Foreign Policy

*Joseph S. Tulchin**

When Raul Alfonsín became president of Argentina in 1983, the central issue as far as foreign policy was concerned was the reinsertion of the country into the international arena. In the forty years since World War II, Argentina had suffered a severe identity crisis. It had not demonstrated any self-confidence in its role in international affairs and had changed foreign policies and its posture on international issues more frequently than Diego Maradona scored goals. The country reached bottom after the Malvinas War, when it had been converted into a pariah state, frustrated in its principal objectives, alienated from its traditional allies, enmeshed in quarrels and disputes with its neighbors, bereft of logical and loyal friends, and demonstrably uncomprehending of the world around it.[1]

Argentina's every move in international affairs in the years before 1983 seemed clumsy and confused. Rhetoric and action often seemed in conflict. Was Argentina a country that defended Western and Christian values, or was it the country in which the human rights of its citizens were most at risk? Was it a country closely tied to the United States, helping it in the semiclandestine struggle in Central America, or a nonaligned nation and the country, after Cuba, with the largest commerce with the Soviet Union? Was it a country of pacifist principles or an aggressor ready to go to war with its neighbors or with European powers to settle territorial disputes that were not resolved in its favor? Was it all of these? None? How was the nation going to define itself before the rest of the world?

*I want to thank Alberto Föhrig for his incisive and constructive comments on this paper. His advice was extremely helpful to me in understanding the evolution of Argentine policy under Alfonsín.

The reinsertion of Argentina into world affairs was a vital facet of the nation's transition to democracy and a central element in its quest for modernization. Foreign policy became a key element in the nation's redefinition of itself. Since the return of democracy in 1983, for the first time in the nation's history there has been an intense public debate over the nature of foreign policy as well as over the correct foreign policy line for the country. Several research centers have devoted at least part of their energies to the analysis of the nation's international affairs, and several new ones were created for that purpose. Questions concerning foreign policy were added to the regular public opinion polls. In the decade after the Malvinas War, there were frequent expressions of the idea that the country had come through a bad time, that it had been a failure, that it had not been what its leaders had claimed, that it had lost its way. Running through the discussion was the admonition that it was time for the country to get its collective act together, to reform, to put a stop to the period of frustration and disappointment by dealing with the world and with itself in a more realistic fashion. In that way, in the decade and more since 1983, the discussion of foreign policy has come to identify "correct policy" with policies that are realistic and appropriate to the world as it is, not as Argentine leaders might wish it to be. Foreign policy has come to be understood as a reflection of how the nation sees itself and how it wishes to be seen, as well as an instrument for national development.

It is in this sense—foreign policy as a form of self-definition—that I propose to evaluate the experience of the Alfonsín and Menem governments in international affairs. My central concern will be to distinguish between conjunctural or ephemeral features and persistent or enduring features of foreign policy. What is new about Argentine foreign policy in its reinsertion into world affairs, and what is familiar or rooted deeply in the nation's past?

The democratic government led by President Raúl Alfonsín came to power in 1983 with a very positive public image and was welcomed with enthusiasm by the rest of the nations in the hemisphere and the entire international community. It was as if the transition to democracy in Argentina was a case freighted with special significance. As a result, the Alfonsín government, and Alfonsín personally, enjoyed privileged international status. This status created political space for the regime within which it could operate to establish its new image, and it accorded the country a sort of reserve credit of influence in the international arena. At the beginning of its mandate, the government had the luxury of formulating its international policies without strong inhibiting pressures. But, like a political honeymoon for a new administration in domestic politics, the international space proved to be ephemeral. By the end of Alfonsín's term, it was not clear what role he hoped the new Argentina would play, or if the role he seemed to have chosen was realistic. How could the nation achieve a "mature" relationship with the United States while remaining a nonaligned country? How could it lead the move for disarmament while maintaining its own missile and nuclear programs? How would it resolve the touchy issue of sovereignty of the Malvinas Islands if it remained obdurate on the terms of negotiation?

After 1989, the government of Carlos Saúl Menem attempted to distance itself from its predecessor by insisting that the core of its foreign policy would be a new, friendly relationship with the United States. By implication, the Menem administration was critical of the Alfonsín government, suggesting that it had engaged in unnecessary confrontations with the United States and with other powers to the detriment of the nation's economic well-being. Not surprisingly, members of the Alfonsín administration and its friends have sallied forth to defend themselves and to criticize Menem's policy as unnecessarily abject in its subservience to the United States.[2]

Even though the repeated, often extravagant, insistence on following the U.S. lead was given great prominence—Foreign Minister Guido DiTella, in a fit of hyperbole he later regretted because it distracted attention from the serious purpose of his policy, once referred to them as *relaciones carnales*—Menem's foreign policy had other prominent features. Picking up on one of Alfonsín's early phrases, that Argentina was a developing nation with all of its attendant problems, Menem's foreign policy team argued that its policy would take the world as it was, not as the nation's historic pretensions might want it to be. To find the nation's appropriate place in the world while demonstrating its fealty to the United States, Argentina joined many peacekeeping missions sponsored by the United Nations and became one of the strongest proponents of making the Organization of American States an effective organization. By the end of Menem's first administration, it was clear that the multilateral card had become crucial to the strategy to redefine the nation's place in the world and to reestablish its influence among the world's players. And yet, by the end of the first Menem administration, there was disturbing evidence that the alliance with the United States had become yet one more way to establish Argentine exceptionalism in the hemisphere and that the historic drive to be in the lead remained powerful and in conflict with the new realism that tried to find a place for Argentina in the world commensurate with its relatively weak status.

While it is premature to offer a scholarly judgment of the first Menem government, enough time has passed so that it is possible to compare it to its predecessor and to evaluate both democratic governments in terms of

Argentina's long-term foreign policy tendencies and in terms of their differences from the nondemocratic regimes that ruled the country prior to
1983. Seen in that perspective, there are some curious continuities between the democratic governments—continuities that help to explain the
differences between them—and between them and the military regime
that preceded them. Of course, there are fundamental differences between
the Alfonsín and Menem foreign policies, and important differences between the democratic governments and the nondemocratic governments.
Regime type, as Roberto Russell argues elsewhere, does make a difference. The question is, What kind of difference does it make?[3]

My purpose is to suggest that, despite the differences, the continuities across administrations and even across regime changes indicate profound tendencies within Argentine foreign policy that appear to be part of
the nation's collective sense of self, elements of the nation's political culture. They represent the foreign policy expressions of the nation's image
of itself. The purpose of this essay is to explore the ways in which the
Alfonsín and Menem governments have expressed these tendencies, and
how, in turn, these elements of Argentine political culture help to define
the limits within which policy is formulated, and how they affect the evolution of a democratic society.

The Alfonsín government had some important successes and was able
to reestablish a constructive international position for the nation. On the
other hand, there were instances in which the government was unable to
accomplish its goals, and others in which the policies of the government
were not in keeping with its stated ethical and moral values. More seriously, on more than one occasion the government, consciously or un-
consciously, imitated the military government it had succeeded, a
government that had showed itself to be ignorant of the world, irresponsible in its behavior, and insensitive to the international consequences of
its actions.

How can we explain this contradictory record by a government that
insisted so often and justifiably on the moral and ethical differences that
separated it from its predecessors? How can we account for the series of
confrontations that characterized the first three years of the administration and the string of frustrating failures in the achievement of its goals?
My view is that the contradictions in Argentine foreign policy are part of
the century-old Argentine legacy of confrontation with the United States,
a tradition that attributes to Argentina significant status in world affairs
in spite of or in defiance of the United States, a position based on the
significance of Argentine exports in the global market and the fabled success of the Argentine development model and its corollary insertion of
the nation into world affairs. This tradition may no longer reflect reality,

but it continues to influence the view of the world held by many Argentines and their leaders. I am speaking of the tradition of the exceptional country, the country exempt from the consequences of its international actions when those actions are not linked directly to the fundamental purpose of its insertion into the world system.

In official thinking from 1880 to World War I, there was a presumed separation between internal and external events, except in one single field or subject, the maximization of the sale of the nation's primary products for the best possible price and the consolidation of the nation's greatness that its insertion anticipated. Across the years, government after government assumed that if the matter at hand did not deal with this issue, it was not vital to the national interest and, therefore, whatever consequences might accrue would not be of material significance to the nation. It would appear from actions by the Alfonsín and Menem administrations that, despite radical changes in the nation's development model and the nation's move into the world arena, this tradition continues to exercise influence over those who formulate the foreign policy of Argentina and to affect the definition of the nation's reinsertion into the world system. More specifically, one dimension of this tradition, relations with the United States, is the key to understanding the apparent contradictions in the foreign policy of the Alfonsín government, as well as the efforts of the Menem administration to correct them. As the Alfonsín government sought to distance itself from the United States, to show itself independent and autonomous, the Menem government has attempted the reverse: to show itself in league with the United States, its fate linked to that of the United States. In its rhetoric and in many of its objectives, the Alfonsín government seems to have been trapped within the tradition of exceptionalism. The Menem government rejected that rhetoric and those objectives for the precise reason that they were unrealistic and inappropriate. Yet in its cavalier style and insistence on being in the lead, even as it acts multilaterally, it appears to be expressing the same tradition. The question is whether democratic Argentina can break with this tradition to carve out a more modest position for itself in the modern world community.

In the nineteenth century, the Argentine insertion in the world was defined without reference to the United States or, even, in spite of the United States. The central element of the nation's emergence into world affairs was the economic ties to those nations that purchased Argentine products. Export markets were the key to Argentine well-being, and the United States simply was not a major player. Relations between the two countries were characterized over the years by mutual incomprehension, a high degree of tension, and severe asymmetry of interests and priorities. This traditional policy, perfectly valid at its formulation at the end of the nineteenth century, distorted and complicated the reinsertion of the nation into the world system following the disaster of the Malvinas War. Whether it wished it to be so or not, the Alfonsín government could not successfully reinsert the nation into the world arena without previously or simultaneously defining its relations with the United States. The lack of resolution in its relations with the United States slowed the evolution of a new international role for the nation during the Alfonsín administration, although enormous progress was made.

In fairness, it should be pointed out that given its obsession with Central America and with Irangate, the United States was not a useful partner for Argentina during this difficult transition stage. The Menem policy of slavishly following the United States is not sustainable either, because the United States simply refuses to pay enough attention to Argentina to justify the policy over the long term. Unless and until Argentina can come to terms with the United States in a stable and sustainable relationship, its foreign policy will continue to be characterized by contradictions, a confrontational tone in the face of minor crises, an idealism that is not congruent with other aspects of the international comportment of the nation, and an exaggerated tendency to protagonize issues, to seek a high profile on the world stage that undermines its relations with its peers and neighbors.

The position of defiance toward the United States that Roque Saenz Peña and Manuel Quintana took at the first Pan American Conference in Washington in 1888–89 was a coherent expression of the Argentine insertion into world affairs at the time. Argentine national interest was defined by concentration on commercial links with its primary markets in Europe, the maximization of its exports, and their sale at the best possible price— together with maintaining an open door to the foreign capital necessary to finance the nation's growth. Economic orthodoxy at the time sanctified this international division of labor, which seemed to be a perfectly realistic reflection of Argentina's position in world affairs. Such an insertion into the world suggested closer relations with the nations of Europe than with the United States, which appeared to produce many of the same things produced in Argentina. At the same time, it was a position that carried few, if any, risks. While the United States, by that time, already was an established industrial power, its military capacity was unproved and its influence over the international market was far from dominant. The fact that there were other nations in the hemisphere that looked askance at U.S. pretensions in the region only buttressed the Argentine position.

Scarcely twenty-five years later, the Argentine insertion into world affairs was unsettled by events suggesting that its relations with the United States were in the process of fundamental change, whether Argentina welcomed that change or not. The Argentine position of neutrality in World War I, completely consistent with its foreign policy principles and protective of its national interests, was called into question once the United States entered the war. There even had been hints earlier that the Argentine position in world affairs, based upon total and faithful adherence to the concept of an international division of labor, was threatened by the geopolitical considerations of the belligerents. Right after the outbreak of war, the British had refused to ship coal to Argentina, even though such action was painfully prejudicial to Argentine well-being.[4]

The situation became more complicated after the United States declared war on the Central Powers. President Woodrow Wilson assumed the leadership of the Western Hemisphere and called on the other nations of the region to join with him and with the United States in the defense of democracy. Now the maintenance of neutrality had a very different meaning than it had had previously. The Argentines responded to the Wilsonian invitation with an invitation of their own to the nations of the hemisphere to attend a meeting in Buenos Aires to study the question of neutrality in the hemisphere. The official explanation was President Hipólito Yrigoyen's high moral approach to international affairs. But Yrigoyen enjoyed tweaking Uncle Sam's nose, and the fact that only Mexico chose to attend made the challenge to Yankee hegemony—and its feebleness—quite clear. The consequences of independent action, of open defiance of the United States in the international forum, had changed dramatically since 1889, but the Argentine government appeared unaware of the changes.

The fact that Argentina was not invited to the Peace Conference in Paris following the war was a surprise and a source of irritation to the Argentine government. They considered it their due, not only for the importance of their foodstuffs in the world, but also because of the weight their ethical posture during the war should exercise in forging the peace. None of the allies was convinced. On the contrary, Argentine behavior, especially its precipitous withdrawal from the first session of the League of Nation's assembly, only convinced the nations of Europe that Argentina was an irresponsible actor in world affairs. The potential role that Yrigoyen wished to play, of a moral leader, had no impact; not because his position was not moral but because his policy had no influence over other nations in the world. In attempting to reform the League, Argentina consulted with no one, tried to convince no one. It merely threw its cards on the table and left the game. There was an assumption underlying these gestures that because of its foodstuffs Argentina was a significant player on the world stage and that its principled posture enhanced its significance and its prestige in the world forum to the extent that the major powers would listen to Argentina. That simply was not the case.

If World War I was a warning bell that Argentina's initial insertion into world affairs was threatened, the Great Depression was clear proof that the international division of labor was no longer what it had been. From the Argentine perspective, the worst consequence of these events was that the nations of Western Europe, especially Great Britain, lost power and influence, while the United States increased its power on the world stage. At the same time, Argentina's influence in Great Britain declined dramatically, leading to the humiliation of the Roca-Runciman Pact as a result of changes in the Commonwealth. The continued independence of action in foreign affairs, based on the presumption of Argentine importance in European and world trade, was bound to create tension in relations with the United States and might logically be expected to create moments of confrontation. Thus it was almost inevitable that during the 1930s, a Wilson-like secretary of state, Cordell Hull, with the conviction that his views of the world were moral, correct, and universal, would look upon differences with him and with U.S. policy as serious lapses and a perverse opposition to truth. In such a situation, Argentine neutrality in World War II was seen in Washington as nothing short of the work of the devil. That the United States did not directly attack and subjugate Argentina to its will during the war was the result almost entirely of British influence and to the relative insignificance of Argentina, but it was taken by some in Buenos Aires as renewed proof of Argentina's significance. After the war, British influence over the United States diminished sensibly and its position in the world economy deteriorated to the point that it was no longer able to serve as a buffer between the United States and Argentina.

In the years following World War II, Argentine foreign policy gyrated between open defiance of the United States and ambiguous friendship. These shifts were made more as a function of internal political struggles and internal instability than as the expression of a coherent vision of the world and a rational analysis of world affairs. Each posture was intended to enhance the nation's prestige. There did not exist a general consensus behind the policy, and each major initiative or shift was the cause of a bitter and divisive debate. This confusion reached its most extreme point during the military governments following the *golpe* of 1976. Those who formulated and executed foreign policy during those years had lost the capacity to perceive reality in the international arena or to analyze the consequences of their actions in the international context.

The culmination of this Alice in Wonderland mentality was the decision to invade the Malvinas. It was based on a porous foundation of myths.

In retrospect, the assumptions upon which the decision to invade the islands was based read like a list of nostalgic yearnings rather than the calculations of rational leaders. Listing them suggests just how out of date those assumptions had become and how far out of sync with the rest of the world the Argentine leadership was:

— the belief that their old natural ally, Great Britain, would not take amiss the invasion of the islands;
— the belief that the European nations would consider Argentina one of them;
— the belief that the government of the United States would treat Argentina on a par with Great Britain, given the support Argentina was providing in the conflict in Central America, thereby pardoning and forgiving all of the historical difficulties that had come between them;
— the belief that Argentina was a leader among the Latin American nations and that the other nations in the region would support Argentina in its anti-imperialist crusade;
— the belief that, in any dispute, a democratic government and a non-democratic government were essentially the same in the eyes of third parties.

The Argentine leaders lived in a world of dreams constructed over the course of a century by distorted perceptions of the world around them and by a tradition of acting without taking account of the possible consequences of their actions, convinced that their importance in the scheme of things, measured by the export of their foodstuffs and not by other measures of power then in use by nations around the world, would protect them from harm, and that their human rights atrocities would not be held against them. In the case of the war in the Malvinas, the results of their misperceptions were tragic. The soldiers who fought on the islands or who went to the bottom with the *General Belgrano* paid the consequences of that foreign policy action with their lives. The question is whether any of these myths continued to adhere to Argentine foreign policy after the transition to democracy, and how they affect the continuing effort to consolidate the nation's democratic government.

The challenge for the democratic government of Raúl Alfonsín in 1983 was to define a new role for Argentina in the international system. The old role no longer served a useful purpose. To do so, as both the president and foreign minister Dante Caputo stated publicly, it was necessary for the country to define its purpose. To declare that it is a democratic country was a first step, but that was not sufficient in and of itself. Political instability and economic stagnation continued to be serious obstacles. The linkages between internal cleavages and international behavior continued to create painful difficulties. And, finally, the outside world itself was a major factor in the process—how others saw Argentina was an important factor in the creation of a national image. Good intentions are not always enough. These are the givens with which the new democratic government had to begin. What was the Alfonsín administration's record in the field of foreign policy, and how does it compare with that of Menem?

From the first moment, in his inaugural address, to the inglorious close of his administration, President Alfonsín maintained the same priorities in foreign affairs. He declared unequivocally that Argentina was a Western nation, nonaligned and developing. By this he meant that the nation was historically, culturally, and politically associated with the countries of the West, but that it was not going to form part of any military bloc. He added that the posture of the nonaligned was not or should not be passive. They would be affected as much as the members of the military blocs by a nuclear war or any conflict between the great powers. Therefore the nonaligned nations had the right to fight for disarmament and the denuclearization of the world.[5]

The phrase "developing nation" signified two important things. In saying it, the president recognized the nation's economic reality. Whatever the potential of the country might have been at some point in the past, it was necessary to recognize its present reality: vulnerable, weak, insecure, and of no particular strategic importance to any other nation or group of nations. There are those who call themselves realists and who insist that Argentina is a poor country, a Third World nation, and that it should behave as such.[6] Alfonsín did not want to identify Argentina in quite so harsh a fashion. He believed that to admit publicly that the country was not yet developed was a sufficient dose of cold water. Even in opposition, he remained harshly critical of these so-called realists and hewed to the line he had spelled out during his presidency.[7]

The second significance of the phrase "developing nation" was political. With it, Alfonsín intended to link Argentina with the group of nations in the Southern Hemisphere, which implied an actual or potential opposition to the countries of the Northern Hemisphere. As such it was a powerful rejection of the nation's traditional posture of standing apart from Latin America as a self-styled "superior, European" nation. On the other hand, it served to push Argentina into a position of leadership in the region, taking full advantage of the special space accorded Alfonsín as the restorer of his nation's democracy.

The principal goal of the new government was to maximize the autonomy of the nation in its project of reinsertion into world affairs. To achieve that goal, Alfonsín maintained contacts with as many states as possible, to broaden the nation's linkages with the world and to facilitate cooperation among the nations of Latin America. Minister Caputo realized that these measures might create tension with the United States. Using the same argument they had in discussing Argentina's potential role in the arms race, Alfonsín and Caputo insisted that Argentina, along with the other nations of Latin America, had the right and perhaps the duty to take part in the quest for peace in the hemisphere because conflicts are going to affect all the nations in the region. With this argument, the Argentine government, always in conjunction with other governments, supported efforts to resolve Central American conflicts, sometimes in very public opposition to the United States.[8]

On the face of it, the foreign policy of the new administration didn't appear confrontational or unrealistic. There were, however, certain echoes of the past that require comment. In his inaugural address, Alfonsín reiterated some Yrigoyenist refrains of international moralism. Three years later, in his lecture at the Universidad de Buenos Aires, Caputo declared that Argentina supported ethical values in its foreign policy. Although his policy is pragmatic, he said, "it is realistic to support principle and the moral position. Ethics, morals, principles, have practical force." Later, he mixed morality with a touch of realpolitik: "I believe that a country like ours that is never going to be a military power, nor wishes to be a military power, which has a long way to go before it is even an economic power, can be a moral power." While Caputo emphasized his government's concern for moral values mainly to distinguish it from its predecessors, the issue remained a constant theme throughout the administration.[9]

What does it mean to be a "moral power"? The experience of Woodrow Wilson in the United States suggests that the international projection of trumpeted moral values is not always understood in the same manner by all the participants. Wilson showed that military power together with ethical fanaticism could be dangerous to the health, and that actions self-defined as moral could have consequences that were quite different from those anticipated. The history of Yrigoyen's foreign policy suggests that morality disconnected from power and exercised without concern for those acted upon is a romantic gesture, with little international impact, and, in certain circumstances, irresponsible and damaging to the nation's own interests. Perhaps what Caputo had in mind is that when a nation recognizes that it does not have sufficient military and economic power to exercise influence over other international actors, even if only to defend itself, then to define it as a moral power and to have others recognize it as such can give the country greater influence than it otherwise might have. In that case, the question becomes, Moral force for what purpose? Here Caputo was clear: Argentina would attempt to maximize its international autonomy and to reinsert itself into the world in such a manner as to favor its economic development and the well-being of its people. Its moral force would facilitate accomplishment of those goals. This was the platform on which Caputo ran for the presidency of the UN General Assembly, while his representatives to the same body were compiling a voting record of hostility to the United States exceeded only by Cuba, Yemen, North Korea, and Libya. Assuming Caputo knew how his ambassadors were voting, what did he expect to demonstrate by this peculiar voting pattern, and how was it congruent with his posture as a leader of a moral power?

When it assumed office in December 1983, the civilian government faced the central problem of the monstrous external debt and the economic stagnation that accompanied it. Assigned the task of dealing with the problem was an intimate friend of the president's, Bernardo Grinspun. A man of strong personality, never timid in expressing his opinions, Grinspun represented the international face of the new government, not by any conscious decision, but because of the press coverage he received in Europe and the United States.[10] Critics have argued that Grinspun was unnecessarily confrontational. Indeed, he was confrontational in his posture and truculent in his public statements, but the posture won space for the new government, both at home and abroad, and accomplished its purpose.

Grinspun, like the other members of the government, must have been aware of the deep and persistent public hostility to the United States, and of the intensity of the public support for his position. The first statement by the new minister was that the foreign debt inherited from the military government was monstrous and that the new government could not pay it—that the new civilian government certainly would not undermine democracy by exacting payment of the military's debt at the expense of the Argentine people. From the very start, the other participants in the international dialogue were patient in their dealings with the Argentines. Major figures in the banking world and public officials in the U. S. government visited Buenos Aires as if it were some sort of political mecca. All expressed their support for the new democracy; no one complained about the stance assumed by Grinspun. We know now that while the public declarations by Grinspun and others indicated that no progress was being made or would be made on the question, negotiations were going on behind the scenes paving the way for a settlement.

Grinspun knew that paying the debt was both economically and politically impossible in 1984, and, by making a public issue of it, he was able to take advantage of the situation to win greater support for the government on other issues then stirring acrimonious debate. Alfonsín was determined to bring the question of the pope's proposal concerning the Beagle Channel before the public at the earliest opportunity. Through public opinion polls conducted by his government, he knew that a majority of the public favored a peaceful and reasonable solution to this vexing problem. In his own mind, he was convinced that Argentina had to accept the pope's plan. But he also knew that the nationalists, civilian and military, were capable of undermining the most reasonable proposal by sticking an antinational label on the government. Such a label would make it impossible for him to govern and would ease the way for an alliance between the most reactionary elements among the labor unions and the military, who could join forces in destroying the nascent democracy. Grinspun's tactics protected Alfonsín's nationalist flank. Beyond the referendum over the Beagle itself, Alfonsín knew that his capacity to effect domestic reforms would be conditioned or constrained to a significant degree by specific international problems, such as the Beagle and the Malvinas. If they could not resolve those disputes, or at least make some progress toward a solution, the government would be held hostage by extremist groups no matter how small they might be. In this sense, Grinspun's policies were wonderfully apt for the domestic political situation in which the government began its term in office, even though his posturing was never a deliberate strategy by the government.[11]

Grinspun's policy had another virtue. It was a shrewd negotiating technique. In 1984, the creditor nations did not have a concerted policy on the debt. The major banks really feared that their clients, among them Argentina, were not going to repay their debts. During 1983 and 1984, the financial press spoke openly about the possible bankruptcy of some giant banks, and there were even persistent rumors of the collapse of the international banking system. Grinspun offered a solution to the impasse. Obviously, it was not an agreeable option for the banks, but it imposed upon them the necessity of coming to an agreement among themselves. Once the banks had come to an agreement, and once they had reached an understanding with the governments of the developed nations, it was necessary to change the Argentine position on the international debt question. The referendum on the Beagle was held in November. Alfonsín's visit to Washington was announced in January 1985, and Grinspun resigned in February. It was time for another policy, and for a less aggressive personality, one not committed to a heroic stance. His successors as spokesmen for the Argentine government in economic matters, Juan Sourrouille, Mario Brodersohn, and Adolfo Canitrot, were frank and direct, but never aggressive.[12]

In its relations with the United States, the new Argentine government was candid in recognizing the historical difficulties between the two countries. Caputo told reporters during a visit to the United States, "We share with the United States the values of individual liberty and social justice. On the other hand, Argentina is also a nonaligned nation and that is an area of discord. In addition, Argentina is a developing nation, not an industrialized one, and that is an area of conflict of interest."[13] One of the areas in which Argentina was willing to disagree publicly with the United States was the situation in Central America. From his very first conversation with President Reagan to his very last, Alfonsín did not let the opportunity go past without informing the North American leader that his policy in Nicaragua was an error. Caputo's public statements carried the same message.

It is important to note that these disagreements were markedly different from earlier episodes. There was nothing confrontational or quixotic about the manner in which they were expressed. Nor could they be called a romantic gesture or mere rhetoric. The words of the nation's leaders and their actions were congruent and realistic because they were acting in concert with the majority of the nations of the hemisphere, an association that strengthened other positions taken by the government in support of hemispheric cooperation, something that the previous Argentine posture of presumed leadership in the hemisphere never contemplated. The Argentine position was actually quite moderate and reasonable in the context of the debate over Central America. Far from advancing blind support for the Sandinistas simply to irritate the United States, the Argentines declared their support for pluralist democracy in Nicaragua and argued in favor of the participation of the democratic opposition in a clean and open contest for power. Further, their perspective on the conflict was not idiosyncratic. It was shared by the majority of nations in the hemisphere and in Europe. It was a position shared by many people in the U.S. government itself. In this case, it was the White House that had lost touch with reality, having become obsessed with its own perspective on events. The Argentine position served to remind those surrounding President Reagan that their vision was not shared, by friend or foe. It helped the evolution of the Reagan administration toward a policy of more consistent support for democracy in the hemisphere.[14] And, most important of all, given the long history of tension between the two nations and the residual suspicion of Argentine intentions in the State Department, Argentine officials went out of their way to keep open channels of communication with their counterparts in Washington. There is evidence that the Argentine position was received with equanimity in the State Department.[15]

It is worth repeating that the policy of Argentina in the Central American dispute was realistic and moderate, both in its analysis of the situation and in its diplomacy. Argentina never attempted to push its position on the United States by itself; it always acted in concert with other Latin American nations. This is important because, in the long run, the most significant foreign policy initiative of the Alfonsín government is likely to prove to have been the rapprochement with Brazil and Latin America. If the integration with Brazil goes forward, it will increase the autonomy of both nations more than any gesture or neutrality policy, no matter how ethical it might be. The Menem administration gave the integration policy a dramatic push by signing the Treaty of Asunción creating MERCOSUR. Effective identification as a Latin American nation may be the only way Argentina can reinsert itself into world affairs without first coming to terms with the United States. A cynic might point out that much has been written in the past about how cooperation among the Latin American nations is the most efficacious way to protect themselves against the imperialism or the hegemony of the United States—without having much to show for such efforts. It remains to be seen if this latest effort will be more than pious rhetoric.

In evaluating the foreign policy of the Alfonsín government, it should be pointed out that if economic integration with Brazil posed a challenge to the United States and the other industrialized nations, and thereby pandered to deep-seated urges within many Argentines, it was a good moment for such a move. Beginning in 1985, the Reagan administration had not had either the interest or the energy to pay much attention to bilateral cooperation between Brazil and Argentina, nor to consider how such cooperation might curtail U.S. influence in the hemisphere. In private, U.S. officials responsible for following the events were convinced that little would come of the integration effort. They admitted that even if there were much progress, their superiors would not pay any more attention than they were at the time—which was very little indeed.[16] This lack of attention—and the nations of Western Europe did not appear to be any more interested in what was going on in Latin America than was the United States—made it easier for Brazil and Argentina to advance their schemes for cooperation. During the Bush administration, the same situation held. Officials in the office of the U.S. Trade Representative acknowledged they could not deal with each country in Latin America separately, and that MERCOSUR was a convenient grouping for them.[17] The Clinton administration adopted the same cautious yet positive posture toward MERCOSUR. In the aftermath of the Cold War, the United States was preoccupied with events in the former Soviet Union and with trade policy with Japan, so that movements among Latin America nations seeking combinations of forces were not considered threatening.

Of course, the lack of attention on the part of the industrialized nations had a negative aspect as well. They did not go beyond rhetoric in helping the new civilian government in its Herculean efforts to re-create the basis for democracy in Argentina. At the beginning of the Alfonsín administration, the lack of European support also constituted a form of political space for Argentina. But it proved to be a false space. It wasn't the autonomy of action sought by the regime. It was a form of isolation, an isolation not wished for by the Argentines. In the case of the dispute over the Malvinas, the lack of support by the industrialized nations, especially the United States, has hurt Argentina. When the European nations turned their backs on the dispute still open between Argentina and Great Britain, the Argentine government felt compelled to act on its own and precipitated the most serious confrontation since the war in the Malvinas. The open wound of the Malvinas represented the sword of Damocles over the collective head of the Alfonsín regime, complicating its internal and external capacity to act. The Argentines could not allow the matter to rest, even for a short period, and yet without external support they were not capable of bringing the British to compromise. The official position of the United States in the dispute was that it was the friend of both parties and would not become involved. As in the period before the war of 1982, that ostensibly evenhanded posture favored the British.

The government of Margaret Thatcher insisted for years that the hard line it had adopted in refusing to negotiate the issue of sovereignty over the Malvinas was due to the fact that the Argentine government was a dictatorship that could not possibly respect the rights of its citizens. Under such circumstances, how could anyone expect that the British would facilitate the transfer of the islands to such a regime? The other part of the great public opinion campaign conducted by the British to justify their steadfast refusal to negotiate with the Argentines was that they had to respect the interests of the inhabitants on the islands. After 1983, however, no one doubted the democratic character of the new Argentine government or its passionate defense of human rights. And still the British remained totally inflexible in the face of repeated attempts by the Argentines to reopen a dialogue on the future of the archipelago. The new airstrip was opened in 1986 at the cost of $1 billion. The cost of "Fortress Falklands" has been extremely high, as had been predicted. But Prime Minister Thatcher did not budge. It would take new administrations in both countries in 1990 to break the diplomatic impasse.

Constantly frustrated in its efforts to open a dialogue with Great Britain, the Argentine government lost patience in 1985. The tone of its diplomacy became confrontational. Sinking a Taiwanese fishing boat and signing contracts with Russian and Bulgarian fishermen could not have had any result other than the one it had. When Great Britain responded by declaring an exclusion zone around the islands, the Argentine government stimulated the latent nationalism of the issue through a series of public declarations of outrage. The public reaction nearly got out of hand. There was a brief moment of near-hysteria in Buenos Aires. The most charitable explanation of the government's headstrong behavior is that the government felt itself hemmed in by the internal nationalist groups and could not allow the British initiative to pass without some strong protest. Caputo stated that his actions were designed to isolate Britain diplomatically, but they had the opposite effect, winning sympathy for the British and antagonizing Argentina's friends, none of whom wanted to see further bloodshed over the islands.[18]

The worst feature of the crisis was that the United States did nothing to relieve the tension. The official position of the United States continued to be that it had no position on the matter. The least it could have done to strengthen the fragile democracy in Argentina would have been to encourage the British allies to soften their rigid position even a little. The slightest movement by the British, however insignificant in the long run, would have been interpreted in Buenos Aires as a great triumph for the government; it would have been the most effective way to disarm the extreme nationalists on the left and on the right, expanding the political space available to the government. It is not unreasonable to suggest that the rebels led by Colonel Aldo Rico were either emboldened by the government's failure to move the British or angered by that failure. They revolted during Easter Week 1987, forcing Alfonsín to deal directly with the rebels and lose face in appearing to accept several of their demands.[19]

The Reagan administration was not capable of constructive action in its dealings with the Argentine democratic government. Representatives of the U.S. government stated over and over again how much they favored democracy in Argentina, how much they wanted the new government to succeed. On more than one occasion, Treasury Department officials called for greater flexibility on the part of private banks in negotiating with the Argentine government so that Argentine democracy would not be compromised, but it did not have much effect. Certainly, the prestige of the executive was not involved. Since Irangate, if not before, the U.S. executive has been detached from international situations not in crisis or that did not directly threaten U.S. national interest. Whether from the strength of his conviction or from internal pressure, Alfonsín could not leave the Malvinas issue alone. And yet, without support from the

United States or from the European nations, his actions served only to make a bad situation worse.

Foreign Minister Caputo stated that in its reinsertion in the world, Argentina sought autonomy of action. Of course, international autonomy never can be absolute. It is defined in the context of international relations. For that reason, it was necessary for Argentina to redefine its relations with the United States, Europe, Latin America, and the Third World. The brusque changes in policy and the lamentable episode in the Malvinas had reduced the confidence of the international community in Argentina. A critical element in the reinsertion after 1983 was the restoration of that confidence, reestablishing the sense of responsibility of the nation as an actor in the international system. Lack of confidence is a major element in the heavy, sad legacy of the military regimes. Alfonsín did not recognize that legacy, or refused to be bound by it. Throughout his administration, he acted and made statements as if he were representing a nation without such a past, without such a legacy, declarations that were counterproductive and that restricted rather than broadened the government's autonomy in international affairs. He miscalculated in assuming it was not necessary to win autonomy, that his government would have it automatically as an intrinsic characteristic of a democracy.[20]

A clear case of a foreign policy action in which the legacy of Argentina's conflicted past confused instead of clarified the Argentine reinsertion was Alfonsín's visit to Cuba in 1986. It appears at first glance to have been a challenge to the United States in the best Yrigoyenist style—without positive results and without potential beneficial consequences. It was added as a technical stop after Alfonsín's visit to Russia and Western Europe. From one point of view, it is possible to see both visits as part of a single, traditional strategy of independence and defiance aimed at the United States. But that was not the Argentine purpose. The stop was made to talk face to face with Fidel Castro, to induce him to influence the armed radical group in Chile that was attempting to kill General Pinochet or undermine his military regime. The Argentines believed that their sovereignty was endangered by the actions of the terrorists, and they were concerned that the political stability of the entire Southern Cone would be undermined if the violent actions continued. According to participants in the conversations with Castro, representatives of the U.S. government were informed of the true reasons for the stopover in Havana in a full and timely fashion. And Castro apparently did cooperate, because the terrorists ended their use of Argentine territory.[21]

Unfortunately, even though the Argentines did everything they could to avoid having their actions misunderstood, they suffered tremendous criticism in the U.S. press, and State Department officials, whatever their private assurances, indicated their displeasure. The problem was twofold. First, the Argentines appeared then, and later, to be ignorant of the special place Cuba holds in U.S. domestic politics. Second, had the stop been made by the leader of another Latin American nation, the reaction in the United States might well have been different. Chancellor Caputo said that one of the government's objectives was "to disconnect internal conflicts from world conflicts."[22] The visit to Havana and the treaty with the Soviet Union to fish in the troubled waters of the South Atlantic could not have been calculated taking that disconnection into account, especially since there is no foreign policy issue more closely linked to U.S. domestic politics than the fate of Cuba.

Another Argentine public posture that reflected its tradition of standing apart from and above world struggles and that complicated its new insertion in the world was the insistence on calling for disarmament by the great powers. While such a policy was consistent with its posture as a moral nation, the policy was not perceived as the Argentine government wished because it came too soon after the period in which Argentina was one of the most heavily armed nations in the world, and one of the most bellicose. Again, Alfonsín was caught up in the legacy of the military governments as well as the older Peronist legacy of the Third Position. While Alfonsín personally did not have to prove his democratic and pacifist credentials, the nation certainly did have to reconstruct its international confidence and goodwill, and it would continue to have to do so for some time to come. President Menem also would have to deal with this problem as the United States pushed Argentina to dismantle its Condor II missile program.

Linked to the theme of disarmament was the persistent refusal of the Argentine government to join the international antinuclear movement. Again, Alfonsín declared that Argentine purposes were entirely peaceful. And, no doubt, they were. But, it was not Alfonsín whose word was questioned, it was the historical memory of the developed nations, filled with episodes that caused doubt and uncertainty concerning the objectives of Argentine foreign policy.[23] Furthermore, the position taken was inconsistent with that of a moral nation. A moral and ethical nation must be cleaner than other nations. It is not sufficient to declare yourself clean; you must demonstrate it by your actions. Refusing to participate in or to take the lead in the antinuclear movement made little sense in the context of Argentina's reinsertion into the world as a moral and nonaligned nation. In the minds of the world's nations, it emphasized Argentina's pretensions to leadership and its exceptionalism. At the same time, however, it is important to remember that Alfonsín began the policy of peaceful nuclear cooperation with Brazil. Undersecretary of Foreign Relations Jorge Sabato

conducted secret negotiations in Brazil that led to President Sarney's visit
to Argentina's nuclear facilities in 1987, including the top secret nuclear
plant in Pilcaniyeu in Patagonia.

The key to Argentina's reinsertion into the world arena today, as it was in
1983, is its relations with the United States. Given the history of the ties
between the two countries, it is difficult if not impossible for Argentina
to accept a bilateral arrangement in which it is forced to play the role of
inferior or subordinate partner. However, given the economic and political reality in the world at the time, there was no other viable option open
to the Alfonsín administration. A U.S. government interested in or sensitive to Latin America might have facilitated or eased Argentina's reentry
into the community of nations. The Reagan administration showed itself
incapable of playing a positive role. The Bush administration was little
better. The only avenue open to the Argentines was the Latin American
option, but it was not clear where this would lead. At the same time, to
identify itself primarily as a Latin American nation with its new role in
the world as a member of the Latin American community was still to
define itself in terms of its relationship with the United States, because,
while much was said in the 1980s of the relative deterioration of the economic hegemony of the United States, it remained the dominant economic
power in the Western Hemisphere. Furthermore, Argentina was weakened
by three decades of political instability and economic stagnation and would
have considerable difficulty in asserting its autonomy of action until it
had put its domestic house in order. In the end, economic instability undermined the Alfonsín government and in 1988 abruptly curtailed its influence in world affairs. Overcoming that instability would become
Menem's top priority.

While critics urged a realistic approach that suggested a rapprochement with the United States, there was no evidence that the Alfonsín regime accepted the suggestion. In this sense, it remained a prisoner of the
rhetoric and the posturing of the nation's traditional diplomacy. The most
serious shortcoming of the foreign policy of the new democratic government was that it declared its definition of an ideal role for itself but was
unable to create the bases to play that role on the world's stage. Without
those bases, the foreign policy of Argentina continued to be characterized
by inflated rhetoric, by gestures disconnected from the behavior of the
country in the international arena, and by confused signals in disputes, all
of which reduced the nation's capacity to influence other nations in international forums. The political culture underlying foreign policy had not

changed and was still dangerously detached from a hard, objective analysis of the world around Argentina.

To some extent, the Alfonsín government, like so many before it, civilian and military, was a prisoner of old policies and old rhetorical positions. The danger that this implies is that it, too, remained under the spell of a vision of the nation's role in world affairs that was anachronistic, a vision of the near-great and about-to-be-great power with significant influence over world affairs through the export of its foodstuffs and through its universally recognized potential and innate moral force. According to this vision, the nation enjoyed great influence without possessing power in the conventional sense of the term. Whether such a role in world affairs actually existed in the past is a matter for discussion. Clearly, it does not exist today. In the context of high internal political tension and economic debility, the Krausian rhetoric of the president and the public declarations of the foreign minister served mainly to confuse. Worse, it diminished the efficacy and the impact of the many excellent policies of the government and, in certain cases, actually stimulated internal or international tension.

On balance, the Alfonsín government merits very good grades for its foreign policy. It ruled at a time that would have been extremely difficult for any government. As Caputo stated at a FLACSO seminar in 1992, many things were impossible for him that were possible for his successors. As his successor, Guido DiTella, acknowledged, the Menem government was able to do certain things in the foreign policy arena only because of the heroic efforts of Caputo and his colleagues. If the political space and the international influence enjoyed by the government was slightly less in 1989 than had been hoped in December 1983, because of the ignominious manner in which it had been forced to hand power to its successor, it was still much greater than that of the preceding government, or at any time in the previous fifty years. Relations with the United States were better than at any time in that period, and the capacity to improve them still further was in the hands of the Argentine government. In that sense, Argentina enjoyed far more autonomy than at any time in this century and can be said, therefore, to have achieved most of its foreign policy goals. On the negative side of the ledger, the government had stumbled in its effort to reinsert the nation into the world community. That task, along with the challenge of achieving economic stability, would await the next government.

When Menem took office in July 1989, his principal concern was economic policy. The country had just suffered an episode of hyperinflation and would suffer another, six months after he took office. There was real danger that the economy would collapse. The new government's main goal was to hold the economy together and to convince the international community that it was serious about undertaking an economic reform or restructuring program consistent with the tenets of what was coming to be called the "Washington Consensus." Menem's first foreign minister was Domingo Cavallo, a Harvard-trained economist with strong support in the private sector. As ambassador to the United States, he appointed Guido DiTella, also an economist, and, like Cavallo, a member of the Peronist party's reformist wing. These appointments underlined Menem's use of foreign policy to achieve his basic economic goal, a tool to facilitate Argentina's advantageous reinsertion into the world economy. After a short period, during which Menem's first economics minister died, it became clear that Cavallo was the dominant figure in the cabinet. Before the end of the year, he became minister of economics and DiTella returned to Buenos Aires to become foreign minister.

From the very beginning, Menem decided that it was necessary to hitch Argentina's star to the United States. While Alfonsín had sought a "mature" relationship with the United States, Menem wanted a preferential, privileged relationship. He and his advisers were struck by the collapse of the Soviet Union and the dramatic triumph of the United States in the Cold War. They were convinced that the United States was the dominant power in the hemisphere and would play what they called a "protagonistic" role in the new international order. Even though they recognized that their trade ties to Europe were still more important than those with the United States, the latter would be critical in their efforts to modernize Argentina.

Here was a foreign policy consciously attempting to correct the errors of the twentieth century by returning to the successes of the nineteenth century. Foreign policy was designed to follow and strengthen the economic model and thereby protect Argentina's national interests. This is what Menem meant by realism, what DiTella meant by pragmatism.[24] In a manner reminiscent of the nation's insertion into the international economy at the end of the nineteenth century, foreign policy would be the handmaiden of the nation's essential economic model.

So long as Cavallo was foreign minister, the emphasis was on doing what was necessary to pave the way for economic restructuring and lining up on the side of the United States. What appeared to Menem as an ideal opportunity came during the Persian Gulf crisis, when, without consulting his congress or anyone in Latin America, he decided to send two naval vessels to join the blockade of Iraq. No other Latin American nation did as much. Publicly, the president made much of his unquestioning support of the United States. Privately, he complained that his efforts had received very little appreciation from the U.S. government.[25]

While Cavallo was still foreign minister, DiTella made a series of quick trips to Buenos Aires to deliver lectures to a variety of audiences, explaining the nation's foreign policy. The goal was nothing less than a change in political culture. DiTella deliberately exaggerated the purposes of the government's foreign policy in order to stimulate discussion. His most famous hyperbole, delivered when he already was installed as foreign minister, was that the government wanted close relations with the United States, so close that they would be "carnal relations." The press had a field day with that quotation, and it became the slogan of those who opposed what they termed Argentina's subordination to the United States, even among some factions of the Peronist party.

What was significant about DiTella's speeches, both as ambassador and, later, as foreign minister, was that he specifically referred to the errors of Argentina's past. He said all of the things that Alfonsín understood but refused to say—that Argentina was not what it once was, that it was an economically weak, vulnerable nation—and then he went further. He stated that Argentina was strategically insignificant and should comport itself consistently with that insignificance, and that the nation's history of confrontation with the United States had left a legacy of suspicion among the developed nations that would have to be overcome in time through good works. DiTella referred to the need for Argentina to enter "the club" of modern nations and said that, in order to enter the club, it had to behave correctly; it had to become a reliable, predictable partner, something it had not done for more than fifty years. Specifically, he noted the three most sensitive issues in U.S. relations with Argentina: nuclear energy and arms proliferation, patent protection, and bureaucratic confusion, including corruption. He stated that the country had to do whatever was necessary to behave properly.

On the issue of nuclear proliferation, Menem acted swiftly and in a manner that enhanced his credentials in Latin America. Building on the foundation established during the Alfonsín administration, Menem called on his Brazilian counterpart, José Sarney, to sign a joint declaration of their common nuclear policy at the Falls of Iguazú on November 28, 1990. In it, both nations committed themselves to confine nuclear energy to peaceful uses, to adhere jointly to the Treaty of Tlatelolco, and to submit jointly to the International Atomic Energy Commission for verification of their peaceful use of atomic energy.[26]

By acting together with Brazil, Menem strengthened the move toward integration begun by Alfonsín and undercut the nationalist opposition to Argentina's adherence to the Treaty of Tlatelolco. He pushed the integration effort further with the Treaty of Asunción, which created MERCOSUR, the free trade market that included Uruguay and Paraguay as well as Brazil.

While backing away from the independent nuclear policy that had frustrated U.S. officials for nearly a generation was a major step, the next step, giving up the development of the Condor missile, was much more difficult and of much greater significance. DiTella and Cavallo pushed hard, while the armed forces and an unholy alliance of political forces on the left and the right screamed and complained. Here was a true test for DiTella's characterization of the new Argentina—a weak, economically vulnerable nation with modest resources and pretensions to match. The new Argentina had no need of an independent missile capability and should certainly not allow the production of that missile to endanger its relations with its neighbors Chile and Brazil, or threaten the link with the United States. Argentina had to convince all of them that it had become a "dependable partner." The advocates of the new Argentina won their battle, but not without a tough, bruising fight, and some favors in return for the military.

The argument that won the debate within the government, the argument that convinced the president to put his prestige on the line and expose himself to military threats, was that without demonstrating that Argentina had become a dependable partner, without pushing constantly to become more and more transparent in its international dealings, especially its commercial dealings, the new economic model would collapse and all of the government's efforts would be nullified. There was a similar internal struggle over the issue of corruption, with repeated scandals tarring members of the president's circle. Two cases, the so-called Swift and Ezeiza episodes, dragged U.S. Ambassador Terrence Todman into the limelight and made the nation's sensibilities the subject of ferocious public debate.[27] In the Clinton administraton, the corruption issue was given the highest priority and was focused on *insegurídad juridica*, or the lack of judicial responsibility and probity. The penchant displayed by Menem and his justice minister, Enrique Barra, for packing the federal courts with unqualified Menemista faithful did not help matters.[28]

Menem kept asking when the United States would respond in some concrete fashion to the Argentine efforts. DiTella and Cavallo were embarrassed to answer that the principal response from the United States in the short term would come from the private sector, not from the government, and that it would take the form of investments in the Argentine stock market, of investments in the newly privatized public utilities, and new portfolio investment that would help to stimulate the Argentine economy and pull it out of the recession in which it had been stuck for so many years. Privately, officials in both the foreign and defense ministries asked American officials when they might expect something in return for their good behavior. Theirs was the complaint of Job: How long do I have to suffer before I get back in your good graces?

Finally, after Menem's visit to Washington in November 1991, official Washington seemed to get the message, at least for a while. Within a few months of the visit, Secretary of Defense Dick Cheney, Senator Richard Lugar, and a brace of other political figures made pilgrimages to Buenos Aires and issued public statements praising the Argentine reform program and recognizing the great value of Argentine friendship to the United States. The U.S. government considered these mere gestures, but they were important to the Argentines. More significant in the long run were the painfully slow negotiations to include Argentina and the rest of MERCOSUR in the free trade area contemplated by the United States in its treaty with Mexico and Canada, and the frustrating talks with the General Agreement on Tariffs and Trade (GATT) and the European community that denied Argentine exports entré into the markets of the developed nations of the Northern Hemisphere. DiTella might have been correct that friendship with the United States was vital to the defense of Argentine national interests, but it was unsettling to many Argentines that the United States and its European allies would continue to shut out of their markets the primary products that had been the pillars of Argentine wealth for a century. The new economic model called for a transformation of the Argentine productive machine, but in the short run the nation's traditional exports were the difference between good times and bad. Public recognition of the Argentina "miracle" in the private sector of the United States and Western Europe was the success that Cavallo and DiTella were hoping for. And it did not hurt that at the end of the first Menem government, the U.S. Department of Agriculture declared Argentina to be free of aftosa (hoof-and-mouth disease) for the first time in seventy-five years. DiTella and Ambassador Granillo Ocampo immediately asked for and won permission to export beef to the United States. Perhaps these were the *relaciones carnales* to which DiTella had referred.

As part of the general strategy to win the trust of the United States, the Menem administration had sent ships to the Persian Gulf. At the same time, it sent an intelligent, energetic ambassador, Juan Pablo Lohlé, to the Organization of American States, where, as luck would have it, he soon joined forces with the Chilean, Brazilian, and U.S. ambassadors there, Heraldo Muñoz, Bernardo Pericas, and Luigi Einaudi, to make something of that organization. Not long after, Lohlé was replaced by Hernan Patiño Mayer, who continued the policy of constructive cooperation.

At the outset, making something of the Organization of American States was intended principally as part of the policy of pleasing the United States, because it was in hemispheric affairs that the Cold War emphasis on democracy and human rights seemed to have its greatest possibilities. Nevertheless, when Lohlé was replaced by Patiño, the OAS card began to take on a form and meaning of its own, and was expanded to include the United Nations, where Ambassador Emilio Cárdenas proved supremely effective. Under Patiño's dynamic and shrewd leadership, the Organization of American States began to discuss reform of the Inter-American Defense Board and to consider proposals for "cooperative security."[29] Meanwhile, Argentine troops participated in as many peacekeeping efforts as any member of the United Nations, which had the double benefit of keeping large numbers of Argentine officers employed in a constructive fashion while building for Argentina, step by step, a new reputation as a team player committed to multilateral efforts to keep the peace. Slowly, a coherent image of the new Argentina was emerging. Cárdenas capped this effort with a high-profile dynamic presidency of the Security Council in January 1996.

Still, problems remained in the bilateral relations with the United States. The Clinton administration sent James Cheek to Buenos Aires as ambassador. Cheek, a career foreign service officer who had served on the transition team, focused his public comments on the issues of democracy and judicial corruption, which had the effect of highlighting the most sensitive issues between the two countries. Meanwhile, in Washington, Menem's ambassador Raul Granillo Ocampo pushed hard for some U.S. recognition of Argentina's good behavior, some explicit acknowledgment that the special relationship with the United States was of benefit to Argentina.[30] The problem, as it had been since World War II, was that the bilateral relationship between Argentina and the United States is asymmetrical. Episodes or issues that seemed very important to Argentina scarcely caught U.S. attention. Conversely, the United States insisted on applying pressure on Argentina over issues that were central to Argentina's political or economic existence, while they were never that important for the United States. Argentina kept hoping for reciprocity or at least some gesture, while reciprocity was out of the question from the U.S. perspective.

There remain to consider the exaggerated gestures and the obsessive focus on the United States of the Menem government. If we grant the soundness of the underlying strategic goal of reinserting Argentina in the world community as a democratic nation and a reliable partner—and Caputo insisted it was his goal as well—then how do we evaluate the strategic device chosen to achieve that goal, the unconditional alliance with the United States, and the tactics used to carry out the strategy? The problem is not DiTella's rhetorical flourishes, even when ill conceived and exaggerated. The problem is the gestures that Menem chose to demonstrate his commitment to the United States and his avowal of an alliance with the United States itself. These gestures are not only exaggerated. They may also prove in the long run to have been counterproductive. For example, sending naval vessels to the Persian Gulf was designed to show how much a part of the U.S. alliance Argentina had become. Aside from the fact that the ships may have made an insignificant contribution, the way in which they were sent—without the prior approval of Congress—was counterproductive in the effort to solidify the institutional basis of Argentina's democracy. Further, it was seen around Latin America and even by some officials in Washington as capricious, the very opposite of what the government had wanted. Worse, several members of the Menem government assumed that the United States would "give" them something in return, so that it became the cause of bitterness in some government circles.

By this thinking, Argentine leaders suggested that they might still be caught in the traditional pattern of Argentine exceptionalism. But now, instead of leading the world against the United States, or in competition with the United States, Argentina would lead the world in supporting the United States. Similarly, Menem's meeting with the president of the Cuban-American Foundation, Jorge Mas Canosa, in Miami, was an exaggerated gesture, as was his public criticism of the nonaligned movement. Ambassador Lúcio Garcia Del Solar noted in the FLACSO seminar that the emphasis on MERCOSUR may in a similar fashion be exaggerated to the point of losing sight of the rest of Latin America, although Menem's courting of Chile through 1996 and DiTella's determined effort to resolve the few remaining border disputes with Chile suggest that there is a sense of balance in the thinking in Buenos Aires. By contrast, Argentina's defense of democracy within the Organization of American States and its activities within the smaller groups of Latin American nations have been self-effacing, constructive, and consistent. So, too, have been the efforts of both democratic goverments to improve what Ambassador Felix Peña called the *tecnología de administración*, which makes Argentine actions more predictable and transparent.[31]

The problem with the exaggerated gestures is that they are consistent with a truly disturbing interpretation: that one of the most enduring myths of Argentine foreign policy lives on in new form, the myth of Argentine world influence, of Argentine exceptionalism. Ambassador Garcia Del Solar referred to this as Argentine "megalomania" and commented that he thought it was disappearing. President Alfonsín sought to establish Argentine exceptionalism through his assertion of Argentine "moral power." Caputo echoed that idea when he insisted on using foreign policy to defend the "dignity of the nation." The issue is not whether having a nuclear program is right or wrong; it is whether, given Argentine political culture, such policy gestures are designed to trumpet to the world that Argentina is a great power, that it has great influence in the world, as it did in the past. Is there something peculiar about Argentine governments that drives them to have a high international profile? Is it part of the nation's political culture? Or is it part of a darker picture in which Argentines, deep down, still do not really believe that their nation is not one of the most powerful on earth, that it is not one of the world's major powers, and that its influence over world affairs is not the equal of that of any other nation in the international community?

The international gestures of the Menem government are disturbing, too, because they appeared capricious—they were decided without consulting Congress and without consulting other nations in the region, thereby gainsaying the assertion that Argentina was a Latin American nation. As DiTella had said on many occasions, capriciousness was precisely the opposite of the image Menem was seeking to create. And yet, virtually everything Menem did in foreign affairs was designed to set himself apart from the rest, not to become one of the crowd. That seemingly insatiable desire to stand out was harder to justify in the 1990s than at any other time in the nation's history.

Until Argentina overcomes its historical legacy of capricious behavior, the nation will increase its international autonomy more by a low-profile foreign policy than by a policy with a high profile. The lower profile fits better with the country's current level of economic and political resources. And staying off the international stage and not drawing attention to itself should provide the time necessary to help reconstruct the tattered fabric of relations with the United States. At the same time, it would serve to make foreign policy less salient in the internal political debate, defusing it to some degree and actually weakening the extremist elements arrayed against the consolidation of the democratic regime. The vision of its future that the Argentine people have is important to the internal debate. Until the coming of the Menem adminstration, that vision was inflated and unrealistic, distorting public discussion of foreign policy and putting severe constraints on any government. The task of the democratic government must be to moderate the vision and adjust it to the realistic possibilities of the nation—the nation of today, not the nation of yesterday.

For several years, leaders of the Argentine foreign ministry asked anyone who would listen, "What will we get for our gestures of friendship toward the United States?" The answer seems to have been given by the Clinton administration, after several years of hard effort by the Argentines: Argentina is now recognized throughout the U.S. government as a special friend in Latin America and is spoken of publicly on many occasions as a nation deserving of special treatment. In the State Department and in Treasury, it is often said, "We must do something for Argentina." That "something" was the designation in 1997 of the country as a non-North Atlantic Treaty Organization military ally.

The point is that the Menem government has won a significant victory within the U.S. bureaucracy by erasing or neutralizing years of ill will and suspicion. The country also has come to occupy a position of growing prestige within the international community, in financial centers such as New York, and in the international organizations. Its influence in the United Nations never has been greater as a result of the active participation of Argentine troops in peacekeeping operations and the scintillating success of Ambassador Emilio Cárdenas in the Security Council.

Argentina has become a reliable partner, but not without having paid a significant cost, both in terms of international relations and in terms of domestic politics. To convince the financial and investing communities that Argentina would not lapse into inflation and fiscal irresponsibility—and to convince the Argentine populace—it was deemed indispensable to lock the government into a fully convertible peso. Many people in the government and outside of it feel that the convertibility policy is a little too rigid for dealing with short-term economic shocks or temporary aberrations in trade flows or tax revenues. As far as the nation's foreign policy is concerned, there is no need for an economic straitjacket; the economic model appears firmly in place.

Since the basic international goals of Menem's first government have been achieved, foreign policy in the second administration has run the risk of seeming like more of the same. Friend and foe alike kept asking DiTella with increasing frequency, "What have you done for me lately?" That suggests that the Menem government's foreign policy in the president's second term either had to make a virtue of its new position in world affairs and derive political benefit from that accomplishment or look for another rabbit to pull out of the hat—something like a magical solution to the Malvinas question. That has not been easy, and depending on tricks and surprises carries considerable risk for the minister and the government.

Bilateral Relations Becoming Dense

The most serious bit of bad news for Minister DiTella is that having become a reliable partner does not mean that there are no problems between the two countries. On occasion, if we read the local press, it appears as if there are more difficulties in the relationship now than there were two, five, or ten years ago. "Why," members of the Argentine government muse, "do the Americans bug us so much about intellectual property rights, or corruption, or juridical security? Are those really such critical issues? If we are such great friends, why do they keep pushing us?"

The answer to those questions is simple and can be captured in one word: density. It is both the good news and the bad news for Argentina that relations with the United States are becoming more dense. The bad news is easy to see; the good news is harder to understand.

Density in international relations simply refers to the frequency and variety of interactions. That bilateral relations are dense means that there are very frequent and many different kinds of interactions between two nations. In the case of Argentina and the United States it means, first and foremost, that there are more and more nongovernmental ties: trade, investment, cultural exchanges, telecommunications, mass media, transportation, contracts, agreements, commitments, and plans. In short, after nearly a century of separation and mutual alienation, relations between the United States and Argentina are becoming normal—normal relations between friendly nations with compatible levels of development.

Problems That Remain

In the long run, there is no question that this normalization of relations with the United States will be of estimable and growing benefit to Argentina. In the short run, however, there are five implications for Argentine foreign policy that carry considerable risk. These might be considered problems that remain in the bilateral relationship.

The first of these is that increasingly dense private sector economic relations—trade, investment, stock market transactions, banking, and the like—bring into high relief anomalies between the ways in which people do business in the two countries. These are issues or anomalies that existed previously, but, because of the nature of the relations between the two countries, were of relatively low salience. Now, however, because Argentina is eager to deepen its insertion into the world market and is consciously courting the United States, the fact that the United States remains the dominant economic member of the dyad and the source of capital, technology, and so forth almost inevitably means that the Argentine way of doing things is put under pressure to change. One obvious example of this disparity is the difference between the way things are done on the New York Stock Exchange and the way they are done on the

Buenos Aires BOLSA. While negotiations may be held to resolve the differences, when push comes to shove it is likely that the New York Stock Exchange will prevail.

Mature international markets play by clear rules. New players joining the market must abide by those rules, which generally include resolution of disputes without reference to the courts of the home countries. When arbitration or other dispute-resolution fails, however, the courts will become involved.

Therefore a second dangerous implication for Argentine foreign policy is that normal, dense, private-sector interactions inevitably produce legal conflicts, and that puts a spotlight on the Argentine legal and judiciary system. For example, in U.S. relations with France or Germany, there are literally thousands of suits under way at any time. Virtually all of these are resolved within the legal systems of the countries considered the domicile of the commercial entities or individuals at loggerheads. Of course, when the stakes are high, lawyers and corporations bring as much pressure for help to bear on their governments as they can. The North American Free Trade Agreement (NAFTA) has done the same for U.S. relations with Mexico. The legal profession in south Texas is going through explosive growth as the number of legal disputes mounts into the thousands. As economic relations between Argentina and the United States become more and more dense, issues like juridical security, corruption, and the political manipulation of court appointments take on increasing significance for the nation's international role.

The third intimation of difficulty in the growing density of bilateral relations is that intellectual property—patents—becomes more important. This issue is closely related to the question of juridical security. Both keep coming up in the official relations between the two countries because they are not getting resolved in the private sector. As our economic relations become more important, these issues will come up with greater frequency. In order for bilateral relations to evolve along natural paths, like those of the United States and France, for example, Argentina must bring its judicial system and its handling of intellectual property into line with the nations with which it wishes to have normal, dense relations.

Fourth, as Argentina becomes more important for the United States, it will become more deeply inserted into the complex matrix of U.S. domestic politics and the U.S. economy. That is not necessarily bad, but it requires that Argentine officials and diplomats become increasingly sophisticated in their understanding of American politics and society. Over time, the relationship will give greater emphasis to private transactions, so that, ironically, official or political relations may become less salient than they are now. That is both the good news and the bad news.

The final and most delicate problem confronting the new relationship between Argentina and the United States is that Argentina will continue to be burdened with the fact that it is not a high priority for the
United States and that there remains a wide asymmetry of power between
the two countries. This asymmetry provokes great irritation in Buenos
Aires.

The debate within the Argentine scholarly community and within the
political leadership of the nation centers on the appropriate role for Argentina in world affairs. That debate hinges on the definition of Argentine power and influence, both real and potential. The most powerful legacy
of the "old" foreign policy is that no matter how unrealistic it may have
been, no matter how dysfunctional it was, it was exquisitely coincident
with the deep-seated belief in Argentine exceptionalism. According to
that belief, Argentina is superior to the other countries in the region and
deserves a prominent place in the family of nations. If that prominence
was denied Argentina for some years, most Argentines believed that it
was the result of incompetent leaders, temporary inconveniences, or the
hostility of a few competitors, principal among them, of course, the United
States.

The residue of this exceptionalism is the most disturbing feature of
the Menem government's foreign policy. It sneaks out of Menem's
speeches. It crops up in conversations with business leaders, with jour-
nalists, with students, and with professors. It exists on the political left
and on the right. It is even part of the discourse of the self-defined realists
among Argentine specialists in international relations.

For all those Argentines who see themselves as exceptional, the new
relationship with the United States will continue to be frustrating. It will
continue to be difficult to catch the attention of the United States, either
its private or public sector. The U.S. government will remain Eurocentric
in its geopolitical concerns, and relations with Latin America will continue to be in the hands of able professionals who will have their own
difficulties in catching the attention of the political leaders. In normal
relations, that is not necessarily bad, but it does not provide the attention
and warmth that Argentines want. Argentines still pursue their lost future, and the more they focus on what might have been, the more frustrating they will find their new relationship with the United States.

The Future

If it is true that Argentina will remain a middle power in international
affairs over the next decade, that Argentina, along with the rest of Latin
America, will remain a low priority for the United States, and that the

Argentine economy is not likely to assume a position of great significance for the private sector in the United States and Europe, how then is Argentina to carve out an appropriate place for itself in the international community? How is Argentina to create a "presence" in world affairs?

The answer has to do with how much leverage Argentina can create for itself in four areas:

1. The leverage of power: military capacity and economics.
2. The leverage of good behavior on the global stage.
3. The leverage of good behavior in domestic affairs.
4. The leverage of cooperative action.

The Menem government has scored highest on the second of these, its citizenship in the emerging post-Cold War world. It is doing quite well on the first, although Argentine economic progress is quite a bit short of the dramatic levels of the Asian tigers in the past two decades. At the current rate of growth, it will take generations, not years or even decades, for Argentina to enter the ranks of the first-rate world economies. The third area is a subject of some concern, but only egregious levels of instability or corruption will cause the nation to trip itself in international affairs. The fourth is the area in which Argentine exceptionalism operates. And, on that subject, we shall have to wait and see.

Notes

1. Carlos Escudé, *La Argentina: Paria internacional?* (Buenos Aires: Editorial Belgrano, 1984).

2. See the exchange between Guido DiTella and Dante Caputo in Roberto Russell, ed., *La política exterior: Argentina en el Nuevo Orden Internacional* (Buenos Aires: GEL, 1992); and Atilio Borón, "Las desventuras del 'realismo perférico,'" *America Latina/Internacional* 8, no. 29 (July–September 1991): 1–15. Another, somewhat exaggerated critique of Menem's policies, from the nationalist perspective, is Alfredo Bruno Bologna, "Dos modelos de inserción de Argentina en el mundo: Las presidencias de Alfonsín y Menem," CERIR, *Serie Informes* 2 (December 1991): 9–95.

3. See Roberto Russell, "From Videla to Alfonsín: Domestic Sources of Argentina's Foreign Policy" (Ph.D. diss., Johns Hopkins University, 1992).

4. See Jospeh S. Tulchin, *Argentina and the United States: A Conflicted Relationship*, chap. 4: "Between the Wars: Collapse of the Argentine Growth Model" (Boston: Twayne, 1990).

5. Alfonsín's speeches are reprinted in the press. The speeches of Foreign Minister Dante M. Caputo are collected in *Discursos del Señor Ministro de Relaciones Exteriores y Culto Dr. Dante Mario Caputo* (Buenos Aires: Congreso de la Nación, 1987).

6. See Carlos Escudé, *Realismo periférico* (Buenos Aires: Planeta, 1992).

7. Alfonsín considered Escudé a person who hated his own country. Interview with author, Washington, DC, January 26, 1993.

8. For a sample of Argentine principles in foreign policy, see Alfonsín's speech before the 39th General Assembly of the United Nations, September 24, 1984; Caputo's talk to the National Press Club, Washington, DC, April 12, 1984; Caputo's lecture to the Jornada Académica, "Treinta meses de política exterior en democracia," June 4, 1986; and Caputo's speech before the 41st General Assembly of the United Nations, September 22, 1986. Among the early analyses of the new government, see Manfred Wilhelmy, "Argentina: Política exterior argentina en 1984," in *Las políticas exteriores latinoamericanas frente a la crisis,* ed. Heraldo Muñoz (Buenos Aires, 1985); Russell, "La nueva política exterior argentina: Rupturas conceptuales," *America Latina/Internacional* 8, no. 29 (July–September 1991); and Carlos Perez Llana, "Mirar creativamente al mundo," *Creación* 1, no. 1 (June 1986). The quarterlies *Cono Sur* (Santiago, Chile) and *America Latina/Internacional* (Buenos Aires) have shrewd commentaries by Carlos Portales and Roberto Russell in nearly every issue. Russell's views of this period are set forth in his Ph.D. dissertation, cited above.

9. This was explained in a communciation of July 30, 1991, to the author from Francisco Diez, who worked with Caputo in the Foreign Ministry. Diez insists that whenever principle and interests were in conflict, interests predominated, although in the same paragraph he says that "it was necessary to sustain principles to support concrete interests, because when you don't have economic, strategic, or military force, you've got to rely on something, and principles were always esteemed by the Radicals, so it fit very well" (author's translation). Caputo's lecture at the university was June 4, 1986, and is reprinted in *Discursos del Señor Ministro.*

10. *New York Times,* January 13, April 1, and June 1, 1984. Alfonsín never supported the radical position of forming a debtors' cartel. See *La Nación,* December 16, and December 17, 1984.

11. Francisco Diez insists that there was never any thought given to using Grinspun's style as a foreign policy ploy and that the debt negotiations and the Beagle referendum were never linked in their discussions. A senior member of the economic team who requested anonymity supported this assertion. The fact remains that the juxtaposition benefited the government.

12. From an interview with an official of the World Bank who had conducted negotiations with the Argentines during the period between 1984 and 1985, Washington, DC, June 15, 1990. His name is withheld by request.

13. Reprinted in *Discursos del Señor Ministro.*

14. See Thomas Carothers, *In the Name of Democracy* (Berkeley: University of California Press, 1992).

15. Statement by former Undersecretary of Foreign Affairs Jorge Sabato during the FLACSO seminar on foreign policy, Buenos Aires, March 1992.

16. Interview with a senior official in the U.S. embassy in Buenos Aires, June 10, 1988.

17. "Trade Opportunities in the Western Hemisphere." Comment by Don Adelson, deputy assistant U.S. trade representative during seminar held November 16, 1990, Woodrow Wilson International Center for Scholars.

18. *El Pais,* October 6, 1986. For a summary of the Argentine press, see Southern Cone *Ten Days Report. Argentina* (October–November 1986), mimeograph. Sabato insists that it was not the government's intention to precipitate a confrontation (interview with author, Buenos Aires, April 22, 1991). There is evidence that Caputo came to understand the need to sidestep the sovereignty issue and that the strategy of the "umbrella," which was the basis of the agreement signed in 1990, was discussed and agreed to in the Foreign Ministry in

1988 and 1989. It could not be made public because of the difficulties confronting the administration on the domestic front.

19. Diez states that all of the points conceded to the rebels had been negotiated with representatives of the armed forces prior to the uprising. On the other hand, a member of the crisis cabinet stated that Alfonsín did negotiate some points with the rebels when he took the helicopter to the base on Sunday. While it is true that the points negotiated were minor, this source, who requested anonymity, felt that the negotiations created a popular perception of a deal, if not a sell-out.

20. Carlos Escudé, "Una analisis critica," *America Latina/Internacional* 8, no. 29 (July–September 1991).

21. Both Caputo and Sabato discussed this episode during the FLACSO seminar in Buenos Aires in 1992. In addition, Sabato provided the author with details in an interview, April 22, 1991. When pressed, Sabato admitted that they could have advised the State Department as to the details of the trip before stopping in Havana, but that it did not seem necessary.

22. Remarks made during the FLACSO seminar, Russell, "From Videla to Alfonsín," 207–8.

23. The most comprehensive treatment of this episode is Rut Diamint, "El gobierno norteamericano ante el caso del Condor II: Sistema burocrático y toma de decisiones," Woodrow Wilson Center, Latin American Program, Working Paper no. 224, 1997.

24. Escudé, *Realismo periférico.* See also the comments by DiTella in Russell, "From Videla to Alfonsín," 261–74.

25. Interview with Undersecretary Perez Anzaur, Buenos Aires, November 15, 1989. Menem expected an immediate, material quid pro quo for his efforts.

26. For a comprehensive review of the events, see Julio C. Carasales, "En el final de un largo camino: Argentina y Tlatelolco," *America Latina/Internacional* 9, no. 32 (April–June 1992): 1–2.

27. Todman's activities are the subject of Martin Gronovsky's *Misión cumplida* (Buenos Aires: Planeta, 1992).

28. See articles on Ambassador James Cheek's first public speeches upon arriving in Buenos Aires in *La Nacion,* October 7, 1993; and comments by L. Ron Scheman at the V. Foro Argentino Norteamericano, November 2, 1993, Airlie House, Virginia. On the need for judicial reform, see Emilio Cárdenas, "Poder político y poder económico en la globalización de fin de siglo," in *ABRA, Banca y Producción: 6 Jornadas Bancarias de le República Argentina* (Buenos Aires: ABRA, 1995); and Chapter 8 in this volume.

29. See presentation by Hernan Patiño Mayer at the seminar "Cooperative Security: Challenges in the Americas," Washington, DC, September 27–28, 1993.

30. Ambassador Granillo and his staff put together a massive record of their efforts in Washington in Raul Granillo Ocampo, ed., *Las relaciones entre la Argentina y los Estados Unidos, 1989–1995, una nueva etapa* (Buenos Aires: CARI, 1996).

31. See Russell, "From Videla to Alfonsín."

III

The Economic Transformation

10

Critical Junctures and Economic Change

Launching Market Reforms in Argentina

*Juan Carlos Torre**

It is likely that Argentina-watchers have not recovered from their surprise in the face of the economic changes made in that country since 1989. In a relatively short time the institutional context of economic development has undergone changes of great scope. Two features particularly characteristic of this process have been the streamlining and curtailing of state intervention in markets, and a greater opening to international trade. Just as important as the direction of the economic changes is the fact that they have been sustained over time. In Latin America, Argentina has stood out for its ability to frustrate the expectations it has sparked throughout its history. On more than one occasion in recent decades the country seemed on the brink of taking a new direction in its development, only to quickly lose momentum.

In order to sort out the keys to the structural change occurring today, it is useful to review Argentina's recent experience. The notable performance of the Argentine economy in the first decades of this century facilitated a wide-ranging process of modernization, which set it apart in Latin America, a region marked by inequalities and the weight of tradition. Argentina was able to weather the 1929 international crisis more easily than the other countries of the region. Later on, the higher prices its products fetched in a world at war and in need of food provided the resources for a new wave of social integration into an industrial economy more geared to the domestic market during the decade of rule by Perón. In the 1950s, Argentina developed the institutions of an expanded state and an urban civilization that took several more decades to be acquired

*This article is part of a research project undertaken in collaboration with Vicente Palermo, whom I thank for his authorization to use ideas and arguments that draw heavily on his contribution.

elsewhere. Its later history was an unfolding of those institutional
foundations.

Studies on comparative political development indicate that once a
country chooses an institutional path, that path tends to perpetuate itself
and to shape future options.[1] Institutions created at a given juncture later
take on a life of their own, drawing societal resources, socializing individuals, and creating vested interests around them; all these factors shaped
the repertoire of strategies available for dealing with changes in the wider
world. This means that a strategy theoretically more functional to the problems a country faces at a given moment may be excluded from its real
options. The weight of institutional arrangements is affected by the density and extent of the fabric of social relations on which they rest. In
other words, the constraints in adjusting to the changing conditions will
be more formidable in countries in which the shadow of the past, with its
burden of interests and deep-rooted expectations, projects its light on future developments. Argentina is an eloquent example.

An overview of Argentina's history since the 1950s yields the image
of a society held back. This image does not deny that alternative sources
were sought to compensate for the drainage of resources that had made
possible economic growth and expanded social participation, and which
by that time had lost their original dynamism. In effect, an effort was
made in the early 1960s to further import-substitution industrialization.
While Brazil would later take this path in a sustained fashion, as
developmentalism ushered in a vigorous modernization effort, soon after
Argentina got started such development ground to a halt. The search was
renewed in the mid-1970s, in a direction opposite that of economic liberalism. And whereas Chile dismantled the institutions of state-protected
and -promoted development at the same time, as part of its effort to attain
renewed growth, Argentina, also after paying high social costs, headed
down a dead-end path. Independent of its immediate causes, the lack of
continuity of such varied efforts reflected a more enduring reality, the
tenacious resistance to change on the part of the distributive coalitions
formed under the postwar economic institutions.

The fact that alternatives were sought refutes any notion that this
tenacious resistance was the expression of an effort to defend a satisfactory equilibrium. Actually, once the favorable economic conditions of the
1930s and 1940s had subsided, Argentina was swept up in an ever deeper
and more intractable flurry of conflicts. With this, Argentina's peculiarity
among Latin American nations changed: From the modern and progressive nation of the early years of the century it became known as particularly unstable and prone to conflict. At the same time, a persistent
discontent permeated the collective consciousness of Argentines. Few

countries of the region experienced economic and social performance in such a self-critical manner. Nonetheless, even in the face of widespread dissatisfaction with its institutions, it was not obvious that the decision to change them was a rational one. The perceived costs of change, coupled with uncertainty as to the possible benefits of the new rules of the game, can create powerful incentives to maintain existing institutions. Novel approaches are always at a disadvantage when judged at the tribunal of the status quo.

This reality helps explains why institutional change, far from being gradual and adaptive, is instead discontinuous and episodic and follows major upheavals that discredit the existing institutional structure and dissolve the alliances that underpin this structure. On this point, Argentine historian Tulio Halperín Donghi in 1994 published a book entitled *La larga agonía de la Argentina peronista.*[2] He reconstructs the series of traumas that marked the postwar period, up to the hyperinflation of 1989. In 1989, amidst unprecedented economic crisis, the institutional order, which had survived so many challenges, was shaken to the ground, and a new institutional arrangement tumultuously began to emerge in its place. The resolution of this prolonged agony that Halperín Donghi so masterfully examines highlights a historic irony: The current administration, which has taken it upon itself to dismantle the existing economic institutions and put in place market reforms, is also Peronist.

This background is the context for the pages that follow, which analyze the political conditions for launching the economic transformation now under way. The idea of "critical juncture" (*coyuntura crítica*), understood as those moments in history when there is an opportunity to change both institutional rules and social coalitions significantly, is central to this analysis.

The time that has elapsed allows us to take a look back to the critical juncture of 1989 to identify the elements that combined to give way to the new institutional arrangement defined by the market reforms. No doubt economic adversity was a major incitement to institutional change. But the process of transition to a more open economy, to a reorganized state with new functions, and the incentives for a more autonomous capitalism should be considered first and foremost as a political operation. That is because the creation of the new economic institutions was determined by the circumstances, political resources, and institutional capabilities available to or created by governmental leaders.

When accounting for the political factors that set the context for the economic reforms, there is a widely held view that tends to limit this type of analysis—that is, the opinion that holds that the key to explaining capability to adopt and implement reforms lies in the existence of political will (or lack thereof) on the part of the government leadership. Certainly having governmental leaders committed to change is a crucial ingredient in any initiative to alter the status quo. Consequently, it is especially important to clear up the question of the reformism. But often the analysis does not end there. The problem with this view is that it is based on the assumption that public decision makers always exercise a substantial degree of control over their institutional and political environment. That is not necessarily so, however, and needs to be verified. Strictly speaking, the first challenge facing political leaders who embarked on economic reform programs was how to mobilize adequate capacity on the part of the government to initiate, define, and sustain policies over time. In other words, structural change was not just a matter of political will, but also one of governmental capability. In each case this question met with historically contingent responses depending on different governmental capabilities.

The Choice for Market Reforms

The external debt crisis, which precipitated a serious emergency for the countries of Latin America in the early 1980s, provided the backdrop for the economic reform under way. In Argentina, the effects of the external debt crisis were felt in an economy already developing under the weight of serious and persistent disequilibria. As a political correlate to the combination of old and new problems, in 1982 the military withdrew to their barracks, but not without first presiding over the military fiasco of the Malvinas War. Argentina thus found itself facing the challenges of two transitions: the transition to democracy, and the transition to a new economic order through structural adjustment.

In the face of the demands of this twofold transition, in 1983 the first democratically elected government, under the presidency of Raúl Alfonsín, placed priority on rebuilding democratic institutions. Alfonsín's strategy involved a constant effort to moderate or delay the distributive costs of the economic emergency, with a view to ensuring that the different social and political forces would continue to be identified with political democratization. This initiative, which sought to elude the harsh economic measures that nonetheless proved necessary to get past the crisis, clearly had a mixed outcome. In 1989, when Alfonsín passed the presidency on to Carlos Menem, for the first time in sixty years a democratically elected government was able to transfer executive power to another president also elected by popular vote. But it was done amid a nationwide economic and social crisis of unprecedented proportions.

Reform policies tend to emerge as responses to crises. They have the virtue of pulling countries out of their traditional policy patterns, and they encourage governmental leaders to try new alternatives. The literature has identified several mechanisms by which crisis facilitates innovation of public policy.[3] The first mechanism reinforces the mandate for new presidential leadership. Thus the crisis has the effect of discrediting the postures and ideas of the previous administration and predisposes public opinion to giving the new entrants to government an opportunity to solve the emergency. Further, the outbreak of crisis instills fear over the fate of public order, for not only are economic problems aggravated, but also there are stepped up conflicts and episodes of violent protest. In addition to all of that is another phenomenon that helps create an institutional framework more open to implementing reforms. That is the well-known sense of urgency that the crisis brings about in public opinion, bolstering the belief that a lack of initiatives can only help make things worse.

When these various mechanisms that the crisis sets in motion combine, and the new president's mandate is reinforced by the sense of urgency and fear of social and political chaos, an extraordinary context is created that is highly propitious for innovative decision making. Carlos Menem acceded to the presidency in July 1989 precisely amid an acute crisis characterized by market dislocation, capital flight, riots and looting in large urban areas, and the collapse of the Alfonsín administration—Alfonsín stepped down prior to the conclusion of his term. In the face of the political earthquake caused by hyperinflation, Menem's decision to stop preaching against the economic adjustment, which in large measure accounts for his electoral victory, ripened swiftly and schematically. In its place, to the surprise of both friends and adversaries, he did not hesitate to embrace the policy of market reforms as the economic strategy best suited to calm the financial markets so as to get his new administration safely past the emergency and its aftereffects.

Menem renounced his programmatic baggage so suddenly and completely that it is hard to speak of a change in economic policy preferences. One would have to look elsewhere to account for Menem's turnabout. In this context, it is important to recall that government elites have their own noneconomic motivations for following the counsel of economic doctrines. By this line of reasoning, Menem's option for market reform resulted from a strategic calculation—that is, it was aimed at winning over the acquiescence of the economic actors, both domestic and foreign, who held decisive veto power over the economic program and the stability of his administration.

Closing the Credibility Gap

The persuasive effect of the hyperinflation crisis appears to have been determinant in Menem's turnabout once in government. But when the change in direction had been made, he had to face an additional challenge: how to make his new policy credible. A key factor in the outbreak of hyperinflation had been the extended period of uncertainty that took hold of the financial markets in early 1989, when pre-election polls indicated an imminent victory for the Peronist candidate. That information had the virtue of conjuring up the memory of the last—and the traumatic— experience of Peronist government from 1973 to 1976. Neither the image nor the message of Menem during the election campaign alleviated fears. Once elected, therefore, Menem's first task was to put an end to the uncertainty regarding his administration's economic policy. With that in mind, he made promises that flew in the face of the arguments that had been instrumental in garnering him votes. And so a credibility problem ensued.

In effect, it would be difficult for the economic actors to behave in a manner consistent with the promises of the new policy unless they believed that these promises were firm and would be sustained over time. Menem displayed manifest weaknesses when it came to clearing up these doubts. If the business world had attributed populist ideas and beliefs to Menem prior to the elections, now there were justified concerns as to the authenticity of his sudden conversion to economic rigor and freedom in the marketplace. Why trust in Menem's new commitments and his consistency? The doubts grew stronger because, as was apparent to everyone, the new president's room to maneuver in choosing policy options had been severely curtailed by the economic crisis. In other words, it was feared that the new policy could be reversed, as it appeared to have been imposed by need, not dictated by conviction.

The literature on reform policies underscores the fact that when a government leader faces such circumstances—that is, when his will to reform is shrouded in suspicion and reservations—he is forced to go further than he would have chosen to in the absence of a credibility gap. More specifically, he needs to overreact, burning bridges and making an abrupt break with the past. Consequently, the scope and pace of his reform policies will serve as a sign of present commitments and future intention. Finding himself in such a situation, Menem undertook to highlight just how profoundly and genuinely convinced he was of his new ideas, how audacious he would be in carrying them out, and—an important signal—how much capacity for political control he had for taking up the challenge.

There were several political operations through which Menem tried to gain the confidence of the business community. In his policy statements, Menem rationalized his ideological turnabout by reference to what he called the "popular market economy," exalting economic principles traditionally foreign to the Peronist tradition: privatization of public companies, liberalization and deregulation of trade, fiscal austerity, and condemnation of state interventionism. This ideological conversion was accompanied by two highly significant political gestures: a clear convergence with big business along with key cabinet appointments, and bringing Argentine foreign policy into line with U.S. positions. Similarly, he assumed a personal commitment quickly to privatize the publicly owned airlines and telecommunications enterprises, which were of symbolic importance.

Indeed, Menem's bold about-face in his ideas, policies, and alliances was (in the incisive language of markets) directly proportional to the rate of risk associated with the return of Peronism and a candidate of populist origins being at the helm of government. At first these initiatives were convincing: The financial operators, who had been turned into key political actors by the crisis in public finance, responded favorably. Having emerged triumphant from his first challenge, Menem turned to his mass of supporters to convince them of the virtues of the new policy.

Menem's Leadership over the Peronist Movement

In a country in which the familiar phantoms of public life have been the political weakness of its governments and their inability to choose a path and stick to it, it was especially urgent for the new administration to show it had the authority to choose market policies and sustain them over time. Whether economic expectations would stabilize around the new policy depended fundamentally on whether Menem would be able to keep the loyalty of his followers: They had been at the vanguard of resistance to the economic adjustment initiatives put forth by the previous administration, which were ultimately frustrated. Hence the second unknown that it was essential to clear up was how the Peronist movement would react. There was a notorious lack of affinity between, on the one hand, the beliefs and expectations of those who had elected him president and, on the other, the direction he sought to give the government. This gap could have become a source of conflict which, in turn, could have spurred renewed distrust.

Menem's new policies and alliances, however, did not draw sharp political reactions among his Peronist grassroots base of support. This turn of events can be viewed in a broader context. Analyzing the acquiescence of the Indian Congress party to reorientation—in the same direction but more modest in scope—of its economic policy by Indira Gandhi in 1981–82, Atul Kohli has noted that "when leaders are judged by their followers, what they seem to stand for turns out to be as important over the short run as the substance of the politics they pursue."[4] Taking advantage of her image as a leftist and nationalist leader and the policies she had implemented that benefited the poor, the Indian prime minister was able to shift the course toward economic liberalization without incurring appreciable political costs.

In this respect, Menem's credentials among the popular Peronist sectors were well established. He emerged as the movement's leader in the 1988 internal elections to designate the presidential candidate for the 1989 general elections. Menem then raised the traditional antipolitical and movement-oriented banners in his confrontation with Antonio Cafiero, chairman of the organization and a politician more closely associated with republican practices and a more modern conception of the party. These contrasting postures, combined with the public opinion of the time, influenced the outcome. The negative views of broad sectors of the population regarding President Alfonsín's economic performance affected not only the popularity of the Radical party, which went down to defeat in the 1987 legislative elections; it also had a negative impact on the political class in general, which Cafiero was closely identified with, considering his history. This political climate created the conditions for Menem's rise. Menem succeeded in portraying himself as set apart from the discredited political class, and he filled the void in the Peronist political consciousness. He was seen as a popular leader who emerged outside of the party structures, and he called on the grass roots to bypass those structures and to rescue the original essence of the movement. Involved in the rituals and slogans of a plebeian and messianic populism, surrounded by trade union leaders, Menem first won his party's nomination and was then voted into office, bringing with him a considerable sum of political capital to confer legitimacy on his policy options.

Had they been carried out by a political leader without Menem's credentials, his innovations in discourse, policies, and alliances once in government would not have been well received. In the critical hours of 1989, we see an old political paradox come to life, according to which leaders of the Left can readily adopt right-wing policies without unleashing the wrath of the Left—or vice versa. Menem's successful turnabout proved that a president from a populist tradition can put forward a nonpopulist economic strategy and come through with flying colors.[5]

However, the Peronist party cadres had a hard time assimilating and digesting Menem's innovations. Some pressed for oppositional strategies, but most were mindful of the fact that there were limits to the expression of dissidence and that an elementary political calculation advised against transgression: Disloyalty to President Menem could jeopardize access to the resources of state patronage which, after thirteen years, were once again within their grasp. Menem exploited this opportunist stance and, skillfully applying carrot-and-stick politics, managed to keep his followers in line. In November of 1989, the deputies and senators of the Peronist party gave legislative approval to the government's first two major initiatives, the Economic Emergency Law and the State Reform Law, providing Menem with the tools he needed to initiate fiscal adjustment and market reforms.

Menem's new economic policy did not meet with consistent and unified labor opposition. The best reflection of this situation was the decline and political isolation of the trade union leadership who had successfully carried out thirteen general strikes to oppose Alfonsín's earlier adjustment efforts. When Menem's economic policies were launched, the Confederación General de Trabajo called for confrontation, consistent with its strategy in the recent past. Its appeal met with a limited response and led to the creation of a rival union federation that advocated collaboration with the government. Menem, in turn using the many mechanisms available to him by which unions depended on the state corporatist arrangements, distributed incentives and applied sanctions with a view to erecting barriers to collective action. In addition, it should be kept in mind that, as had occurred from 1973 to 1976, the presence of a government whose election they had backed modified the political landscape within which the trade union leaders determined their options. Most responded with the same spirit of understanding that trade union leaders elsewhere offered governments friendly to them in the face of similar emergencies and policy swings. Typically, that was the case of the Spanish socialist unions toward the government of Felipe González in his first periods in power. The primacy of politics in guiding the action of the Argentine unions was translated into a labor truce, which was all that Menem urgently needed in order to show that he had the authority to govern, and in so doing to close the credibility gap with the business community.

Social Tolerance for Structural Adjustment

The disciplining of the Peronist party by Menem, and the labor truce agreed upon by the majority of unions, while facilitating the embrace of a new policy in theory entailed a serious risk: that the popular sectors traditionally organized by the Peronist movement would express their discontent with the structural adjustment policy in a direct and inorganic manner.

The primacy of politics, by subordinating the defense of social interests to party loyalties, created the potential for a crisis of social and political representation.

That happened in 1973, when, after eighteen years of existence on the periphery of legal politics, Peronism and Peron returned to government.[6] Nonetheless, this time the attitude of the Peronist politicians and unionists in the face of Menem's turnabout did not appear to betray or fail to respect the will of their grassroots base of support. Actually, the structural adjustment policy was adopted and implemented without major social resistance.

Analyzing the conditions under which market reforms can be launched and sustained in the context of democratic regimes, Adam Przeworski asks why the population may favor policies that entail an immediate decline in their well-being.[7] His conclusion is that this outlook requires confidence in the future: The greater the population's confidence that their lot will improve in the future through the reform, the greater their support for implementing such a reform. A key concept in this argument is what Przeworski calls the costs of the transition and what Ralph Dahrendorf, in more colorful language, calls "the valley of tears."[8] In this context, it is argued, the population will be ready to bear the costs of the reforms and to cross a "valley of tears" insofar as they trust that after the journey their socioeconomic situation will improve.

Following this reasoning, it is useful to note that the starting point from which Menem won social tolerance for his structural adjustment policy was quite different from what is contemplated in the above argument. In effect, in the hyperinflation episodes the valley of tears did not lie ahead in the collective experience; rather, the deterioration in standard of living was already evident. It could be said that the costs were being paid in the present, which radically alters the perception of reform policies. In a major crisis, the most drastic economic reforms are judged not on their own terms but in comparative terms—that is, for the promise they hold of making the population's emergence from the "valley of tears" swifter and more definitive. Under such circumstances, public acquiescence to adjustment policies is based less on the confidence in a better future and more in the urgency to flee from an unbearable present. One could say that support for the reforms can be guaranteed if the break with the status quo is seen as an alternative bringing an end to the economic decline, despite entailed sacrifices that are definitely more moderate than those associated with the persistence of hyperinflation.

And so, in mid-1989, the political dynamics generated by the outbreak of hyperinflation came to solve a key dilemma of the reform policy. Since the need to foster change in the economic institutions was already becoming apparent during the Alfonsín administration, the development of the structural adjustment programs turned on the question, What can be done to garner popular support for the reform policy? The Radicals' response was pessimistic, in large measure because of the wave of general strikes initiated by the Peronist unions in the name of pro-growth policies that offered an alternative to Alfonsín's attempts at economic adjustment.

In contrast, with the change in administration it was no longer thought that there was an alternative; at the same time, there was a dramatic decline in expectations. Many polls revealed a widespread consensus in public opinion that the structural adjustment policy was the way to avoid greater evils. As Víctor Paz Estenssoro had done in the Bolivian hyperinflation of 1985, Menem took advantage of the willingness of most of the population to accept policies that promised to leave the economic emergency behind and transform it into a crucial resource for bolstering his ability to govern.

The Formation of a New Governing Coalition

The issues discussed thus far were all in play in solving a crucial problem for initiating reforms within a democratic framework—that is, forming a governing coalition. The credibility of structural change policies depends on their viability. In that regard, it should be pointed out that the governing coalition crafted by Menem was a novel one, as it put together the support of economically powerful groups along with the institutional power provided by a popular electoral majority. As such, Menem's governing coalition represented an ambitious effort to alter the historical asymmetry of Argentine policies.

One of the keys of Argentina's endemic governability problem has been the divorce between parties with electoral potential and economically powerful groups. This separation of votes on the one side and resources on the other was reflected historically in a dispersal of government power. The government elites were often under threat of a deficit of legitimacy or a deficit of effectiveness. By bringing together what for so long had been separated, Menem joined the ability to govern as conferred through the institutions of the popular vote and the ability to govern based on control of extra-institutional resources that influenced the development of the economy.

Certainly the weight of the different components in this broad and novel government coalition has not been even. The political and financial needs of the Menem administration gave the major economic groups considerable influence when it came to defining the rules of the game and distributing the costs of the structural change. In view of the circumstances under which the market reforms were launched, this influence is not surprising. Of particular interest was the fact that the weight of private capital demands over the government did not entail a loss of support from the popular sectors traditionally mobilized by the Peronist movement. This made it possible for Peronism, with Menem in the presidency, to ratify as never before its claim to being "the natural governing party"—that is, to having in its hands the key to governability of a conflict-prone society such as Argentina.

The formidable concentration of power articulated by his governing coalition provided Menem a crucial input for handling the emergency gripping the country. The other important input came from the rules and practices of the presidentialist system in place, putting at his command the institutional resources needed to monopolize planning and implement the reform policies in the executive branch. When it came to taking action, Menem fully exploited these resources, in large measure thanks to the discipline he was initially able to impose upon his followers.

The first two government initiatives noted above, the Economic Emergency Act and the State Reform Act, were clear-cut delegations of legislative powers by the Congress to the executive. Under this arrangement, the executive was practically given a blank check to decide on key aspects of the economic reforms without having to be accountable to the legislative assembly. The Peronist deputies and senators also authorized expanding the number of members of the Supreme Court; this enabled Menem to designate judges whom he trusted politically and so pack the high court to prevent it from becoming a veto opportunity for interests adversely affected by the reforms. Furthermore, he added the large-scale use of what are known as "decrees of necessity and urgency"—that is, para-constitutional legislative capacity, which became routine. The policymaking style was increasingly centered on the president's powers, similar to those characteristics of a state of emergency. Writing on the political logic of processes of economic change, Stephan Haggard and Robert Kaufman have held that beginning the reforms entails a break with the status quo, and that this will be the more likely the greater the discretionary power of government elites.[9] The launching of market reforms by Menem was a good example of this logic.

The Political Sustainability of Market Reforms

Inasmuch as structural change threatens so many vested interests and challenges so many well-established beliefs, if it is to become part of the public agenda it must meet a very specific and demanding set of factors.

In retrospect, that was what happened in the critical juncture of 1989. There we observed a situation of acute economic crisis, a new government's need to overcome a credibility gap with the economic actors, a leadership invested with considerable political capital, great social tolerance for the cost of the adjustment, and the formation of a powerful governing coalition. The presence of these factors made it possible for Argentina to begin the laborious process of dismantling the economic institutions under which it had developed for the previous fifty years.

Dictated more by need than by conviction, and as the result of a pragmatic commitment to the economic and political constraints under which it operated, Menem's reform policy underwent several tests between 1989 and 1995. One important asset he held for addressing challenges was having associated himself with producing a crowd pleaser—that is, economic stability. The market reforms were introduced along with fiscal and monetary adjustment measures aimed at leaving hyperinflation behind. After almost two years of frustrated attempts, inflation was sharply curtailed, thereby galvanizing popular support for the new economic path. This accomplishment occurred at the same time as the appearance of an auspicious circumstance, the change of trends in international capital flow. External voluntary financing, which had come to an abrupt halt in 1982, was resumed in 1991 because of the effect of the recession in the countries of the Northern Hemisphere; a new wave of capital flowed into Latin America. Considering that slowing inflation can have diminishing returns in public opinion if not accompanied before too long by growth, these funds arrived in Argentina at a crucial moment. Between 1991 and 1994, the Menem administration took advantage of the favorable external conditions by using foreign financing to bolster domestic demand. Thus stability and economic boom provided positive incentives that, although unevenly distributed, helped to lubricate adjustment costs and garnered political support for the reform process.

Reform policies are generally in a race against time, a race between the destruction they provoke and the creation they foster, between the disarticulating effects associated with the end of the old economic institutions and the opportunities for implementing new rules of the game. The Argentine experience of recent years has not been an exception, as revealed by the major increases in unemployment that accompanied economic restructuring. The consequences of this gap for the legitimacy of the reform policy may be cushioned if the economy is able to return to the path of growth within a reasonable period. The problem Argentina faces today is that, economic reforms notwithstanding, its sources of growth are still dependent on resources such as international movements of capital that are volatile and unpredictable, raising serious questions about the future. This vulnerability became apparent in 1995, when the country suffered the impact of the December 1994 Mexican peso crisis—the so-called "Tequila effect"—which caused a massive outflow of capital and led the economy into a deep recession from which it is now recovering. While the well-known slogan *no hay alternativa* ("there is no alternative") may be useful for withstanding the first stages of structural adjustment, it does not solidify an enduring consensus. Actually, continuity of social tolerance is associated with tangible improvements in well-being. To the extent that these are not consolidated, the process of transformation runs the risk not of sliding backward but of producing a sort of adjustment fatigue that can take it to a standstill.

Another possible source of uncertainty, more institutional in origin, is the decision-making style with which Menem led the country through the turbulent periods of structural adjustment. While this type of public policy management helped to solve certain problems at first, as it did so it also raised other problems. Kaufman and Haggard, after having associated initiation of the reforms with the discretionary power of the government elites, hold that the sustainability of reforms, in contrast, requires other conditions. Briefly, rules need to be fashioned that restrict the discretion of rulers to set the rules of the game, so as to consolidate expectations around the new incentives. In addition, no economic transformation can have lasting effects under a permanent state of emergency because the results that flow from this logic of decision making create uncertainty—the economic actors know that the current administration, or perhaps the next, will be in a position to change the rules of the game when and as it chooses. To avoid that risk, the decision-making process would have to be made more institutionalized, transparent, and depersonalized than when the reforms were initiated.

Nonetheless, the transition to this more desirable environment should not be taken for granted. The problem here lies in the existence of incentives capable of stimulating a change in the government's style of decision making. Institutional practices have an inertia of their own that makes them insensitive to the logic of normative reasoning. In addition, relative success in carrying out the economic transformation may prompt government leaders to perceive more drawbacks than advantages in political innovation. Those who have governed in an exclusionary and unilateral style and have enjoyed the benefits of such governance are very likely to resist the checks and balances of a more institutionalized system. This is not conjecture; rather, it is a worrisome corollary to a review of Menem's six years as president. Initially, the need to ensure governability through the term of the emergency was argued to plead for understanding of an unconventional political style. Over time, however, the persistence of that style threatens to hinder consolidation of the structural changes.

The structural transformation now under way must continue to address economic as well as institutional issues. Those issues must be resolved if Argentina is to hold its course over time. This will make possible the stability Argentine society needs to renegotiate the distributive costs of the structural change and bolster its political sustainability within a democratic framework.

Notes

1. See Kathleen Thelen and Sven Steinmo, "Historical Institutionalism in Comparative Politics," in *Structuring Politics*, ed. S. Steinmo, K. Thelen, and F. Longstreth (New York: Cambridge University Press, 1992), 1–32.
2. Tulio Halperín Donghi, *La larga agonía de la Argentina peronista* (Buenos Aires: Editorial Ariel, 1994).
3. John T. S. Keeler, "Opening the Window for Reform: Mandates, Crises, and Extraordinary Policymaking," *Comparative Political Studies* 25, no. 4 (January 1993): 433–86.
4. Atul Kohli, "The Politics of Economic Liberalization in India," *World Development* 17, no. 3 (March 1989): 305–28. The quotation is taken from p. 310.
5. Dani Rodrik has called this paradox the "Nixon-in-China syndrome." In his words:

> It is a truism that only President Richard M. Nixon, with his impeccable anti-Communist credentials, could have made the overtures he did to Mao Tse-tung's China. Since Nixon was a trustworthy character to the American right, he could be relied on not to sell out U.S. national interests. The translation of this principle to reform strategy is that it may take a labor-based government to undertake reforms that would be otherwise unacceptable to labor and other popular groups. And for the same well-founded reason: it is easier to convince organized labor that the changes are needed ones that will pay off in the long run, even if they hurt a bit now, when the argument is put to them by a government that *prima facie* has their interest in mind.

Dani Rodrik, "Comment," in *The Political Economy of Policy Reform*, ed. John Williamson (Washington, DC: Institute for International Economics, 1994), 213.
6. Juan Carlos Torre, *Los sindicatos en el gobierno, 1973–1976* (Buenos Aires: Centro Editor de América Latina, 1983).
7. Adam Przeworski, *Democracy and the Market: Political and Economic Reforms in Eastern Europe and Latin America* (New York: Cambridge University Press, 1991).
8. Ralph Dahrendorf states that "the basic economic changes cannot be undertaken in just a few months. In any event, they will not be effective immediately. Rather, the economic reforms inevitably lead to a valley of tears. To improve, the situation must worsen initially." In *Reflexiones sobre la revolución en Europa* (Barcelona: Emece, 1991), 100.

9. Stephan Haggard and Robert Kaufman, "The State in the Initiation and Consolidation of Market-oriented Reform," in *State and Market in Development*, ed. L. Putterman and D. Rueschemeyer (Boulder, CO: Lynne Rienner, 1992), 221–40.

11

The Road to
Sustainable Growth, 1983–1993

Daniel Marx*

The Republic of Argentina had sixteen presidents and thirty-four ministers of finance between 1955 and 1983. Finally, after several experiences with military governments and unstable political and economic regimes, a civilian government was inaugurated at the end of 1983. The new administration came into power with a strong mandate to restore the democratic political institutions established in Argentina's constitution. The new civilian government faced a daunting challenge—to restore democracy and political stability while fostering economic development and growth.

While the new democracy functioned quite well from the start, economic progress has been slower. To begin, the economic situation in 1983 was not favorable. Inflation was close to 430 percent on an annualized basis; and, internationally, the recycling of petrodollars was over and commodity prices, highly relevant to Argentine export revenues, were falling. Stubbornly high interest rates in the early 1980s added to the change in direction of capital flows, while commercial lending to sovereign debtors virtually disappeared with the debt crisis: The government had accumulated $3.2 billion in arrears to external creditors. At the same time, low levels of international reserves, at $1 billion, both underscored the lack of market liquidity and strained currency stability. The public sector deficit reached 11 percent of GDP. Furthermore, the country's public sector account woes showed a marked trend toward continued deterioration—taxes and other forms of government revenues were shrinking while spending commitments and outlays were increasing.

These factors characterized the end of a long period marked by easy financing of costly domestic imbalances. Equally important, these

*With the collaboration of Jorge Rodríguez, Jorge Castillo, and John Friend.

domestic imbalances had perverse dynamics; the accumulated commitments of various members of the society, individuals, and corporations were such that they required additional expenditures without a revenue counterpart. These expenditures were growing over time.

The beginning of this period was marked by confusion in economic ideas. The Argentine populace in general, and its political leaders specifically, were less inclined to adhere to sound policies and public management for two principal reasons:

1. Ingrained perceptions based on previous experiences: Specifically, some of the military regimes had employed rhetoric that favored orthodox financial management, but the policies actually utilized were far from consistently orthodox. The results were consistent only with management failures.
2. Misperception of the actual economic situation: The rate of deterioration of the country's economy was not clearly perceived. In addition, the restoration of democracy was accompanied by a wave of optimism that overshadowed the prevailing economic trends. Finally, the incoming civilian leaders expected to receive generous external aid, which never materialized.

In a country in which people with unsatisfied basic needs were becoming more politically important, there was pressure to satisfy them as quickly as possible. The best way to take care of those needs was by creating opportunities to increase production. The previous situation had been characterized by a state that could not control itself, that was trapped by promises it was unable to fulfill, and frustrations accumulated. Recent changes have made possible the creation of more wealth to be spread throughout the society.

Given the confluence of internal and external economic and political factors facing the new civilian regime, it is not surprising that Argentina's economy has traveled a bumpy road since 1983. Using the evolution of real GDP as an indicator, one can see periods of some growth along with some declines and a significant crisis by the end of the decade. If that performance is overlapped with the inflation rate, a pattern emerges. For most of the 1980s, Argentina suffered poor economic performance while inflation rates averaged 280 percent annually. In 1989 hyperinflation arrived, and inflation jumped to nearly 3,300 percent. Inflation subsequently fell to roughly 1,340 percent in 1990, 84 percent in 1991, and then 18 percent and 7 percent in 1992 and 1993, respectively. At the same time, real economic growth resumed and accelerated.

One can conclude that periods of low inflation rates, or a credible tendency toward them, are associated with improved performance in the real economy. For example, when the rate of inflation fell from nearly 3,300 percent in 1989 to 84 percent in 1991, real growth resumed. The growth rate reached 8.9 percent in 1991; it was 8.7 percent in 1992 and fell slightly to 6.0 percent in 1993. This pattern was also in evidence earlier. In 1986 inflation dropped to 82 percent from 385 percent a year before, helping GDP grow 7.3 percent one year after a 6.6 percent decline. Graphing GDP performance against the rate of inflation corroborates the previous analysis (see Table 1 and Graph 1). It appears that, contrary to some economic opinions, it is not necessary to relax the variables that give rise to inflationary pressures in order to boost the growth

Table 1. GDP Growth and CPI Inflation

	GDP Growth	*CPI Inflation*
1980	0.7	87.6
1981	-5.4	131.3
1982	-3.2	209.7
1983	4.1	433.7
1984	2.0	688.0
1985	-7.0	385.4
1986	7.1	81.9
1987	2.5	174.8
1988	-2.0	387.7
1989	-7.0	3,297.9
1990	-1.3	1,343.9
1991	10.5	84.0
1992	10.3	17.5
1993	6.2	7.4

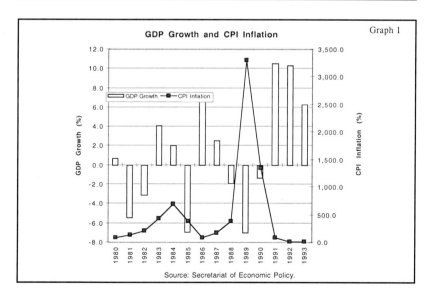

Graph 1

Source: Secretariat of Economic Policy.

of GDP. In the recent Argentine experience the opposite is true—economic agents perform well during price stabilization.

The real challenge is to create an environment for sustainable growth. In the short run, GDP increases can be obtained through a variety of means. In the long run, investment is required as an engine for real growth. In Argentina, investments as a percentage of GDP have varied up and down. During the early 1980s, however, investments were often motivated by substantial, but not necessarily sustainable, tax breaks. For example, a plant might be constructed that would not operate profitably. The same plant would end up being profitable, though, if its products were exempt from the Value Added Tax (VAT). Estimates of the total amount of such tax promotion vary, but the magnitude was certainly important. Such incentives were required under conditions of economic instability to maintain a certain level of investment. But, as noted, while the incentives did spur investment, the investments themselves were often inefficient (see Table 2 and Graph 2). Today, investment allocations are more appropriate because they are undertaken under conditions of stability and are designed to take advantage of competitive advantages rather than merely tax incentives.[1]

Table 2. Gross Domestic Investment (% of GDP)

	Private	*Public*
1980	19.08	6.08
1981	16.86	5.77
1982	14.72	5.21
1983	14.25	6.05
1984	14.20	5.04
1985	13.21	4.83
1986	13.36	4.05
1987	12.65	6.19
1988	13.34	5.30
1989	11.59	3.92
1990	11.03	2.97
1991	12.53	2.11
1992	14.82	1.89
1993	16.16	2.23

In a world that is increasingly and unavoidably integrating, being and staying competitive is of utmost importance. Allocating resources for investment and maximizing the efficiency of that investment is the driving force in generating wealth, and private income increases during that process. In the long run, the basic needs of the population can be met only through the creation of wealth.

Toward that end, Argentina has made significant progress in becoming more competitive, through the process of modernization and struc-

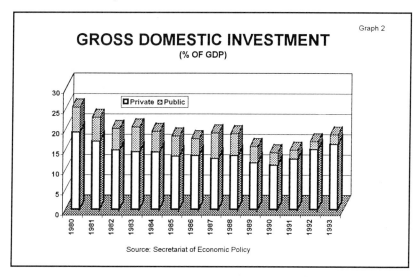

GROSS DOMESTIC INVESTMENT
(% OF GDP)

Graph 2

Source: Secretariat of Economic Policy

tural reform, including deregulation, privatization, and the opening of the economy. A leaner government is a cornerstone of this process. The government is unique in that it is not only a part of the production function of society, but it is the ruling body as well.

Fiscal Performance

Aggregate Fiscal Accounts

Available statistics are not entirely reliable, because of varying accounting procedures and inflationary distortions. Nevertheless, the statistics show a fiscal deficit roughly equal to 11 percent of GDP in 1983.[2] Subsequent government efforts aimed at bringing the deficit down to approximately 2.5 percent of GDP by 1986. After that time the tendency reversed, with a clear deterioration accompanied by increases in inflation until the stabilization programs of the early 1990s.

The federal government's inability to maintain budgetary control was principally the result of commitments to several bodies or agencies that had budgetary implications but that were not easily accountable for their expenses. A set of these were open-ended commitments of the government to society that would eventually appear in treasury or central bank accounts. For example, the central bank was the source of last resort of funds for the National Mortgage Bank, which was autonomously offering credit to home builders and dispersing those funds while work progressed (see Table 3 and Graph 3).

Table 3. Fiscal Accounts (% of GDP)

	Expenditures	Revenues	Financial Result	Rediscounts	Adj. Financial Result
1981	21.4	12.6	-8.8	2.3	-11.1
1982	20.5	10.5	-10.0	16.1	-26.1
1983	20.1	10.5	-9.6	2.2	-11.9
1984	17.7	10.8	-6.9	2.1	-9.0
1985	21.5	17.5	-4.0	3.4	-7.5
1986	19.4	16.3	-3.0	1.6	-4.6
1987	20.1	15.1	-5.0	2.7	-7.7
1988	20.0	13.9	-6.0	1.5	-7.5
1989	18.3	14.5	-3.8	1.1	-4.9
1990	16.7	13.9	-2.8	0.9	-3.7
1991	17.3	16.4	-0.9	0.6	-1.5
1992	19.0	18.7	-0.4	0.1	-0.5
1993	20.1	20.0	-0.1	-0.1	0.0

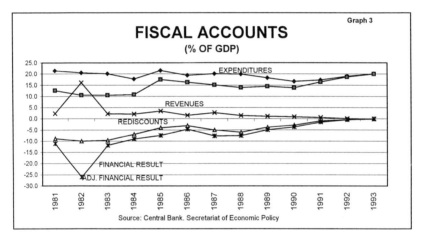

Source: Central Bank. Secretariat of Economic Policy

There were three principal institutions that functioned as brokers or intermediaries for the open-ended commitments of the federal government and central bank. These were (not in order of their importance) public sector companies, provincial governments, and the pension system. Examining each one sheds light on the issues and dynamics of the overall fiscal situation.

The first intermediary or set of intermediaries were the government-owned companies, or *parastatals*. As late as 1990, nearly 25 percent of federal government spending was incurred through the *parastatals*.[3] These companies were often attacked because of poor productivity standards, and they were also often major beneficiaries of transfers from the treasury. In fact, during the 1980s, the cumulative annual deficit of the *parastatals* never dropped below 2.2 percent of GDP.[4] The *parastatals* proved to be difficult to control, particularly in terms of budgetary restraint, for the following reasons:

1. Management Information Systems (MIS): Public companies suffered from a lack of accounting statements and economic analysis, and the information that was available was unreliable.

2. Pricing distortions: Some of the rates or prices charged by the *parastatals* were determined politically, which gave the organizations the incentive to request additional governmental funding in order to compensate them for reduced revenue, rather than pursuing cost efficiency.

3. Key appointees: The criteria for appointments to management positions in *parastatals* was often heavily weighted to pay back political favors. Another important factor was the assessment of how accommodating the administrator would be to advancing political objectives. Partially as a result of these two considerations, and also because of the constant flux of politics, management in the state companies was prone to high turnover and a lack of continuity.

4. Loyalties: The *parastatals* were generally managed with an orientation toward satisfying the needs of their own employees or certain interest groups. The managers saw themselves as responsible for delivering the maximum possible funding and resources; these managers did not see themselves as accountable for the most efficient use of the available funds. Additionally, some public companies incurred expenses payable over time but did not report them until due (at which time they asked the treasury to bail them out).[5]

5. Diluted responsibilities regarding debt servicing: In some cases, public companies were used to front for the borrowing of other governmental agencies. In any event, the firms had little incentive to comply with the repayment terms of their debt, particularly if the instrument had implicit or explicit governmental guaranties. Moreover, by having budgetary appropriations but not servicing their debt, companies had additional cash flow available for other uses. Even with supplier financing, it was not unusual that the treasury had to bail out the companies. Consequently, to avoid pressures on the money supply, the treasury would often issue debt instruments to honor *parastatal* commitments.

The provinces were another important source of unexpected transfers from the federal government (see Graph 4). Real current expenditures

by the provinces grew 41 percent between 1982 and 1990.[6] The procedures and dynamics, especially regarding MIS, appointment of managers, and debt servicing, were comparable to those described above
regarding *parastatal* companies, with the additional possibility of the
extensive use of the overdraft capabilities of provincial banks at the central bank. Only in 1987 and again in 1989 did the central bank authorities
take appropriate countermeasures, in the second instance removing banks
that were abusing their overdraft privileges from the check-clearing
system.

Finally, the pension system had annual net outflows of around 4 percent of GDP during the early 1980s. After 1984, the net outflows tended
to rise, reaching 6.9 percent of GDP in 1993 (see Table 4 and Graph 4).

Table 4. Federal Government Transfers (% of GDP)

	Provincial Governments	Pension Systems	Other
1985	4.52	4.80	1.26
1986	4.95	4.82	1.23
1987	4.90	4.52	1.46
1988	4.92	4.36	1.35
1989	4.78	3.47	1.47
1990	4.33	4.75	0.96
1991	5.03	5.14	0.98
1992	5.68	6.22	0.91
1993	6.40	6.92	1.34
1994	5.64	6.50	1.07

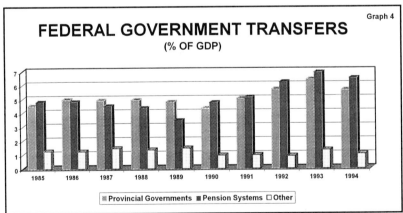

Graph 4

FEDERAL GOVERNMENT TRANSFERS
(% OF GDP)

Provincial Governments Pension Systems Other

SOURCE: Secretariat of the Treasury

The pay-as-you-go system was a source of inequalities, and it was increasingly bankrupt. The inequalities were evident in the payment of benefits: People closer to the power structure received more money. At the
same time, firms "promoted" employees to high-level positions immedi-

ately prior to retirement, not necessarily to give them greater responsibilities but rather to increase the pension to which they would be entitled. Pensions were linked to the wages earned during the years immediately before retirement. The system was thus increasingly facing financial difficulties because benefits were unrelated to either past or current contributions. Besides, the implicit subsidy in the system was, generally speaking, not received by the needier segments of the population, creating a perverse incentive scheme. Moreover, during the 1960s and 1970s, the system had cash surpluses, enabling the government to increase entitlements without considering the future cash-flow implications.

Dynamics

Without specific policy action, the imbalances outlined above could only worsen. In the first instance, public administrators or public companies had few incentives to lower costs or improve their efficiency. Actually, the incentive was to invoice the treasury for increased funding, as there was usually no penalty for doing so. Thus, public expenditures were bound to spiral higher.

Incentives related to spending by provincial governments were similar. Access to taxes collected by the federal government and other federal resources became competitive: Individual provinces had incentives to make spending commitments and to draw on the "collective pot" before other provinces could do so. By acting that way, a province could ensure itself a share of funding in the short term. Needless to say, this skyrocketed expenditures. As provincial governments grew, the private sector shrank.[7] This was both because public employment pushed up wage scales and because government interference increased. The result in some provinces was that the private sector became too small to support the burgeoning public sector, which increased the provinces' need for external (that is, federal) funding assistance.

In the early stages of the pension system (1950–1970), the government was able to use its net cash surplus as a cheap and growing source of its own financing. However, in the 1980s benefits paid began to exceed contributions. To make things worse, because of the generous legal framework of the system or occasional amnesty programs, some individuals would contribute only toward the end of their working lives but receive full pensions, as if they had contributed fully. The system provided incentives for individuals to avoid contributing after a certain time. For example, if one contributed for twelve years, one received the same pension that would have been available after five years. It was only after contributing for fifteen years that one could expect benefits that would exceed those received after five years of contributions.[8] This higher amount was also capped.

The context, then, was one of broad external and internal forces pulling away from fiscal equilibrium. As described, internal incentives led to spiraling public expenditures. Tax compliance was declining in the face of measures perceived as arbitrary, short-term fixes. Moreover, agricultural and commodity prices were trending lower, which translated into lower revenues from the collection of export taxes. And international and domestic interest rates were going up. In this context, the changing pension equation was critical, because the government could no longer finance itself from pension surpluses. Instead, the government was forced to borrow in the domestic and international capital markets.

Management

The imbalances and dynamics described were further reinforced by difficulties inherent to public sector management in Argentina. A first requirement for a solution to any problem is the awareness and understanding of the issues. Regular information and good accounting systems, however, were rare within the public sector. Preparation of information relevant to making decisions was usually the result of individual initiative. It was rare that a public administrator was required to make a decision based upon cost-benefit analysis. Only very recently has the Argentine goverment begun to re-create systems that follow budgetary execution and the treasury cash accounts. Regular statements that match flows and stocks of monetary accounts as well as commitments are an important step; they are currently being implemented.

A second requirement is being willing to follow a comprehensive solution. The political demands at the time were for making up for lost wealth and revenue. Within that context, few people were interested in presenting a wide-ranging diagnosis, and even fewer were interested in listening to it, not to mention acting accordingly. It is no coincidence that, after six decades, only in 1991 was a federal budget passed on time.

The third element is an appropriate administrative framework. Lack of information and political will aside, the Argentine government was also hindered by diluted responsibilities and a cumbersome decision-making process, particularly in the executive branch. Not only did the appointment of decision makers not sufficiently emphasize professional and ethical background, but, in addition, the system did not grant the minimum authority to perform tasks efficiently. For example, below the ministerial level, consent from several areas was required for regular administrative decisions. This multiple consent structure created significant delays and granted a de facto veto to several persons while at the same time diluting responsibility and accountability. To the extent allowed by the legal framework, the president could issue decrees to resolve issues caught in the approval process. Still, under even the best of the circumstances, this method overburdened the executive branch. Moreover, the widespread use of presidential decrees was distracting, requiring the president and his office to make decisions on less important subjects and administrative matters instead of focusing on important issues.

In Argentina, as in any democratic country, the reform process required timely, albeit heavy, action by Congress, not always easy to bring about. Even when the governing party had a majority, it was always difficult to pass legislation reducing entitlements or other perceived benefits, or diminishing expenses. It can be tempting for the opposition to abandon the government in order to see how they handle an almost unmanageable situation. It was only after the hyperinflationary crisis, and with a new government and a partially new Congress, that the executive branch and Congress collaborated to pass legislation that set the groundwork for a more realistic economic framework.

Consequences

The poor initial diagnosis of the condition of Argentina's economy and fiscal position in the early 1980s, coupled with self-imposed urgency to show quick improvements in personal income levels, resulted in a failure to put the economy on a growth path or to resolve imbalances that with the passage of time could only worsen. When the economy did not respond as expected and it became evident that long-run prospects had not improved, the new civilian government began to lose authority.

At those moments during the period between 1983 and 1989 in which the fiscal accounts reached an unsustainable imbalance, each time the solution came more from the executive branch and less from Congress. The government utilized schemes that brought some temporary relief to the fiscal accounts, and through this a respite was achieved from inflationary pressures. However the measures were disruptive of growth potential because the private sector viewed them as arbitrary and as punishing income-generating activities such as increased production. Moreover, the private sector lost faith with each new round and focused more and more on subsequent efforts. Examples of the temporary measures thus employed include taxes on exports of agricultural products, taxes on bank account debits, forced savings, and exchange rate differentials by which the government would profit by paying lower than market rates for foreign exchange (see Table 5 and Graph 5).

Table 5. Exchange Rates (Official rate=100)

	Official Rate	Free Market Rate	Effective Rate for Corn Exports
1984	100.00	112.52	73.36
1985	100.00	106.79	69.54
1986	100.00	129.42	69.50
1987	100.00	128.60	98.51
1988	100.00	120.62	98.50
1989	100.00	186.17	73.90
1990	100.00	100.00	78.50
1991	100.00	100.00	98.70
1992	100.00	100.00	100.00

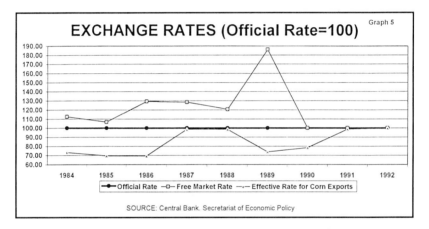

Graph 5

EXCHANGE RATES (Official Rate=100)

SOURCE: Central Bank. Secretariat of Economic Policy

In the short run, these measures had several advantages. First, a revenue stream was generated almost immediately. The appeal for the executive branch was that no negotiations with Congress were required, making the measures relatively easy to implement. Second, most revenues were directed to the federal government. Unlike regular taxes, these revenues were not shared with the provinces. And third, these executive measures were relatively effective in reducing inflation, at least in the short run.

Together with these revenue "fixes," the federal government pursued a mix of price-related policies. Price increases were granted to certain public sector companies in order to attempt to limit their drain on fiscal resources. At the same time, price guidelines or controls were imposed on the rest of the economy. Again, these pricing measures helped dampen general price increases in the short run because, in addition to macroeconomic effects, the relative prices of products that affect the consumer market basket were reduced.

In fact, the type of measures implemented did not necessarily reduce inflation in either the medium or the long run. The actions emphasized the intrinsic weakness of the fiscal accounts by making use of measures that were perceived as arbitrary and not precursors to a long-term solution. Additionally, by affecting wealth creation, the government eroded the future tax base. Finally, the harm done to confidence in the market triggered capital outflow, which in turn led to lower demand for money and higher inflation.

The end result of the various economic programs and regimes was the hyperinflation of 1989. In that year, a new administration was inaugurated. The new administration benefited from the fact that its party controlled Congress. With the executive and legislative branches functioning together, a new strategy was enacted to meet the country's various problems.

Significant progress was made in the early 1990s:

1. The passage of the Economic Emergency Law, the Reform of the State Law, and other key pieces of legislation enabled the government to address deeply rooted issues such as streamlining budgetary and procurement procedures, starting the privatization process, eliminating investment restrictions, and suspending distortionary subsidies and taxes.
2. Movement toward a more equitable, comprehensive tax system, coupled with improved administration, closed loopholes and increased compliance. As an additional consequence, real incentives were created for the private sector to invest in productive activities with true competitive advantages, rather than politically favored sectors. (In the previous regime, a certain producer might receive a tax break for 20 percent of sales by means of an exemption from VAT, while another producer was penalized by 30 percent of sales through export taxes.)
3. Confidence was restored by putting public sector liabilities into order. The debt restructuring provided for a lasting solution with a thirty-year time horizon and significantly reduced tensions, related to the ongoing negotiations on the public sector debt. Those tensions had been generated because of the uncertainty linked to the nature of the negotiations and their potential effects on transfers within and outside the economy. At the same time, prior to restructuring, the government redeemed enough debt to reduce its service to more manageable levels. As such, the new administration's strategy reinforced the trend toward balanced accounts. Last but not least, the government contributed to

confidence by renouncing the use of arbitrary mechanisms such as price controls.

4. Structural reforms, in which the government increasingly concentrated on the private sector were made. Measures utilized toward this end included deregulation, privatization, and pension reform. The pension reform put the system on a self-sustaining footing. It also significantly reduced liabilities accumulating into the future, although at the expense of having to handle in just a few years accumulated costs that had been incurred over an entire generation.

External Factors and Capital Markets

Issues

Given the amount of capital movement, it has a significant impact on the performance of the Argentine economy. As mentioned, domestic factors were important determinants of capital flow in the 1980s, but it was also affected by the level of interest rates and the nature of external negotiations. From this perspective, the experience of that decade can be characterized as follows:

1. Diagnosis: Given the internal situation at the beginning of the decade, Argentina was particularly vulnerable to external factors. Accordingly, it was no coincidence that the so-called debt crisis was triggered by an unprecedented level of dollar interest rates. At the time, the "crisis" was diagnosed by international financial institutions as a short-term liquidity problem as opposed to an exhaustion of the previous economic model.

2. Solutions and dynamics: Argentina, like several countries with debt problems, designed programs by which it tried to solve them in accordance with the previously noted diagnosis: The goal was to create short-term breathing room rather than to correct the deeply rooted problems that had caused the situation. Necessary so-called structural policies were not sufficiently emphasized. Some programs bought time but had built-in dynamics that were seeds for future problems. Given a certain level of committed expenses, and given a deficit and limited financing alternatives, the intended solution was to try to achieve a revenue increase through unusual methods, such as forced savings, taxes on bank debits, or utilizing exchange rate differentials. These measures deepened the private sector's view of the system as both artifi-

cial and arbitrary. With that justification, attempts followed to avoid the new measures, possibly by changing the reporting system of economic transactions (sometimes by employing the black market).

3. Timing and capital movements: Time management, from a number of perspectives, was far from ideal. In the first place, some international financial institutions made an important assessment through the application of the concept of "financial assurances," which intended to match the sources and uses of funds during the implementation of a lending or assistance program without taking into account its later effects. Moreover, there was no intention to close the financial gap over the longer term. In the second place, the horizon of the programs was insufficient to factor in the results of structural measures. The short-time horizon imbedded in the program increased skepticism over the sustainability of these programs and had negative effects on capital flows. To the extent that decision makers expected the programs to be revised, or expected another round of corrective measures, they would not take the risk of longer-term investments. Rather, economic agents sought to hedge against uncertainties by taking money out of the country. As a result, the financial gap fed on itself, and the amounts that had to be covered under the new circumstances spiraled ever higher.

4. Public authority: Authority was significantly eroded during the succession of short-term programs. The lack of sufficiently long time horizons coupled with the failure to resolve structural imbalances weakened the public authorities in the eyes of the political and business communities. The so-called short-leash approach taken by the international financial institutions also resulted in a low level of confidence, which in turn undermined the possibilities for endorsement of costly measures within the country.

5. International politics: The external political circumstances related to the debt crisis were also confusing. Authorities of the borrowing countries complained about the perversity of the system. These borrowers argued that their newborn democracies could be in danger. In response, sympathetic counterparts, from authorities in developed countries to international financial institutions, would promise to change their lending arrangements. The proposed modifications varied from greater and speedier disbursements to debt forgiveness. Regardless of the merit of the proposals, as the changes failed to materialize, the borrowers

diverted their attention from working on the main issues: sound domestic economic policies and restoring creditworthiness.

6. Contingencies: The short-term focus also left the country exposed to additional unforeseen events with no room for such contingencies. A natural disaster, such as the floods of 1987, that affected exports and corresponding tax collection created needs that were temporary by definition. In this context, the quarterly monitoring of financial targets, even when all measures were correctly factored in, could make matters worse. When a target was not met, disbursements were halted at the moment when the needs were greatest. Even if disbursements were resumed later on, the government's credibility had already been affected, and the financing needs were not necessarily covered in aggregate terms.

Consequences

Generally, economic isolation is very costly in the long run because of reductions in standards of living and the slowing of economic progress. But to the extent that a country does not isolate itself, it is more dependent on external factors, and when borrowing from international lenders it will receive policy suggestions. To reduce such vulnerability, it is necessary to establish a strong domestic base through the elements of a sound economic program and to take the initiative to reduce exposure to external forces to the greatest extent possible. In that regard, the aspects relevant to Argentina in the 1980s were the following:

1. Growth possibilities resumed when authorities took a long-term structural approach while also resolving everyday problems. The authorities then obtained backing from the population. These new dynamics produced favorable results. When the government began to reduce the size of the state, opportunities were opened for private enterprise. The introduction of what was perceived as a much more equitable tax system, and improvement in administration at the same time, began to regularize the economy and increase tax income. The resulting perception, of a system that would not be forced to undergo regular revisions with unpredictable outcomes, brought capital and economic transactions back into the formal economy.

2. Another necessary feature for making the program sustainable was "clearing the horizon"—that is, eliminating the process of

ongoing negotiations that could constantly reopen issues affecting the country's economic life. The debt strategy is the critical element in this regard. Reducing the external debt through market operations when values were well below par brought the debt to a level at which interest payments became affordable. At the same time confidence was rebuilt, thanks to low but consistently regular payments. The renewed confidence in turn gave the republic the necessary authority to ask for longer tenors and reduced cost of servicing. Finally, the execution of the strategy took advantage of lower market interest rates. One objective became to obtain a fixed interest rate to the maximum extent possible as an insurance against future fluctuations.

Even for small countries, there is never enough public money available to finance all needs. As a result, a strategy that in the end made borrowing countries increasingly dependent on international loans or forced financing was not sustainable. The use of private capital, however, is sustainable over that time frame. Private capital can be attracted if economic stability prevails and opportunities for growth are available.

The future utilization of public sector borrowing must be carefully monitored. An increase in expenditures coupled with a reduction in tax collection is normally accompanied by debt accumulation, unless there is a significant fiscal surplus to begin with. On the other hand, regular expenditures can only temporarily be supported by the sale of assets. At some point in the past, a segment of society utilized the government to siphon money from another segment, which was setting it aside for the future. When that was over, Argentina asked the rest of the world for financing. Today, the figures of public debt and debt service are manageable, by international standards. Nevertheless, developing a local market capable of providing consistent financing is an important element that is still in the process of development. A capital market with consistently responsible players will significantly improve the country's ongoing creditworthiness.

More decentralization of decisions within society leads to improved economic organization, which in turn gives rise to more efficiency, more production, and fewer frustrations. Simply stated, the government cannot manage economic production as efficiently as individual, private economic agents can. As discussed previously, Argentina has made significant strides with economic policies based on these presumptions, maintaining the socioeconomic equation with some degree of equilibrium. However, challenges still remain.

The Socioeconomic Equation

Long-Term Trends

Public sector behavior has historically had a powerful impact on private sector decisions and on the performance of the Argentine community. Today, because of deregulation, privatization, the elimination of price controls, and the general opening of the economy, there are more individual opportunities to succeed than there have been for decades. The new framework is based on a shift in responsibilities in which the public sector continues supervising the areas it is uniquely responsible for while avoiding the mismanagement seen in the past, at the same time continuing to remove barriers to private sector competitiveness. The job of the private sector is to achieve competitiveness and make sustainable growth a reality.

The present policies are necessary to reverse the underlying trends of the previous decades, during which per capita income remained stagnant at best. Analysis of the available statistics (see Table 6) leads us to the following conclusions:

1. Productivity: Taking GDP per employed person as a proxy for productivity, it is evident that Argentina was consistently losing ground in both absolute and relative terms between 1970 and 1990. The absolute loss represents a sharp contrast with the performance of a number of other countries during the same period. The 22 percent recovery during the current decade is quite remarkable, but there still is significant room for improvement.

2. Employment: The growth of the labor force (employed and unemployed people) has exceeded both population growth and the job-creating capacity of the economy. In the last ten years, the employment creation rate exceeded the rate of growth of the population (16 percent vs. 13 percent), while productivity gains were achieved at the same time. In absolute terms, nearly 1.5 million jobs have been created. The unemployment index nevertheless increased because the labor force expanded, and it did so relatively rapidly in the face of numerous economic changes.

3. Pensioners: The increase in this segment of the population has outpaced by far any of the previous categories. The number of employed people per pensioner declined from 5.46 in 1970 to 3.36 in 1994. In a system that was functioning as a distribution mechanism in which wage earners maintain the retired, the burden on the active population increased at a pace difficult to sustain.

Table 6. Socioeconomic Indicators

	1970	1985	1990	1994
Population	23.4	29.9	32.2	34.0
Labor Force	7.3	9.9	10.7	12.1
Employed	7.1	9.3	10.0	10.8
Unemployed	0.2	0.6	0.7	1.3
Pensioners	1.3	2.7	3.1	3.2
GDP*	$8,027.0	$9,303.3	$9,430.4	$12,419.6
Ratio Analysis				
GDP/Employed	$1,130.6	$1,003.6	$944.0	$1,154.2
Employed/Pensioner	5.46	3.38	3.19	3.36
Labor Force/Population	31.2%	33.0%	33.1%	35.5%
Unemployed/Labor Force	2.7%	6.1%	6.3%	10.8%
Employed/Population	30.3%	31.0%	31.0%	31.6%

*Expressed in thousands of pesos at 1986 prices.

Consequences

Analyzing the 1970s and 1980s as a single period, GDP grew more slowly than the population. If real wages were to follow productivity, they could only fall. In addition, wage earners ended up paying more out of pocket, directly or indirectly, to support pensioners, further reducing the purchasing power of their incomes. If wages did not decrease accordingly, employment opportunities would diminish, because fewer jobs would meet the higher productivity standards. The paradox is that those lesser jobs would still have to support the same number of retired people. A new iteration of this cycle would lead to an even less acceptable situation. Borrowing is an expensive way of coping with this situation.

The challenge is how to increase employment, knowing that a relevant part of income must be set aside to take care of the retired population. Increasing the number of employed without altering remuneration while maintaining the current output is not viable. One possibility is having a more flexible labor contract that will open opportunities that do not exist under current restrictions. In any event, the productivity standards for the currently employed should and can increase further to accommodate expansion of real incomes.

More Challenges

Another area that still has not been resolved is the relationship between the federal and provincial governments. In fact, the distribution of rights and responsibilities among these entities is neither as clear nor as balanced as it should be. The federal government is obligated to share the taxes it collects with the provinces, an obligation with which it has not always complied. Despite today's laws mandating sharing provisions and the restriction of overdraft privileges with the central bank, the strain between federal and provincial governments is becoming more difficult to resolve because of the suffocation of productive activities in some provinces and continued reliance on the federal government as the provider of funds of last resort.

It remains difficult to generate the understanding that it can be more efficient for the provincial units to delegate certain tasks to a more neutral, comprehensive body, rather than performing them individually. Issuance of currency is a good example. To avoid abuses, currency has to be issued by one entity under a sound rule, and no one should have the right to draw on that entity, either directly or indirectly. As described, the mechanisms for dealing with provincial governments have imbedded in them the potential to destabilize the system, either through the threat that failure of one province would drag down the republic or simply in that one province would increasingly draw on resources that belong to others.

There are other areas that require the attention of the federal government. The need exists to:

—prioritize and subsequently establish the framework for new infrastructure projects;

—monitor the privatized monopolies and their regulatory bodies, and try to spur these newly private firms into providing their services at internationally competitive prices;

—further streamline public sector activities;

—continue to strengthen the public sector accounting systems as a management tool; and

—create and foster conditions that will encourage the domestic savings pool.

Several of the challenges mentioned above require further reforms, such as in provincial finances or streamlining the administration. There are still other areas in which results will be evident only after a time, such as pension reform, and others that will require constant work, such as preemptive bank supervision. The private sector is also undergoing major restructurings that require time and capital to show the returns. Financing is therefore key. Domestic financing is preferable, because suppliers of funds are closer and may thus monitor the results of their actions, and they are less prone to unpredictable behavior. Under any circumstances, trustworthiness is the key to obtaining financing and diminishing the costs of transactions.

Tremendous economic and political improvements have been achieved since the end of military rule in 1983. If Argentina remains on the same route mapped out at the beginning of this decade, continued progress is possible. Overcoming difficulties will still demand significant effort, but, in the end, the only limit to what can be achieved will be that of the skills and desires of the people.

Notes

1. The World Bank has published statistics that differ slightly from those summarized in Graph 2. The principal difference in the World Bank figures is the greater magnitude of the decline in investment over the 1980s. For example, the World Bank estimates show Gross Domestic Investment falling to less than 10 percent of GDP between 1988 and 1990.

2. As estimated by the World Bank. The overall fiscal balance, including rediscounts and extrabudgetary items, was a deficit equal to 16.5 percent of GDP.

3. World Bank.

4. World Bank.

5. Given their legal status, these companies were considered part of the sovereign government and therefore not liable for bankruptcy procedures.

6. World Bank.

7. One author estimates that the number of employees in provincial government grew from 750,000 in 1983 to 1.1 million in 1990.

8. World Bank.

12

The Third Stage of Argentine Economic Growth

Juan José Llach and Fernando Cerro

Economic Reforms and Convertibility

The organizational problems of the Argentine economy, with rising fiscal imbalances and expanding domestic debt, exploded in the form of hyperinflation in 1989, at which time consumer prices rose 4,923.6 percent. Hyperinflation demonstrated that it was impossible to achieve growth and stability within a regulated economy that was closed to the world and by means of a deficit-ridden public sector that performed a multitude of functions that should have been delegated. After this diagnosis was made, an economic program was implemented to balance public finances and reassign functions to achieve efficient resource allocation and improved income distribution.

The State Reform Law of 1989 was the starting point of an extensive restructuring of public finances and a redefining of the tasks of the public sector. The law established a new division of roles between the public and private sectors. The supply of national public goods, the defense of competition, and the regulation of nonprivatizable monopolies and investments were entrusted to the state. The provision of local services was transferred to the provinces to ensure that they were overseen by the level of government closest to the beneficiaries.

During the period between 1985 and 1989, the practice of financing the fiscal deficit through the placement of the Banco Central de la República Argentina's (BCRA, or central bank) remunerated debt with the financial markets became the rule. At first this was done voluntarily, but later it was mandated. Quasi-fiscal activity, which in the last stage of the period reached nearly one-third of the combined deficit, was carried out not only for the monetary financing of the fiscal deficit but also as an instrument to finance the various sectors' credit selectively and to subsidize differential exchange rates.

Changes in the tax system were intended to bring about efficiency and equality within a framework of continuously increasing tax collection. Neutrality in the allocation of resources was achieved by coordinating the tax burdens among the different government levels and through a simplification of the system into just a few taxes. In addition, economically distorting emergency taxes were eliminated. Fairness was to be achieved through strict rules against evasion and by broadening the tax base to increase the number of people paying income and value added taxes.

The privatization process, understood as the transfer to the private sector of the production of goods and services supplied through market mechanisms, was the final focal point of the reform program to eliminate the structural causes of the deficit. The privatization program produced a considerable flow of funds into the public sector, leading to a repayment of a considerable portion of the public debt, and the transfer of the liabilities of state-run companies to the consortia that received the operating concessions for those companies. Apart from the fiscal aspects, however, the process aimed at achieving much more significant goals and permanent results: channeling private investments into activities with excellent profit potential, contributing to a strengthening of the capital markets, and reducing the public utility rates for basic services, which added greatly to overall production costs.

The Convertibility Law of March 1991 established the convertibility of the austral with the U.S. dollar at a 10,000-U.S.$1, obligating the BCRA to sell foreign exchange at this parity and to withdraw from circulation the local currency exchanged in the transactions. At the same time, it forced the government to permanently maintain freely disposable international reserves (of gold and foreign currencies) equivalent to at least 100 percent of the monetary base. These reserves are the backing of the monetary base and cannot be seized. The law also abolished all legal or regulatory rules that established methods of monetary updating, price index-linking, debt revaluation, or changes in costs, even if a debtor's payment is overdue.

Market reforms were meant to eliminate the multiple mechanisms, developed over a number of decades, that distorted the free operation of the markets. The process began with the approval of the Economic Emergency Law of 1989, which suspended the industrial and mining promotion regimes, local procurement requirements and subsidies aimed at creating differential prices or tariffs.

Deregulation measures were intended to establish a market economy and encourage a restructuring of production based on a general renewal of competition. The main agricultural, mining, wholesale, and export markets were deregulated. Trading monopolies were suppressed in the wholesale markets, and the opening of new markets was authorized in large urban centers throughout the country. At the same time, restrictions on the development of retail trade, which had prevented the growth of new forms of retail organization, were removed. Finally, competition was introduced into the professional services market, which was subject to price controls over its services and had entry conditions mandated for new professionals.

Labor legislation progressed at a slower pace. The approval of some "flexibilization" measures was noteworthy, however, such as the encouragement of temporary employment, especially for youths and women, and incentives for compliance with labor legislation. An integral compensation system for the unemployed was established.

The pension system, which had worked on a pay-as-you-go basis, was transformed into an "integrated" system that combined share-out with privately funded pension benefits. The new system established that the worker may choose whether to stay in the public system or join a private one.

The boost given to the capital markets was marked by increased trading volumes of public and private securities. New rules provided greater market transparency, guaranteed equal information and publishing requirements, and promoted deregulation by establishing freely negotiated commissions instead of the prior fixed charges that had made entering and leaving the market excessively expensive.

A substantial unilateral reduction in tariffs on foreign trade was implemented through a reduction of the average import tariff, an almost complete elimination of nontariff barriers, and the suppression of export duties. Import tariff policy became a mirror image of tax reimbursements, in an effort to avoid disparities between the incentives either to sell to the domestic market or export. The sequence shows that, as indirect taxes that differentially affect production are lowered, the level and dispersion of reimbursements is reduced, thus permitting import tariffs to converge at a lower level. In March 1991, MERCOSUR, a common market among Argentina, Brazil, Paraguay, and Uruguay, was established. The fundamentals of the accord have been a trade liberalization program, the establishment of a common external tariff, coordination of the member countries' macroeconomic policies, and the adoption of sectional accords.

Since the Convertibility Program was implemented, there has been a continuous deceleration of inflation in retail and wholesale prices, as well as in costs and sectional prices, all of which have converged on the international levels (see table). In 1995 the annual increase in consumer prices was 1.6 percent and that of wholesale prices was 5.9 percent, with deflation recorded during some months. Linked to the stability achieved, there was an unprecedented revival of the real economy. Between 1991 and 1994, GDP grew at a cumulative annual rate of 7.7 percent, based at first on strong growth of gross domestic investment and later on exports.

Macroeconomic Indicators, 1989–1995

Indicator	1989	1990	1991	1992	1993	1994	1995
Inflation Rate (%)							
Consumer Prices	4,923.6	1,343.9	84.0	17.5	7.4	3.9	1.6
Wholesale Prices	5,386.4	798.4	56.7	3.1	0.1	5.8	5.9
Combined Prices[a]	5,146.5	1,069.1	70.3	10.3	3.7	4.9	3.8
GDP Growth (%)	-6.2	0.1	8.9	8.7	6.0	7.4	-4.6
Investment Growth (%)	-24.4	-9.9	25.1	30.9	14.5	19.5	-16.3
Trade Balance (millions of dollars)							
Exports	9,579	12,352	11,978	12,235	13,118	15,839	20,968
Imports	42.03	4,077	8,276	14,872	16,786	21,590	20,124
Balance	5,376	8,276	3,702	-2,637	-3,668	-5,751	844
Capital Goods and Parts Imports	1,446	1,327	2,672	5,686	6,924	9,428	8,119
Urban Employment (1990 = 100)	99.0	100.0	104.3	107.0	108.4	108.1	105.2
Open Urban Unemployment (%)							
May	8.1	8.6	6.9	6.9	9.9	10.7	18.4
October	7.1	6.3	6.0	7.0	9.3	12.2	16.4

Source: Secretaría de Programación Económica
[a]CPI (50 percent), WPI (50 percent)

The reduction in the relative price of capital goods and the lengthy period during which investments had been put off constituted a propitious framework for the addition of new assets to the economy, which registered an annual growth rate of around 22 percent. The investment maturation process and MERSOCUR were two of the sources of strong export growth, exceeding U.S.$20.9 billion in 1995, with a sharp upward trend.

The comprehensive restructuring of public finances brought about the return to fiscal solvency. For the first time in decades, the Argentine public sector achieved a fiscal surplus after paying interest, and without including privatization revenue.

Structural reforms and rising real wages contributed to a significant increase in rates of urban labor. Ample private investment opportunities caused the economy, at first, to absorb the induced increase in the supply of labor. However this process did not take place at the desired rate, as the approval of legislation promoting labor market deregulation was delayed, thus resulting in high levels of unemployment.

The Extended Fund Facility of the IMF enabled Argentina to have renewed access to that organization's resources, and it facilitated the return of the Argentine government to international capital markets. This established the basis for an agreement with the commercial banks over the Argentine foreign debt. The Brady Plan enabled a considerable portion of the foreign debt to be rescheduled at favorable rates and terms. As a result, the capital of both residents and nonresidents returned to the country, to take advantage of the ample investment opportunities. This inflow of capital and restored confidence in the national currency were manifested by the strong growth of monetary resources, within the framework of currency convertibility, which has led to the accumulation of freely available international reserves of around U.S.$19 billion.

The Response to the Mexican Crisis

The promising progress of the Argentine economy between 1991 and 1994 was strongly affected by the confidence crisis brought about by the devaluation of the Mexican peso toward the end of 1994. The visible repercussions of that event in Argentina were a significant and rapid drop in bank deposits, equivalent to that recorded in the U.S. economy in the first three months of the Great Depression, with the consequent contraction in the financial system's loaning capacity. Rising interest rates and postponed investment decisions, brought about by greater uncertainty, had a strong impact on activity and employment levels. GDP fell 4.4 percent during 1995, and the unemployment rate soared to 18.4 percent in May, dropping to 16.4 percent in October of that same year. This severe recession led to a considerable loss of tax revenue. The intensity of the recession also had important origins in the considerable political uncertainty surrounding the presidential elections of 1995.

Economic policy responded with neither inflation nor deflation. The value of the peso, convertibility, and the financial system were defended, public expenditure was reduced to the levels at which there was available financing, and, even more important, the reforms that had been already implemented were extended. For the first time in decades, a crisis was surmounted without infringing on property rights (those that bet on the peso and the Argentine financial system were clearly the winners) and by persevering with the ongoing policies, with the approval of a set of vitally important reforms that were viable only in the crisis. Among others, these included the following:

1. The Pension Solidarity Law, which fixed a ceiling on pensions and prevented automatic adjustment. In its first year in force, the new pension system had a yield of over 10 percent.
2. Reforms to the BCRA's statutory code and to the financial organizations law.
3. The establishment and implementation of fiduciary funds in the financial sector, which boosted the merger and takeover process and helped to increase the system's solvency. In the provinces, the fiduciary fund enabled progress to be made in the privatization of two-thirds of the provincial public banking sector.
4. Reductions in employer contributions to the social security system of 30 to 80 percent, depending on location.
5. The Labor Accidents Law, which introduced mandatory insurance but imposed limits on disability lawsuits.
6. The Small- and Medium-Sized Company Law, which promotes development and growth through easier access to credit, making it easier to form exporting consortia, and which spreads the supplier development program.
7. The Insolvency and Bankruptcy Law, which enables productive activity to continue (analogous to Chapter 11 in the United States).

In the last few months of 1995, and particularly in the first quarter of 1996, the first clear signs of an improvement in some of the main macroeconomic indicators were noted. In the financial sector, there was a recovery of bank deposits and of stock and bond prices to levels slightly higher than those prevalent before the Mexican Crisis, as well as renewed access to international capital markets. In the real sector, there were increases in production and sales by some industries and public utilities, as well as higher imports. Fiscally, the results of the tax moratorium amply exceeded expectations; the provinces were forced to reduce spending levels through cuts in salaries and staffing levels. More important, they have stepped up the privatization process of their public companies. The flexibility thus demonstrated by the economy in modifying prices and moving toward increases in productivity supports the contention that conditions are right for a return to economic growth.

A Look at the Models (External Shocks)

The "Tequila Crisis" gave rise to old debates, and analogies were rapidly established. Orthodox and Keynesian economists alike agreed in linking convertibility to the gold standard. The first group recommended that the deflation mechanism be helped by drastically reducing public spending. The Keynesians, however, said that public spending should be kept as high as possible. It was also argued that the rapid economic growth between 1991 and 1994 was only a "natural" rebound after the previous intense crisis, but that it was temporary because distorted relative prices were generated that caused an external imbalance that could not be financed. Carried into the present, this argument would say that if there is an economic recovery, the trade deficit will return and the overvaluation of the currency (currently hidden by the recession) will become evident. If there is no recovery, the fiscal accounts will not balance.

On the fiscal front, this view maintains that convertibility will last as long as "Granny's jewels" and the boom in fiscal revenues associated with a cycle of capital inflows. However, while on the one hand a unilaterally expansive fiscal policy is recommended, along with social spending and industrial and export promotion, on the other hand, the consequent currency overvaluation is deplored. The inconsistency, relevant to a discussion of alternative economic policies, should not cause any surprises, because the implied reasoning is the old structuralist model of stop-go cycles. However, there is no acknowledgment that this led to hyperinflation in Argentina or that convertibility was the only alternative to a savage and disorganized dollarization.

Either of the devaluation-inflation and deflation-depression alternatives would have been more socially costly than the path chosen to deal with the crisis. The basis for these decisions, drawn up partly in the heat of battle, are the following:

1. The mechanisms to deal with a crisis are specific to each period. It is a mistake to believe that adjustment mechanisms for foreign shocks are valid forever. They are specific to each stage of development of the world's economy and to individual national economies.

2. There are crucial differences between the gold standard and convertibility. The main difference is that there are no generalized deflations. During the days of the gold standard, there was a somewhat rigid international division of labor. In countries such as Argentina, everything depended on the export sector. When a

crisis blew up in the leading countries, there was heavy price deflation, mainly of primary products. Exports and capital inflows contracted simultaneously. The "automatic adjustment" through deflation was extremely costly. In Argentina, GDP fell 30 percent between 1913 and 1917 and 19 percent between 1929 and 1932.

3. Keynesian policies were designed for a closed economy in a protectionist world. That was the cradle of practical Keynesianism, with its active state intervention. Later, Keynes conceptualized it as a closed economy in which neither foreign trade nor capital flows (which were both in retreat in those days) were relevant in the determination of the level of economic activity. Everything depended on domestic demand, and, given the reigning pessimism and mistrust, only the government could and should "prime the economic pump." Balance-of-payments problems were solved with devaluations—that is, "priming the export pump." Sooner or later, the price of both policies was inflation.

4. With the globalization of the economy and the new international cycle, the world is now very different, made up of an economy that is increasingly open in trade and finance. But it is also different from the *belle époque* in that there is no longer a rigid division of labor, and emerging countries are growing year by year at a faster rate than the industrial countries. The international business cycle is also different. When there was a recession in the world centers, as between 1991 and 1993, more capital flowed to emerging countries, but it was more difficult to export. When the economy revived in the industrialized countries, as it did from 1993 onward, the opposite happened: there was less capital, international prices rose, and more was exported.

Argentina's relationship with the world is changing completely. Its main axes are MERCOSUR plus Chile, the Americas in projection, and an expansion toward Asia that has just begun. This new relationship is also based on a long-lasting change in the value of a vast set of agricultural by-products as a result of increased world consumption and the crisis of protectionist policies.

The Third Stage of Argentine Economic Growth

A merely fiscal understanding of the reforms, in the light of another frustrated attempt at stabilization, ignores that the decisions made include extensive structural changes as a result of a proper diagnosis of the causes of the chronic stagnation of the Argentine economy over the last twenty years. If conditions are adequate, it will soon be proven that the rapid growth of the period between 1991 and 1994 has been the first chapter of a new stage and not just another temporary boom. There are two facts that augur a strong increase in investments: the existence of a large number of profitable projects and the fact that for a country like Argentina that is relatively small in the world economy, the possibility of attracting capital (including the sizable Argentine funds currently abroad) and technology can be almost unlimited.

According to the phases of the international cycle, alternating periods of investment or export could predominate until they have achieved a critical mass that would lead to growth. Circumstantial drops in investments that depend on domestic demand can be more than offset by an increase in investment driven by supply and linked directly or indirectly to foreign trade. With convertibility, not only the public sector economy is subject to strong discipline; all private activities are forced to invest to increase productivity and improve quality. As has been happening since 1993, this push from the supply side will increasingly be channeled into exports. In this framework, inflation and deflation can be avoided, and the "adjustment variable" is an increase in productivity. A system of relative prices has now been set up that is sustainable in the long term and that backs a return to growth. This is the link between the short and the long term that must not be ignored. The new era is dominant, while the new phase of the cycle is an accessory.

Convertibility arose more out of necessity than virtue. However, it gradually changed from being a mere retaining wall to becoming an independent variable of behavior. As escape routes are cut off, it generates conditions for the flight toward productivity as the only outlet for both the public and the private sectors. A look at the responses of the different sectors to the economic measures adopted since convertibility was implemented can thus be useful in evaluating the behavior of the different markets in response to the changes in the economic rules of the game.

Mergers, Acquisitions, and Agreements

One of the main consequences of economic liberalization has been the increased size of potential markets, which led to improvements in business organization through important changes in the structure of the companies. This has occurred in the form of partial or total acquisitions, mergers, the purchase-sale of specific segments (brand, productive unit, business unit), joint ventures, or the establishment of new companies.

The projects, financed largely with foreign capital, show important investment commitments in activities aimed mainly at exports.

The trade liberalization program of MERCOSUR has multiplied the number of partnerships, mergers, and acquisitions between Argentine and Brazilian companies to take advantage of the extended market. These joint ventures have had an impact on trade and on the production of goods and services.

The Reduction of Business Costs

Company cost structures to date show significant reductions in areas such as financial costs, taxes, public services, and expenditures on imported raw materials. These reductions improve the profitability of tradable goods without resorting to changes in the nominal exchange rate. The accelerated investment in infrastructure services, with the consequent increase in quantities offered and productivity, has led to important reductions in production costs (for example, for electricity, gas, telecommunications, ports, transport, and postal services).

Technological Progress and Diversification of the Agricultural Sector

Current programs are based on the offering of technical and credit assistance to small farms and smallholders in low-productivity areas. The Rural Change Program was designed to help farmers find ways to diversify. The target group is small- and medium-sized agricultural companies, and the program's specific aim is to help the farmer in areas related to the modernization of production. The Farming Social Program is designed to increase the income of smallholders and to encourage their participation in policy, program, and project decisions. The purpose of the credit and technical support program for smallholders in northeastern Argentina is to raise the income of smallholders through their competitive, equitable, and sustainable integration into the markets.

Natural Resource-based Industries

The controls, regulations, norms, and specific taxes that have burdened these industries in the last few decades restricted potential for their growth and diversification. A series of measures have been adopted to improve farming profitability, encourage investment, and increase agro-industrial exports. In response to competitive stimulus, there has been a remarkable increase in the range of natural resources exported. From a few products from the pampas region and industrial crops, this has expanded to a wide range of crops, fish, and timber. Technological advances and the development of new products are equally important. This is true both in traditional industries and in newer industries such as organically grown foods, production of fragrances, wild animal breeding, fish farming, vegetable and fruit cultivation, and handicrafts.

Deep-sea fishing has been one of the most rapidly growing sectors since convertibility began, particularly because of its increasing contribution to total exports. Catch volume in 1995 was around one million tons, almost double that of 1990, and it is one of the country's main foreign exchange earners, bringing in close to U.S.$850 million. Agreements signed with the European Union and other negotiations under way with other countries have laid the groundwork for important advances—opening up new markets, a greater product diversification, and an emphasis on the increase in value added. These developments support a forecast of continued growth.

Mining and Petroleum

Mining policy seeks to mobilize risk capital through measures to increase the exploitable area, to reduce the transfer periods from the public to the private sector, and to modify the time allotted to exploratory work and auction rights to publicly held natural resources. Since this sector has a huge export potential, rules have been adopted to increase and diversify the volume of sales abroad: financing of VAT for investments in physical infrastructure, project planning, and the establishment of consortia to use the road or rail network in order to reduce freight costs.

The new petroleum policy included the free disposal of hydrocarbons, the privatization of secondary areas, the installation of additional refining capacity, and creation of sales outlets. Freedom to export and import was granted, and Yacimientos Petrolíferos Fiscales was privatized after turning it into a statutory company.

In 1995 crude oil and natural gas production reached levels of 41.7 million cubic meters (of which one-third is exported) and 30.5 billion cubic meters, respectively, almost a 50 percent increase over the figures recorded in the 1980s. Oil companies have announced investments of U.S.$15 billion over the next five years, to be channeled into prospecting for new reserves, improving extraction at existing sites, refinery modernization, launching of new products, and improving quality. The 420-kilometer gas pipeline that will link Mendoza to Santiago de Chile will require an investment of over U.S.$300 million and will be able to carry seventeen million cubic meters of gas per day.

Industrial Specialization

The policy developed has consisted basically of creating a competitive environment in which to stimulate an increase in production and encourage a relative price structure in line with international prices. To achieve these objectives, all the special subsidy regimes to various industrial sectors that enabled their beneficiaries to elude competition (despite the tariff modifications that had been introduced) were abolished. The new competitive climate led to an intensive process of acquiring capital equipment, for which procedures for joining tariff-exempt import regimes were speeded up. The programs and regimes in force make possible greater specialization and the incorporation of imported components.

The purpose of the industrial modernization and specialization regime (REI) is to allow companies to achieve greater specialization and to make possible an increase in the value of their exports by allowing industry to import at a reduced tariff (2 percent) goods in the same chapter of the harmonized nomenclature, up to the same amount as the increase in exports. The auto regime required the car companies to submit a modernization plan for a three-year period and made it possible for established factories to import finished vehicles with a preferential tariff of 2 percent. Imports, however, have to be offset with an increase in exports. The auto companies specialized, reducing their output of old models and increasing the production of high-quality and advanced-technology vehicles.

The reimbursement regime for domestic manufacturers of capital goods freed up the importation of capital goods, granting a 15 percent compensation on the sales of locally produced capital goods. This stimulated competition through an increase in the scale of production and encouraged prices to converge on international levels. The three-year program to support, encourage, and promote small- and medium-sized businesses facilitated their insertion into the world market, improved their access to credit, and provided advisory and training tools. A law was also passed that brought interest rates for working capital and capital goods purchases into line.

The consequence of the policies implemented is that we are leaving behind the practice of producing goods with no economies of scale and with little attention to large-scale production, specialization, quality control, or trade within industries. Argentina will continue to have industrial output in every area, but it will now be specialized and of better quality.

Investment and specialization are occurring in the commodity industries such as steel, with a doubling of capacity; forestry by-products; petrochemicals; construction materials; textiles; and aluminum. The food-processing industry is also playing a leading role. The important growth in food exports recorded in 1995 has led Argentine companies to invest in new technology and factories for the production of such foods as prepared and frozen meats, dairy products, vegetable oils, beer, flour, soft drinks, chocolates, and candy. There is also innovative change, although less visible because it is occurring in small- and medium-sized companies, taking place in specialized industries such as tailoring, leather manufacturing, printing and book production, fine chemicals, light metallurgy, and capital goods.

Modernization of the "Nontradable" Sectors

The production of goods and services in the economy also includes a set of important activities defined as nontradable in the dynamic sense of the term. Even though they have not been directly affected by trade liberalization, they have shown clear signs of expansion and modernization. These sectors of the economy involve commodities that cannot be obtained from the rest of the world but for which there is local demand.

Private Investment in Privatized Sectors

The privatization of state-run companies has transferred to domestic and foreign private investors a significant portion of the responsibility for savings and investment in infrastructure and fuel and public utilities, decisions that had traditionally been in the hands of the government. The electricity sector, for example, was organized on the basis of centralized state planning, with vertically integrated public companies that handled 90 percent of electricity production, 100 percent of transport, and 50 percent of distribution. For electrical generation, a competitive system has been set up characterized by production that must adapt instantly to demand, which is why a system to determine prices with penalties for failure has been established. This has encouraged a noticeable improvement in efficiency. Even though the transport and distribution systems are monopolies, a set of measures have been implemented that provide incentives for concession operators to include efficiency in their criteria for technology selection and investment programs. Information about direct agreements between generators and large users has led to a significant reduction in rates.

The National Plan for Potable Water and the privatization of the Obras Sanitarias de la Nación (National Sanitary Works) and other provincial companies were the instruments chosen to achieve 90 percent coverage for potable water and 80 percent for sewage systems. Other programs, run by the municipalities, finance projects in suburban and rural areas of fewer than five hundred inhabitants aimed at eliminating waterborne diseases.

Commitments made by the companies that were awarded public service concessions, the inclusion of new activities as a result of deregulation, and heavily unfulfilled demand have caused the telecommunications sector to become one of the main recipients of private investment. The total digitalization of the network and the use of fiber optics and new satellites are the main pillars of the development of new technologies for standard telephone service, cellular networks, and satellite links.

The official policy on deregulation has been oriented toward establishing market conditions and encouraging the restructuring of production based on the re-creation of competition. Although the measures have affected the goods and services market as a whole, their effects have been felt by some industries more than others. The wholesale trade in agricultural products, new retail trade outlets (malls), the professional services market, road freight, mid- and long-distance passenger traffic, river and maritime traffic, and the post and telecommunications industries have been especially affected.

The construction industry, even though it is not subject to foreign competition, needed to be modernized extensively. Its backwardness was especially noticeable in the intensive use of labor, the machinery employed, and the level of technology, all of which have a strong bearing on salary costs and construction times. Investments in the construction sector between 1991 and 1995 recorded a cumulative growth of 91 percent. However, despite this improvement, it is still 8 percent below the level of 1980, the previous record. In the coming years, the construction field is expected to grow at a faster rate than overall GDP.

The retail trade sector is undergoing an extensive modernization process. There has been a growth in the number of malls and supermarkets, substantial drops in trading margins, and a remarkable increase in overall product quality and customer service. In addition, efforts are currently being concentrated on greater diversification in the supply of financial services: the financing of mortgage operations, loans for the purchase of cars and durable consumer goods, credit cards, the incorporation of capital goods and technology, and financing of foreign trade transactions. There has also been a significant expansion and diversification caused by the implementation of the privately funded pension system operated mainly by banks and insurance companies.

Imports

The evolution of the level and composition of imports shows particular consequences for each domestic sector. The levels reached for some imports reflect, in the light of the production costs revealed by the companies in those sectors, a tendency to reduce the local component of their manufacturing processes. This is especially evident in processes in which there is a considerable amount of trade within industries—that is, the simultaneous import and export of similar types of merchandise. In this context, the consequence of the opening of the economy is not the displacement of production but increased specialization, to take advantage of economies of scale. Imported capital goods have had a growing importance in durable production equipment, making possible access to international technology at competitive prices.

Increases in the Output/Capital Ratio

Historical data show that a combination of an acceptable investment rate (Net Investment/GDP) with a low rate of growth in GDP has for decades been a reflection of a totally distorted allocation of investments and a significant sacrifice in current consumption. The structural reforms that have been implemented were aimed at the decisions affecting profitability, efficiency, and growth: They brought transparency into the system of incentives and penalties, they stimulated the inclusion of "risk capital," they eliminated distorted signals, they eliminated corporatist advantages, and they encouraged selective training. This is why the Argentine economy is now able to achieve significant GDP growth rates with investment levels that are between 20 and 22 percent of GDP.

The Driving Force behind Growth, 1996–1999: Investments and Exports

Forecasts indicated that signs of recovery would become evident in the second quarter of 1996 and that GDP would grow at a rate of around 5 percent with good price stability (retail inflation of around 2 percent per year). The continued implementation of structural reforms and the reduction in labor costs strengthened the prospects for increased investment and supported the ongoing efforts to reduce unemployment.

The declining real exchange rate, a product of the reforms, made possible solid export performance in 1995. The progressive reduction of rigidities in the labor market and other reforms also contributed to improvements in competitiveness. The large number of projects under way in, among others, the mining, forestry, food, automobile, energy, and petrochemical sectors, and the improving trade prospects within MERCOSUR, suggested a high level of exports during 1996.

Facing the Future: Pending Challenges

The interruption of the progress was caused by the crisis over the Mexican peso. Afterward, the veil of uncertainty that inhibited investment was the result of political factors and delays in the implementation of reforms. Because of these conflicts there was excessive savings, resulting from consumer uncertainty that must be resolved in terms of consumer expectations and confidence. Even the supply-side economy might otherwise be in danger. Notwithstanding the progress that has been achieved, long-awaited reforms are still pending. The first few steps toward a second stage of state reform is a fundamental move.

As to fiscal issues, in the framework of increased austerity, a reduction in the tax burden on taxpayers will be attempted through a broadening of the tax base and a more efficient use of funds, particularly those assigned to improving income distribution. Even in a recessionary year like 1995, the Argentine economy had a fiscal deficit of the public sector as a whole that was well within the Maastricht criteria (3 percent of GDP). The same also applied in the case of public debt (30 percent of GDP versus 60 percent) and inflation (1.6 versus 3.0). This means that, under full employment, the Argentine public sector is in equilibrium.

In addition, few economies in the world have the margin for potential tax increases as that of Argentina. VAT revenue accounts for only 6.2 percent of GDP, compared with a potential share of 10.5 percent, indicating 4.3 percent of GDP in possible additional resources. Similar considerations apply to income taxes. This wide margin must be used mainly to lower tax rates and, at a subsidiary level, improve some social programs.

The taxes/public spending ratio compared to GDP is not high in Argentina (26 percent), in a structural sense. An efficiency problem exists, however, and there can and must be selective reductions. But selective increases are also necessary in the medium term. Thus, the virtues of convertibility are revealed once again. There will be a de facto efficiency shock in public spending because of financing restrictions, followed soon, it is hoped, by an alteration de jure.

The gravest aspect of the provincial crises was concentrated on the financial situation into which the provincial banks had been dragged: They took on large deposits in the short term at high rates and with an excessive concentration of depositors. These were then channeled into the financing of public spending, rather than productive regional activities. The withdrawal of deposits caused by the Mexican peso crisis, with its consequent financial strangulation, demonstrated the fragility of this financing method.

The establishment of the Fiduciary Fund for Provincial Development was aimed at helping provincial banks in the process of privatization and at encouraging the privatization of provincial public enterprises. The provinces that participate in the program find an alternative to substitute short term and highly onerous debt in long-term rates and conditions, which help to relieve the public debt burden and improve finances.

Health Insurance

The trade-union sponsored health insurance system covers 60 percent of the Argentine population. Its expenditure levels are around 2.4 percent of GDP. Despite the magnitude of the resources involved, the system is under scrutiny because of its elevated costs and the deterioration of the quality of its services. Legislation in 1995 provided valuable guidelines for regulating the Redistribution Solidarity Fund, as well as taking other measures to improve the system. Freedom of choice for the beneficiaries and the standardization of services are steps that will ensure that the system operates with greater equity and transparency.

Unemployment and Labor Reform

The change in relative prices has worked in favor of the selection of capital-intensive techniques. The rising trend in wages has had the same effect on decisions about investments and forms of organization. The consequence has been that a phenomenon of "growth without employment" occurred and was reinforced by the presence of considerable idle capacity at the beginning of the expansionary process, brought about by the progressive disappearance of hidden or redundant employment and the reduction of illegal forms of self-employment as a result of the crackdown on tax and social security evasion.

The institutional framework is decisive. Important reforms have been carried out, but only in the last year. Thus, a high price is being paid for previous inaction. A reform of the collective wage bargaining system is

crucial so that companies may again negotiate directly with their employees and take advantage of modern work systems (such as horizontal
methods of production and quality circles). Two-thirds of the problem
originated in increased supply. The slope of the supply curve is positive
and is a function of market opening. This indicates a degree of social
distress that is substantially less than that revealed by the 16.4 percent
unemployment rate. In any case, there is a serious problem. Growth from
now on will be different. Most of the reductions in company staffing levels have already been carried out, and growth in the construction industry
and regional exports will lead to the creation of increasing numbers of
jobs.

13

The Impact of Market Opening on Argentine Industry

A Survey of Corporate Impressions*

Margaret Daly Hayes†

S ince the late 1980s, Argentina has been swept up in a process of profound economic restructuring. The government has privatized state
enterprises, reduced tariff and nontariff barriers to trade, gradually increased Argentina's integration with Brazil, eliminated subsidies, increased
tax collection, and achieved an unprecedented degree of macroeconomic
stability, particularly compared with the previous turbulent decades. Beginning in April 1991, when the Convertibility Plan was launched,[1] Argentina experienced a consumer market boom. Industrial output expanded
by 11.9 percent in 1992 and by another 7.3 percent in 1993, while in 1994
output retreated to a 6.0 percent expansion level. Between 1990 and 1994,
auto production quadrupled while production of consumer appliances
doubled. In contrast, the steel and petrochemical industries, which had
led expansion in the 1980s, shrank in the domestic market and under distinctly unfavorable international market conditions. Through 1993, Argentina maintained a positive trade balance until imports, needed to satisfy
consumer demand and to modernize the country's aging industrial plant,
began to rise precipitously, fueled by massive foreign capital flows. Figure 1 summarizes the pattern of Argentine growth over the past decade.

*This study was funded by a grant to the Wilson Center's Latin American
Program by Fundación Atlantis of Buenos Aires. An initial work plan was re-
viewed with Dr. Robert Frenkel and Carlos Bonvecchi of the Centro de Estudios
de Estado y Sociedad (CEDES), Buenos Aires.
    †I am grateful to Roberto Frenkel, Carlos Bonvecchi, and Dr. Lucio Simpson
of CEDES for their assistance with this project. Lucio Simpson accompanied me
on most of the interviews. I am especially grateful to him for both good compan-
ionship and running commentary on what we learned.

While GDP has increased dramatically, industry has tracked a more modest although still positive growth trend. Agriculture's contribution to GDP growth has remained stagnant at about 10 percent of GDP, as the result of both internal production problems and international price fluctuations in key commodities.

The private sector is the engine of growth in the new, open, global economic environment. Argentine industry had been experiencing profound transformation since the late 1970s, when Finance Minister José Martínez de Hoz introduced a first round of trade liberalization policies. Further adjustment took place under the gradual liberalization of the Raúl Alfonsín government (1983–1989). But the extent of policy shift under Carlos Menem (1989–) and the Convertibility Plan introduced in April 1991 by Finance Minister Domingo Cavallo has been unprecedented, with the potential for wrenching impact on firms of all dimensions. Most analysts have studied this phenomenon from the macroeconomic perspective. It seemed appropriate to begin to probe precisely what impact market opening and structural reforms had on business as practiced by individual firms of the Argentine private sector.

Figure 1. Argentine Growth, 1985–1994

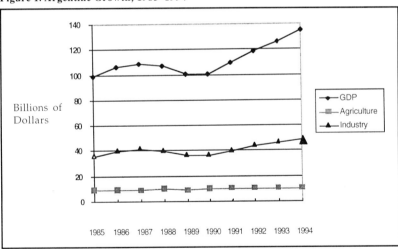

Source: World Bank, *World Development Report* (in billions of dollars) (Washington, DC: World Bank, 1995).

Methodology

This study reports the results of a series of interviews with senior management of some twenty-eight Argentine firms in 1994 and early 1995. The interviews were based on a detailed, open-ended questionnaire that requested opinions on the following issues: the impact of market opening and structural reforms on Argentine business management; competitiveness under the new rules of the game; competitiveness with respect to other regional and international firms, and the outlook for the future.[2] The goal was to learn how quickly and effectively Argentine business was adapting to a new business environment and which adjustments firms were finding most easy or most difficult.

Michael Porter's research into the competitive advantages of ten industrial nations guided the questioning in this study.[3] According to Porter, competitiveness depends not so much on the classic factors of land, labor, and capital, but, rather, on the ability of industry constantly to innovate and upgrade. Four national attributes were associated with competitiveness in his formulation: 1) the presence of skilled labor and supportive infrastructure; 2) discriminating home market demand; 3) competitive supporting industries; and 4) strong rivalry among local firms.

Clearly, in 1994, Argentina still did not offer the competitive environment described by Porter. But were there signs that such competitive attributes might be evolving? If not, how differently was Argentina's business environment evolving, and what might be the implications for its future competitiveness in regional (MERCOSUR) and global marketplaces? In Argentina's favor were her relatively well educated labor force and sophisticated consumers. Other attributes in Porter's paradigm, necessary to stimulate competitive industry, would clearly still be lacking in Argentina, though perhaps some components would be improving.

The competitiveness of supplier industries and the question of linkages and rivalries among local firms (or in the evolving regional market) were key themes to be probed. Neither condition held historically in Argentina, where industry developed during three distinct periods of economic growth: the 1880s period of European immigration, the pre- and post-World War I period, and finally, the import substitution era of the 1940s and 1950s. Companies formed in the 1880s and the period between 1910 and 1925 evolved through mergers and marriages of entrepreneurial capital and traditional large landholder interests; today they share highly interlocking directorates and ownerships. The same is true of post-1940s firms, though to a lesser degree, and the two generations of firms tend not to overlap.[4] Those that emerged after 1940 tended to be or become heavily dependent on import substitution policies and large-scale state-financed projects. Severe distortions in business practices were created by poor management of state enterprises; government policies that promoted a proliferation of small, inefficient, and widely dispersed firms; inadequate protection of contractual rights; and other factors. Chronic inflation in the 1970s and 1980s forced firms to focus their attention on preserving their capital base instead of modernizing their enterprises. Profitability depended on continued inflation. In the late 1970s and 1980s, Argentine industry suffered major contractions. Many smaller firms disappeared, and large conglomerates expanded both vertically and horizontally. One source noted 665 firms in the steel industry in 1973 and only 260 in 1984, with approximately 85 percent of production being done by the largest firms in each period.[5] Major industrial groups acquired all or significant parts of the most important private banks during the 1980s. During the recession of the 1980s, some of the firms that had been most dependent on large state-financed projects began to shift their orientation successfully toward the external market.

It is no longer "correct" to be protectionist, but as the economy has opened, smaller firms have born the heaviest burden of long years of protection from competition. The struggle for defense of their interests has played out in public in the postures taken by rival leaders within the Argentine Industrial Union (Union Industrial Argentina, UIA) and other representative chambers. Nevertheless, for the most part, Argentine firms have struggled alone to survive the wrenching economic changes of the 1980s and 1990s. In this study, we were particularly interested in how those that did survive had managed to do so, and what their future outlook might be.

Profile of Firms Interviewed

We conducted extended interviews (one to two hours in length) with twenty-eight chief executive officers or operations or financial managers, and with several representatives of sector chambers. Most of the firms figured among the 100 to 150 largest in Argentina according to annual rankings by the economic press.[6] Table 1 gives a rough profile of the firms interviewed.

Table 1. Profile of Firms Interviewed

	Domestic Firms	*Multinational Firms*
Consumer nondurables	4	6
Consumer durables	7	1
Intermediate goods	9	3
Capital goods	3	2

The consumer nondurable sector includes firms in the food, beverage, and tobacco industries, which together account for one-third of the sales of Argentine industrial firms; also included are pharmaceutical laboratories and cleaning and beauty products. We interviewed companies in each of these sectors. The consumer durables sector includes manufacturers of textiles and clothing, leather goods, autos, and tires. We did not conduct interviews in the tire sector, most of which is run by multinationals like Goodyear, Pirelli, and Michelin, and we did not have access to the textile and clothing manufacturers, most of which remain small enterprises operating outside of metropolitan Buenos Aires. Intermediate goods include paper, chemicals, petrochemicals, paint and enamels, and nonmetal manufacturers. We interviewed one or two companies in each of those sectors. Several of the sectors, including paper and petrochemicals, have been profoundly transformed as a result of Argentina's nearly completed privatization of state-owned enterprises. The capital goods sector includes heavy equipment and construction materials, as well as high technology manufacturers. In the latter area we interviewed two very interesting small enterprises (Pequeña y Mediana Empresas, or PyMEs). While a number of the firms interviewed were multinational, all operated under Argentine management and had done so for many years. In these multinational firms, ownership remained 75 to 100 percent foreign. Some of the largest firms (in terms of sales) were Argentine multinationals—that is, domestic capital corporations with major overseas exposure.

The firms interviewed reflected a number of characteristics of Argentine industry. For example, most of those we interviewed, including the PyMEs, ranked among the leaders in their sectors. The firms interviewed figured among the top two to five in the sector and for the most part held 60 to 80 percent of the market for their primary product. Only one, in the meat processing industry, reported significant dispersion in its industry. Thus, the firm profile reflected the high degree of concentration of Argentine industry. Even in those sectors in which only one or two firms operate, they compete in different market niches to such an extent that there is very little domestic competition for their product. Finally, most firms reported a dramatic consolidation of the sector in which they operated. The consolidation resulted from a combination of mergers and the demise, over the past decade, of many—often a majority —of the small firms operating in the sector.[7]

The Impact of Market Opening

Reports of Argentine economic performance since 1991 underscore the consumer boom that drove economic growth. Firms acknowledge the tremendous impact that the introduction of the Convertibility Plan had on their business. With the end of inflation came stable prices on the one hand and a dramatic expansion of credit on the other. Firms in the consumer goods sectors reported a sharp increase in consumer demand for their products, willingness to buy on credit, and greater demand for finer products. The food and beverage industries led the boom, accompanied by small appliances, white goods, and automobiles. Firms able to respond to these new dimensions of consumer demand saw their sales increase dramatically—from 10 to 40 percent—between 1991 and 1994. Meeting expanded demand was not a problem for most firms, because capacity utilization was at a low in 1991. At the same time, products and manufacturing processes were outdated, and, with easy access to imported goods, many firms experienced an initial loss of sales before they could compete effectively in the new marketplace. One firm, which produced a low-end product, saw its market share slip dramatically in favor of its only competitor, which produced the more expensive variety of the same product. Some firms began to import higher quality products from their multinational headquarters, or sought to market higher quality products under license. Critics of government policy expressed concern that Argentine firms would become mere traders of goods that were formerly produced at home.

The end of inflation and market opening put downward pressure on prices. Firms reported a 30 percent reduction in prices overall following the introduction of the Convertibility Plan and its associated reductions in taxes and tariffs. Most firms reported that prices had remained stable since 1992. Few expected to raise prices in the near term, because imports continued to pressure their market share. All of the firms reporting said that they had experienced reduced profits, and some were expecting to find their way out of red ink for the first time in 1994. Nearly all firms reported diminished expectations for 1995 and beyond. The consumer bubble could not last forever.

While many individual firms benefited handsomely from the economic recovery of 1991–1994, not all sectors fared well. But the glass sector, the printing industry, the porcelain and ceramic manufacturing sector, nonmachine metal products, nonmetal minerals (cement), miscellaneous chemical products, and the transport sector (which includes the auto industry) all fared well, with stronger positive growth rates in 1993 than 1987. On the other hand, the clothing and textile sector, nonelectric machinery, professional and scientific products, and the petroleum derivatives sector all declined between 1987 and 1993.[8]

The change in production output per sector reflects the dramatic changes taking place. Companies in a variety of sectors reported the dramatic consolidation of their sectors as a result of the market opening. Many small companies simply could not compete with international products. One firm in the consumer nondurables sector reported that the number of firms operating in his sector had fallen from two hundred to one hundred since 1991, and that ten firms held 50 percent of the market. In five years there would only be ten to fifteen firms operating in his sector, he predicted; many would go under and others would be taken over by the sector leaders. A similar phenomenon has occurred in the auto parts sector, in which of 377 firms operating in 1991 to supply the large assemblers only 30 remain. Those in the heavy equipment industries reported that the ongoing crisis of Argentine agriculture—many farms are too small to be competitive—had profoundly affected sales of tractors. Indeed, tractor sales had been declining for more than fifteen years. A producer of precision instruments noted that his three competitors had gone out of business, leaving him as the sole producer in the sector. One firm reported, "The only way we can improve productivity is by applying technology and producing in volume. Small firms can't achieve volume."

Modernizing the Firm

Perhaps the most salient characteristic of Argentine firms interviewed in this study was the profound restructuring and modernization that most had experienced and were continuing to experience. For most, restructuring had begun in the 1980s with the need to adjust to the domestic market recession brought on by the debt crisis. But restructuring in the 1980s was a requirement for survival. Restructuring in the 1990s responded to a new market dynamic—greater competition from imports and a need to lower prices, increase productivity, and raise quality to compete both internally and externally.

All of the firms we interviewed had reacted quickly to improve their productivity. They did this by introducing new management techniques, incorporating new technology into production and management, and reducing their labor force (a process that was already under way in the 1980s as a result of the prolonged recession).

Many of the new managers had been trained abroad in U.S. business schools, but whether trained abroad or not, management as a whole was fully in tune with current international business practices. Several had introduced Total Quality Management and Just-in-Time delivery practices to their firms. Many were experimenting with worker-management teams and plant floor-based management. Some firms began to out-source processes they had previously undertaken in house; others sought to bring into the plant processes they had contracted out. Most firms with multiple site operations began to consolidate production in one or two large, modern facilities.

Managers agreed that the only way to stay in business in the new, more competitive marketplace was to increase productivity. For most manufacturers this meant modernizing existing plants with the addition of imported capital-intensive machinery. Following the reduction of import tariffs in 1987, it was possible for the first time to import the best overseas technology for use in Argentine plants. Most large firms began to add new equipment and automate production lines in the early 1990s, when inflation ended. Incorporation of technology was not possible for many small ones, and in every sector business leaders reported dramatic numbers of firms going out of business.

Rising unemployment has accompanied Argentina's restructuring since the beginning, and it shows no sign of tapering off. National unemployment statistics reported 6 percent unemployment nationwide in 1991. By 1994, the figure has risen to 13 percent, the highest level of unemployment ever recorded in Argentina. October 1995 figures exceeded 16 percent. Reduction in force in the government bureaucracy and layoffs among state-owned firms being privatized contributed greatly to unemployment, as did the ongoing restructuring of industry. Most firms we interviewed indicated that, between the late 1980s and 1994, their labor force had been reduced dramatically. Table 2 summarizes the results.

Table 2. Change in Labor Force

	Number of Companies Reporting Change in Employment			
Sector	*Reduced 1–25 percent*	*Reduced 26–50 percent*	*Reduced > 50 percent*	*Increased*
Consumer nondurables	3	4	2	1
Consumer durables			1	
Intermediate goods	2	5	3	1
Capital goods	1	3	3	1

Most firms reported a 25–33 percent reduction in personnel from the mid-1980s to 1994. Work-force reductions targeted both workers and middle management. Workers were displaced by automation, and middle management by the incorporation of computer technology into management practice. Market opening and the end of inflation facilitated both these changes. Those firms that took on new workers did so as a result of new plant acquisition.

Most firms reported the need to reduce labor costs in order to have a competitive product. Argentine labor costs (wage levels) and benefits were often cited as "the most expensive in Latin America," or "two times international costs." Costs of middle management were even more burdensome. One manager observed that while Argentine labor was expensive, it was expensive only in comparison to other Latin American labor, not in comparison to U.S. or European labor. Management, on the other hand, cost as much in Argentina as it did in Europe, and it was not as productive. Management layers and perks had to be eliminated if companies were to remain competitive. His firm had closed its executive offices in downtown Buenos Aires and moved senior managers out to the plant.

Most firms reported that while they had traditionally maintained a long-term relationship with their labor force, achieving greater productivity demanded lower labor costs. Many companies said that they had tried to retrain older employees. Nevertheless, one such firm had seen employment drop by 30 percent between 1990 and 1994.

Changing labor requirements put a premium on a well-educated work force. Unskilled labor was particularly hard hit by force reductions. Most firms reported no interest in any worker who had not completed secondary education. Many technicians working on machinery on the plant floor were reported to have had university preparation. Several managers lamented the "deficit of well-trained technicians in Argentina." Secondary-level education was believed to have deteriorated dramatically, producing poorly prepared graduates for the work force. The incorporation of high technology into the production and inventory management process will mean a continuing premium placed on skilled technical workers. Managers acknowledged that while a better-educated work force costs more, the result is vastly greater productivity.

Companies consistently reported that Argentine labor costs were high—two to three times the cost in Brazil. Most complained that Argentina's social benefits package was high and "out of line." "Unfortunately," one manager observed, "the worker doesn't get most of those benefits. The worker's take-home pay is not that great after social charges have been deducted." Thus, the Argentine worker's purchasing power is not commensurately greater than that of other Southern Cone workers. Nearly all employers interviewed believed that labor reforms being discussed by the government would increase Argentine cost competitiveness.

Despite the fact that they were engaged in reducing the labor force, most employers reported a positive relationship with their plant labor unions. One firm that had undergone a major restructuring spent several million dollars buying out union contracts, but in the aftermath it reported a good relationship with the remaining union workers. Most managers reported that "union attitudes have changed; they are more cooperative." Union leaders now recognize that the old system of caretaker government is gone for good: "There is a recognition that neither government nor management is ever again going to subsidize work." Now the unions are interested in working with management to achieve productivity. Several managers observed that management attitudes about working with labor had also changed, making it possible to experiment with worker teams on the plant floor and involving workers in management decision making.

Finally, restructuring and market opening also brought dramatic changes to the way products are marketed in Argentina. These changes have had a particularly dramatic effect on the small business sector. Most commerce had been done through small "mom and pop" shops throughout the country. Many of those shops could not survive the price competition that came with the end of price controls in 1991.

One firm described the "ferocious competition" that has evolved in the food trade over the past few years. Small shops buy goods with suppliers' credit, but don't pay. The suppliers now have long and burdensome lines of accounts receivable with these shops. A manufacturer of precision instruments observed that he and his partners had decided that they could no longer service some of their oldest customers. That meant fewer invoices. At the same time, the new supermarkets use integrated, computerized control systems that do not require stand-alone scales, and sales declined still further.

The arrival of large supermarket chains has brought other changes in marketing practice. One manager observed that, while the supplier is in control of pricing to the small shops, the supermarket controls prices by selling space on its shelves. The net price to the customer is lower at the supermarket, and the producers' margins are reduced accordingly. One manufacturer of cleaning and beauty products observed that "we would be broke if we had to sell all of our product to Carrefour. Lots of firms prefer not to sell to them. That is why Carrefour has little variety in its products." The manager estimated that five thousand shopkeepers (*minoristas*) disappear for every supermarket that opens in Argentina.

A positive impact of the globalization process has been the incorporation of environmental concerns into the plant modernization process. Manufacturers in diverse sectors commented that in modernizing plants over the past four years they had incorporated environmental controls—primarily effluent controls—that brought their plants up to global standard. Attention to environmental issues affected costs, especially vis-à-vis competition with other Third World producers (notably Brazil), but it was viewed as necessary to establishing a reputation for First World production standards.

Market Orientation

Figure 2 depicts the shifting pattern of Argentine exports and imports between 1985 and 1994. During the 1980s, under the constraints of the debt crisis and IMF-imposed austerity measures, Argentina posted strong positive trade balances. Recession and hyperinflation curtailed imports severely after 1987, but exports expanded sharply, led in part by the successful export efforts of Argentina's steel and petroleum industries. Exports have continued to expand after a modest dip in 1991 and 1992, but the dramatic influence on Argentina's trade balance has been its sharp increase in imports. In 1994 the country's trade balance was negative. A recession in 1995 brought the trade balance more closely into line.

Figure 2. Argentine Exports and Imports, 1985–1994

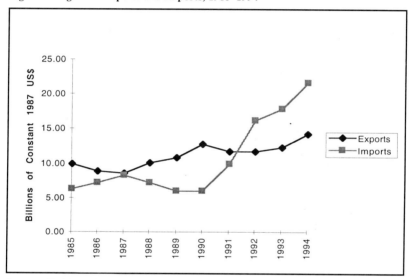

Source: World Bank, *World Development Report* (Washington, DC: World Bank, 1995).

While Argentina has been mostly an agro-exporting country, during the late 1970s and early 1980s a dynamic industrial sector also began to export, so that by 1990 the export coefficients of the industrial and agriculture sectors were nearly similar. At the same time, however, industrial exports are dominated by a very few sectors. Iron and steel, refined petroleum products, and chemical products accounted for 47 percent of industrial manufacturers' exports between 1988 and 1990.[9] Moreover, most exports in each of these sectors are dominated by a handful of large Argentine multinational firms that entered the export market in the 1980s in order to survive the austerity regime brought on by the debt crisis and subsequent years of high inflation. The vast majority of Argentine producers participate little in the international market.

A survey of one hundred firms conducted in 1994 by UADE (Universidad Argentina de la Empresa) indicated that some 50 percent were "investing to export," but 67 percent still found the domestic market more lucrative.[10] Twenty-nine percent of industrial firms believed that their product was very competitive in the export market.

As can be seen in Table 3, many of the firms that we contacted did not export at all. Of those that did, most reported that about 10 to 15 percent of their production went to export. Many firms had exported more at the beginning of the decade but had cut back to attend to domestic market demand. Others were only beginning to explore exports to neighbors. Several firms complained that export costs have been high, making Argentine goods less competitive. Most firms' ability to export have been constrained by lack of price competitiveness and the lower quality of technology used in Argentine manufacturing, the latter a consequence of still-ongoing modernization. Many firms mentioned that the exchange rate was too high. One manager, a producer of precision weights, observed that he used to export to Colombia and Mexico, but there was no financing so he gave it up. He had found that his product was marketable in the United States, but bureaucratic obstacles (certification of standards) made it too difficult to pursue. He would concentrate on Brazil in the immediate future.

Table 3. Export Orientation of Argentine Firms

| | *Number of Firms (Product Lines) Reporting Exports* | | | |
	None/negligible	*MERCOSUR*	*Asia/SW Asia*	*U.S./Europe*
Consumer nondurables	5	4	2	2
Consumer durables	2	1	1	1
Intermediate goods	2	3		1
Capital goods	1	4	1	2

Another firm, a PyME process-control manufacturer, reported that its product was competitive in the global market. The president and founder said that he sold in Germany, Japan, and other developed markets, rarely missing a sale when he set out to target a market. The product was a winner wherever it was marketed, but exports were down, he reported, because he had made a personal decision to cut back on travel.

One industrialist, in the meat packing and packaging sector, observed that the Convertibility Plan had been "disastrous" for the beef sector and that his exports had dropped from 45 to 25 percent of sales. Another manufacturer, in the intermediate goods sector, noted that despite an internationally competitive product, his exports were down because of high domestic demand and high export costs. He expected exports to recover in the near term.

The automotive and heavy equipment sectors have had a different experience. One manufacturer of heavy equipment observed that his company had been exporting to Brazil since the Convertibility Plan was put in place: "We sell half of our product's components to our sister plant in Brazil." An automotive sector representative observed that the Brazilian auto market is three times that of Argentina and will be a market of ten million vehicles. Argentina exports many mechanical devices (such as motors, gear boxes, axles), and Brazil does not do as much of that; Brazilian workers tend to do the assembly. Thus, Argentina's advantage is in the high quality of its product. "We don't go for volume, but for quality." A sector representative said, "Our goal is to have a product that is equivalent to European or American production. Scania products made in Tucumán are indistinguishable from products made in Stockholm or in Hamburg."

MERCOSUR, or more precisely, Brazil, was seen as both an export challenge and an opportunity for Argentine exporters. Brazil was the most dynamic regional export market for most firms, with the rest of Latin America and extraregional exports playing a relatively smaller role. Many firms believed that Argentine manufacturers would enjoy a favorable "quality"-oriented niche in the Brazilian market. Brazilian firms, which were behind in incorporating new technology and production processes, would manufacture for the mass market while Argentina would produce the higher-priced, higher-quality products. Argentine exports would benefit by an end to Brazilian inflation. Most firms saw the advent of MERCOSUR (which came into being shortly after most of these interviews were completed) as an unqualified good for Argentine business. The Brazilian market is many times bigger than Argentina's, and Argentine producers were seen to have a comparative advantage in servicing the dynamic southern and southwestern regions of Brazil, where transportation factors favored Argentine shippers.

A small manufacturer reflected many opinions in saying that to market in Brazil, Argentine companies would "have to find a niche." They would also have to find ways to cope with contraband, and would be assisted by government policies to help move products through customs. A food products manufacturer argued that MERCOSUR would be a major opportunity, but Argentine firms would have to work with the local base (that is, a Brazilian partner) to overcome prejudice against Argentine products.

In spite of the fact that MERCOSUR was to come into effect on January 1, 1995, not much thought was being given to exploiting the market opening. Some businessmen still expressed pessimism regarding Brasilia's ability to contain inflation, the sine qua non for making Argentine products competitive in that market. A number of manufacturers expressed concern at Brazil's greater installed capacity. For some, Brazilian producers could simply overwhelm the regional market with their production, so direct competition was to be avoided for as long as possible. Other managers worried that competition with Brazil's state-owned firms would be difficult. Some manufacturers were more sanguine, arguing that once Brazil was on the road to economic recovery, domestic demand would absorb all of her installed capacity and more; Argentine firms could then compete successfully in that more dynamic marketplace. In spite of these different perspectives, most companies agreed with the high-tech exporter who summarized the challenge of MERCOSUR by saying that it is "causing a revolution in this market. There is no excuse not to take advantage of this tremendous market."

Given the retrenchment in the capital goods industry in Argentina, one manufacturer of heavy equipment, committed to retaining his Argentine manufacturing base, observed that "growth will depend on selling outside Argentina, primarily to Brazil." A multinational operating in the consumer nondurables sector observed that MERCOSUR would evolve into a regional block in which large manufacturers would consolidate production in one plant. His own firm was slowly closing independent operations in other Latin American countries to manufacture exclusively out of Brazil. One technology-oriented capital goods manufacturer argued that his firm had sought to establish relations with a Brazilian counterpart, in part because he feared that Brazilian firms would resist competition from foreign manufacturers and would use ISO 9000 technical standards to freeze foreigners out of the market. (ISO 9000 standards refer to the standards of technical quality established by the Geneva, Switzerland-based International Standards Organization [ISO]. ISO 9000 pertains to the basic definitions of quality and standards. A company is "certified" when its products meet ISO 9000 standards, and many companies will use only ISO-certified components.)

Chile also was seen as a market opportunity by most Argentine firms, though competition with other exporters and a Chilean preference for "national" products were viewed as obstacles. The producer of precision instruments also observed that Argentine products are viewed as "shabby (*chata*)" in Chile, and that Argentine industry would have to overcome this powerful bias to exploit the Chilean market. Most firms reported a minuscule percentage of their production going to Chile, and only a few firms were even contemplating marketing there.

Financing and Credit

Investment

Nearly every firm we interviewed had been investing at least since 1991 to enhance its productivity, and many had begun before that. "We have to lower our costs," reported one firm. "The new regime is allowing us to incorporate the latest technology." Most capital goods acquisitions were imported. Most, but not all, were imports of the latest technology, but some modernization was just to "a more recent technology than we had." One producer of consumer nondurables invested in consolidation of its four plants, dispersed across Argentina, to one central plant. Another firm in the same sector reported investment to "expand capacity, acquire firms, diversify, improve profitability, and to rationalize production lines." One supplier began investing in automating his plant, introducing a sophisticated robotics system, when management first recognized the dramatic change in marketing practices that was coming to Argentina with the arrival of the supermarket and shopping malls. The Wharton School-trained manager acknowledged that he had not seen the changes coming, but the company was able to capitalize on the changes with timely investments.

Nearly every producer of consumer products emphasized the need for modern, high-quality packaging. Several manufacturers of consumer nondurables reported investing in packaging and labeling to raise their product to international standards. One manager observed that the paper and paper products sector in Argentina, until recently state controlled, was very out of date. To export, Argentina had to have a paper and packaging industry that operated at international standards.

One domestic firm invested in a franchise product line as a means of retaining a unique product line in the more competitive open market. Most multinational firms began to import items from their international product line that had not previously been available in Argentina; some would subsequently produce those products in the country. Many multinational corporations (MNC) foresaw a consolidation in one country of production platforms for South America, or at least for MERCOSUR. The open Argentine market would become part of the firm's global strategy.

Financing Investment

Almost all firms reported using working capital to finance their investments and many reported providing financing to their clients. Table 4 summarizes the reporting of the firms interviewed.

Table 4. Patterns of Financing

Numbers of Firms Reporting Use of Various Financing Modes

	Self-Financing	Local Bank Credits	MNC Finance	Long-term International Credit	Client Financing
Consumer nondurables	4	2	1	2	3
Consumer durables	1	1			
Intermediate goods	5	3		2	2
Capital goods	1	2		2	1

"No one wants to increase debt, and access to bank credit is difficult and costly," several managers reported, describing their current approach to financing expansion. Large firms reported no lack of credit in the market, but still found local bank credit costly. Small firms reported more difficult relations with their banks, often stressing the importance of a personal relationship with one's banker, a relationship that was not necessarily transferred if the banker moved on. Even the larger firms were using working capital to finance expansion and modernization.

Most firms reported that relations with the local banking community were changing. One producer of capital goods reported that "what we buy in the local market is financed with supplier credits and bank credit. There are various lines of credit, each one more expensive than the previous one, and the more money, the higher the interest rate." But things are changing, the manager said. Whereas four to five years ago there was only one source of loans in his sector, Banco de la Nación, private banks are now beginning to come looking for clients for their own loans. "We used to finance our clients, but now most pay cash, or come with bank financing." A PyME reported that it maintained several lines of credit with its local bank, but "the bank credit lines are too expensive. We are financing out of cash flow."

One firm, which had recently gone public on the Argentine stock exchange, reported that this action dramatically increased its access to international venture capital and to long-term external financing: "Our new machinery was financed with long-term credit from the Austrian Export-Import Bank."

Few businesses had a good word for the banking system in Argentina. Most multinational firms were able to access international lines of credit and did not rely on local banks, particularly for long-term capital. But many firms reported that the lack of long-term industrial credit in Argentina is a major problem. Firms complained that the "banks don't help." There is no risk credit. Two well-placed firms in the paper and packaging industry complained that "credit lines are too short. Argentina does not have long-term credit for industry." The financial manager for the firm receiving Austrian EX-IM support observed that "(local) long-term credit is still a problem." Another manager complained that he was using short-term credit to finance capital goods. A manager of a major Argentine multinational was more explicit: "Argentine banks are inefficient and costly; they lack service and hurt the local market with their lack of credit." Several firms complained that credit is much easier to acquire in Brazil, and this places Argentine firms at a disadvantage vis-à-vis their principal export market.

This study's findings echo responses reported to Universidad de Administración de Empresas (UADE) in their 1994 survey. When asked whether firms encountered difficulties in accessing local credit, 45 percent of respondents said "no," but 22 percent said "yes" and 33 percent responded "some." Forty percent of respondents in that survey reported that they had increased their debt "moderately," while 48 percent reported little or no increase in debt. Forty-three of UADE's respondents reported using their own funds to finance their firm. Seventy-nine percent of firms reported that their firm's debt would remain the same (58 percent) or decrease (21 percent).

The responses reinforce the conclusion that, in spite of the more stable economic environment, Argentine firms in 1994 were still not ready to contemplate long-term expansion plans. Modernization to date has generally taken place within existing plant structure, not through expansion of installed capacity. Recently, the Argentine research firm Fundación de Investigaciones Económicas Latinoamericanas announced that Argentine industry has achieved optimal capacity utilization; to grow, it will have to invest in additional plant capacity. This will require investments well beyond the scale of the early modernization and consolidation phase of Argentine recovery.[11]

Most firms reported that financing clients continued to place a serious burden on firm balance sheets. Small firms and those working with small shops were most affected. The continuing financial decline of the small trade sector threatened the livelihood of many of the consumer products firms whose managers we interviewed.

Government Policy

Firms were nearly uniform in their praise of government policy, even when it hurt their own operations. Opening of markets and controlling inflation were the two policy changes cited for their impact. "Stability brought credit and credit brought consumption," observed one manager.

And stability also made it easier to "do business." Firms can invest, now that inflation is past. They can take a longer view to product development. Other policy changes—privatization of Yacimientos Petrolíferos Fiscales (the national oil company) and of telecommunications and liberalization in the information sector—also affected firms by allowing them access to technology that improved management productivity or communications with customers. In many cases, however, privatization resulted in increased costs for services. Many complained that energy costs are high and disproportionate compared with costs in neighboring Brazil. Despite this, most managers said, "Don't change the process."

We asked managers whether they believed the government understood and was sympathetic to the problems firms were having in adjusting to the new market environment. The responses were mixed. Some managers felt that government did not listen to business and pointed to the low profile of the ministry of industry. Others were more generous, arguing that "Cavallo understands but can't do anything about it" because he has to worry about overall stability.

Managers cited a number of policies that still need to be addressed. In particular, firms interested in exporting argued that Argentina needs to develop an export-support infrastructure. An export bank is needed. Several firms reported that Argentine firms were disadvantaged in competition with Brazilian producers by their Brazilian rivals' access to export financing credit. "For small firms to survive, government needs to support PyME exports." The firms in the precision instrument and high-technology sectors argued that an industrial standards certification capability at home would help Argentine exports. "ISO 9000 standards are a burden. We can't export to First World countries without having our products certified," said one manufacturer. "First World countries won't approve a product for use unless the full production cycle is certified. There has to be demonstrated quality control in the whole process, and you have to be able to show the records." The National Institute for Technology (INTI) used to do this, but it was the manager's impression that it has been abandoned. The government must support INTI. Again, Argentine firms cited more favorable Brazilian policies in this area.

Argentine firms also asked for greater assistance in meeting international customs standards. One firm noted that the new tariff nomenclature (Harmonized Tariff Schedule) prejudiced his company by reallocating a key imported input from capital good (0 percent tariff) to intermediate good (15 percent tariff). That raised the cost of the product and meant that the domestically produced product now costs more than a similar product wholly produced outside Argentina. Other customs procedures need to be developed to permit companies to send samples abroad and to recover parts that don't work. One manufacturer making this argument noted that "we still have to send the replacement parts, so we just absorb the additional costs. Other countries don't operate that way, and that gives them advantages."

Several exporters cited "mixed" support for their export effort from Argentine embassies abroad. Performance clearly varied from one individual commercial attaché to another, but the support of the commercial office was generally perceived to lend prestige to the exporter and to be a sought-after asset. Several firms wanted greater help from embassies in running the bureaucratic gauntlet in new markets.

Throughout our interviews we questioned managers on the impact of the fixed exchange rate. While several managers felt that the exchange rate made their products more costly, none would forgo the stability brought about by the fixed rate. While acknowledging the exchange rate to be a factor, the fixed exchange rate was not generally speaking viewed as a major problem.

Firms also noted that the continuing reform of labor legislation would be helpful. Argentine social costs are higher than those of other countries' and they limit firms' ability to reduce costs to competitive levels. Most managers believed that tax reform would have a positive effect on the business environment. Still, several managers observed that although their firms paid taxes, they were not sure that their competitors did. Most firms noted that tax and other reforms remained to be institutionalized in the interior.

Continuing Obstacles

Firms were questioned about continuing obstacles to doing business in Argentina. Most mentioned in passing the high costs of Argentine products caused both by the fixed exchange rate and the high cost of labor. They also mentioned the continuing high costs of energy and other recently privatized services.

Complaints of lack of access to capital for modernization and that the banking system does not have a probusiness attitude were frequent. Many regretted the lack of long-term vision in the country. Several firms observed that lack of finance capital meant that firms take longer to adjust than is necessary. Most managers would have been supportive of government-supported industrial and export credit programs. Several small firms argued that government needs a special program to help small businesses, the PyMEs.

Education of the work force was another program that firms argued government needs to address.[12] Managers recognized that the ongoing restructuring of Argentine industry would create fewer jobs per peso invested in the future, and that industry would not be an outlet for unskilled labor. Even secondary-school graduates need technical skills and computer literacy. Most plants were engaged in on-the-job training for long-time employees, but standards for hiring new employees would be high.

Continuing reform of the regulatory environment was high on the list of remaining obstacles to doing business in Argentina. Many firms mentioned the need to straighten out provincial finances and provincial regulations. The cost of services continues to be a detriment to international competitiveness. Companies cited the cost of energy, communications, taxes, and labor benefit packages as higher than those of their competitors.

Many companies, particularly smaller ones, mentioned that Argentine business itself needs more effective business lobbies. Most chambers of commerce were viewed as weak and ineffective, in part because companies do not fund them. At the same time, many managers believed that the government does not pay much attention to business anyway, so representative organizations would not be effective. But they agreed that business needs to be increasingly proactive to defend sector interests. Some firms, operating in sectors still dominated by a monopoly or oligopoly, argued for further regulatory changes to remove restrictions on free-market activities. Pharmaceutical laboratories, for example, have excessive influence on drug prices because pharmacists cannot substitute generic brands.

While most of the firms we interviewed had been notable for their efforts to modernize both management and production processes, it remained clear that many managers had still not adjusted to new market conditions. An association executive who had spent many years in the textile industry compared management foresight in that industry to the initiative that the auto assemblers had demonstrated around 1989–90. Auto sector management had undertaken a study of how their industry had changed worldwide and its implications for Argentina. Out of that review came the industry's proposal for gradual opening: a strategy based on accords between assembly plants, parts suppliers, and unions, and, finally, full integration with Brazil, a market three times the size of Argentina's today. MERCOSUR will be a market of ten million vehicles in the near future. The textile industry has still not conducted an adequate assessment of where it needs to go to become competitive.

Conclusion

Despite a long list of continuing needs, most Argentine businessmen interviewed were optimistic about prospects in the long term. As one owner said, "This country is beginning to do business like a First World country." Nevertheless, most also foresaw difficulties in the near and medium term. Few expected their markets to continue expanding in 1995–96 as they had in 1993–94. Indeed, most foresaw a mild contraction. From the food manufacturers to the capital goods producers, expectations were that growth in 1995 and for the next several years would be slow, or flat. That said, none may have anticipated the severity of the recession that ensued in 1995, in part, but not entirely, as a result of the shock that the Mexican peso crisis dealt to the international marketplace. Despite cautions about the near-term future, no one believed that the policy process could or would be reversed, or that doing so would be good for Argentina.

In 1994, Argentina ranked twenty-seventh on the World Economic Forum's World Competitiveness Index.[13] This reflected a continuing gradual improvement on almost all components of the index over the preceding four years. Our interviews revealed both strengths and weaknesses in Argentina's competitive profile, as evaluated against Michael Porter's four determinants of competitive advantage: factor conditions, demand conditions, related and supporting industries, and firm strategy, structure, and rivalry.[14] On the one hand, Argentina's factor endowments were cause for concern. Firms complained of the scarcity of well-trained workers and technical personnel, and, more important, no longer saw a demand for unskilled labor. Yet the educational system was not yet able to address the demand for skilled labor, nor were universities or other research institutes well plugged into the industrial cycle. Access to capital resources was still deficient, though perhaps improving. Finally, the national infrastructure, though in the process of change, still did not enhance competitiveness.

Argentina clearly did have a discriminating home market. Consumers were aware of and demanded higher quality products once they were made available. Companies by and large responded to the demand for quality, but often, at least in the short run, by importing products made abroad. Argentina did seem to have identifiable advantages in MERCOSUR's marketplace.

Perhaps the greatest test of Argentina's competitive position will be its supplier industries. Porter argues that supplier and related industries must also be internationally competitive. The smaller and specialized firms that constitute suppliers to most of the large manufacturers that we interviewed were among the least competitive segments of Argentine industry—and often the most overwhelmed by market opening. The process of consolidation evident in the auto parts industry, in which only thirty firms remained of more than three hundred some five years earlier, was occurring in every segment of Argentine production. Competitive advantage emerges from close working relationship between world-class suppliers and the industry. While the pattern of consolidation does not suggest that the remaining firms will not be world class, it does imply a continuing massive displacement of workers, employers, and shopkeepers that can no longer compete in the open market. This adjustment is manifested in Argentina's current record unemployment levels.

Firm strategy, structure, and rivalry is Porter's fourth determinant of national competitive advantage. Argentine firms interviewed in this study were clearly changing management practices to become more competitive. No manager had any confusion about what needed to be done to improve his firm's position in the marketplace. Many firms continued to focus primarily on the domestic marketplace, when economists and others thought they should be more actively engaged in positioning themselves in MERCOSUR. Beginning on January 1, 1995, that challenge would confront managers directly.

Porter regards domestic rivalry as particularly important for stimulating competitive innovation: "Strong domestic competitors create particularly visible pressures on each other to improve. Vigorous local competition not only sharpens advantages at home but also pressures domestic firms to sell abroad in order to grow; toughened by domestic rivalry, the stronger domestic firms are equipped to succeed abroad. Domestic rivalry not only creates pressures to innovate but to innovate in ways that upgrade the competitive advantages of a nation's firms."[15] The pattern among Argentine firms was not one of strong domestic competition. Rather, firms tended to dominate niches within a sector. Again, MERCOSUR will bring direct competition from the Brazilian market. Many of the firms interviewed expressed concern about their ability to compete against their Brazilian counterparts.

Porter also notes that "government can influence . . . each of the four determinants either positively or negatively. . . . Government's role in national competitive advantage is in influencing the four determinants." While Argentine businessmen were enthusiastically supportive of the Menem government's efforts to "get out of business" and return productive activities to the private sector, they also identified a number of areas—national education, tax structure and collection policy, continuing deregulation but with new regulations in trade and finance, and support for small business—that are clearly important to leveling the playing field as Argentine firms adjust to the competitive international marketplace.

We have studied firms that were, for the most part, still in the process of adjusting to the changed business environment. Some were just beginning to see the fruits of a difficult adjustment, while others had not yet begun to benefit. These were the survivors of the adjustment process. Most knew of colleagues who had not survived. For the most part, the members of the Argentine private sector we interviewed were well aware of what they needed to do to lower costs and improve productivity in their operations. Despite some concerns about the near-term future, all of the firms interviewed were optimistic about their longer-term prospects. Their next challenge would be to consolidate their position and begin the process of investment in expanded plant capacity, both to create employment op-portunities and to provide Argentine firms with economies of scale for competing effectively in the larger MERCOSUR and international marketplaces.

Notes

1. Among other things, the Convertibility Plan, introduced on April 1, 1991, tied money supply to reserves and permitted the free convertibility of pesos to dollars. In addition, domestic interest rates would be determined by the market and indexation of wages, prices, and utility charges ended. Tariffs were established in three bands ranging from 0 to 22 percent. Moreover, government spending could not exceed available receipts.

2. In an effort to expand the number of firms surveyed, a written questionnaire was developed and circulated to an additional sixty firms, Argentine and American, through the courtesy of the American Chamber of Commerce of Argentina. Returns were abysmal, as predicted by a number of professional survey experts. This was consistent with the recent experience of Argentine Industrial Union (Unión Industrial Argentina, UIA) economists and others who had from time to time attempted to survey the private sector. The fact that the questionnaire circulated in the difficult aftermath of the Mexican peso crisis, which hit Argentina heavily, may also help explain the poor return.

3. See Michael E. Porter, "The Competitive Advantage of Nations," *Harvard Business Review* (March–April 1990): 73–93; or *The Competitive Advantage of Nations* (New York: Free Press, 1990).

4. See, among others, Paul H. Davis, *The Crisis of Argentine Capitalism* (Baton Rouge: Tulane University Press, 1990); and Bernardo Kosakoff et al., *El desafío de la competitividad: La industria argentina en transformación* (Buenos Aires: CEPAL/Alianza Editorial, 1993).

5. Eduardo M. Basualdo and Daniel Aspiazu, *Cara y contracara de los grupos económicos: Estado y promoción industrial en la Argentina* (Buenos Aires: Cántaro, 1989).

6. See, for example, *Prensa Economica, Negocios,* or *Mercado,* all published in Buenos Aires and all of which produce annual rankings of firms overall and by sector.

7. Inter-American Development Bank, *Economic and Social Progress in Latin America, 1995 Report* (Washington, DC: Inter-American Development Bank, 1995), notes rather blandly that "although small businesses in Argentina account for 45 percent of the gross domestic product and 65 percent of the labor force, in recent years they have declined because of outdated practices and structural macroeconomic changes." Our exposure to this sector, both direct and indirect, suggests that the impact has indeed been quite profound.

8. This reporting is taken from Carlos Bonvecchi, "La industria argentina en los años noventa," draft manuscript, 1994. Bonvecchi compares the gross value of production per sector in 1993 to 1987 production levels projected into 1993. The calculation describes the change in sector performance resulting from structural changes within the sector. When this research was being performed, 1987 was the date of the last national survey. A subsequent survey was conducted in 1993, but results were not yet known when this research was conducted.

9. See Robert Bisang and Bernardo Kosakoff, "Las exportaciones industriales en una economia en transformación: La sorpresas del caso argentino, 1974/1990," in Kosakoff et al., *El desafío*, 134, table 4.

10. "Situación y perspectivas de las empresas argentinas," *Report of 11 August 1994*. Universidad Argentina de la Empresa, Buenos Aires.

11. Reported in *Latin American Economy and Business*. London: Latin American Newsletters. LAEB-96-04 (March 1996): 6.

12. The problem of educating the work force has been the subject of considerable debate in Argentina. See Asociación de Bancos Argentinos (ADEBA), "Educación y mercado de trabajo en la Argentina," Working Paper of the Fundación de Investigaciones Económicas Latinoamericanas, FIEL, Buenos Aires, August 1994.

13. Porter, *Competitive Advantage of Nations*, 103.

14. Ibid., 77.

15. Ibid., 118–19.

IV

The Social Question

Building Human Capital

14

Higher Education Reform

Meeting the Challenge of Economic Competition

Jorge Balán

Higher education should play a fundamental role in any program of economic reform that considers international competition a dynamic element in growth. To fill this role, universities face the challenge of making thoroughgoing reforms in their educational programs. Inertia is very strong in this institutional system, which was formed over many decades by governmental and institutional actions whose results were rarely either anticipated or desired. The system has become very complex and the sometimes gigantic institutions within it have enormous difficulties proposing, deciding on, or implementing plans to transform their programs.

Although the "crisis" in Argentine university education has been discussed for a long time, only in recent years has discontent with the quality of university education, and with the failure of the institutions responsible for improving it, been made explicit.[1] Until recently, the failures of higher education could be attributed directly and unequivocally to external factors, creating the illusion that correcting them would be the path to recovery. Political turbulence, police control, and intervention by the executive branch in the life of the universities prevented the exercise of autonomy and academic freedom, without which improvement in academic quality was unthinkable. However, since the normalization initiated in 1984, the national universities entered a period— unusually long for Argentina—of freedom and autonomy. The serious financial difficulties during the years of extremely high inflation (1988 to 1990) made it hard to imagine that changes could be launched and sustained in response to the challenges currently presented by higher education. In recent years, however, monetary stability and the national government's heightened interest in university affairs are creating a new mood with respect to university reform.[2]

The financing of higher education—and indeed of basic education—is far from adequate, and there is little possibility of a significant increase in the short and medium term, although an upward trend in government funding has accompanied price stability and economic growth in the last few years.[3] It is now possible to ask how the institutions themselves can solve their multiple management problems and set out to improve the quality, efficiency, and relevance of their educational and scientific performance. Can universities independently mobilize their many academic and administrative talents to make the changes needed to improve academic excellence, competitiveness, and relevance in the professional training and research they conduct? Or are other external changes needed (beyond the absence of police control or the stifling economic limitations that they endured) to make this possible?

International experience in recent decades includes numerous reform efforts initiated by central authorities with varying degrees of cooperation by institutions and academic communities.[4] Governments, often under pressure from important sectors of society (such as business associations and politicians, in addition to consumers and taxpayers), have generated wide-ranging reform programs in higher education based on sometimes radical changes in the linkages between the institutions and the state. This has been particularly true in Western Europe, where the public sector weighs heavily in institutional management and financing of the dominant model of higher education. Currently, similar plans have been announced by many Latin American governments; in Latin America, state university institutions typically enjoy greater political autonomy (that is, self-government) than their European counterparts.

This essay will discuss a few of the inherited characteristics of Argentine higher education that are inadequate for the current demands of international competitiveness. It begins with an assessment of the reforms implemented in the 1960s, to emphasize how and why their continuation in the 1990s, vis-à-vis a much larger and more complex institutional system, necessarily requires a change in relations between the state and the universities to enable the state to play a different role in the coordination of the system and in institutional reform. This change is essential for influencing the overall context in which autonomous universities, both public and private, make and implement their decisions.

The 1960s Reform Program

In 1965 and 1966, experts from the Organization for Economic Cooperation and Development (OECD), within the framework of the Argentine National Development Council (CONADE) and with financing from the

Ford Foundation, carried out an exhaustive survey of the Argentine educational system regarding the needs for qualified workers for the country's future development.[5] A key chapter in the study was devoted to an analysis of higher education, in particular at the eight national universities (Buenos Aires, La Plata, Córdoba, Litoral, Tucumán, Cuyo, Nordeste, and Sur), with some notes about the then-recently created alternatives—that is, the National Technological University, nonuniversity institutions of higher education, and private universities.

The overview sketched by those experts is surprisingly familiar to current readers. Realizing the chronic nature of some problems in higher education is fundamental to avoiding attributing them to the effects of certain perverse policies. We will consider some of the key points in that report.

Enrollment grew at an extraordinary pace between 1947 and 1954, 14.8 percent annually, the highest rate in the secular history of the system. The enrollment growth rate fell sharply afterward, although it continued to exceed the growth rate of the population. This expansion was a direct result of growth in the number of secondary-school graduates and their high rate of enrollment in higher education. The increase was possible because admission, formerly limited to academic high school graduates, was expanded to include graduates of vocational schools, and because quotas and entrance exams were eliminated. Three out of four high school graduates enrolled in some institution of higher learning, the vast majority in the national universities, with no need to pass any qualifying examination.

In 1956, schools of the University of Buenos Aires again introduced entrance exams, which were later adopted by other universities throughout the country. In 1962, for instance, the University of Buenos Aires received sixteen thousand applications (one thousand more than in 1953), and admitted only 38 percent of those seeking admission. A growing percentage of students enrolled in higher education were absorbed by the National Technological University, first known as the Workers' University, primarily a technological institute geared to professional training. Also, private universities, which had been authorized since 1958, represented a new choice for many students. Enrollment in nonuniversity institutions of higher education, such as teacher training colleges, grew faster than university enrollment. A process of institutional diversification was under way that suggested that the system had grown in pace with the innovations being introduced in advanced countries.

Argentina during the 1960s had some of the highest rates of enrollment in higher education in the world, above those of the European countries. The authors of the OECD report compared Argentine figures with

British data. While Great Britain had few students and many graduates relative to the population, the opposite was the case in Argentina, where generous access diluted quality, resulting in high dropout rates and few graduates. The general frustration among students was easy to imagine: The percentage of graduates ranged from 10 to 25 percent of the number of students who had enrolled eight years earlier, while programs of study theoretically lasted four to six years. Many continued studying, but many more dropped out. A survey of three universities (Córdoba, La Plata, and Litoral) revealed that more than half of enrolled students had not taken any exams during a three-year period. Figures from the five major universities showed that the percentage of graduates who had received their degree during the period specified by their programs was never more than 30 percent of total enrollment; approximately half took three or more years more than what is formally required to graduate.

The report attributed these facts to two major causes. First, there were many "phantom" students, who only registered or attended a few classes and then withdrew or switched department or university but continued to appear on the rolls. University education was very attractive, but that did not mean that enrolled students were prepared to continue their studies. The lack of remedial courses or intermediate degree programs concentrated enrollment in lengthy programs beyond the capabilities of many of these students. Second, the vast majority of students were part-time. The general norm (except in a few schools, such as medicine and engineering) was to combine study with some other occupation. While most such cases reflected economic necessity (there were hardly any scholarships), this phenomenon also occurred in families with high incomes. It was, apparently, a life-style fostered by student culture, fitting in amid the laxity of the study programs and the lack of incentives to devote oneself exclusively to study. Moreover, a large majority of professors worked only part-time at the university; their real jobs, with the exception of a few new programs, were in their professional offices and businesses.

Public universities had made strides toward democratization by opening up access, which was frustrated by limited revenues and the low rates of compensation for an incomplete degree. However, they were the central institutions in the socialization of the members of the vast middle-class population as they entered into adult life, politics, and the work world, whether during the course of their studies or upon graduation, that often failed to produce a fundamental change in their career paths.

The changes then introduced by some national universities, in particular the prestigious University of Buenos Aires—such as new degrees in the sciences, departmental organization by discipline, enhanced professional training for teaching and the possibility of full-time research, and the development of graduate programs—reached only a small sector within the university system. The dominant model remained that of professional schools with lengthy degree programs, part-time professors, students who combined studies with other work, scarce resources, and lack of incentives for research, the funding for which tended to be separate from rewards for teaching. There was a general awareness of the shortcomings of this university system, which were assessed and quantified in the report. It was clear that a reasonably broad-based investment and reform plan would not be possible without alternatives, within or outside the public universities, capable of absorbing the growing demand for higher education. In the absence of such an initiative, the public university would have both missions at the same time.

As already stated, some alternatives to the comprehensive public university emerged at this time. But these alternatives absorbed only part of the growing demand and on the whole introduced few innovations: They did not create shorter programs for professional training, nor did they increase the time devoted by students or teachers. In addition, the loss of quality in secondary education was not offset by the creation of a period of basic study prior to professional specialization, as is typical in the U.S. system. The Argentine university was inspired by the European model, which assumed that basic general education was acquired in preparatory schools. Compared to its European counterparts, Argentine secondary schools had very low levels of academic performance. The very high attrition rate reflected that phenomenon.

Innovative groups seeking renewal of the national universities in the 1960s recognized the crucial importance of distinguishing among levels of academic study and focusing on the development of graduate programs. This was perhaps the most difficult and costly innovation. Linked with scientific and humanistic research, it allowed research to move to the center of university life, institutionalizing teaching in higher education as a professional course of study (instead of being a part-time, parallel activity of people identified with other professions), and laying the groundwork for reform in undergraduate teaching. This was no doubt the greatest theme of renewal in the 1960s and 1970s in all of Latin America, but only Brazil was able to implement it with any degree of success at the time. The Brazilian innovation is significant in that, unlike what occurred in Argentina, it was based in a sector of public institutions to which there was limited access, enabling the private sector to play a more active role in absorbing the demand, as had been recommended by international specialists at the time and since.

The Argentine system of higher education in the mid-1960s was clearly atypical in Latin America: It had definitively entered the phase that

Martin Trow dubbed "massive."[6] Yet it was typical in its professional orientations. Although the system outwardly proclaimed its public vocation to serve the needs of national development—which were often identified exclusively as public sector needs—system supply and student demand were channeled almost entirely to professional training geared to the private market.

The university modernization program of the 1960s was not backed by a stable economy or a financially strong government. Argentine growth displayed marked fluctuations and successive fiscal crises that affected the entire public sector; education, including higher education, was especially hard hit. System reforms presupposed an improvement in public finances, as well as the political will favorable to the public universities. The 1966 military coup brought the former but not the latter: It meant a dramatic end to this program of change from within, severely limiting academic autonomy and the capacity for self-management of these institutions.

The New Reform Movement: Autonomy without Coordination

A few months after the inauguration of the constitutional authorities late in 1983, the Argentine Congress passed a law establishing a one-year period for normalization of all the national universities, restoring the model of autonomy and self-government of the 1960s. Since then they have been governed by collegiate bodies with representatives elected by tenured professors, alumni, and students, who choose the executive officers without any intervention by the national authorities.

The climate of political participation, channeled by the two majority parties, immediately brought with it pressure to adopt policies in opposition to those of the former military government. An open admissions policy was established in all public universities; their schools could no longer enforce entrance exams or limit the number of students. The idea of open admissions emanated from the former quota system and the academically irrelevant exams administered by the military authorities merely to limit the number of students. The immediate result was a large increase in the number of applicants admitted at all universities nationwide, which made it necessary to hire more teaching staff and increase investment in classrooms.

Another policy of the public university system was free undergraduate study. Although at different times in the past it had been common to establish moderate fees, a free tuition policy was now instituted. As a result, university budgets were totally dependent on payments from the national government, since their own revenues were always very limited. Programs undertaken since 1987 to allow institutions an increase in their nonbudgetary income have had limited success.

When the universities became fully autonomous and self-governing, the budget became the core policy issue and the main point of university conflict with the government.[7] Financing for the national universities increased from 1984 to 1987, although not on a per-student basis, and quickly found a ceiling in the severe constraints imposed on federal spending by the fiscal crisis of the state. In the best of cases the increases made it possible to expand hiring but did not allow for salary hikes, which had long been promised, nor did they leave any funds for investment (see Table 1). In addition, the financing of each institution, determined by

Table 1. Republic of Argentina, 1972–1995: Credits from the National Budget to National Universities, and Numbers of Students

Year	In Current Money	Budget 1994 Pesos	Period	Change	Number of Students	Budget per Student
1972	1,381,259	927,647,451	1972–73	31.89%	245,789[a]	3,774
1973	2,863,943	1,223,450,696	1973–74	19.74%	312,110[a]	3,920
1974	4,215,382	1,464,999,456	1974–75	−8.87%	417,876[b]	3,506
1975	10,975,787	1,335,092,237	1975–76	−46.68%	447,380[b]	2,984
1976	32,746,922	711,884,091	1976–77	−0.23%	461,187[b]	1,544
1977	87,555,816	710,264,888	1977–78	33.43%	407,125[b]	1,745
1978	310,571,960	947,672,232	1978–79	3.53%	402,422[b]	2,355
1979	823,360,746	981,096,018	1979–80	22.50%	397,643[b]	2,467
1980	1,931,160,242	1,201,807,310	1980–81	−11.31%	302,110[b]	3,978
1981	3,533,522,083	1,065,835,426	1981–82	−27.09%	301,085[b]	3,540
1982	7,518,206,000	777,085,390	1982–83	38.79%	318,299[c]	2,441
1983	4,682,570	1,078,544,071	1983–84	3.22%	337,998[c]	3,191
1984	34,367,691	1,113,258,611	1984–85	−5.44%	443,441[c]	2,510
1985	250,022,778	1,052,650,668	1985–86	0.52%	524,590[c]	2,007
1986	455,403,313	1,058,077,001	1986–87	30.70%	581,813[c]	1,819
1987	1,359,400	1,382,926,820	1987–88	−4.58%	618,651[c]	2,235
1988	6,029,775	1,319,556,968	1988–89	−25.81%	652,997[c]	2,021
1989	146,856,238	979,035,016	1989–90	−3.04%	661,315[c]	1,480
1990	3,066,280,688	949,267,351	1990–91	2.80%	679,403[c]	1,397
1991	7,734,689	975,839,615	1991–92	19.69%	681,990[c]	1,431
1992	1,074,017,092	1,168,023,346	1992–93	8.12%	699,293[c]	1,670
1993	1,233,000,000	1,262,817,219	1993–94	10.54%	657,545[d]	1,921
1994	1,395,958,000	1,395,958,000	1994–95	7.57%	615,796[e]	2,267
1995	1,501,607,000	1,501,607,000	1990–95	58.19%	574,048[f]	2,616

Source: Secretaría de Hacienda (Treasury Ministry), Harvard Club of Argentina, *La Nación*, budget laws and laws of the Ministry of Culture and Education.
Current monetary units: 1972–1982: Thousands of pesos, law 18,188. 1983–84: Thousands of Argentine pesos. 1985–86: Thousands of australs. 1987–1990: Thousands of australs. 1991–1995: pesos (one peso is equal to one dollar).
[a]Number of students according to the Statistics Department, Ministry of Education
[b]Number of students according to the Council of Presidents of National Universities

ᶜNumber of students according to Ministerio de Cultura y Educación, Secretaría de Políticas Universitarias, *Estadísticas básicas de universidades nacionales; Años 1982–1992, 1985–1994* (Buenos Aires: MCE, 1994, 1996)
ᵈInterpolated number of students
ᵉNumber of students covered in census
ᶠExtrapolated number of students

Congress in the Budget Law, largely reflected the number of its students, although it also was dependent upon the pressure brought to bear by representatives to favor one or another university. The institutional innovations proposed lacked incentives, and the funds needed for implementation were not available.

Academic and administrative reforms, and program innovation in general, became rare throughout the 1980s. The problems of the traditional model, already diagnosed in the 1960s, were aggravated by open admissions and budgetary constraints, which resulted in a very high student dropout rate and the lack of professionalization in most of the teaching staff, made up of part-time personnel with no graduate-level training. The continued concentration of enrollment in long-term professional programs of study was further aggravated by the relative decline in the number of students in scientific and technological areas, which are more demanding and costly than are the popular programs of study in "soft" areas. This trend suggests that the response of higher education to the demands of economic competitiveness, strongly voiced by the economic reformists in government and elsewhere, was totally inadequate.

In this context, the government took few initiatives to reform coordination of the university system, in both the public and private subsectors, until recently. The only mechanisms of coordination, the *consejos de rectores* (councils of university presidents), were consultative; their decisions were not binding on the participating universities. Until 1993, the Ministry of Education had only an archaic structure with which to deal with the universities, along with old functions of bureaucratic control and no capability to supervise results. The government contained demands to authorize new institutions, public or private, protecting until 1989 the already-existing private institutions from competition and expanding still further the giant public sector universities, which greatly expanded their programs without becoming accountable for their academic quality or economic feasibility.

One sign of the worsening of the crisis, which at the same time makes it difficult to obtain quantitative indicators of its scope, was the interruption of the flow of university statistics between 1987 and 1994. Any initiative to coordinate the system or plan teaching tasks ran up against the insurmountable barrier of a lack of information. But some censuses of students and teaching staff in the late 1980s suggested that the long-term trends were continuing, taking their toll on quality. The complex national university system was thus left without any coordinating body, at the same time as the institutions that constitute it found it impossible to make substantive decisions regarding their educational and scientific plans. Restoration of the reformist ideals of the 1960s—professionalization of teaching staff, strengthening of the scientific disciplines, and development of graduate-level studies—was limited to empty rhetoric with no financial or political potential for implementation. The situation could be described as institutional paralysis, an inability to take initiative on the part of both institutions and government, who entered into repeated conflicts around the budget problem.

Reform in the Relationship between the Government and the Universities

The proposals to transform coordination of the systems of higher education that developed in Europe in the 1980s arose in an international context marked by four principal features: expansion and differentiation of systems of higher education, constraints on public financing, failure of centralized planning efforts, and the strengthened role of the market in the public policy framework. These same conditions, in the extreme, are present in Argentina, and so it is not unusual for these proposals to find an ever louder echo in government and among selected sectors of the academic, political, and business elite. Since the mid-1980s, certain issues fundamental for changing relations between the state and the institutions, such as quality evaluations and competitive financing of educational and scientific programs, have become part of the debate in Argentina.

The system of higher education has undergone notable expansion, in terms of both enrollments and growth in the number of its institutions. From 1980 to 1995, the number of students doubled; today the system has just over one million students, 70 percent of whom are enrolled in the universities, the rest in nonuniversity institutions (see Table 2).

Beginning in 1989, moreover, the government responded favorably to pressures to authorize new institutions. Congress was sensitive to local and provincial interests pressuring for their new universities to be paid for out of the federal budget; it passed laws creating eight national universities in a matter of years. At the same time, the executive authorized approximately twenty new institutions in a few short years. Similarly, the nonuniversity higher education sector, under the authority of provincial and municipal governments, also saw rapid growth in the number of its institutions.

Table 2. Number of Establishments and Students in the Argentine System of Higher Education, 1994, by Sector

Regime	University	Nonuniversity	Total
	Establishment		
Official	National[a]: 31	956	992
	Provincial[a]: 5		
Private	36	693	729
Total	**72**	**1,649**	**1,721**
	Students		
Official	National[a]: 615,796	235,089	853,488
	Provincial[a]: 2,603		
Private	124,749	93,983	218,732
Total	**743,148**	**329,072**	**1,072,220**

Source: Partial results from the National Census of Teachers and Educational Establishments, 1994 (General Bureau of the Federal Educational Information Network, Ministry of Culture and Education); and Argentina, Ministerio de Cultura y Educación, Secretaría de Políticas Universitarias, Consejo Interuniversitario Nacional e Instituto Nacional de Estadística y Censos, *Censo de estudiantes de universidades nacionales 1994; Resultados definitivos; Totales por universidad*, Serie A NS1 (Buenos Aires: MCE, 1995); idem, *Censo de estudiantes de universidades nacionales 1994; Resultados definitivos; Totales por rama de estudio y disciplina*, Serie B NS1 (Buenos Aires: MCE, 1995); idem, *Censo de estudiantes de universidades nacionales 1994; Resultados definitivos; Totales por carreras y universidad*, Serie C NS1 (Buenos Aires: MCE, 1996); and Ministerio de Cultura y Educación, Secretaría de Programación y Evaluación Educativa, Dirección General Federal de Información Educativa, *Censo nacional de docentes y establecimientos educativos '94; Informe I; Resultados provisorios* (Buenos Aires: MCE, 1995).
[a]Figures for mid-1995

As a result of all these changes, in 1995 the system of higher education included more than eighty universities, more than half of them private, and over sixteen hundred nonuniversity institutions of higher learning distributed throughout the country. Even leaving aside the vast and heterogeneous world of nonuniversity institutions of higher learning, the eighty public and private universities constitute a heterogeneous mix of educational settings. Despite intersectoral differences, the notion of system generally applied today to take in the set of postsecondary teaching institutions denotes many interdependent and necessary interactions among the different sectors. This system is weakly integrated, because of both the lack of mechanisms for overall coordination and the ineffectiveness of many of the currently existing mechanisms. The old bureaucratic mechanisms of control, inefficient in the past, cannot possibly be applied by a deteriorated state apparatus to such a complex set of institutions. The associations of public and private universities have specialized in negotiating with the government, and have assumed only a few coordinating functions. Competition among institutions for resources, students, professors, and prestige is very limited because there is little transparency and there are arbitrary budget allocations and severe limitations on autonomy.

In effect, the institutions often find their latitude in decision making constrained by bureaucratic forms of control that deprive them of financial autonomy. They cannot decide freely, for example, on salary policies or hiring, policies to expand sources of funding, or how to invest such funds. Decision making in the public universities relies upon the operation of collegiate bodies that are diverse and decentralized, yet no mechanisms are in place to foster institutional responsibility. In the larger universities, the capacity for coordination at the higher levels of academic authority is limited by the powerful professional schools. The complexity and variety of disciplines gives greater legitimacy to the effort to coordinate decisions made by the operational units. Autonomous management of the operational units with respect to the office of the president is clear when one analyzes how they operate when linked with the productive sector, one of the few areas in which major innovations were made in the late 1980s. The efforts of university presidents to coordinate activities for the transfer of technology and delivery of services in large universities whose units have won their own recognition from outside have generally met with little success. Furthermore, the programs developed by many academic divisions or schools within universities to increase their own revenues by providing services, with no coordination, increase institutional dispersion while yielding scant academic benefits.

The best evidence of the crisis in the coordination of the system is in the dizzying array of degrees and diplomas now offered by university institutions. The proliferation does not ensure diversity, but in contrast it poses serious risks to the students and weakens the necessary control over the exercise of the regulated professions. The current structure of supply of university programs of study is the result of the sum of decisions made by each university individually, with no coordination between them. The national universities are free to create new programs of study, as they enjoy academic autonomy, often committing as yet uncertain resources with no consideration of possible overlaps with other public universities. Programs are analyzed and approved by the top collegiate bodies of each university and then reported to the Ministry of Culture and Education. In theory, the private universities require prior approval, but the procedure often occurs after the fact, when the program of study has already begun to operate, or it results in mere red tape without a clear evaluation of the institution's ability of offering the new programs. Although bureaucratic controls are more stringent in the case of academic degrees that automatically qualify the holder to one of the professions (such as medicine, law, or civil engineering), they have no capability whatsoever to guarantee the professional competence of graduates.

The autonomous capacity of the national universities to determine their course offerings, the lax state regulation of private universities, and the major expansion since the early 1990s of institutions of higher learning, especially private ones, have led to a doubling in the number of academic degrees awarded in recent years.[8] The university subsystem currently has more than two thousand undergraduate programs of study. Approximately one-fourth of the degrees that were created have been the effect of institutional expansion. It is very likely that some of the new programs offered end up disappearing, inasmuch as there is no significant demand, posing serious risks to enrolled students. The proliferation of certain degrees, especially in new programs of study, may reflect not a real diversification of supply, but a mere terminological distinction that may be somewhat artificial. This is particularly the case in degrees related to management, computer science, and social communication, especially in the private sector.

Conclusion

The adaptation of university education to the present-day demands of Argentine society cannot proceed spontaneously as a result of the decisions made by all the institutions, nor will it result automatically from an increase in public and private resources earmarked to them. It requires profound changes in offerings, admission systems, dedication on the part of students and professors, and the very processes of academic work and administration within the universities. That cannot occur in the current institutional context. Reforming the system involves fundamental changes in the rules that regulate the workings of the institutions, both public and private. These rules refer to relationships among institutions and with their markets (student, academic, and financial), but above all to their relationships with the state.

State reforms in education, and particularly in higher education, are very different from those that have been called for with respect to the state role in production. Here it is not a question of "less" state, but of a state with different capabilities and functions. It must take the initiative in the reform process, creating the conditions to provide incentives for more appropriate institutional conduct from the standpoint both of efficiency in the use of resources and in adapting to new social demands.

Some authors have referred to these new functions in light of the concept of the "evaluative state," which attributes responsibility to government not only for monitoring and evaluating the results of public investment but also for providing incentives to improve the quality and relevance of university programs. The institutions have scant initiatives of their own to innovate, and in isolated places where there are such initiatives they are commonly drowned out by cultural and organizational barriers. It is a current responsibility of the state to recognize such initiatives, to protect them, and to encourage them within the university system. The specific mechanisms are highly diverse; they differ depending on the institutional setting (public or private, old or new institutions, comprehensive and specialized, teaching only, or teaching and research). Their implementation is politically complex and risky, since it is impossible to provide incentives without the active and voluntary participation of the universities, which no doubt harbor well-founded fears of the risks inherent in such changes. Even so, international experience clearly indicates that it is possible to change the basic rules governing the linkage between governments and institutions when there is sufficient trust, over time, in academic autonomy and the merit of the universities' decisions.

Notes

1. Jorge Balán, "Argentina," in *The Encyclopedia of Higher Education*, vol. 1, ed. Burton Clark and Guy Neave (Oxford: Pergamon Press, 1992), 19–29; Emilio Fermín Mignone, "Educación en los años 90 : El desafío de la calidad, la pertinencia, la eficiencia y la equidad," in Academia Nacional de Educación, *Reflexiones para la acción educativa; Incorporaciones, presentaciones y patronos, (1993–1994)* (Buenos Aires: Academia Nacional de Educación, 1995), 81–104.

2. Jorge Balán, "Políticas de financiamiento y gobierno de las universidades nacionales bajo un régimen democrático: Argentina, 1983–1992," in *Políticas comparadas de educación superior en América Latina*, ed. Hernán Courard (Santiago, Chile: FLASCO, 1993), 131–84.

3. José Luis de Imaz, Juan Carlos Auernheimer, María Nicholson, and Antonio Paz, *Informe blanco sobre el sistema educativo argentino* (Buenos Aires: Fundación Banco de Boston, 1993).

4. Guy Neave and Frans A. van Vught, eds., *Prometheus Bound: The Changing Relationship between Government and Higher Education in Europe* (Oxford: Pergamon Press, 1991).

5. Argentina, Presidencia de la Nación, Secretaría del Consejo Nacional de Desarrollo, *Educación, recursos humanos y desarrollo económico-social; Situación presente y necesidades futuras*, Tomo II, Serie C NS73 (Buenos Aires: CONADE, 1968), 33–57.

6. Martin Trow, "Problems in the Transition from Elite to Mass Higher Education," in OECD, *Policies for Higher Education* (Paris: OECD, 1974), 51–106.

7. Balán, "Políticas de financiamiento."

8. Ana M. García de Fanelli and Jorge Balán, *Expansión de la oferta universitaria: Nuevas instituciones, nuevos programas*, Documento CEDES 106 (Buenos Aires: Centro de Estudios de Estado y Sociedad, 1994).

15

Restructuring the Argentine Educational System, 1984–1995

Cecilia Braslavsky*

In an article written in mid-1993,[1] I stated that Argentine education was undergoing a process of profound transformation that was recognized by a wide array of authors, albeit with different interpretations. According to some, it resulted from the implementation of a neoconservative agenda;[2] others saw it as the result of years of work to bring about consensus-based programmed change.[3]

I suggested that the educational transformation under way in Argentina is actually the result of a multifaceted movement that sought to respond to many different needs and demands with elements drawn from many sources. Today, one can also note that its consequences include the emergence of an educational system markedly different from that which was regulated, put in place, and expanded[4] from approximately 1880 to 1910.[5]

It is now possible to state that, just as at that time, the federal government is speeding up the process, and to some extent playing a leadership role. Now, however, the type of linkage among the federal government, the provinces, the associations, and the social actors engaged in the various sectors appears to be different from that of the earlier period, particularly given the balance between the persistence of traditional relations of competition and the strengthening of cooperation, which has usually been weak.

The educational needs stem from individual and collective challenges that neither the educational system as a whole, nor any of the institutions in particular, are in a position to address; they involve widespread dissatisfaction with Argentine education. Once the criticism is focused on how

---

*The opinions are the author's and do not necessarily reflect the views of the institutions with which she works.

people are educated, there is a general agreement that the educational system is not providing the basic skills for adequate individual development and social performance, nor is it providing training in the attitudes valued by the more dynamic economic groups.[6] Around 1984 the demands were associated with the effort to democratize the system and institutions, which were considered highly elitist and authoritarian. Today they are more strongly associated with proposals for reconversion of the productive apparatus and participation in an increasingly globalized society.[7]

At the beginning of the transition to democracy, the need for change in education was faced by a variety of actors including the Ministry of National Education—at the time in the hands of the Radical party—broad sectors of *progresismo*,[8] and religious and other private schools.[9] This need for change was initially expressed in the framework of a "restoration perspective"—that is, most discussions were anchored to conditions and issues that belonged to the past. After almost two decades without a serious educational debate, the new debate was begun almost exactly in the same place it had been left in the 1960s. For the Radicals and some of the progressives, the need was felt to return to the regulatory principles of the "golden age" of Argentine public education. At that time, the federal government was responsible for education, with free public education at all levels, and education was secularized and compulsory. On the other hand, many privately owned schools felt a need to limit the power of the federal government, and some sectors linked to Catholic schools wanted to set a metaphysical direction for the entire educational system.

The restoration approach reached its high point in February 1988. During the Congreso Pedagógico, which took place from 1986 to 1988, it was clear that this approach imposed a gridlock, making it difficult to build consensus to put forth creative alternatives for addressing both long-standing unsolved problems as well as emerging ones.

Among the long-standing problems were the exclusion of 5 percent of the school population from compulsory primary education; a dropout rate that ranged from 12.1 percent in the city of Buenos Aires to 58.1 percent in the province of Corrientes; historically low teacher salaries, in some sectors less than U.S.$300 per month; and a labor regime for teachers that awarded seniority more than training and on-the-job performance. All these had unfolded in a context in which little priority was accorded to investment in education and poor use was made of now scant resources.[10]

Among the new emerging problems were fragmentation of the system, the increase in anomic institutional behavior, and an ever greater need to review the selection of subjects and to articulate them within the new comprehensive educational proposals, designed from perspectives very different from the conventional ones. Within the Congreso Pedagógico, an effort began to build consensus and to seek out or create new policies and action strategies. From that moment on, the importance of the past in education diminished, and changes already under way in the Argentine educational system increasingly became part of the international effort to restructure national educational systems. This occurred mainly through initiatives to bring about a National Educational Reform,[11] delineated in the Federal Law on Education passed in April 1993. Passage of this law completed the legislative process for regulation of the new educational system and ushered in the adoption of a complementary set of guidelines and public policies for its new structure.

The Challenges of Restructuring Educational Systems Both Internationally and in Argentina

Human societies, and even the survival of their members, are inconceivable without education—that is, without the systematic and intentional transmission of a series of cultural forms from adult generations to younger generations. As these cultural forms have become more complex, institutions have had to be "invented" that were specially dedicated to transmitting culture and to providing training in certain skills. These institutions were schools, founded by many different social actors who competed among themselves for relevance and effectiveness in transmitting knowledge. In this way, educational systems developed as the most functional means of systemicatically putting into place a diverse supply of schools. Educational systems are thus complex organizations of relatively recent historical creation; they have emerged through complex processes of establishing cultural control over the population; without them, addressing the challenges that have come in the wake of the industrial and democratic revolutions would prove inefficient.

National governments have made use of educational systems to guarantee the direct provision of educational services to ensure their own legitimacy, power, and domination. Educational systems were invented only 150 or 200 years ago, and they have operated in their present form for only about fifty years.[12] They emerged in response to the impact of modern technologies, the first stage of the industrial revolution, and the invention of republican democracies as the best form of governance for nation states. In the Western world, they expanded and consolidated both as a result of and as a determining force behind effective modernization. Great strides were made in that undertaking, yet at the same time its limits were revealed.

The fate of educational systems, with both their achievements and limitations, is linked to modernity, and in particular to the possibility of reforming them anew as a means of fostering integration and social cohesion that enshrines and seeks to implement fundamental human rights and relies on rationality.[13] In contrast, the centripetal forces that tend toward its dissolution are associated with both the persistence of premodern phenomena and the emergence of postmodernity in the Western world.[14] Both the persistence and emergence entail destructuring, marginalization, and the expansion of irrational ways of approaching the world. In this context, the potential for survival of educational systems is closely linked to their capacity to restructure so as to overcome their weaknesses and solidify modern education under new conditions.[15]

Of great concern is that the effectiveness and efficiency of the schools depend in large measure on the supply of a wide variety of inputs: making massive and intensive use of new technologies, curricular designs, textbooks, well-trained teachers, comparable information on the achievements of their graduates, and so on. These inputs cannot be produced by the educational establishments themselves; only in countries with a strong tradition of involvement of social organizations in education will some of these inputs be produced with the requisite quality outside of the educational system.[16]

In contrast to what happened in many European countries, where the models of Latin America's national educational systems find their roots, in Latin America the national governments did not create the educational systems to systematize a varied and expanded supply of institutions. Rather, they were developed to foster a scant or nonexistent number of educational opportunities, which was essential for the liberal modernization program of the late nineteenth century and, in some countries, that of the early twentieth century.

Yet the federal government was not the only actor; it was highly dynamic but not omnipresent. In Argentina schools were founded, resulting in the existence, by 1960, of at least four types of primary schools and almost always three types of secondary schools as well, including public national schools, public provincial schools, and private schools supervised by the provincial government. Each had its own plans, programs, standards, supervisors, and salaries.[17] In that context, schools situated two thousand kilometers from the federal capital and two kilometers from a provincial capital had to operate as part of a subsystem with its center in the federal capital and no connection to the provincial government.

Also in contrast to the European experience, over time most of the Latin American national states tended to neglect regulation and structuring of the system, focusing instead on the routines of providing the service. In the case of Argentina, that had a particularly negative impact on quality and hindered equity in education. The federal government concerned itself only with "its" schools, and in many cases just part of them, through pilot projects.[18] The schools in general, and education as a whole, did not receive the same attention.

The national state's tendency to focus on the service-delivery function, and almost exclusively on the services of a fraction of the institutions directly under it, was aggravated under military rule, especially during the period between 1976 and 1983. This stemmed from lack of interest in knowledge as a factor of development; distrust in school education as a means of authoritarian socialization; and the low likelihood of many social sectors to voice demands, including demands for education, in an authoritarian context. The emphasis on the service-delivery function was accompanied by the gradual deactivation of many devices that had been set up to monitor and support the everyday operations of educational institutions, such as quarterly exams in secondary education and the practice of supervision. The focus on service-delivery also stemmed from several factors, including the weakening of the service-delivery function itself through the reduction of time dedicated to teaching within the school schedule, the impact of teacher strikes, and the limited ability to get talented youth to choose careers in teaching.

As a result of this dynamic, the Argentine educational system embarked upon a process of *desconfiguración*, "destructuring," that stemmed from the loss of efficacy of existing norms, the persistent inability to change them, the withering away of shared systems and processes, and, perhaps even more serious, the nonexistence of forums for debate and interaction among different social, economic, political, and educational actors who would be needed to frame educational issues as part of an agenda of public issues. In the context of a weak society, this contributed to the fragmentation of educational supply and the weakening of each of the fragments. In other words, it contributed to the institutionalization of postmodernization of the sector, in a society that had yet to accede fully to modernity.

In the face of this destructuring, there were two alternatives. The first was to permit anomie to worsen, with the consequent proliferation of strategies for routinely carrying out activities as the hegemonic form of operation of the educational system and most of its institutions, with few favorable results in terms of quality and equity.[19] The second was to design a reform aimed at regulating and structuring education, once again with a view to pursuing modernization, meaning reconverting the educational system which, having begun to deteriorate, was delegitimized and questioned.

The new approaches to regulating and structuring educational systems worldwide are organized along two lines. The first, which could be called "minimal regulation," focuses attention on the demands for education and on the results expected of the educational process. The second, in contrast, can be called "necessary regulation."[20] It also focuses attention on the inputs and processes necessary for covering educational needs from the standpoint of bringing them up to date in the context of the profound technological changes and transformations in organization of work internationally, and in the search for equity and democracy as intrinsic values.[21]

The alternatives of "regulation and minimal structuring" make the national state responsible for determining the demand for and establishing information and evaluation systems, as well as systems for promotion or accreditation. In operational terms, the need for and functions of state intervention are rejected; instead, the emphasis is on the trend toward decentralization of education, including municipalization and privatization.

The alternatives of "regulation and necessary structuring" suggest that the state should define the skills for which training should be provided, create information systems, and even, at a later point, create evaluation systems for promotion and accreditation. Yet these alternatives do not tend to diminish the role the state will play in education. They do not dismiss the need for public intervention, but redefine and in some cases modify it. Rather than promoting the existing trend toward decentralization of education with a view to municipalization and privatization, these alternatives would bolster the autonomy and reprofessionalization of educational institutions and strengthen the core areas;[22] further, the inputs need to be assessed and the processes given direction.

As already suggested, the Argentine educational system has been undergoing a lengthy reconversion that began long before there was any systematic analysis of comprehensive alternatives. Rather, this process unfolded with the view that having a single comprehensive course of action nationwide would be effective. This single approach was decentralization, understood mainly as transfer of the traditionally large educational sector dependent on the federal government to the provinces and to the municipal government of Buenos Aires, strengthening the potential for putting initiative into the hands of other municipalities through new constitutional or statutory provisions, or by implementing unapplied articles from older ones.

Trends in the Reform of the National Educational System and the Proposed Curriculum

Transfer of Schools and Reconversion of the Educational System

In the late 1960s, the military government (1966–1973) took the first steps to transfering the schools created by the federal government to the provinces.[23] The lack of consensus regarding these steps meant that, with the return to democracy in 1973, this transfer was discontinued until the rise of the next military government (1976–1983). In 1978 practically all primary education was in the hands of the provinces and the municipal government of Buenos Aires. Under the first Menem administration (1989–1995), secondary schools and teacher-training schools were transferred to the same school districts.

The justification for this transfer was that it was a decisive step and the best possible way to guarantee a more complete constitutional federalism, to make better use of ever more scarce resources and to enhance reorganization of a large number of overlapping educational systems in the same area. It also brought decision making closer to each school, facilitating community participation.

The constitutional argument is based on interpretation of an article in the constitution that gives the provinces the power to take charge of general education, which today includes at least primary and secondary schooling. Assistance from the federal government compensated for the temporary inability to found schools, but there is no longer any reason for it to continue in its present form, according to the argument.

The administrations that have promoted the transfer, and public finance specialists,[24] who have argued that rational use must be made of scarce resources, assumed that bringing decision making closer to services would result in more careful use of resources. Their critics, generally educators, though also including economists of different persuasions, held that, beyond streamlining, an effort was made to diminish the resources earmarked by the federal government to education.[25] Finally, a significant part of the sectors not guided by fiscal logic (or at least not exclusively by it), who supported decentralization and see the transfer as a necessary part of it, thought that it would facilitate participation of the educational communities in decision making.[26]

It is possible that the process of transferring educational responsibilities from the federal government to the provinces would continue, in some provinces, in a process of municipalization. In at least ten provinces, the main rules governing the institutional organization of education provide for, but do not impose, municipalization of education. In seven, these provisions were issued after the return of democracy in 1983. In some cases, such as the city of Mar del Plata in the Province of Buenos Aires, and Córdoba, greater municipal government involvement in creating and maintaining educational services—but not in formulating proposals for teaching or working conditions—is a reality.

In the late 1980s and early 1990s, the transfer of services, yet with no articulation with other educational policies, appeared to have set off and coexisted with at least four problems that it had been expected to help solve.[27] The first was the consolidation of provincial organizational and administrative styles, which are often as bureaucratic and distant from schools as the federal government had been before. The second problem is the strengthening of clientelistic mechanisms at the base of the system. The third is the increase in certain costs without a clear improvement in the quality of services—for example, through the creation of technical teams with scant experience and training and consequently low efficiency. And the fourth problem is the tremendous difficulty in promoting the participation of parents, students, and teachers.

Provision for social participation in education is made in the constitutions or educational laws of twenty of Argentina's twenty-four educational districts. All provide that direction of the educational system must be in the hands of boards of education, with some type of community participation, at least of the educational community. Chaco, Río Negro, and Salta provide for the formation of school councils in their primary school regulations. In none of these provinces, however, were they actually organized—in contrast to the province of Buenos Aires, where they were created and chartered by decree, though the experience did not receive a positive evaluation.[28] Independent of the debate on participation, in recent years the need to strengthen the autonomy of educational institutions has been raised from several perspectives,[29] though it had not been fully perceived that the schools had already initiated such a process. At least two recent studies[30] include explanations that account for the transformation of schools as described above. Based on these studies, one can conclude that the institutions are increasingly autonomous in various areas of decision making. Nevertheless, the scant evidence available suggests that the exercise of autonomy does not always translate into improved educational proposals.

Explaining the many reasons for the paradoxical effects of the transfer and for the limitations to institutional autonomy is extremely complex. Under one hypothesis, these effects can be explained at least in part by the absence of new regulations and a new proposed configuration for the educational system, as well as the lack of mechanisms for coordination and consensus-building, in conjunction with the definition and implementation of a new role for the federal government and its Education Ministry, which, once the transfer was completed, did not operate schools.

The first administration after the return to democracy (that of President Alfonsín, 1984–1989), organized a forum for negotiation and consensus-building on the issue, the Congreso Pedagógico. But this administration failed to create coordination mechanisms or to implement a new concept for the national Ministry of Education. This was due, among other factors, to the lack of political will to accelerate and complete the transfers, which was necessary for culminating the process of *desconfiguración* and for drawing up a coherent plan for restructuring the system. The Alfonsín administration helped frame proposals to create systems that could be part of the restructuring, such as to evaluate the quality of education, but it focused again on formulating and implementing a series of policies aimed at improving those educational services under its direct responsibility—that is, the 36 percent of the secondary schools nationwide that were federal schools. This decision can be attributed to the fact that there were Justicialista party administrations in most of the provinces, the immaturity of a political system that did not allow for public policy conceptions that went beyond differences in party affiliation, and to the immaturity of policy proposals for restructuring the federal educational system as a whole.

In 1993, under the Menem administration, the Federal Education Act was passed. It incorporates many proposals and concluded the regulation of a markedly federal educational system in which all of the provincial educational systems, both public and private, are brought together in a process of coordination and consensus-building. The act sought to enable the educational system to share systems to facilitate the circulation of information, to promote training, to receive technical assistance and to have a "reparation" function—that is, to assist the most underprivileged populations and schools.[31]

The Federal Education Act also served as a work plan for a new education minister, who took office in November 1992. His administration created two federal systems and a network that are fundamental in restructuring the national educational system. These are the federal systems for information and for evaluating quality in education, and the federal network for permanent teacher education. The same administration has helped get several other initiatives off the ground, with a special focus on the initiative for curricular reform.

The Federal Council of Culture and Education is the entity created to negotiate agreements—that is, to restructure the system. The council must reach agreement on all issues not addressed in the law in its assembly, which is made up of the ministers of the country's twenty-four educational jurisdictions and is presided over by the federal minister of culture and education. It is to be assisted by two assistant councils, a technical council, in which interest-group representatives are to participate, and an economic and social council.

Furthermore, the Federal Education Act anticipates a "ministry without schools" whose main functions, consistent with what was being developed at the regional level,[32] should be to contribute to policy making and monitoring, along with technical assistance, compensation for inequalities, information and evaluation, promotion of research, external representation, and recognition and equivalence of titles. In other words, the ministry produces drafts of the framework agreements that make it possible to enforce the law as well as the designs for operation of the systems, while also guaranteeing the operation of such systems and providing technical assistance to the provincial ministries in order to increase their capability to implement policies consistent with the federal agreements.

In summary, the Federal Education Act is aimed at making the transfer of federal schools to the provinces part of an educational reform that determines the design and workings of the new structure of the national educational system. It provides that, in addition to the successive transfer laws, which for the most part bring about "destructuring," and the Federal Education Act itself, the agreements of the Federal Education Council shall make it possible once again to regulate the educational system in a manner that addresses the new challenges, attempting to correct the tendency toward fragmentation through a dual tendency to re-create an active center spurred on by the federal government and to strengthen a type of autonomy that produces quality. In this way, the law embraces the alternative of "necessary regulation." It was anticipated that federal curricular reform would play an important role. Its starting point should be a federal agreement on Common Basic Contents, as stipulated in article 66 of the law. The next section refers to the curricular reform in the context in which it took place.

Curricular Aspects

Of 225 programs undertaken in recent years and surveyed in a recent study, most (61 percent) were concentrated in three priority areas: curricular and school reform; classroom learning; and teacher training, continuing education, and teacher support.[33] This has been interpreted by the author of the study as an indicator that education has found its place on politicians' and planners' agendas. It is likely that this process, which the author calls *pedagogización*, has resulted from a perceived need to focus attention once again on curricular contents and educational methods. *Pedagogización* is also fostered by the realization that decentralization should not be the only strategy, and by the failure of community participation initiatives that are dissociated from proposals for educational reform.

From the outset of the democratic period of government in 1983, a movement for curricular reform and innovation in teaching developed in several provinces and institutions of Argentina. This movement was the starting point for drawing up the Basic Common Contents of the Republic of Argentina, approved at the November 29, 1994, assembly of the Federal Council of Culture and Education. This movement, parallel to the transfer process, was not part of the overall process of restructuring the educational system. As a result, it was heterogeneous and not articulated. In some provinces the main thrust was on updating the curriculum. In others, more attention has been devoted to reworking methodologies. In still others, the institutional organization of the schools has been revamped. Some proposals were more complete than others, and certain objectives were put forth more forcefully in some than in others. As a result, some provincial curricula place greater emphasis on training in language for communication and expression; in others, ethics and civics are stressed, with a focus on human rights. And there are further variations.

In addition to helping to motivate and mobilize, this movement has also had paradoxical effects. Emphasis was placed on the difficulties in moving from one province to another. It was difficult to get adequate textbooks for all students, especially in the small provinces, which proved to be an unattractive market for publications. Further, installed technical capacity was not used in such a manner as to make it accessible to the population nationwide, and certain risks were taken regarding the contribution of education to national unity.

The growing awareness of these unanticipated effects and of the problems of quality surrounding all the curricular proposals highlighted the need for common curricular contents nationwide, which was translated into an obligation to have Common Basic Contents approved by the Federal Council of Culture and Education. Determining that there was a need for the Common Basic Contents was another step in the process of developing a new structure, which strengthened the initiative to adopt the needed regulations.

The process of drawing up Common Basic Contents was designed to pick up on ideas that emerged from the already-existing movement for curricular reform and innovation in teaching methods, and to strengthen the ties of the educational system to society as a whole, both the work world and academia. In other words, an effort was made to situate the process of creating the new structure of the educational system in the broader field of symbolic regulation. To do so, a methodology was developed at the Ministry of Culture and Education that was later discussed in the provincial ministries and approved at the assembly of the Federal Council of Culture and Education. It set up a structure for reviewing contributions from five sources through three circuits of work. This effort was overseen by a small Technical Advisory Commission of the Ministry of Culture and Education and coordinated by a small drafting team. The methodology made it possible to consult more than eighty thousand people and to allow for broader participation by two thousand people from different institutional settings, geographical areas, and theoretical, political, religious, and ideological identities. All pitched in to develop the proposal, and, after a year's work, it was approved by the Federal Council of Culture and Education.

In contrast to the vast majority of existing curricular designs, the Common Basic Contents are guided toward training in basic and fundamental skills, introducing many procedural contents, and placing emphasis on training in conceptual thinking more than on factual contents. The following merit special mention: procedures for understanding and producing discourse; for problem-solving; for mathematical analysis; for collection, organization, analysis, and communication of information; for reflective, analytical, and critical thinking (analogical, deductive, and inductive); for analyzing products and project design; for creativity; and for discerning the moral dimension of human actions.[34] Diverse institutions that traditionally did not share views, such as private school associations and teacher unions, were supportive in principle of what was approved, even though critical voices were heard in both sectors. Qualified opinion makers commented, "It is the result of an effort to coordinate and update that reflects the current state of knowledge."[35]

No doubt, some factors that have contributed to agreement on the Common Basic Contents may be attributed to the methodology and process adopted. Nonetheless, other factors that probably weigh more heavily in reaching agreement are to be found outside the process. First, wide ranges of Argentine society and the political system are seeking forms of democratic consolidation that look for consensus. Certainly it is not by mere chance that it was possible to reach agreement on the Common Basic Contents in the same year that a National Constituent Convention unanimously approved major reforms, including the granting of constitutional status to the international agreements on human rights and other matters traditionally considered hard to reach consensus on.

Second, the management style of the educational sector in the period during which this agreement was being developed has been clearly characterized by a significant curtailing of clientelism and sectarianism, a new combination of professional skills and experiences in the state apparatus, and a certain administrative heterodoxy. Clientelism and sectarianism are characteristic features of Argentine political life that have not been eradicated. In education they inhibited the entry into the state apparatus of highly qualified technical personnel not identified with the political party in power or with the powerful political figures. In the Ministry of Culture and Education, the efforts for curbing clientelism and sectarianism made it possible to ensure coordination in the exercise of major responsibilities for education on the part of political officials sensitive to technical issues, all of whom took on a new awareness and set out to strengthen efficient and effective management. In this vein, they provided information, met deadlines, and offered public explanations of problems. There was also a certain trickle-down effect to several provincial administrations, which were encouraged to foster an increasingly professional leadership style. Furthermore, this more professional style was accompanied by the use of unorthodox management methods that made it possible to skip bureaucratic procedures that tended to frustrate public policies, and to implement those public policies in a reasonable time.

Third, investment in education, for carrying out the recently approved compensatory, remedial, or social assistance functions of the national government, in-service training plans, and other such actions, lent credibility to sector managers and reinforced the potential for reconversion of the national educational system.

Fourth, and finally, studying similar processes in other countries has made it possible to gain perspective on local educational reform, which provided more inputs, thereby making possible greater creativity.

During several decades of hardship and one of return to democracy, no school or educational institution, public or private, no network of institutions, no provincial government on its own, nor any university was able to produce even a partial synthesis of what should be taught that would suffice for the entire country. The proposal prepared at the initiative of the federal government does not alone improve the quality of education in the day-to-day life of the schools. Yet it does help strengthen expectations regarding the potential for reconversion of the entire

educational system and is essential for its new structure. But the new
structure is being put in place in the context of a transformation fraught
with risks and subject to change.

The Federal Government in the Restructuring
of the Educational System

The federal government promoted, helped coordinate, and took an initiative that only it could have taken to move from destructuring and fragmentation of the Argentine educational system to a new structure based
not on any particular ideological orientation but on social practice. This
development appears to corroborate a recent hypothesis according to which
it is useless to debate whether national government should or should not
be involved in changes under way in Latin America, because in fact it
will intervene.[36] Nonetheless, several factors suggest that the transformation still entails risks and is volatile, and that diminishing the risks and
overcoming the volatility require a thoroughgoing restructuring of the
federal government itself, and of the provincial governments. Not only
must the role of the public sector in society and education be examined,
but also the internal workings of the governments.

The main risk in the current reconversion of the educational system
is that only private schools attended by the higher-income population,
and public schools that participate in plans and projects for offering targeted assistance, will be able to gain the kind of autonomy needed to
adopt their own proposals for restructuring the system. Indeed, the results of federal assessments in 1993 and 1994 suggest that improvements
occurred nationwide, but especially in private schools and schools that
received benefits from the "Plan Social Educativo," which included re-
furbishment of infrastructure and training. If these evaluations are accurate, a small fraction of the population benefits more from improvements
in the quality of education.

The restructuring effort is volatile because not only education but
also the entire public sector is in need of modernization. The fact that the
federal government had been an extremely active player does not mean
that it had been or is now strong, as some were led to believe.[37] To the
contrary, the whole public sector had become ever weaker in terms of
professionalism, effective planning, efficient implementation, and capacity
to sustain initiatives for democratic consensus-building.

The first two and one-half years of restructuring of the educational
system were sustained with a large quota of voluntarism, and the process
is subject to the leadership style of those who hold principal responsibility in the sector. This situation has been dubbed "administrative hetero-

doxy." It consists of the lax use of rigid operational norms that have been laid down to promote state intervention that asphyxiates institutional autonomy. In other cases, an ad hoc approach to nonexistent standards is employed to avoid state paralysis.

On the other hand, steps have been taken to overcome obstacles that stand in the way of modernization of the federal state, such as institutionalizing competitive hiring for the selection of executive personnel; moving from planning focused on the "Plan Libro" to directive, situational, and operational planning;[38] shifting from actions focused on short-term circumstances and exclusively on means to actions that seek to balance short-term with medium- and long-term planning; and harnessing resources to address underlying problems. Nonetheless, one might question whether those steps have begun an irreversible process of reform that makes the public sector more professional and democratic, and in all likelihood they will still prove insufficient to sustain reconversion of the system.

The situation of the provincial governments is very mixed, but few are in the same situation as the federal government and many are held up by their own institutional reforms. As they too are hard pressed by the productive, social, and financial crisis, there is a risk that they might abdicate part of their responsibilities in the design and implementation of the restructuring. Indeed, the provincial governments demand from the federal government more than is to be expected when exalting the virtues of federalism, which might be reasonable in light of Latin America's historic experience, particularly from the Argentine perspective. It is as though it were neither possible nor desirable to try to establish new approaches to educational policymaking that represent a clear break with national traditions. Rather, it may be necessary to recover effective traditions by finding new ways of making them work. The dynamism of the federal government is part of these traditions. The difference now is that more thought should be given to the notion that dynamism, strength, and democratization are not synonyms, but rather three distinct and necessary dimensions of federal government intervention in the overall process of reconverting the educational system.

Notes

1. C. Braslavsky, *Las transformaciones en curso en el sistema educativo argentino, 1984–1993* (Buenos Aires: FLACSO, Programa Argentina, 1993).

2. N. Paviglianitti, *El Neoconservadurismo y educación: Un debate silenciado en la Argentina de 1990* (Buenos Aires: Libros del Quirquincho, 1991).

3. G. Cantero, *La transformación y la innovación de la educación en las provincias y en la MCBA. Prioridades políticas, opciones estratégicas y*

modalidades de gestión (Buenos Aires: Ministerio de Cultura y Educación. Dirección Nacional de Planeamiento e Investigación/PRONATASS, 1991).

4. Throughout this article the following terms will be used with the meanings noted here: *Regulation*: general definition of the purposes and principles and therefore of the possibilities and limitations of the different educational institutions and actors, through the invention or legitimation of certain models of macro- and micro-institutional functioning that are set forth in statutes, decrees, regulations, and other formal rules. *Structuring, or structure*: development of the macro- and micro-institutional models through the organization of means for pursuing the purposes and transforming the normative models into everyday styles. These definitions are my own, but are inspired mainly by B. Bernstein, *Class, Code, and Control*, vol. 4, *The Structuring of Pedagogic Discourse* (London: Routledge, 1990); and T. S. Popkewitz, *A Political Sociology of Educational Reform: Power/Knowledge in Teaching, Teacher Education, and Research* (New York: Teachers College Press, 1991).

5. See, among others, A. Puiggros, ed., *Historia de la educación en la Argentina*, vol. 4 (Buenos Aires: Editorial Galerna, 1993).

6. P. Gentili, "Poder económico, ideología y educación" ("A Study of Entrepreneurs, Enterprises, and Educational Discrimination in Argentina in the 1990s") (Master's thesis, FLACSO, 1993); E. Zuleta Puceiro, *La Sociedad Argentina ante el reto de la reforma educativa* (Buenos Aires: UBA-UBE, SOFRES-IBOPE, 1994); and Ministry of Culture and Education, *Demandas de transformación educativa* (Buenos Aires: Ministry of Culture and Education, 1994).

7. G. Tiramonti, C. Braslavsky, and D. Filmus, *Las transformaciones de la educación en 10 años de democracia* (Buenos Aires: Tesis Norma Editorial, 1995).

8. In Argentina this term is generally used to designate a diffuse movement that embraces partisans of the principles of equity and lay education in primary schooling, of democratic forms of organization of government, of authorization for the work of teachers' and students' organizations, and of a conception of quality that emphasizes education for citizenship over education for work. This perspective is shared by political and trade union leaders with affinities to political liberalism and with socialist ideas, as well as some members of the Partido Justicialista. They all agree when it comes to "defending public education."

9. See the description of the Congress and various assessments in C. De Lella and P. Krotsch, eds., *Congreso Pedagógico Nacional: Evaluación y perspectivas* (Buenos Aires: Editorial Sudamericana, Instituto de Estudios y Acción Social, 1989).

10. For a more detailed assessment, see, among others, Braslavsky, *Las transformaciones*.

11. "Reform" here is understood as the "mobilization of the public estates and relations of power" within a process of educational change that involves it and goes beyond it (T. S. Popkewitz, *Sociología política de las reformas educativas* [Madrid: Morata Ediciones, 1994], 13).

12. See for example, for Spain, A. Viñao Frago, *Innovación pedagógica y racionalidad científica* (Madrid: Akal Universitaria, 1990); and for France, F. Furet and M. Ozouf, *Lire et écrire* (Paris: Minuit, 1994).

13. J. Habermas, *La modernidad, un proyecto incompleto*, in H. Foster, J. Habermas et al., *La posmodernidad* (Barcelona: Kairós, 1986).

14. J. F. Lyotard, *La condición posmoderna* (Madrid: Rei, 1987).

15. Guaranteeing a modern education means offering access to shared codes that make it possible to transmit equivalent basic, fundamental skills in an equitable manner to the entire population so as to render insignificant the role of

education in processes of social exclusion, and so as to prevent and overcome this problem.

16. One such case appears to be the United States, where for example the American Association for the Advancement of Science, after a joint effort with universities and educational institutions, produced a consolidated and graduated proposal of subject matters in science to be taught throughout the educational system (*Benchmarks for Science Literacy* [New York: Oxford University Press, 1993]).

17. J. C. Tedesco et al., *El proyecto educativo autoritario* (Buenos Aires: Grupo Editorial Latinoamericano/FLACSO, 1983).

18. One example was implementation of what was called Project 13 in a group of national secondary schools in the early 1970s. At that time it was already thought that the secondary schools had an inadequate institutional model, among other reasons because teachers were not hired to full-time positions. This situation affected all the national, provincial, and private establishments. Nonetheless, the innovation was introduced in only a few national schools.

19. Braslavsky, *Las transformaciones*.

20. This classification is inspired by another more general one proposed by Adolfo Gurrieri, "Validity of the State planner in the current crisis," *ECLA Review*, no. 31 (1987): 201–17.

21. The question of financing education is intentionally set aside in these positions, as it requires special treatment.

22. N. Luhmann and K. Schoor, *El sistema educativo (problemas de reflexión)* (Guadalajara, Mexico: Universidad Iberoamericana de Guadalajara, Instituto Tecnologico y de Estudios Superiores de Occidente, 1993).

23. Puiggros, ed., *Historia de la educación en la Argentina*.

24. H. Piffano, *Economía y finanzas en la educación* (Buenos Aires: PRONATASS, 1987).

25. P. Narodowsky, "La decentralización como política," *Realidad Económica*, no. 99, 2do. bimestre (1991): 111–35.

26. Consejo Interprovincial para la Educación, la Ciencia y la Tecnología, *El peronismo participa del Congreso Pedagógico* (Buenos Aires: n.p., 1986).

27. S. Señén González, *Políticas estatales y programas de decentralización educativa* (New York: ILO, WHO/PAHO, NESCO-Latin America, 1989); G. Tapia de Cibrián, *Federalización política y descentralización de la educación* (Buenos Aires, 1989); and M. Kisilevsky, *La relación entre la nación y las provincias a partir de la transferencia de los servicios educativos del año 1978* (Buenos Aires: Ministry of Education and Justice/Organization of American States, 1990).

28. G. Tiramonti, "Nuevos modelos de gestión: El caso de los Consejos Escolares de la Provincia de Buenos Aires," *Propuesta Educativa*, no. 9 (1993): 36–49; and S. Cigliutti, "La participación en los Consejos Escolares de la Provincia de Buenos Aires," *Propuesta Educativa*, no. 9 (1993): 27–35.

29. S. Dutchatzky et al., "El programa de mejoramiento de la calidad de la enseñanza media, con énfasis en los CBU de Río Negro," *Revista Latinoamericana de Innovaciones Educativas*, no. 13 (1993): 102–72.

30. Dutchatzky et al., "El programa"; and UEPC (Teachers' Union of the Province of Cordoba), *Escuelas urbano marginales, Ciudad de Córdoba* (Córdoba: Programa de Formación y Capacitación de los Trabajadores de la Educación, 1992).

31. Popkewitz, *Sociología política*.

32. J. C. Tedesco, "The Role of the Nation-State in Education," *Prospect* 19, no. 4 (1989): 489–51.

33. Cantero, *La transformación y la innovación de la educación.*

34. Argentina, "Common Basic Contents" (Buenos Aires: Ministry of Culture and Education, 1995).

35. "Revista *Criterio* Editorial," *Criterio*, no. 2153 (1995): 183–85.

36. Gurrieri, "Validity of the State."

37. E. Faletto, "The specificity of the Latin American State," *ECLA Review*, no. 38 (1989): 69–87.

38. G. Matus, "Planning and Government," *ECLA Review*, no. 31 (1987): 161–77.

16

Notes on Structural Reform of the University System

Juan Carlos Del Bello

Argentina emerged from the economic crisis of the late 1980s with a more solid foundation for taking on the challenges of modernization and sustained development. As the country advances, production and employment are now geared to a more flexible and competitive form of organization. The initiative to take advantage of MERCOSUR and to open up to other international markets is moving forward. Primary and secondary education have begun to frame responses to this challenge; there is a clearer need to give impetus to structural reform of the university system so that it may be part of this transformation.

All indications suggest that if the shortage of qualified workers is not addressed, and if the national universities are not strengthened, economic development could become sluggish. Therefore, to sustain renewed growth, decisions must be made regarding the role assigned the university in the social agenda, and they must be implemented swiftly. This is crucial given not only the potential of the university but also the time it takes to train the people the country needs and to compete economically.

The recent history of many countries, including Argentina, appears to indicate that as a new economy emerges, reforms are needed in higher education. The reforms should make it possible to attain greater effectiveness in teaching and in scientific research so as to create a labor force adapted to the new situation, which is marked by greater demands and heightened competition. At the same time, and as a result of the current distortion in the distribution of wealth, the next decade is expected to see greater tensions brought to bear on the labor market. Much of the effort to transform university education in Argentina is aimed at preparing young people for this new situation. This essay outlines recent efforts in Argentina to reform university education.

The University in Argentina and
Its Main Structural Problems

The national universities in Argentina are part of a broader set of institutions that constitute the system of higher education. Argentina now has: thirty-three autonomous national universities, financed by the national government and focused primarily on research and undergraduate education (*enseñanza de grado*); forty-four private universities, without state financing, with a mixed supply including undergraduate and short-duration programs; and some eight hundred nonuniversity institutions of higher education under the provincial governments, both public and private, mostly specializing in teacher training. Short programs for training professionals have been developed only to a limited extent in Argentina.

The national universities are especially important among institutions of higher education because they are associated with the beginnings of the country and its political and social evolution. The first university in the Southern Cone was founded in 1613, in Córdoba, two centuries before independence. Today, these institutions enjoy significant social preference among college applicants. In 1992, for example, the national universities had seven hundred thousand students, or 70 percent of all students enrolled in higher education nationwide. Therefore, any reference to the main structural problems of higher education in Argentina and the challenges of its modernization necessarily calls for an analysis of the national universities and their structural reform.

One of the main challenges faced by the universities today regarding modernization is improving the quality of teaching. This challenge is closely associated with the issue of autonomous management and the system for designating professors and governing the university. Further, the prevailing structure of governance and management appears not to have been very effective in reversing the high dropout rate or the low entry rates, or in fostering curricular reform so as to stay abreast of changes in other areas of society.

Selection of Teachers and University Autonomy

The autonomy of the universities goes back to the 1918 university reform, though in practice it operated at full force only during the period between 1957 and 1966. Since then, and until 1983, the universities were controlled by successive military dictatorships (with the exception of a short democratic period in 1974 and 1975). In Argentina, with the exception of one provincial university, all government universities belong to the national jurisdiction. With the reestablishment of democracy in 1984, the national universities regained their autonomy. Beginning that year the previously existing system of public competitions, with a tribunal of peers for the appointment of faculty members, was reinstalled again. Nonetheless, in most of the national universities only a small percentage of teaching staff have been selected by this system; the rest work on a temporary basis until a competition is called. The university government is elected; the members are teaching staff chosen through the competitive process, students, and accredited graduates. Therefore the center of attention of university life in the first years of the return to democracy was on "normalization"—that is, on the designation of professors by competition based on past record and on the democratic election of the university government, both individual posts and collective bodies. The quality of teaching and research depends mainly on the transparency and competitiveness of the system of selecting faculty members.

The Demands of Democratization and University for the Masses

There is currently an explosion in the demand for higher education that has led to a deterioration of the teacher-student ratio and has made it harder to achieve excellence, as "normalization" was the only instrument for selecting teaching personnel. To illustrate the increase in demand, in 1980 only 6.8 percent of the total number of students were in higher education, while in 1991 that figure had jumped to 11.4 percent. The percentage of the population between eighteen and twenty-four years of age who were students rose from 9.3 percent in 1980 to 19.9 percent in 1991.[1]

The increase in the percentage of the school-age population in higher education can be verified by consulting the census data for 1980 and 1991, which show that the number of students in the national universities increased from 318,000 in 1982 to 700,000 in 1992. This occurred after an open admissions system for all high school graduates was adopted in 1984 (with the elimination of explicit admission systems, courses, and entrance exams); in addition, some disciplines were reopened (mainly in the social sciences) as a result of the democratization process. The number of students in private universities rose from 81,000 in 1982 to 103,000 in 1992, indicating that most of the expansion has been in the state universities.

The increase in enrollment that began in 1984 has been associated with the social demands for democratization. In just ten years, the university system has evolved into a "mass access" institution,[2] without a parallel reform in the systems of government and management that would facilitate swift adaptation to the new conditions.

Performance Indicators

As a result of the factors mentioned above, the increase in enrollment in state universities was accompanied by a decline in all performance indicators for the system. In 1992, the ratio of graduates to entry-level students was 19 percent—that is, there was only one graduate for every 5.2 entry-level students. This means that the cumulative dropout rate is 80 percent; it is believed that half of those who enter leave before completing their first year.

It has been argued that the main reason for the high dropout rate in the first year is poor skills among the young people graduating from secondary schools. While there was a notable increase in the school-age population attending primary and secondary schools in the 1980s, the quality of graduates did not improve. A recent survey to evaluate the quality of students in the last year of high school shows that 70 percent of the students about to graduate do not adequately interpret written texts, nor do they solve basic math equations correctly.[3] But it may be that the lack of an institutional response to the challenges of access to the university for the masses has contributed to the learning difficulties students face in their first year. Prior to 1984, selective entry systems eliminated a large part of the demand for higher education. With the indiscriminate opening of the university came the "mirage" of a supposedly "democratic university" that guaranteed equal opportunity; its flip side has been very low performance levels. An effort was made to incorporate the "principle of equity" through a misguided admission policy that does not consider the "principle of meritocracy."

On another level, it is found that those few who do graduate take 60 percent more time to finish their programs of study than it should take, which suggests that many students are repeating courses and that their dedication to study is limited. One of the main reasons for this situation is that a large number of students study and work simultaneously. While many students work, they do not necessarily do so for economic reasons. The data from the Permanent Household Survey (the source of information used for calculating unemployment rates) indicate that 75 percent of Argentine university students are from upper-income homes, and thus that only 25 percent are from low-income homes.[4]

Hypothetically, one factor that might have an impact is the long duration of undergraduate university studies. The structure of university curricula in Argentina is focused on long-term undergraduate training:

One enters with a secondary school degree to undertake a program of study five or six years in duration. For example, the expected duration of the program of study in engineering is six years. The supply of graduate-level training is very limited, and the short programs of study in technical and professional fields are hardly developed.

Even though finances could be one of the causes of this situation, the long duration of the undergraduate programs of study certainly contributes to dropout rates and to early entry into the job market: These people are twenty-two years old, in the best of cases, and will have concluded the fourth year of their studies. Youth seek independence from their parents, and one of the means of achieving it is through economic independence. This could explain why many of the students work while they are in school.

The universities have also promoted this practice. There is a prevalent "protective-populist" view: Not only were direct-entry systems put in place, but, in addition, the academic organization is based on protecting students who work (supposedly out of economic need) through a low course-load requirement and a permissive policy on staying enrolled. In the best of cases, state universities may require passing just one course in the previous annual academic calendar to maintain regular status. In summary, the high dropout rates plus the high incidence of students having to repeat a course explains how it is that practically two-thirds of educational resources are invested in students who never graduate.

Nor does the historic development of the private universities or technical institutes provide an option of significant quality, and only recently have they come to be considered as an alternative to the traditional public universities. In fact, while no detailed information is available about nonuniversity institutions of higher education, there are indications of sustained growth in enrollment and in the number of such establishments in the last five years. At the same time, the private universities, which had not increased in number since 1973 because of regulations that prevent their creation, have experienced appreciable growth since 1991: Fourteen new private universities have joined the twenty-six already existing in 1991. Nonetheless, as we have seen, private universities have not had a significant impact on the market for higher education.

There has been an explosion of demand on the state universities. If the private universities are to broaden their participation in the sector, the lack of financial incentives, which stands as a major barrier, must be overcome, either through subsidy payments to the students or directly to the institutions. Private suppliers tend to focus their academic supply on the "soft" sciences, the only area in which they can be self-financing with student fees.

The Distributive Impact

Qualitative issues that have to do with the distribution of demand, mainly in the various areas served by the national universities, should also be considered. Growth in demand has been concentrated in the social sciences and humanities, which increased their relative share by 10 percent, while basic and technological sciences dropped from 49 percent to 33 percent of students.[5] These figures are a warning sign from the standpoint of the human capital requirements for sustainable economic development in a globalized world economy.

Although there are no systematic studies of the curriculum for all university studies, it has been confirmed that study plans are obsolescent. For example, engineering studies still have a structure based on superspecialization from the start, with a major professional bias, while internationally there is a trend toward a standard first two years, with solid basic training. Later there is a choice of specialty with a duration of not greater than three years, which is then linked to graduate-level training in academic centers or other specialization.

There has been an apparent decline in the quality of educational services, the result of more than twenty years of disinvestment in fixed and human capital. The most conservative estimate suggests that disinvestment in the minimum laboratory equipment required for the basic sciences is on the order of $100 million, and the most recent university statistics confirm that only 10 percent of the personnel in the national universities have had graduate-level studies.

In conclusion, the structural problems of higher education in Argentina are of various sorts and cover a wide spectrum, including the limited supply of nonuniversity higher education, imbalances in supply and demand, a low level of enrollment per age group in higher education in large parts of the country, the limited quality of education, and backwardness in academic organization.

One must then inquire into the instruments and policy measures for structural reform of the system of higher education that would make it possible to reverse this situation.

Notes for Structural Reform of Argentine University Education

The following is a basic set of issues that should be part of a priority working agenda for overcoming the structural problems of higher education in Argentina. The issues are presented with a view to action.

Reform of Primary and Secondary Education

Higher education will always be compromised until structural reform is carried out in primary and secondary education. The Federal Law on Culture and Education of 1993 opened the way to reforms to expand compulsory basic education and develop a multimodal teaching level as a stage prior to higher education.

These reforms have begun to be implemented and will become fully operational in the year 2000. The multimodal level, which follows on the cycle of compulsory education (ten years) and will further expand the main components of the personal and social education of youths, will also provide students the tools needed to work in production and to continue their studies. Multimodal education will be a synthesis stage aimed at addressing apparent dysfunctions that stem from current secondary education. The recent reform seeks to introduce multimodal education to overcome the dichotomy between schooling that promotes a general, encyclopedic education, and that which provides what is thought to be practical training. To this end, multimodal education will be organized to enable students graduating from this level to get job training, and that should make possible a real linkage with higher education studies. The likelihood of success of this reform effort will depend mainly on according the proper rank to teaching staff, on bolstering their education and training, and on changing the basic curriculum.

Development and Diversification of Nonuniversity Higher Education

Historically, higher education has been concentrated in universities. Except for teacher training, which relies primarily on the upper-level teacher training institutes (it would, in fact, be more logical for the university to do its own teacher education and training), nonuniversity technical and professional training takes place in institutions of average or low quality. In view of this situation, some universities have introduced short-duration technical courses lasting two to three years, a strategy in opposition to what international experience indicates at best. In effect, this has brought about a contradictory specialization: Instead of focusing efforts and resources on graduate-level education and scientific research, the university has become *tecnicatura*, or a sort of advanced technical institute. This implies an allocation of resources that brings scientific development and higher-level training to a halt, and steps have been taken to reverse this trend.

The recent experience of the Instituto Tecnológico Universitario in the province of Mendoza, as an alternative model for institutional development, seeks to place the responsibility for short courses not exclusively on the university. The Instituto, for example, is a joint undertaking of the Universidad Nacional de Cuyo, the government of the province of Mendoza, and the business sector. It points to a nonconventional path (or third way), the "inverse reconversion" of certain universities. This institutional setup, patterned after the experience of the Instituts Universitaires Technologiques of France, is accompanied by other initiatives in different parts of the country to form "community colleges" and other alternative forms of institutional organizations. Thus, in the context of expanding and diversified nonuniversity higher education, there will be less pressure on the universities.

Opening of the Higher Education Market

Growth in the demand for higher education has created expectations in the private sector. There has been growing interest in private university education, and recent regulatory changes have ended the prohibition against private universities. Such measures will prove insufficient if not accompanied by incentives for the private sector. Argentina does not finance loans or fellowships for students. Demand is focused on state supply and it is segmented, with only the highest-income social sectors having access to private education services.

In the wake of the deterioration of the state universities, the result of a long period of disinvestment accompanied by the policy of mass access, some students began turning to private educational facilities. Nonetheless, private schools will succeed in acquiring larger numbers of students only to the extent that they can assist their students financially. To that end, the recent introduction of the university loan system (the agreement between the Secretariat for University Policies and the Banco de la Nación Argentina, in the amount of ten million pesos), and the creation of an extensive system of needs-based fellowships, are tools that will enable the private sector to assist in providing educational services. Further, the private sector needs financial support in the form of long-term credit for investments in infrastructure and capital formation, since it is not feasible for capital spending to be financed by student contributions. The development of private institutions will play a fundamental role in the major urban areas, where there is now great demand for state universities.

Reform of the Regulatory Framework for Operation of the System of Higher Education

In order to ensure the stability of the system of higher education, the existing regulatory framework must change. The proposed Law on Higher Education being debated in the congress will bring very significant changes to the organization and governance of the system. The first chapter proposes guidelines for organization of the nonuniversity higher education subsystem, with a view to expanding this as yet little developed educational sector.

A "common regulatory regime" is defined for state and private universities, while recognizing the particularities that differentiate them and that give rise to certain "specific rules" in each case. These are the main common elements proposed in the rule: a) the regime of degrees, associated with how professional practice is regulated;[6] b) institutional evaluation and accreditation of programs of study through the promotion of private accreditation institutions (based on the U.S. experience) and the establishment of a state entity for external evaluation that universities may turn to; and c) university autonomy as a system of governance and academic and administrative management. In summary, university autonomy is strengthened along with the establishment of evaluation and accreditation mechanisms, which guarantee the public's trust in society's educational institutions.

Changes are encouraged in specific rules for the governance of the national universities in order to ensure greater representation of the professors in the governing bodies, and to further economic and financial autonomy, fostering the establishment of foundations and private undertakings. With respect to the private universities, the current regime, which is clearly regulated, is replaced by a provisional authorization system for initial operations (limited autonomy). After six years of limited operations, the new institutions enjoy full recognition and autonomy (through external evaluation), in a manner similar to that of the state universities.

Reform of the System for Financing the National Universities

First, it should be recalled that the national universities are the backbone of the Argentine university system. These institutions are financed almost exclusively by the state, and they cannot collect fees for the educational services they provide.

There is now a prevailing view in favor of lifting this prohibition because most university students are from households that can make some payment, and also because not accepting tuition payments from those who can pay limits the resources available to those who cannot. Argentina, a developing country that is emerging from a period of hyperinflation, economic turmoil, and bankruptcy in public finance, must focus its education expenditures on compulsory basic education. That is another reason to raise money by means of tuition payments.

Moreover, the state contribution to the thirty-two national universities is not consistent with a transparent and objective model of resource allocation as adopted in the rules of many university systems worldwide. The lack of objective criteria for financial distribution leads to situations of economic laxity at some universities and just the opposite at others. An adequate system for secondary distribution of resources would incorporate principles of equity and efficiency, with allocations linked to measures of quality and productivity (concerning students, graduates, publications, and so forth).

Finally, centralized salary regimes used by the management of state universities contributes to inefficiency. While universities are autonomous in regard to the services that they provide, they do not enjoy the same independence with respect to matters involving salary policy. Considering that educational services are human resource intensive (personnel costs account for at least 80 percent of total expenditures), it is not viable to have academic autonomy at the same time as economic and financial autarchy where national universities cannot determine their own form of personnel management, including responsibility for setting their own pay system.

Reform of the Academic Regime in State and Private Universities

The academic regime of universities regulates all the instrumental aspects that define, for example, what goes into an undergraduate degree, the requirements for maintaining regular status, the duration of the curriculum for obtaining a degree, and admission to the university. Clearly there are many changes that must be made to the universities, including the following: a) reformulating undergraduate programs of study, shortening them and linking them to graduate programs; b) reformulating the labor regime for the teaching staff so that teachers devote more attention to students, and making research and developmental tasks compulsory for full-time staff; c) establishing entry regimes that "anticipate" early dropout, especially in the state universities; d) modifying the regimes for remaining in the institution, with a view to encouraging greater dedication to study; e) establishing fellowship systems with the dual purpose of responding to principles of equity in the distribution of educational services and linking the fellowship to reasonable academic performance; f) extending and furthering research and development in technological innovation leading to scientific production; and g) developing an aggressive plan for graduate-level teacher education and training, in the context of the previous point.

In recent months, various incentive mechanisms have been put in place to guide the national universities in the direction of structural transformation. A system of incentives for research teaching staff holds out the possibility of salary increases of up to 30 percent, based on evaluations to date. A project fund is to be endowed with more than U.S.$150 million to improve teaching; and, beginning in 1996, it will help equip teaching laboratories and assist in training the youngest and most promising teachers in the system.

Notes

1. Instituto Nacional Estadísticas y Censos, "Censo Nacional de Población." 1980 and 1991. The rate of higher education in the federal capital is comparable to that of developed countries (40.2 percent), while in the provinces of Patagonia and the northeast it is only 10 percent of the population between the ages of eighteen and twenty-four years.

2. Víctor Sigal, "El acceso a la educación superior," Buenos Aires, mimeograph, 1993.

3. Secretariat for Programming and Educational Evaluation, "Resultados Nacionales 1er. Informe/Sistema Nacional de Evaluación," Buenos Aires, 1994.

4. Cristina de Flood et al., "El gasto público social y su impacto redistributivo," Secretariat for Economic Programming, Buenos Aires, 1994.

5. Secretariat for University Policies, "Censo de estudiantes de universidades nacionales, 1992. Resultados definitivos, totales por universidad," SPU/Series A, no. 1, Buenos Aires, 1995.

6. The university community in Argentina has not attained the degree of maturity needed to assume the separation between academic degree and authorization to practice a profession. Therefore a second-best choice was made, a regime of degrees that authorizes practice, with monitoring in those areas where health, safety, or property is at risk. It is similar to the "community directives" experience of the European Economic Community.

Index

Abstentions from voting, 135
Accountability: of governments, 31
Acquisitions, 247–48
Acuña, Carlos H., 96
Administrative Emergency Law, 47
Administrative framework: in
  Argentine government, 226; need
  for efficiency, 23–25
Administrative heterodoxy, 310
Agricultural sector, 258; technological progress and diversification,
  248
Aggregate fiscal accounts, 221–25;
  deficit in 1983, 221
Alfonsín, Raúl, 5, 46, 109; attempt to
  force democratization, 124;
  coalition, 125; definition of
  Argentine international role, 171–
  72; democracy as priority, 204;
  education under, 305; endorsement
  of Olivos Pact, 139; foreign policy
  contradictions, 166; goal of new
  government, 173; inaugural
  address, 173; international
  reaction to, 164–65; old policy
  restrictions on, 183; resignation,
  137; trade liberalization by, 258;
  visit to Cuba, 180–81
Aliança Renovadora Nacional
  (ARENA), 120
Androgué, Gerardo, 134
Angeloz, Eduardo, 134
Antinuclear movement: refusal of
  Argentine government to join, 181
Argentina: border dispute with Chile,
  44, 189; currency conversion to
  U.S. dollars, 6; democracy 10
  years after restoration, 13–14;
  disposable income in, 64; economic subsectors, 10; elections,
  99; electoral volatility, 105, 106;
  foreign population, 117, 118;

future political structure, 31–2;
  government transition in, 86, 92;
  hostile attitude toward U.S., 174;
  industrialization in, 119; internal
  migrants, 119; lack of European
  support, 178; national interests,
  168; negotiations with Brazil, 38;
  neoliberalism in, 108; overseas
  trade imbalance, 34; political
  parties in, 102; poverty and
  extreme poverty (1970–1992), 94,
  96; presidential elections, 108; as
  society held back, 202; standard
  of living, 64; vulnerability of,
  213–14
Argentine Industrial Union (Union
  Industrial Argentina), 260
Argentine relations with U.S., 36–37,
  166–68, 182; Argentina's leverage,
  195; Caputo's description, 176;
  under Clinton administration, 188–
  89, 190; legal conflicts from
  private-sector interactions, 193;
  problems remaining, 192–95; U.S.
  response to Argentine international
  efforts, 186–87
Argentine University Federation, 51
Aristide, 90
Austral Plan, 47, 135
Australia, 121
Authoritarianism: in Argentina, 124;
  conditions favoring, 16; in Latin
  America, 3–4
Authority: traditional or charismatic,
  42
Auto parts sector, 263, 278
Auto sector, 250; exports by, 269;
  production, 257; study by, 276

Balze, Felipe A. M., 153
Banco Central de la República
  Argentina (BCRA), 239, 244

About the Contributors

EDUARDO AMADEO holds a *licenciado* degree in economics from the Catholic University of Buenos Aires. He was professor of economics at the Catholic University and the University of Buenos Aires. Mr. Amadeo was a member of the parliament and president of the Education Committee. Since 1994 he has served as secretary of social affairs for the government of Argentina. He is the author of various books and research papers, primarily for the IDRC.

JORGE BALÁN holds a *licenciado* degree in sociology from the University of Buenos Aires and a Ph.D. in sociology from the University of Texas at Austin. Currently a senior researcher and former director of the Centro de Estudios de Estado y Sociedad (CEDES) as well as professor at the University of Buenos Aires, Dr. Balán coordinates a comparative research project on higher education policies in Latin America, conducted in five countries under a grant from the Ford Foundation. He is also an advisor to the secretary of university policies of the Argentine Ministry of Culture and Education.

JOSÉ OCTAVIO BORDÓN holds a *licenciado* degree in sociology from the University of El Salvador, Buenos Aires. Since 1994, Senator Bordón has served as president of the party, Política Abierta para la Integridad Social (PAIS). He ran as the Frente País Solidario (FREPASO) candidate in the May 1995 presidential elections and has held a number of elected positions for the Province of Mendoza, serving as senator from 1992 to 1996, governor from 1987 to 1991, and representative from 1983 to 1987.

Senator Bordón has taught at Georgetown University and at Cuyo National University. He has conducted research for CONICET and the United Nations and is a member of the Inter-American Development Bank President's Advisory Council on Integration Issues. He is the author of *La Racionalidad del Peronismo* (1986) and numerous articles. Senator Bordón is currently the president of the Economy and Organization Institute (INSTECO) and the president of the Fundación Andina.

CECILIA BRASLAVSKY holds a *licenciado* degree in educational sciences from the University of Buenos Aires and a Ph.D. in social sciences from the

University of Leipzig, Germany. She is currently national director for research and development of Argentina's Ministry of Culture and Education and professor of the history of education at the University of Buenos Aires. Dr. Braslavsky is also a scientific researcher at CONICET and has recently been named a member of the follow-up committee of the World Conference on Education.

A former director of education at the Facultad Latinoamericana de Ciencias Sociales (FLACSO), she has specialized in education and society, with an emphasis on primary and secondary education. Dr. Braslavsky has participated in many research and development projects focused on the improvement of educational equity and quality in Latin America and in Africa with the support of the IDRC (Canada) and other institutions. She is the author of several books and numerous articles.

EMILIO JORGE CÁRDENAS has been the executive director of Roberts S.A. de Inversiones since May 1996. Ambassador Cárdenas served as permanent representative of the Argentine Republic to the United Nations from 1993 to 1996. Earlier he had been a partner in the law firm of Cárdenas, Cassagney Asociados and has served as chairman of the Section on Energy and Natural Resources Law of the International Bar Association since October 1996. Ambassador Cárdenas was also president of the Argentine Banking Association until 1993. He has taught at the Catholic University Law School, the University of Buenos Aires Law School, and the University of Illinois College of Law.

Ambassador Cárdenas holds degrees from the University of Buenos Aires Law School and the University of Michigan Law School. He also studied at Princeton University and at the University of California, Berkeley. He is the author of several books and numerous articles.

FERNANDO CERRO holds a *licenciado* degree in economics from the University of Buenos Aires and an M.A. in Public Sector Economy and Social Planning Projects from the Torcuato Di Tella Institute. He is currently the coordinator of the Inter-American Development Bank Loan project, "National Accounts System Revision."

From 1991 to 1995, Mr. Cerro served as cabinet aide to Secretary of Economic Programming Juan Llach in the Ministry of the Economy. Mr. Cerro worked from 1987 to 1988 as an assistant to the president of the Economic Commission in the National Chamber of Deputies, Guido Di Tella (currently minister of foreign affairs), with whom he is collaborating on the forthcoming publication, *Economic Cycles*. He served as an expert consultant to the Economic Commission for Latin America

(CEPAL) on national accounts from 1986 to 1989. Mr. Cerro has taught at the University of Buenos Aires, the National University, and the Catholic University of Santiago del Estero, where he is currently teaching applied economics.

JUAN CARLOS DEL BELLO holds a *licenciado* degree in economic planning from the University of Comahue and has undertaken postgraduate studies in regional planning and technological development. He has been a senior consultant to the United Nations Development Program (UNDP), the United Nations Conference on Trade and Development (UNCTAD), and the Inter-American Development Bank. He is professor and senior researcher on the economics of technological change and innovation at the University of Quilmes.

Since 1991, Lic. Del Bello has held the following positions in the federal government: undersecretary of state for economic studies; undersecretary of state for public investment; and secretary of state for university policies, a position in which he had executive responsibility for the recent structural reform of Argentina's university system. Lic. Del Bello is currently secretary of state for science and technology.

LILIANA DE RIZ is a senior researcher and professor of political science at the Instituto de Investigaciones Sociales de la Facultad de Ciencias Sociales of the University of Buenos Aires. In addition to writing numerous articles on Argentina and comparative politics, Dr. De Riz has edited *Retorno derrumbe: El último gobierno peronista*, in its second edition (1987); *Radicales y Peronistas: El Congreso argentino entre 1983 y 1989* (1994); and "Argentina since 1946," which she coauthored with Juan Carlos Torre. She holds a Ph.D. in sociology from the Ecole Pratique des Hautes Etudes, Université de Paris.

TORCUATO S. DI TELLA, an Argentine sociologist, teaches at the University of Buenos Aires and has specialized in the comparative study of Latin American social and political structures, with an emphasis on trade unions and populism. He has held temporary appointments at Columbia University and the Universities of California (Berkeley) and London as well as at Oxford and Kobe Universities. Professor Di Tella is also a vice president of UNESCO's Management of Social Transformations program. He is the author of *Latin American Politics* (1990), *Historia de los partidos políticos en América Latina* (1993), and *National Popular Politics in Early Independent Mexico* (1996), and coeditor of *Diccionario de Ciencias Sociales y Políticas* (1989).

JONATHAN HARTLYN is professor of political science at the University of North Carolina at Chapel Hill. He is the author of *The Struggle for Democratic Politics in the Dominican Republic* (1998, forthcoming) and *The Politics of Coalition Rule in Colombia* (1988; Spanish edition, 1993); he authored, with Arturo Valenzuela, "Democracy in Latin America since 1930," in *Cambridge History of Latin America*, Vol. VI, Part II, ed. Leslie Bethell (1994). He is also an editor, with Samuel A. Morley, of *Latin American Political Economy* (1986); and, with Lars Schoultz and Augusto Vargas, of *The United States and Latin America in the 1990s: Beyond the Cold War* (1992). He has published numerous articles in journals and edited volumes on issues related to democracy in Latin America.

MARGARET DALY HAYES is vice president and senior scientist at EBR Inc., a Virginia-based consulting firm. A political scientist with extensive experience with the Latin American public and private sectors, Dr. Hayes's most recent work has focused on strategies for U.S. military engagement with Latin America and other regions' armed forces, and on U.S. government interagency planning strategies in crisis scenarios. As visiting fellow at the Center for Naval Analyses, Dr. Hayes directed the U.S. Navy's examination of relations with Latin America and developed its Four-Year Plan of Action for Latin America.

Dr. Hayes has served in senior policy positions in Washington, DC, including director of external affairs at the Inter-American Development Bank, director of the Washington Office of the Council of the Americas, and senior staff person for the Western Hemisphere of the Senate Foreign Relations Committee. She also served as the associate director of the Center for Brazilian Studies of The Johns Hopkins University School of Advanced International Studies and as senior scientist at CACI, Inc., a Washington-based consulting firm. She has published widely on Latin American affairs and U.S.-Latin American relations. She holds a Ph.D. in political science from Indiana University and is a member of the Council on Foreign Relations.

JUAN JOSÉ LLACH has held several positions within the government of Argentina, serving as vice minister of economy and public works in 1996, secretary of economic programming for the Ministry of the Economy from 1991 to 1996, and as chief of advisors to the Ministry of the Economy in 1991. He is currently the president of the Institute for the Study of Argentina and the Latin American Reality (IERAL).

Mr. Llach was a research fellow at the Di Tella Institute from 1985 to 1991 and at the Mediterranean Foundation from 1982 to 1985. He is the author of *A Job for Everybody* (1997), *Another Century, Another Argen-*

tina (1997), and *Reconstruction or Stagnation* (1987). In addition, he has written numerous articles on institutional economics, hyperinflation, stabilization, economic reform, labor economics, sociology, and Argentine economic history. Mr. Llach holds a *licenciado* degree in economics from the University of Buenos Aires and in sociology from the Catholic University of Argentina, and he has taught at both schools as well as at the University of El Salvador.

DANIEL MARX is managing director of Darby Overseas Investments, Ltd. His career covers an unusual combination of service in both the private and public sectors. Mr. Marx was appointed undersecretary of financing of the Republic of Argentina in 1992. He managed Argentina's recent positioning in the capital markets through the implementation of the country's external debt agreement, the flotation of shares of companies being privatized (including the YPF offering), and the flotation of bonds, including the first global bond issued by an emerging country. He served as the external debt negotiator and financial representative of Argentina, dealing with banks, multilateral institutions (International Monetary Fund, World Bank, Inter-American Development Bank), and governments. Mr. Marx was also a member of the board of directors of the Central Bank of Argentina from 1986 to 1988.

From 1982 to 1986, Mr. Marx was head of corporate banking of Banco Rio de la Plata, the largest privately owned bank in Argentina, and served as director of the insurance companies La Patagonia and Sur as well as of Citicorp and Rio Banco de Inversión. From 1980 to 1982, Mr. Marx was responsible for restructuring the Arbol Solo-Inversiones Unidas conglomerate. From 1974 to 1979 he served as head of the treasury and planning departments of Banco Tornquist in Buenos Aires. Mr. Marx holds a degree in economics from the University of Buenos Aires.

JESÚS RODRÍGUEZ served from 1983 to 1997 as representative of the Federal Capital to Argentina's National Assembly, where he held a range of leadership positions responsible for the oversight of budget and finance, defense, domestic security and intelligence, and local affairs. He also has held numerous leadership positions within the Radical party. In 1989 he was named minister of the economy. Mr. Rodríguez holds an M.A. in economics from the University of Buenos Aires and is the author of many articles and essays on contemporary economic and political affairs in Argentina as well as of the volume *Tornar Partido* (1994).

FEDERICO STORANI has served since 1983 as a representative of the Province of Buenos Aires to the National Assembly, where he is currently president of the Unión Cívica Radical bloc. He has held numerous leadership positions within the National Committee of the Radical party and within the House of Deputies, including two terms as president of the House Commission on Foreign Affairs. He is currently president of FUTENA, a foundation for the study of national affairs, and teaches at the National University of La Plata, from which he holds a law degree.

JUAN CARLOS TORRE studied sociology at the University of Buenos Aires and received his Ph.D. in social sciences from the Ecole Pratique des Hautes Etudes, Université de Paris. He is currently a researcher at the Social Research Center of the Di Tella Institute and is director of the editorial board of *Desarrollo Económico* (Buenos Aires). Dr. Torre has taught and worked in several universities in Europe and Latin America. He has been a Guggenheim Fellow and a visiting scholar at the Institute for Advanced Study in Princeton.

Dr. Torre is the author of numerous articles as well as *Los sindicatos en el gobierno, 1973–1976* (1983) and *Perón y la vieja guardia sindical* (1990). He is the editor of *La formación del sindicalismo peronista* (1988) and *El 17 de octubre* (1995). With Liliana De Riz, he is the author of the chapter "Argentina since 1946," in Volume VIII of the *Cambridge History of Latin America* (1991). He is now working on the relationship between democratization and economic reform in Argentina and Latin America.

Latin American Silhouettes
Studies in History and Culture

William H. Beezley and
Judith Ewell
Editors

Volumes Published

William H. Beezley and Judith Ewell, eds.,
*The Human Tradition in Latin
America: The Twentieth Century*
(1987). Cloth ISBN 0-8420-2283-X
Paper ISBN 0-8420-2284-8

Judith Ewell and William H. Beezley, eds.,
*The Human Tradition in Latin
America: The Nineteenth Century*
(1989). Cloth ISBN 0-8420-2331-3
Paper ISBN 0-8420-2332-1

David G. LaFrance, *The Mexican Revolution
in Puebla, 1908–1913: The Maderista
Movement and the Failure of Liberal
Reform* (1989). ISBN 0-8420-2293-7

Mark A. Burkholder, *Politics of a Colonial
Career: José Baquíjano and the
Audiencia of Lima*, 2d ed. (1990).
Cloth ISBN 0-8420-2353-4
Paper ISBN 0-8420-2354-2

Carlos B. Gil, ed., *Hope and Frustration:
Interviews with Leaders of Mexico's
Political Opposition* (1992).
Cloth ISBN 0-8420-2395-X
Paper ISBN 0-8420-2396-8

Heidi Zogbaum, *B. Traven: A Vision of
Mexico* (1992). ISBN 0-8420-2392-5

Jaime E. Rodríguez O., ed., *Patterns of
Contention in Mexican History* (1992).
ISBN 0-8420-2399-2

Louis A. Pérez, Jr., ed., *Slaves, Sugar, and
Colonial Society: Travel Accounts of
Cuba, 1801–1899* (1992).
Cloth ISBN 0-8420-2354-2
Paper ISBN 0-8420-2415-8

Peter Blanchard, *Slavery and Abolition in
Early Republican Peru* (1992).
Cloth ISBN 0-8420-2400-X
Paper ISBN 0-8420-2429-8

Paul J. Vanderwood, *Disorder and Progress:
Bandits, Police, and Mexican Develop-
ment*, revised and enlarged edition (1992).
Cloth ISBN 0-8420-2438-7
Paper ISBN 0-8420-2439-5

Sandra McGee Deutsch and Ronald H.
Dolkart, eds., *The Argentine Right: Its
History and Intellectual Origins, 1910 to
the Present* (1993). Cloth ISBN 0-8420-
2418-2   Paper ISBN 0-8420-2419-0

Steve Ellner, *Organized Labor in Venezuela,
1958–1991: Behavior and Concerns
in a Democratic Setting* (1993).
ISBN 0-8420-2443-3

Paul J. Dosal, *Doing Business with the
Dictators: A Political History of United
Fruit in Guatemala, 1899–1944* (1993).
Cloth ISBN 0-8420-2475-1
Paper ISBN 0-8420-2590-1

Marquis James, *Merchant Adventurer:
The Story of W. R. Grace* (1993).
ISBN 0-8420-2444-1

John Charles Chasteen and Joseph S. Tulchin,
eds., *Problems in Modern Latin
American History: A Reader* (1994).
Cloth ISBN 0-8420-2327-5
Paper ISBN 0-8420-2328-3

Marguerite Guzmán Bouvard, *Revolutionizing
Motherhood: The Mothers of the Plaza de
Mayo* (1994). Cloth ISBN 0-8420-2486-7
Paper ISBN 0-8420-2487-5

William H. Beezley, Cheryl English Martin,
and William E. French, eds., *Rituals of
Rule, Rituals of Resistance: Public
Celebrations and Popular Culture in
Mexico* (1994). Cloth ISBN 0-8420-
2416-6   Paper ISBN 0-8420-2417-4

Stephen R. Niblo, *War, Diplomacy, and
Development: The United States and
Mexico, 1938–1954* (1995).
ISBN 0-8420-2550-2

G. Harvey Summ, ed., *Brazilian Mosaic:
Portraits of a Diverse People and Culture*
(1995). Cloth ISBN 0-8420-2491-3
Paper ISBN 0-8420-2492-1

N. Patrick Peritore and Ana Karina Galve-
Peritore, eds., *Biotechnology in Latin
America: Politics, Impacts, and Risks*

(1995). Cloth ISBN 0-8420-2556-1
Paper ISBN 0-8420-2557-X

Silvia Marina Arrom and Servando Ortoll, eds., *Riots in the Cities: Popular Politics and the Urban Poor in Latin America, 1765–1910* (1996). Cloth ISBN 0-8420-2580-4 Paper ISBN 0-8420-2581-2

Roderic Ai Camp, ed., *Polling for Democracy: Public Opinion and Political Liberalization in Mexico* (1996). ISBN 0-8420-2583-9

Brian Loveman and Thomas M. Davies, Jr., eds., *The Politics of Antipolitics: The Military in Latin America*, 3d ed., revised and updated (1996). Cloth ISBN 0-8420-2609-6 Paper ISBN 0-8420-2611-8

Joseph S. Tulchin, Andrés Serbín, and Rafael Hernández, eds., *Cuba and the Caribbean: Regional Issues and Trends in the Post-Cold War Era* (1997). ISBN 0-8420-2652-5

Thomas W. Walker, ed., *Nicaragua without Illusions: Regime Transition and Structural Adjustment in the 1990s* (1997). Cloth ISBN 0-8420-2578-2 Paper ISBN 0-8420-2579-0

Dianne Walta Hart, *Undocumented in L.A.: An Immigrant's Story* (1997). Cloth ISBN 0-8420-2648-7 Paper ISBN 0-8420-2649-5

Jaime E. Rodríguez O. and Kathryn Vincent, eds., *Myths, Misdeeds, and Misunderstandings: The Roots of Conflict in U.S.-Mexican Relations* (1997). ISBN 0-8420-2662-2

Jaime E. Rodríguez O. and Kathryn Vincent, eds., *Common Border, Uncommon Paths: Race, Culture, and National Identity in U.S.-Mexican Relations* (1997). ISBN 0-8420-2673-8

William H. Beezley and Judith Ewell, eds., *The Human Tradition in Modern Latin America* (1997). Cloth ISBN 0-8420-2612-6 Paper ISBN 0-8420-2613-4

Donald F. Stevens, ed., *Based on a True Story: Latin American History at the Movies* (1997). ISBN 0-8420-2582-0

Jaime E. Rodríguez O., ed., *The Origins of Mexican National Politics, 1808–1847* (1997). Paper ISBN 0-8420-2723-8

Che Guevara, *Guerrilla Warfare*, with revised and updated introduction and case studies by Brian Loveman and Thomas M. Davies, Jr., 3d ed. (1997). Cloth ISBN 0-8420-2677-0 Paper ISBN 0-8420-2678-9

Adrian A. Bantjes, *As If Jesus Walked on Earth: Cardenismo, Sonora, and the Mexican Revolution* (1998). ISBN 0-8420-2653-3

Henry A. Dietz and Gil Shidlo, eds., *Urban Elections in Democratic Latin America* (1998). Cloth ISBN 0-8420-2627-4 Paper ISBN 0-8420-2628-2

A. Kim Clark, *The Redemptive Work: Railway and Nation in Ecuador, 1895–1930* (1998). ISBN 0-8420-2674-6

Joseph S. Tulchin, ed., with Allison M. Garland, *Argentina: The Challenges of Modernization* (1998). ISBN 0-8420-2721-1

Louis A. Pérez, Jr., ed., *Impressions of Cuba in the Nineteenth Century: The Travel Diary of Joseph J. Dimock* (1998). Cloth ISBN 0-8420-2657-6 Paper ISBN 0-8420-2658-4

Guy P. C. Thomson, with David G. LaFrance, *Patriotism, Politics, and Popular Liberalism in Nineteenth-Century Mexico: Juan Francisco Lucas and the Puebla Sierra* (1998). ISBN 0-8420-2683-5

June E. Hahner, ed., *Women through Women's Eyes: Latin American Women in Nineteenth-Century Travel Accounts* (1998). Cloth ISBN 0-8420-2633-9 Paper ISBN 0-8420-2634-7

James P. Brennan, ed., *Peronism and Argentina* (1998). ISBN 0-8420-2706-8

John Mason Hart, ed., *Border Crossings: Mexican and Mexican-American Workers* (1998). Cloth ISBN 0-8420-2716-5 Paper ISBN 0-8420-2717-3